CALCULUS
& Its Applications

Larry J. Goldstein, David C. Lay, David I. Schneider, Nakhlé H. Asmar

Custom Edition for Math 16B
Volume 2
University of California, Berkeley

Taken from:
Calculus & Its Applications, Twelfth Edition
by Larry J. Goldstein, David C. Lay, David I. Schneider, and Nakhlé H. Asmar

D0731311

Custom Publishing

New York   Boston   San Francisco
London   Toronto   Sydney   Tokyo   Singapore   Madrid
Mexico City   Munich   Paris   Cape Town   Hong Kong   Montreal

www.pearsonhighered.com

ISBN 10: 0-558-37274-0
ISBN 13: 978-0-558-37274-3

CONTENTS

*Sections preceded by a * are optional in the sense that they are not prerequisites for later material.

v

PREFACE

We have been very pleased with the enthusiastic response to the previous editions of *Calculus & Its Applications* and its Brief version by teachers and students alike. The present work incorporates many of the suggestions they have put forward.

Although there are many changes, we have preserved the approach and the flavor. Our goals remain the same: to begin the calculus as soon as possible; to present calculus in an intuitive yet intellectually satisfying way; and to illustrate the many applications of calculus to business, life sciences, and social sciences.

The distinctive order of topics has proven over the years to be successful—easier for students to learn, and more interesting because students see significant applications early. For instance, the derivative is explained geometrically before the analytic material on limits is presented. To allow you to reach the applications in Chapter 2 quickly, we present only the differentiation rules and the curve sketching needed for those applications. Advanced topics come later when they are needed. Other aspects of this student-oriented approach follow below.

The Series

This text is part of a series consisting of three texts: *Finite Mathematics & Its Applications*, *Calculus & Its Applications*, and *Brief Calculus & Its Applications*. All three titles are available for purchase in three formats: printed text, eBook and as an eBook within the MyMathLab online course.

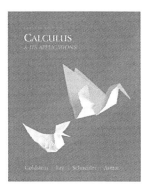
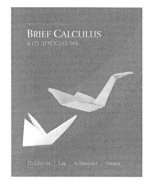

Topics Included

This edition contains more material than can be covered in most two-semester courses. Optional sections are starred in the table of contents. In addition, the level of theoretical material may be adjusted to the needs of the students. For instance, Section 1.4 may be omitted entirely, if the instructor does not wish to present the notion of limit beyond the required material that is contained in Section 1.3.

Review of Prerequisites

In Chapter 0, we review those concepts that the reader needs to study calculus. Some important topics, such as the laws of exponents, are reviewed again when they are used in a later chapter. Section 0.6 prepares students for applied problems that appear throughout the text. A reader familiar with the content of Chapter 0 should begin with Chapter 1 and use Chapter 0 as a reference, whenever needed.

Trusted Features

In this edition, we attempt to maintain our popular student-oriented approach throughout and, in particular, by the following features:

Relevant and Varied Applications

We provide realistic applications that illustrate the uses of calculus in other disciplines. See the Index of Applications at the back of the text. Wherever possible, we have attempted to use applications to motivate the mathematics.

Plentiful Examples

The text includes many more worked examples than is customary. Furthermore, we have included computational details to enhance readability. "Warning!" notes provide tips on common pitfalls and mistakes and appear at relevant times throughout the text.

Exercises to Meet All Student Needs

The exercises comprise about one-quarter of the text—the most important part of the text in our opinion. The exercises at the ends of the sections are usually arranged in the order in which the text proceeds, so that the homework assignments may easily be made after only part of a section is discussed. Interesting applications and more challenging problems tend to be located near the ends of the exercise sets. Supplementary exercises at the end of each chapter expand the other exercise sets and include problems that require skills from earlier chapters.

Practice Problems

The Practice Problems have proven to be a popular and useful feature. Practice Problems are carefully selected questions located at the end of each section, just before the exercise set. Complete solutions are given following the exercise set. The Practice Problems often focus on points that are potentially confusing or are likely to be overlooked. We recommend the reader work them and study their solutions before moving on to the exercises. In effect, the Practice Problems constitute a built-in workbook.

New To This Edition

Among the many changes in this edition, the following are the most significant:

1. **New and Revised Exercises and Examples**

   162 new and updated exercises feature a wide range of levels from those designed to aid students with a limited math background to exercises that challenge the more capable students.

2. **Revised presentation of crucial topics**

   a. The Derivative

   Some content of Section 1.3 has been moved to Section 1.4 and, as a result, Section 1.3 presents the derivative in an intuitive way, before the expanded presentation of limits that appears in Section 1.4. The new presentation offers the instructor the option of spending less time on limits (and therefore more time on applications) by not emphasizing Section 1.4.

   b. Differential equations

   We rewrote Section 10.3 on first-order linear differential equations in order to lead directly into the step-by-step method for solving this type of equation. This new presentation offers a faster track to the applications of equations presented in Section 10.4.

3. **Enhancing pedagogy with graphing calculators**

   As in previous editions, the use of graphing calculators is not required for this text; however, graphing calculators are very useful tools that can be used to simplify computations, draw graphs, and sometimes enhance understanding of the fundamental topics of calculus. Helpful information about the use of calculators appears at the end of most sections in subsections titled Incorporating Technology. The examples in this text use the family of TI-83/84 calculators, which include TI-83, TI-84, TI-83+, TI-84+, TI-83+ Silver Edition, and TI-84+ Silver Edition. Additional graphing calculator support material can be downloaded from pearsoned.com/Goldstein.

Program Supplements

All supplements support both *Calculus & Its Applications* and *Brief Calculus & Its Applications*.

For Students

Student's Solutions Manual (ISBN: 0-321-59901-2)
Fully worked solutions to selected exercises and study tips.

DVD Lecture Videos (ISBN: 0-321-57735-3)
A comprehensive set of topical videos, in which examples for each topic are worked out by an instructor. The videos provide excellent support for students who require additional assistance, for distance learning and self-paced programs, or for students who missed class.

For Instructors

Instructor's Edition (ISBN: 0-321-60012-6)
This version of the text includes answers to all exercises presented in the book.

Instructor Resource Center
All instructor resources can be downloaded from www.pearsonhighered.com/irc. This is a password-protected site that requires instructors to set up an account or, alternatively, instructor resources can be ordered from your Pearson Higher Education sales representative. Instructors may use their instructor's log-in from MyMathLab to access the Instructor Resource Center.

Instructor's Solutions Manual (ISBN: 0-321-59900-4)
Fully worked solutions to every textbook exercise.

TestGen®
TestGen (www.pearsonhighered.com/testgen) enables instructors to build, edit, print, and administer tests using a computerized bank of questions developed to cover all of the text objectives. TestGen is algorithmically based, allowing instructors to create multiple but equivalent versions of the same question or test with the click of a button. Instructors can also modify test bank questions or add new ones. Tests can be printed or administered online. The software and testbank are available for download from Pearson Education's online catalog.

PowerPoint Lecture Slides
Fully editable and printable slides that follow the textbook. Use during lecture or post to a Web site in an online course. For download from the Instructor Resource Center and available within MyMathLab.

MyMathLab® Online Course (access code required)

MyMathLab is a series of text-specific, easily customizable online courses for Pearson Education's textbooks in mathematics and statistics. Powered by CourseCompass™ (our online teaching and learning environment) and MathXL® (our online homework, tutorial, and assessment system), MyMathLab gives you the tools you need to deliver all or a portion of your course online, whether students are in a lab setting or working from home. MyMathLab provides a rich and flexible set of course materials, featuring free-response exercises that are algorithmically generated for unlimited practice and mastery. Students can also use online tools, such as video lectures, and a multimedia textbook, to independently improve their understanding and performance. Instructors can use MyMathLab's homework and test managers to select and assign online exercises correlated to the textbook, and they can also create and assign their own online exercises and import TestGen tests for added flexibility. MyMathLab's online gradebook—designed specifically for mathematics and statistics—automatically tracks students' homework and test results and gives the instructor control over how to calculate final grades. Instructors can also add offline (paper-and-pencil) grades to the gradebook. MyMathLab also includes access to the **Pearson Tutor Center** (www.pearsontutorservices.com). The Tutor Center is staffed by qualified mathematics instructors who provide textbook-specific tutoring for students via toll-free phone, fax, email, and interactive Web sessions. MyMathLab is available to qualified adopters. For more information, visit our website at www.mymathlab.com or contact your sales representative.

MathXL® Online Course (access code required)

MathXL® is a powerful online homework, tutorial, and assessment system that accompanies Pearson Education's textbooks in mathematics or statistics. With MathXL, instructors can create, edit, and assign online homework and tests using algorithmically generated exercises correlated to the textbook's objectives. They can also create and assign their own online exercises and import TestGen tests for added flexibility. All student work is tracked in MathXL's online gradebook. Students can take chapter tests in MathXL and receive personalized study plans based on their test results. The study plan diagnoses weaknesses and links students directly to tutorial exercises for the objectives they need to study and retest. Students can also access supplemental video clips directly from selected exercises. MathXL is available to qualified adopters. For more information, visit our website at www.mathxl.com, or contact your Pearson sales representative.

Visual Calculus

Built from the ground up by David Schneider (University of Maryland), the Visual Calculus software enhances the visualization and therefore the understanding of the *ideas* behind the calculus. With this software students can: analyze a function and its derivatives, examine solutions of differential equations, graph functions, calculate definite integrals, evaluate finite and infinite sums, graph Taylor approximations, plot cosine and sine functions and much more. This software adds further value for you for constructing graphs for exams. Visual Calculus is available for download from the Website www.pearsoned.com/goldstein.

Acknowledgments

The following is a list of reviewers from this and previous editions. We apologize for any omissions. While writing this book, we have received assistance from many persons, and our heartfelt thanks goes out to them all. Especially, we would like to thank our reviewers, who took the time and energy to share their ideas, preferences, and often their enthusiasm with us.

James V. Balch, *Middle Tennessee State University*

Jack R. Barone, *Baruch College, CUNY*

Michael J. Berman, *James Madison University*

Dennis Bertholf, *Oklahoma State University*

Fred Brauer, *University of Wisconsin*

Dennis Brewer, *University of Arkansas*

James Brewer, *Florida Atlantic University*

Todd Brost, *South Dakota State University*

Robert Brown, *University of California, Los Angeles*

Robert Brown, *University of Kansas*

Alan Candiotti, *Drew University*

Der-Chen Chang, *Georgetown University*

Charles Clever, *South Dakota State University*

W. E. Conway, *University of Arizona*

Biswa Datta, *Northern Illinois University*

Karabi Datta, *Northern Illinois University*

Dennis DeTurck, *University of Pennsylvania*

Brenda Diesslin, *Iowa State University*

Bruce Edward, *University of Florida*

Janice Epstein, *Texas A&M University*

Albert G. Fadell, *SUNY Buffalo*

Betty Fein, *Oregon State University*

Howard Frisinger, *Colorado State University*

Larry Gerstein, *University of California, Santa Barbara*

Shirley A. Goldman, *University of California, Davis*

Jack E. Graves, *Syracuse University*

Harvey Greenwald, *California State Polytechnic University*

David Harbater, *University of Pennsylvania*

James L. Heitsch, *University of Illinois, Chicago*

Donald Hight, *Kansas State College of Pittsburg*

Charles Himmelberg, *University of Kansas*

W. R. Hintzman, *San Diego State University*

James E. Honeycutt, *North Carolina University*

E. John Hornsby, Jr., *University of New Orleans*

James A. Huckaba, *University of Missouri*

Samuel Jasper, *Ohio University*

Shujuan Ji, *Columbia University*

James Kaplan, *Boston University*

Judy B. Kidd, *James Madison University*

W. T. Kyner, *University of New Mexico*

T. Y. Lam, *University of California, Berkeley*

Lawrence J. Lardy, *Syracuse University*

Melvin D. Lax, *California State University, Long Beach*

Russell Lee, *Allan Hancock College*

Joyce Longman, *Villanova University*

Roy Lowman, *University of Illinois, Chicago*

Gabriel Lugo, *University of North Carolina, Wilmington*

Gordon Lukesh, *University of Texas, Austin*

John H. Mathews, *California State University, Fullerton*

William McCord, *University of Missouri*

Ann McGaw, *University of Texas, Austin*

Albert J. Milani, *University of Wisconsin-Milwaukee*

Robert A. Miller, *City University New York*

Carl David Minda, *University of Cincinnati*

Donald E. Myers, *University of Arizona, Tempe*

Dana Nimic, *Southeast Community College-Lincoln*

David W. Penico, *Virginia Commonwealth University*

Georgia B. Pyrros, *University of Delaware*

H. Suey Quan, *Golden West College*

Jens Rademacher, *University of British Columbia*

Heath K. Riggs, *University of Vermont*

Ronald Rose, *American River College*

Arthur Rosenthal, *Salem State College*

Murray Schechter, *Lehigh University*

Claude Schochet, *Wayne State University*

Arthur J. Schwartz, *University of Michigan*

Robert Seeley, *University of Massachusetts, Boston*

Arlene Sherburne, *Montgomery College, Rockville*

James Sochacki, *James Madison University*

Edward Spanier, *University of California, Berkeley*

H. Keith Stumpff, *Central Missouri State University*

Bruce Swenson, *Foothill College*

Geraldine Taiani, *Pace University*

Joan M. Thomas, *University of Oregon*

Frankl Warner, *University of Pennsylvania*

Dennis White, *University of Minnesota*

Dennis A. Widup, *University of Wisconsin-Parkside*

W. R. Wilson, *Central Piedmont Community College*

Carla Wofsky, *University of New Mexico*

Wallace A. Wood, *Bryant University*

The authors would like to thank the many people at Pearson Education who have contributed to the success of our books over the years. We appreciate the tremendous efforts of the production, art, manufacturing, and marketing departments. Special thanks go to Bob Walters, who managed production of this book. Many thanks to Jason Aubrey for his contributions to the technology sections. We also thank the accuracy checkers: Damon Demas, Blaise DeSesa, Doug Ewert, Bev Fusfield, Debra McGivney, Theresa Schille, Lauri Semarne, and Tom Wegleitner. The expert skills of our typesetter, Dennis Kletzing, have once again eased the burden of preparing this new edition.

Thanks also to Gracia Nabhane, M.D., for her help with the applications in biology and medicine.

The authors would like to thank our editor, Chuck Synovec, who helped us plan this edition.

Larry J. Goldstein
larrygoldstein@comcast.net

David C. Lay
lay@math.umd.edu

David I. Schneider
dis@math.umd.edu

Nakhlé H. Asmar
nakhle@math.missouri.edu

FUNCTIONS OF SEVERAL VARIABLES

Until now, most of our applications of calculus have involved functions of one variable. In real life, however, a quantity of interest often depends on more than one variable. For instance, the sales level of a product may depend not only on its price, but also on the prices of competing products, the amount spent on advertising, and perhaps the time of year. The total cost of manufacturing the product depends on the cost of raw materials, labor, plant maintenance, and so on.

This chapter introduces the basic ideas of calculus for functions of more than one variable. Section 7.1 presents two examples that will be used throughout the chapter. Derivatives are treated in Section 7.2 and then used in Sections 7.3 and 7.4 to solve optimization problems more general than those in Chapter 2. The final two sections are devoted to least-squares problems and a brief introduction to the integration of functions of two variables.

7.1 Examples of Functions of Several Variables

A function $f(x, y)$ of the two variables x and y is a rule that assigns a number to each pair of values for the variables; for instance,

$$f(x, y) = e^x(x^2 + 2y).$$

An example of a function of three variables is

$$f(x, y, z) = 5xy^2z.$$

EXAMPLE 1   A store sells butter at \$2.50 per pound and margarine at \$1.40 per pound. The revenue from the sale of x pounds of butter and y pounds of margarine is given by the function

$$f(x, y) = 2.50x + 1.40y.$$

Determine and interpret $f(200, 300)$.

Solution $f(200, 300) = 2.50(200) + 1.40(300) = 500 + 420 = 920$. The revenue from the sale of 200 pounds of butter and 300 pounds of margarine is \$920. ■

A function $f(x, y)$ of two variables may be graphed in a manner analogous to that for functions of one variable. It is necessary to use a three-dimensional coordinate system, where each point is identified by three coordinates (x, y, z). For each choice of x, y, the graph of $f(x, y)$ includes the point $(x, y, f(x, y))$. This graph is usually a surface in three-dimensional space, with equation $z = f(x, y)$. (See Fig. 1.) Three graphs of specific functions are shown in Fig. 2.

Application to Architectural Design   When designing a building, we would like to know, at least approximately, how much heat the building loses per day. The heat loss affects many aspects of the design, such as the size of the heating plant, the size and location of duct work, and so on. A building loses heat through its sides, roof, and floor. How much heat is lost will generally differ for each face of the building and will depend on such factors as insulation, materials used in construction, exposure (north, south, east, or west), and climate. It is possible to estimate how much heat is lost per square foot of each face. Using these data, we can construct a heat-loss function as in the following example.

EXAMPLE 2   A rectangular industrial building of dimensions x, y, and z is shown in Fig. 3(a). In Fig. 3(b) we give the amount of heat lost per day by each side of the building, measured in suitable units of heat per square foot. Let $f(x, y, z)$ be the total daily heat loss for such a building.

(a) Find a formula for $f(x, y, z)$.

(b) Find the total daily heat loss if the building has length 100 feet, width 70 feet, and height 50 feet.

Solution **(a)** The total heat loss is the sum of the amount of heat loss through each face of the building. The heat loss through the roof is

[heat loss per square foot of roof] · [area of roof in square feet] $= 10xy$.

Similarly, the heat loss through the east side is $8yz$. Continuing in this way, we see that the total daily heat loss is

$$f(x, y, z) = 10xy + 8yz + 6yz + 10xz + 5xz + 1 \cdot xy.$$

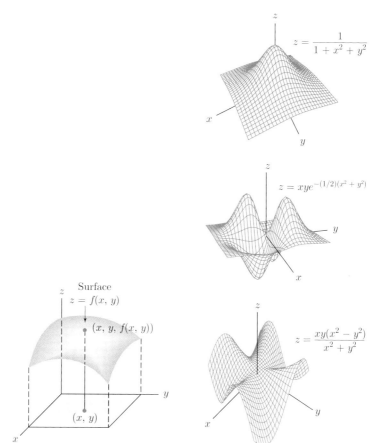

Figure 1.   Graph of $f(x,y)$.   **Figure 2**

We collect terms to obtain

$$f(x, y, z) = 11xy + 14yz + 15xz.$$

(b) The amount of heat loss when $x = 100$, $y = 70$, and $z = 50$ is given by $f(100, 70, 50)$, which equals

$$f(100, 70, 50) = 11(100)(70) + 14(70)(50) + 15(100)(50)$$
$$= 77{,}000 + 49{,}000 + 75{,}000 = 201{,}000.$$

In Section 7.3 we will determine the dimensions x, y, z that minimize the heat loss for a building of specific volume.

Production Functions in Economics   The costs of a manufacturing process can generally be classified as one of two types: cost of labor and cost of capital. The meaning of the cost of labor is clear. By the cost of capital, we mean the cost of buildings, tools, machines, and similar items used in the production process. A manufacturer usually has some control over the relative portions of labor and capital utilized in its production process. It can completely automate production so that labor is at a minimum or utilize mostly labor and little capital. Suppose that x units of labor and y units of capital are used.* Let $f(x, y)$ denote the number of units

---
*Economists normally use L and K, respectively, for labor and capital. However, for simplicity, we use x and y.

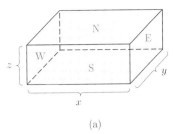

(a)

	Roof	East side	West side	North side	South side	Floor
Heat loss (per sq ft)	10	8	6	10	5	1
Area (sq ft)	xy	yz	yz	xz	xz	xy

(b)

Figure 3. Heat loss from an industrial building.

of finished product that are manufactured. Economists have found that $f(x, y)$ is often a function of the form

$$f(x, y) = Cx^A y^{1-A},$$

where A and C are constants, $0 < A < 1$. Such a function is called a *Cobb–Douglas production function*.

EXAMPLE 3

Production in a firm Suppose that during a certain time period the number of units of goods produced when utilizing x units of labor and y units of capital is $f(x, y) = 60x^{3/4}y^{1/4}$.

(a) How many units of goods will be produced by using 81 units of labor and 16 units of capital?

(b) Show that whenever the amounts of labor and capital being used are doubled so is the production. (Economists say that the production function has "constant returns to scale.")

Solution (a) $f(81, 16) = 60(81)^{3/4} \cdot (16)^{1/4} = 60 \cdot 27 \cdot 2 = 3240$. There will be 3240 units of goods produced.

(b) Utilization of a units of labor and b units of capital results in the production of $f(a, b) = 60a^{3/4}b^{1/4}$ units of goods. Utilizing $2a$ and $2b$ units of labor and capital, respectively, results in $f(2a, 2b)$ units produced. Set $x = 2a$ and $y = 2b$. Then we see that

$$f(2a, 2b) = 60(2a)^{3/4}(2b)^{1/4}$$
$$= 60 \cdot 2^{3/4} \cdot a^{3/4} \cdot 2^{1/4} \cdot b^{1/4}$$
$$= 60 \cdot 2^{(3/4+1/4)} \cdot a^{3/4}b^{1/4}$$
$$= 2^1 \cdot 60a^{3/4}b^{1/4}$$
$$= 2f(a, b).$$

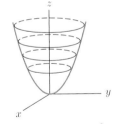

Graph of $f(x, y) = x^2 + y^2$

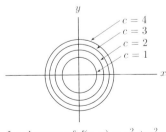

Level curves of $f(x, y) = x^2 + y^2$

Figure 4. Level curves.

Level Curves It is possible graphically to depict a function $f(x, y)$ of two variables using a family of curves called level curves. Let c be any number. Then the graph of the equation $f(x, y) = c$ is a curve in the xy-plane called the *level curve of height c*. This curve describes all points of height c on the graph of the function $f(x, y)$. As c varies, we have a family of level curves indicating the sets of points on which $f(x, y)$ assumes various values c. In Fig. 4 we have drawn the graph and various level curves for the function $f(x, y) = x^2 + y^2$.

Level curves often have interesting physical interpretations. For example, surveyors draw *topographic maps* that use level curves to represent points having equal altitude. Here $f(x, y) =$ the altitude at point (x, y). Figure 5(a) shows the graph of

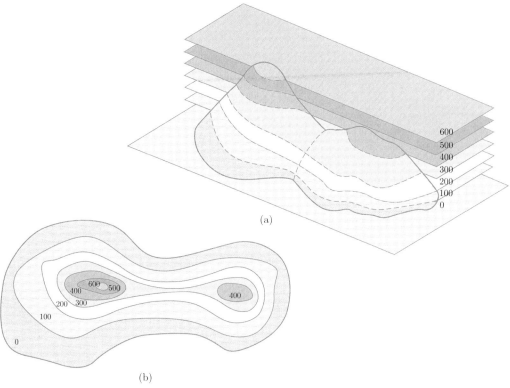

(a)

(b)

Figure 5. Topographic level curves show altitudes.

$f(x,y)$ for a typical hilly region. Figure 5(b) shows the level curves corresponding to various altitudes. Note that when the level curves are closer together the surface is steeper.

EXAMPLE 4 Determine the level curve at height 600 for the production function $f(x,y) = 60x^{3/4}y^{1/4}$ of Example 3.

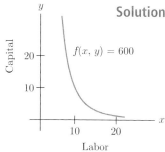

Figure 6. A level curve of a production function.

Solution The level curve is the graph of $f(x,y) = 600$, or

$$60x^{3/4}y^{1/4} = 600$$

$$y^{1/4} = \frac{10}{x^{3/4}}$$

$$y = \frac{10{,}000}{x^3}.$$

Of course, since x and y represent quantities of labor and capital, they must both be positive. We have sketched the graph of the level curve in Fig. 6. The points on the curve are precisely those combinations of capital and labor that yield 600 units of production. Economists call this curve an *isoquant* . ∎

Practice Problems 7.1

1. Let $f(x,y,z) = x^2 + y/(x-z) - 4$. Compute $f(3,5,2)$.

2. In a certain country the daily demand for coffee is

given by $f(p_1, p_2) = 16p_1/p_2$ thousand pounds, where p_1 and p_2 are the respective prices of tea and coffee in dollars per pound. Compute and interpret $f(3,4)$.

EXERCISES 7.1

1. Let $f(x, y) = x^2 - 3xy - y^2$. Compute $f(5, 0)$, $f(5, -2)$, and $f(a, b)$.

2. Let $g(x, y) = \sqrt{x^2 + 2y^2}$. Compute $g(1, 1)$, $g(0, -1)$, and $g(a, b)$.

3. Let $g(x, y, z) = x/(y - z)$. Compute $g(2, 3, 4)$ and $g(7, 46, 44)$.

4. Let $f(x, y, z) = x^2 e^{\sqrt{y^2 + z^2}}$. Compute $f(1, -1, 1)$ and $f(2, 3, -4)$.

5. Let $f(x, y) = xy$. Show that $f(2 + h, 3) - f(2, 3) = 3h$.

6. Let $f(x, y) = xy$. Show that $f(2, 3 + k) - f(2, 3) = 2k$.

7. Cost Find a formula $C(x, y, z)$ that gives the cost of materials for the closed rectangular box in Fig. 7(a), with dimensions in feet. Assume that the material for the top and bottom costs \$3 per square foot and the material for the sides costs \$5 per square foot.

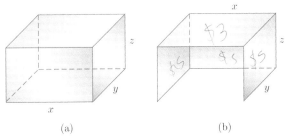

(a)   (b)

Figure 7

8. Cost Find a formula $C(x, y, z)$ that gives the cost of material for the rectangular enclosure in Fig. 7(b), with dimensions in feet. Assume that the material for the top costs \$3 per square foot and the material for the back and two sides costs \$5 per square foot.

9. Consider the Cobb–Douglas production function $f(x, y) = 20x^{1/3}y^{2/3}$. Compute $f(8, 1)$, $f(1, 27)$, and $f(8, 27)$. Show that, for any positive constant k, $f(8k, 27k) = kf(8, 27)$.

10. Let $f(x, y) = 10x^{2/5}y^{3/5}$. Show that $f(3a, 3b) = 3f(a, b)$.

11. The present value of A dollars to be paid t years in the future (assuming a 5% continuous interest rate) is $P(A, t) = Ae^{-.05t}$. Find and interpret $P(100, 13.8)$.

12. Refer to Example 3. If labor costs \$100 per unit and capital costs \$200 per unit, express as a function of two variables, $C(x, y)$, the cost of utilizing x units of labor and y units of capital.

13. Tax and Homeowner Exemption The value of residential property for tax purposes is usually much lower than its actual market value. If v is the market value, the *assessed value* for real estate taxes might be only 40%

of v. Suppose that the property tax, T, in a community is given by the function

$$T = f(r, v, x) = \frac{r}{100}(.40v - x),$$

where v is the estimated market value of a property (in dollars), x is a *homeowner's exemption* (a number of dollars depending on the type of property), and r is the tax rate (stated in dollars per hundred dollars) of net assessed value.

(a) Determine the real estate tax on a property valued at \$200,000 with a homeowner's exemption of \$5000, assuming a tax rate of \$2.50 per hundred dollars of net assessed value.

(b) Determine the tax due if the tax rate increases by 20% to \$3.00 per hundred dollars of net assessed value. Assume the same property value and homeowner's exemption. Does the tax due also increase by 20%?

14. Let $f(r, v, x)$ be the real estate tax function of Exercise 13.

(a) Determine the real estate tax on a property valued at \$100,000 with a homeowner's exemption of \$5000, assuming a tax rate of \$2.20 per hundred dollars of net assessed value.

(b) Determine the real estate tax when the market value rises 20% to \$120,000. Assume the same homeowner's exemption and a tax rate of \$2.20 per hundred dollars of net assessed value. Does the tax due also increase by 20%?

Draw the level curves of heights 0, 1, and 2 for the functions in Exercises 15 and 16.

15. $f(x, y) = 2x - y$ **16.** $f(x, y) = -x^2 + 2y$

17. Draw the level curve of the function $f(x, y) = x - y$ containing the point $(0, 0)$.

18. Draw the level curve of the function $f(x, y) = xy$ containing the point $(\frac{1}{2}, 4)$.

19. Find a function $f(x, y)$ that has the line $y = 3x - 4$ as a level curve.

20. Find a function $f(x, y)$ that has the curve $y = 2/x^2$ as a level curve.

21. Suppose that a topographic map is viewed as the graph of a certain function $f(x, y)$. What are the level curves?

22. A certain production process uses labor and capital. If the quantities of these commodities are x and y, respectively, the total cost is $100x + 200y$ dollars. Draw the level curves of height 600, 800, and 1000 for this function. Explain the significance of these curves. (Economists frequently refer to these lines as *budget lines* or *isocost lines*.)

Match the graphs of the functions in Exercises 23–26 to the systems of level curves shown in Figs. 8(a)–(d).

23.

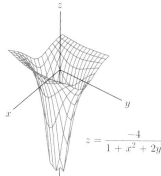

$$z = \frac{-4}{1 + x^2 + 2y^2}$$

24.

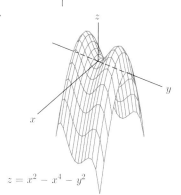

$$z = x^2 - x^4 - y^2$$

25.

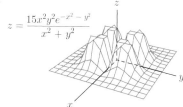

$$z = \frac{15x^2 y^2 e^{-x^2 - y^2}}{x^2 + y^2}$$

26.

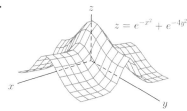

$$z = e^{-x^2} + e^{-4y^2}$$

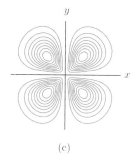

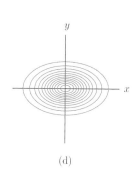

(a)   (b)   (c)   (d)

Figure 8

Solutions to Practice Problems 7.1

1. Substitute 3 for x, 5 for y, and 2 for z.

$$f(3, 5, 2) = 3^2 + \frac{5}{3 - 2} - 4 = 10.$$

2. To compute $f(3, 4)$, substitute 3 for p_1 and 4 for p_2 into $f(p_1, p_2) = 16p_1/p_2$. Thus

$$f(3, 4) = 16 \cdot \tfrac{3}{4} = 12.$$

Therefore, if the price of tea is \$3 per pound and the price of coffee is \$4 per pound, 12,000 pounds of coffee will be sold each day. (Notice that as the price of coffee increases the demand decreases.)

7.2 Partial Derivatives

In Chapter 1 we introduced the notion of a derivative to measure the rate at which a function $f(x)$ is changing with respect to changes in the variable x. Let us now study the analog of the derivative for functions of two (or more) variables.

Let $f(x, y)$ be a function of the two variables x and y. Since we want to know how $f(x, y)$ changes with respect to the changes in both the variable x and the variable y, we shall define two derivatives of $f(x, y)$ (to be called partial derivatives), one with respect to each variable.

DEFINITION The *partial derivative of $f(x, y)$ with respect to x*, written $\dfrac{\partial f}{\partial x}$, is the derivative of $f(x, y)$, where y is treated as a constant and $f(x, y)$ is considered as a function of x alone. The *partial derivative of $f(x, y)$ with respect to y*, written $\dfrac{\partial f}{\partial y}$, is the derivative of $f(x, y)$, where x is treated as a constant.

EXAMPLE 1 Let $f(x, y) = 5x^3 y^2$. Compute

$$\frac{\partial f}{\partial x} \quad \text{and} \quad \frac{\partial f}{\partial y}.$$

Solution To compute $\dfrac{\partial f}{\partial x}$, we think of $f(x, y)$ written as

$$f(x, y) = \left[5y^2\right] x^3,$$

where the brackets emphasize that $5y^2$ is to be treated as a constant. Therefore, when differentiating with respect to x, $f(x, y)$ is just a constant times x^3. Recall that if k is any constant then

$$\frac{d}{dx}(kx^3) = 3 \cdot k \cdot x^2.$$

Thus

$$\frac{\partial f}{\partial x} = 3 \cdot \left[5y^2\right] \cdot x^2 = 15x^2 y^2.$$

After some practice, it is unnecessary to place the y^2 in front of the x^3 before differentiating.

Now, to compute $\dfrac{\partial f}{\partial y}$, we think of

$$f(x, y) = \left[5x^3\right] y^2.$$

When differentiating with respect to y, $f(x, y)$ is simply a constant (that is, $5x^3$) times y^2. Hence

$$\frac{\partial f}{\partial y} = 2 \cdot \left[5x^3\right] \cdot y = 10x^3 y. \qquad \blacksquare$$

EXAMPLE 2 Let $f(x, y) = 3x^2 + 2xy + 5y$. Compute

$$\frac{\partial f}{\partial x} \quad \text{and} \quad \frac{\partial f}{\partial y}.$$

Solution To compute $\dfrac{\partial f}{\partial x}$, we think of

$$f(x,y) = 3x^2 + [2y]x + [5y].$$

Now we differentiate $f(x,y)$ as if it were a quadratic polynomial in x:

$$\frac{\partial f}{\partial x} = 6x + [2y] + 0 = 6x + 2y.$$

Note that $5y$ is treated as a constant when differentiating with respect to x, so the partial derivative of $5y$ with respect to x is zero.

To compute $\dfrac{\partial f}{\partial y}$, we think of

$$f(x,y) = [3x^2] + [2x]y + 5y.$$

Then

$$\frac{\partial f}{\partial y} = 0 + [2x] + 5 = 2x + 5.$$

Note that $3x^2$ is treated as a constant when differentiating with respect to y, so the partial derivative of $3x^2$ with respect to y is zero. ∎

EXAMPLE 3

Compute

$$\frac{\partial f}{\partial x} \quad \text{and} \quad \frac{\partial f}{\partial y}$$

for each of the following.

(a) $f(x,y) = (4x + 3y - 5)^8$ (b) $f(x,y) = e^{xy^2}$ (c) $f(x,y) = y/(x+3y)$

Solution (a) To compute $\dfrac{\partial f}{\partial x}$, we think of

$$f(x,y) = (4x + [3y - 5])^8.$$

By the general power rule,

$$\frac{\partial f}{\partial x} = 8 \cdot (4x + [3y - 5])^7 \cdot 4 = 32(4x + 3y - 5)^7.$$

Here we used the fact that the derivative of $4x + 3y - 5$ with respect to x is just 4.

To compute $\dfrac{\partial f}{\partial y}$, we think of

$$f(x,y) = ([4x] + 3y - 5)^8.$$

Then

$$\frac{\partial f}{\partial y} = 8 \cdot ([4x] + 3y - 5)^7 \cdot 3 = 24(4x + 3y - 5)^7.$$

(b) To compute $\dfrac{\partial f}{\partial x}$, we observe that

$$f(x,y) = e^{x[y^2]},$$

so that

$$\frac{\partial f}{\partial x} = [y^2]\, e^{x[y^2]} = y^2 e^{xy^2}.$$

To compute $\dfrac{\partial f}{\partial y}$, we think of

$$f(x,y) = e^{[x]y^2}.$$

Thus

$$\frac{\partial f}{\partial y} = e^{[x]y^2} \cdot 2[x]y = 2xye^{xy^2}.$$

$\frac{y}{x+3y}$

(c) To compute $\frac{\partial f}{\partial x}$, we use the general power rule to differentiate $[y](x+[3y])^{-1}$ with respect to x:

$$\frac{\partial f}{\partial x} = (-1) \cdot [y](x+[3y])^{-2} \cdot 1 = -\frac{y}{(x+3y)^2}.$$

To compute $\frac{\partial f}{\partial y}$, we use the quotient rule to differentiate

$$f(x,y) = \frac{y}{[x]+3y}$$

with respect to y. We find that

$$\frac{\partial f}{\partial y} = \frac{([x]+3y)\cdot 1 - y\cdot 3}{([x]+3y)^2} = \frac{x}{(x+3y)^2}.$$

The use of brackets to highlight constants is helpful initially to compute partial derivatives. From now on we shall merely form a mental picture of those terms to be treated as constants and dispense with brackets.

A partial derivative of a function of several variables is also a function of several variables and hence can be evaluated at specific values of the variables. We write

$$\frac{\partial f}{\partial x}(a,b)$$

for $\frac{\partial f}{\partial x}$ evaluated at $x=a$, $y=b$. Similarly,

$$\frac{\partial f}{\partial y}(a,b)$$

denotes the function $\frac{\partial f}{\partial y}$ evaluated at $x=a$, $y=b$.

EXAMPLE 4   Let $f(x,y) = 3x^2 + 2xy + 5y$.

(a) Calculate $\frac{\partial f}{\partial x}(1,4)$.   **(b)** Evaluate $\frac{\partial f}{\partial y}$ at $(x,y)=(1,4)$.

Solution (a) $\frac{\partial f}{\partial x} = 6x + 2y$, $\frac{\partial f}{\partial x}(1,4) = 6\cdot 1 + 2\cdot 4 = 14$.

(b) $\frac{\partial f}{\partial y} = 2x + 5$, $\frac{\partial f}{\partial y}(1,4) = 2\cdot 1 + 5 = 7$.

Geometric Interpretation of Partial Derivatives   Consider the three-dimensional surface $z = f(x,y)$ in Fig. 1. If y is held constant at b and x is allowed to vary, the equation

$$z = f(x,b)$$

constant

describes a curve on the surface. [The curve is formed by cutting the surface $z = f(x,y)$ with a vertical plane parallel to the xz-plane.] The value of $\frac{\partial f}{\partial x}(a,b)$ is the slope of the tangent line to the curve at the point where $x=a$ and $y=b$.

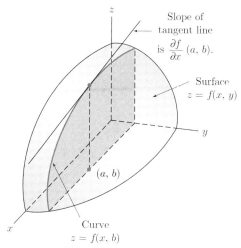

Figure 1. $\frac{\partial f}{\partial x}$ gives the slope of a curve formed by holding y constant.

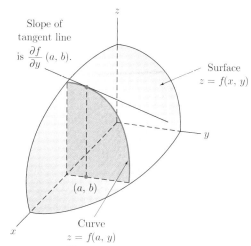

Figure 2. $\frac{\partial f}{\partial y}$ gives the slope of a curve formed by holding x constant.

Likewise, if x is held constant at a and y is allowed to vary, the equation

$$z = f(a, y)$$

└─ constant

describes the curve on the surface $z = f(x, y)$ shown in Fig. 2. The value of the partial derivative $\frac{\partial f}{\partial y}(a, b)$ is the slope of this curve at the point where $x = a$ and $y = b$.

Partial Derivatives and Rates of Change Since $\frac{\partial f}{\partial x}$ is simply the ordinary derivative with y held constant, $\frac{\partial f}{\partial x}$ gives the rate of change of $f(x, y)$ with respect to x for y held constant. In other words, keeping y constant and increasing x by one (small) unit produces a change in $f(x, y)$ that is approximately given by $\frac{\partial f}{\partial x}$. An analogous interpretation holds for $\frac{\partial f}{\partial y}$.

EXAMPLE 5 Interpret the partial derivatives of $f(x, y) = 3x^2 + 2xy + 5y$ calculated in Example 4.

Solution We showed in Example 4 that

$$\frac{\partial f}{\partial x}(1, 4) = 14, \qquad \frac{\partial f}{\partial y}(1, 4) = 7.$$

The fact that

$$\frac{\partial f}{\partial x}(1, 4) = 14$$

means that if y is kept constant at 4 and x is allowed to vary near 1, then $f(x, y)$ changes at a rate 14 times the change in x. That is, if x increases by one small unit, $f(x, y)$ increases by approximately 14 units. If x increases by h units (where h is small), $f(x, y)$ increases by approximately $14 \cdot h$ units. That is,

$$f(1 + h, 4) - f(1, 4) \approx 14 \cdot h.$$

Similarly, the fact that

$$\frac{\partial f}{\partial y}(1,4) = 7$$

means that, if we keep x constant at 1 and let y vary near 4, then $f(x,y)$ changes at a rate equal to seven times the change in y. So, for a small value of k, we have

$$f(1, 4+k) - f(1,4) \approx 7 \cdot k.$$

We can generalize the interpretations of $\frac{\partial f}{\partial x}$ and $\frac{\partial f}{\partial y}$ given in Example 5 to yield the following general fact:

Let $f(x,y)$ be a function of two variables. Then, if h and k are small, we have

$$f(a+h, b) - f(a,b) \approx \frac{\partial f}{\partial x}(a,b) \cdot h,$$

$$f(a, b+k) - f(a,b) \approx \frac{\partial f}{\partial y}(a,b) \cdot k.$$

Partial derivatives can be computed for functions of any number of variables. When taking the partial derivative with respect to one variable, we treat the other variables as constant.

EXAMPLE 6   Let $f(x,y,z) = x^2yz - 3z$.

    (a) Compute $\frac{\partial f}{\partial x}, \frac{\partial f}{\partial y},$ and $\frac{\partial f}{\partial z}$.   (b) Calculate $\frac{\partial f}{\partial z}(2,3,1)$.

Solution (a) $\frac{\partial f}{\partial x} = 2xyz, \ \frac{\partial f}{\partial y} = x^2z, \ \frac{\partial f}{\partial z} = x^2y - 3.$

    (b) $\frac{\partial f}{\partial z}(2,3,1) = 2^2 \cdot 3 - 3 = 12 - 3 = 9.$

EXAMPLE 7   Let $f(x,y,z)$ be the heat-loss function computed in Example 2 of Section 7.1. That is, $f(x,y,z) = 11xy + 14yz + 15xz$. Calculate and interpret $\frac{\partial f}{\partial x}(10,7,5)$.

Solution We have

$$\frac{\partial f}{\partial x} = 11y + 15z$$

$$\frac{\partial f}{\partial x}(10,7,5) = 11 \cdot 7 + 15 \cdot 5 = 77 + 75 = 152.$$

The quantity $\frac{\partial f}{\partial x}$ is commonly referred to as the *marginal heat loss with respect to change in x*. Specifically, if x is changed from 10 by h units (where h is small) and the values of y and z remain fixed at 7 and 5, the amount of heat loss will change by approximately $152 \cdot h$ units.

EXAMPLE 8   **Production** Consider the production function $f(x,y) = 60x^{3/4}y^{1/4}$, which gives the number of units of goods produced when utilizing x units of labor and y units of capital.

(a) Find $\dfrac{\partial f}{\partial x}$ and $\dfrac{\partial f}{\partial y}$.

(b) Evaluate $\dfrac{\partial f}{\partial x}$ and $\dfrac{\partial f}{\partial y}$ at $x = 81$, $y = 16$.

(c) Interpret the numbers computed in part (b).

Solution (a) $\dfrac{\partial f}{\partial x} = 60 \cdot \dfrac{3}{4} x^{-1/4} y^{1/4} = 45 x^{-1/4} y^{1/4} = 45 \dfrac{y^{1/4}}{x^{1/4}}$,

$\dfrac{\partial f}{\partial y} = 60 \cdot \dfrac{1}{4} x^{3/4} y^{-3/4} = 15 x^{3/4} y^{-3/4} = 15 \dfrac{x^{3/4}}{y^{3/4}}$.

(b) $\dfrac{\partial f}{\partial x}(81, 16) = 45 \cdot \dfrac{16^{1/4}}{81^{1/4}} = 45 \cdot \dfrac{2}{3} = 30$,

$\dfrac{\partial f}{\partial y}(81, 16) = 15 \cdot \dfrac{81^{3/4}}{16^{3/4}} = 15 \cdot \dfrac{27}{8} = \dfrac{405}{8} = 50\frac{5}{8}$.

(c) The quantities $\dfrac{\partial f}{\partial x}$ and $\dfrac{\partial f}{\partial y}$ are referred to as the *marginal productivity of labor* and the *marginal productivity of capital*. If the amount of capital is held fixed at $y = 16$ and the amount of labor increases by 1 unit, the quantity of goods produced will increase by approximately 30 units. Similarly, an increase in capital of 1 unit (with labor fixed at 81) results in an increase in production of approximately $50\frac{5}{8}$ units of goods. ■

Just as we formed second derivatives in the case of one variable, we can form second partial derivatives of a function $f(x, y)$ of two variables. Since $\dfrac{\partial f}{\partial x}$ is a function of x and y, we can differentiate it with respect to x or y. The partial derivative of $\dfrac{\partial f}{\partial x}$ with respect to x is denoted by $\dfrac{\partial^2 f}{\partial x^2}$. The partial derivative of $\dfrac{\partial f}{\partial x}$ with respect to y is denoted by $\dfrac{\partial^2 f}{\partial y\, \partial x}$. Similarly, the partial derivative of the function $\dfrac{\partial f}{\partial y}$ with respect to x is denoted by $\dfrac{\partial^2 f}{\partial x\, \partial y}$, and the partial derivative of $\dfrac{\partial f}{\partial y}$ with respect to y is denoted by $\dfrac{\partial^2 f}{\partial y^2}$. Almost all functions $f(x, y)$ encountered in applications [and all functions $f(x, y)$ in this text] have the property that

$$\frac{\partial^2 f}{\partial y\, \partial x} = \frac{\partial^2 f}{\partial x\, \partial y}.$$

When computing $\dfrac{\partial^2 f}{\partial y\, \partial x}$ and $\dfrac{\partial^2 f}{\partial x\, \partial y}$, note that verifying the last equation is a check that you have done the differentiation correctly.

EXAMPLE 9   Let $f(x, y) = x^2 + 3xy + 2y^2$. Calculate

$$\frac{\partial^2 f}{\partial x^2}, \quad \frac{\partial^2 f}{\partial y^2}, \quad \frac{\partial^2 f}{\partial x\, \partial y}, \quad \text{and} \quad \frac{\partial^2 f}{\partial y\, \partial x}.$$

Solution First we compute $\dfrac{\partial f}{\partial x}$ and $\dfrac{\partial f}{\partial y}$.

$$\frac{\partial f}{\partial x} = 2x + 3y, \qquad \frac{\partial f}{\partial y} = 3x + 4y.$$

To compute $\dfrac{\partial^2 f}{\partial x^2}$, we differentiate $\dfrac{\partial f}{\partial x}$ with respect to x:

$$\frac{\partial^2 f}{\partial x^2} = 2.$$

Similarly, to compute $\dfrac{\partial^2 f}{\partial y^2}$, we differentiate $\dfrac{\partial f}{\partial y}$ with respect to y:

$$\frac{\partial^2 f}{\partial y^2} = 4.$$

To compute $\dfrac{\partial^2 f}{\partial x\, \partial y}$, we differentiate $\dfrac{\partial f}{\partial y}$ with respect to x:

$$\frac{\partial^2 f}{\partial x\, \partial y} = 3.$$

Finally, to compute $\dfrac{\partial^2 f}{\partial y\, \partial x}$, we differentiate $\dfrac{\partial f}{\partial x}$ with respect to y:

$$\frac{\partial^2 f}{\partial y\, \partial x} = 3.$$

INCORPORATING TECHNOLOGY

Evaluating Partial Derivatives The function from Example 4 and its first partial derivatives are specified in Fig. 3(a) and evaluated in Fig. 3(b). Recall that the expression $1 \to X$ is entered with $\boxed{1}$ $\boxed{\text{STO} \triangleright}$ $\boxed{\text{X,T,}\theta\text{,}n}$ and indicates that we are setting $X = 1$. The expression $4 \to Y$ has a similar meaning, but the variable Y is entered using $\boxed{\text{ALPHA}}$ $[\text{Y}]$. We can also evaluate other partial derivatives. For example, the partial derivative $\dfrac{\partial^2 f}{\partial x\, \partial y}$ in this case could be found by setting

$$Y_4 = \text{nDeriv}(Y_3, X, X).$$

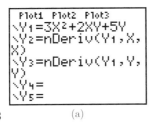
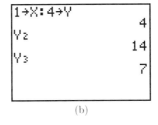

Figure 3   (a)   (b)

Practice Problems 7.2

1. The number of TV sets an appliance store sells per week is given by a function of two variables, $f(x, y)$, where x is the price per TV set and y is the amount of money spent weekly on advertising. Suppose that the current price is \$400 per set and that currently \$2000 per week is being spent for advertising.

   (a) Would you expect $\dfrac{\partial f}{\partial x}(400, 2000)$ to be positive or negative?

   (b) Would you expect $\dfrac{\partial f}{\partial y}(400, 2000)$ to be positive or negative?

2. The monthly mortgage payment for a house is a function of two variables, $f(A, r)$, where A is the amount of the mortgage and the interest rate is $r\%$. For a 30-year mortgage, $f(92{,}000, 9) = 740.25$ and $\dfrac{\partial f}{\partial r}(92{,}000, 9) = 66.20$. What is the significance of the number 66.20?

2   3

EXERCISES 7.2

Find $\dfrac{\partial f}{\partial x}$ *and* $\dfrac{\partial f}{\partial y}$ *for each of the following functions.*

1. $f(x,y) = 5xy$

2. $f(x,y) = x^2 - y^2$

3. $f(x,y) = 2x^2 e^y$

4. $f(x,y) = xe^{xy}$

5. $f(x,y) = \dfrac{x}{y} + \dfrac{y}{x}$

6. $f(x,y) = \dfrac{1}{x+y}$

7. $f(x,y) = (2x - y + 5)^2$

8. $f(x,y) = \dfrac{e^x}{1 + e^y}$

9. $f(x,y) = x^2 e^{3x} \ln y$

10. $f(x,y) = \ln(xy)$

11. $f(x,y) = \dfrac{x - y}{x + y}$

12. $f(x,y) = \sqrt{x^2 + y^2}$

13. Let $f(L,K) = 3\sqrt{LK}$. Find $\dfrac{\partial f}{\partial L}$.

14. Let $f(p,q) = 1 - p(1+q)$. Find $\dfrac{\partial f}{\partial q}$ and $\dfrac{\partial f}{\partial p}$.

15. Let $f(x,y,z) = (1 + x^2 y)/z$. Find $\dfrac{\partial f}{\partial x}, \dfrac{\partial f}{\partial y}$, and $\dfrac{\partial f}{\partial z}$.

16. Let $f(x,y,z) = ze^{x/y}$. Find $\dfrac{\partial f}{\partial x}, \dfrac{\partial f}{\partial y}$, and $\dfrac{\partial f}{\partial z}$.

17. Let $f(x,y,z) = xze^{yz}$. Find $\dfrac{\partial f}{\partial x}, \dfrac{\partial f}{\partial y}$, and $\dfrac{\partial f}{\partial z}$.

18. Let $f(x,y,z) = \dfrac{xy}{z}$. Find $\dfrac{\partial f}{\partial x}, \dfrac{\partial f}{\partial y}$, and $\dfrac{\partial f}{\partial z}$.

19. Let $f(x,y) = x^2 + 2xy + y^2 + 3x + 5y$. Find $\dfrac{\partial f}{\partial x}(2,-3)$ and $\dfrac{\partial f}{\partial y}(2,-3)$.

20. Let $f(x,y) = (x + y^2)^3$. Evaluate $\dfrac{\partial f}{\partial x}$ and $\dfrac{\partial f}{\partial y}$ at $(x,y) = (1,2)$.

21. Let $f(x,y,z) = xy^2 z + 5$. Evaluate $\dfrac{\partial f}{\partial y}$ at $(x,y,z) = (2,-1,3)$.

22. Let $f(x,y,z) = \dfrac{x}{y - z}$. Compute $\dfrac{\partial f}{\partial y}(2,-1,3)$.

23. Let $f(x,y) = x^3 y + 2xy^2$. Find $\dfrac{\partial^2 f}{\partial x^2}, \dfrac{\partial^2 f}{\partial y^2}, \dfrac{\partial^2 f}{\partial x\,\partial y}$, and $\dfrac{\partial^2 f}{\partial y\,\partial x}$.

24. Let $f(x,y) = xe^y + x^4 y + y^3$. Find $\dfrac{\partial^2 f}{\partial x^2}, \dfrac{\partial^2 f}{\partial y^2}, \dfrac{\partial^2 f}{\partial x\,\partial y}$, and $\dfrac{\partial^2 f}{\partial y\,\partial x}$.

25. Production A farmer can produce $f(x,y) = 200\sqrt{6x^2 + y^2}$ units of produce by utilizing x units of labor and y units of capital. (The capital is used to rent or purchase land, materials, and equipment.)

   (a) Calculate the marginal productivities of labor and capital when $x = 10$ and $y = 5$.

(b) Let h be a small number. Use the result of part (a) to determine the approximate effect on production of changing labor from 10 to $10 + h$ units while keeping capital fixed at 5 units.

(c) Use part (b) to estimate the change in production when labor decreases from 10 to 9.5 units and capital stays fixed at 5 units.

26. The productivity of a country is given by $f(x,y) = 300x^{2/3} y^{1/3}$, where x and y are the amount of labor and capital.

   (a) Compute the marginal productivities of labor and capital when $x = 125$ and $y = 64$.

   (b) Use part (a) to determine the approximate effect on productivity of increasing capital from 64 to 66 units, while keeping labor fixed at 125 units.

   (c) What would be the approximate effect of decreasing labor from 125 to 124 units while keeping capital fixed at 64 units?

27. Demand In a certain suburban community, commuters have the choice of getting into the city by bus or train. The demand for these modes of transportation varies with their cost. Let $f(p_1, p_2)$ be the number of people who will take the bus when p_1 is the price of the bus ride and p_2 is the price of the train ride. For example, if $f(4.50, 6) = 7000$, then 7000 commuters will take the bus when the price of a bus ticket is \$4.50 and the price of a train ticket is \$6.00. Explain why $\dfrac{\partial f}{\partial p_1} < 0$ and $\dfrac{\partial f}{\partial p_2} > 0$.

28. Refer to Exercise 27. Let $g(p_1, p_2)$ be the number of people who will take the train when p_1 is the price of the bus ride and p_2 is the price of the train ride. Would you expect $\dfrac{\partial g}{\partial p_1}$ to be positive or negative? How about $\dfrac{\partial g}{\partial p_2}$?

29. Let p_1 be the average price of DVD players, p_2 the average price of DVDs, $f(p_1, p_2)$ the demand for DVD players, and $g(p_1, p_2)$ the demand for DVDs. Explain why $\dfrac{\partial f}{\partial p_2} < 0$ and $\dfrac{\partial g}{\partial p_1} < 0$.

30. The demand for a certain gas-guzzling car is given by $f(p_1, p_2)$, where p_1 is the price of the car and p_2 is the price of gasoline. Explain why $\dfrac{\partial f}{\partial p_1} < 0$ and $\dfrac{\partial f}{\partial p_2} < 0$.

31. The volume (V) of a certain amount of a gas is determined by the temperature (T) and the pressure (P) by the formula $V = .08(T/P)$. Calculate and interpret $\dfrac{\partial V}{\partial P}$ and $\dfrac{\partial V}{\partial T}$ when $P = 20$, $T = 300$.

32. Beer Consumption Using data collected from 1929 to 1941, Richard Stone[*] determined that the yearly quantity Q of beer consumed in the United Kingdom was approximately given by the formula $Q = f(m, p, r, s)$, where

$$f(m, p, r, s) = (1.058)m^{.136}p^{-.727}r^{.914}s^{.816}$$

and m is the aggregate real income (personal income after direct taxes, adjusted for retail price changes), p is the average retail price of the commodity (in this case, beer), r is the average retail price level of all other consumer goods and services, and s is a measure of the strength of the beer. Determine which partial derivatives are positive and which are negative and give interpretations. (For example, since $\frac{\partial f}{\partial r} > 0$, people buy more beer when the prices of other goods increase and the other factors remain constant.)

33. Richard Stone (see Exercise 32) determined that the yearly consumption of food in the United States was given by

$$f(m, p, r) = (2.186)m^{.595}p^{-.543}r^{.922}.$$

Determine which partial derivatives are positive and which are negative and give interpretations of these facts.

34. Distribution of Revenue For the production function $f(x, y) = 60x^{3/4}y^{1/4}$ considered in Example 8, think of $f(x, y)$ as the revenue when utilizing x units of labor and y units of capital. Under actual operating conditions, say $x = a$ and $y = b$, $\frac{\partial f}{\partial x}(a, b)$ is referred to as the *wage per unit of labor* and $\frac{\partial f}{\partial y}(a, b)$ is referred to as the *wage per unit of capital*. Show that

$$f(a, b) = a \cdot \left[\frac{\partial f}{\partial x}(a, b) \right] + b \cdot \left[\frac{\partial f}{\partial y}(a, b) \right].$$

(This equation shows how the revenue is distributed between labor and capital.)

35. Compute $\dfrac{\partial^2 f}{\partial x^2}$, where $f(x, y) = 60x^{3/4}y^{1/4}$, a production function (where x is units of labor). Explain why $\dfrac{\partial^2 f}{\partial x^2}$ is always negative.

36. Compute $\dfrac{\partial^2 f}{\partial y^2}$, where $f(x, y) = 60x^{3/4}y^{1/4}$, a production function (where y is units of capital). Explain why $\dfrac{\partial^2 f}{\partial y^2}$ is always negative.

37. Let $f(x, y) = 3x^2 + 2xy + 5y$, as in Example 5. Show that

$$f(1 + h, 4) - f(1, 4) = 14h + 3h^2.$$

Thus the error in approximating $f(1+h, 4) - f(1, 4)$ by $14h$ is $3h^2$. (If $h = .01$, for instance, the error is only $.0003$.)

38. Body Surface Area Physicians, particularly pediatricians, sometimes need to know the body surface area of a patient. For instance, the surface area is used to adjust the results of certain tests of kidney performance. Tables are available that give the approximate body surface area A in square meters of a person who weighs W kilograms and is H centimeters tall. The following empirical formula[†] is also used:

$$A = .007W^{.425}H^{.725}.$$

Evaluate $\dfrac{\partial A}{\partial W}$ and $\dfrac{\partial A}{\partial H}$ when $W = 54$ and $H = 165$, and give a physical interpretation of your answers. You may use the approximations $(54)^{.425} \approx 5.4$, $(54)^{-.575} \approx .10$, $(165)^{.725} \approx 40.5$, and $(165)^{-.275} \approx .25$.

Solutions to Practice Problems 7.2

1. (a) Negative. $\dfrac{\partial f}{\partial x}(400, 2000)$ is approximately the change in sales due to a \$1 increase in x (price). Since raising prices lowers sales, we would expect $\dfrac{\partial f}{\partial x}(400, 2000)$ to be negative.

(b) Positive. $\dfrac{\partial f}{\partial y}(400, 2000)$ is approximately the change in sales due to a \$1 increase in advertising. Since spending more money on advertising

brings in more customers, we would expect sales to increase; that is, $\dfrac{\partial f}{\partial y}(400, 2000)$ is most likely positive.

2. If the interest rate is raised from 9% to 10%, the monthly payment will increase by about \$66.20. [An increase to $9\frac{1}{2}\%$ causes an increase in the monthly payment of about $\frac{1}{2} \cdot (66.20)$ or \$33.10, and so on.]

---

[*]Richard Stone, "The Analysis of Market Demand," *Journal of the Royal Statistical Society*, 108 (1945), 286–391.

[†]See J. Routh, *Mathematical Preparation for Laboratory Technicians* (Philadelphia: W. B. Saunders Co., 1971), p. 92.

7.3 Maxima and Minima of Functions of Several Variables

Previously, we studied how to determine the maxima and minima of functions of a single variable. Let us extend that discussion to functions of several variables.

If $f(x, y)$ is a function of two variables, we say that $f(x, y)$ has a *relative maximum* when $x = a$, $y = b$ if $f(x, y)$ is at most equal to $f(a, b)$ whenever x is near a and y is near b. Geometrically, the graph of $f(x, y)$ has a peak at $(x, y) = (a, b)$. [See Fig. 1(a).] Similarly, we say that $f(x, y)$ has a *relative minimum* when $x = a$, $y = b$ if $f(x, y)$ is at least equal to $f(a, b)$ whenever x is near a and y is near b. Geometrically, the graph of $f(x, y)$ has a pit whose bottom occurs at $(x, y) = (a, b)$. [See Fig. 1(b).]

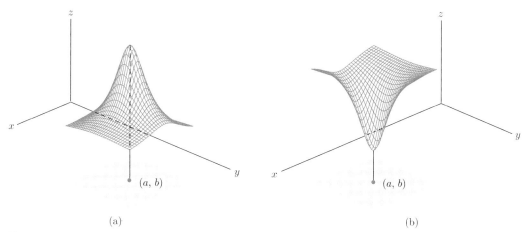

(a)   (b)

Figure 1. Maximum and minimum points.

Suppose that the function $f(x, y)$ has a relative minimum at $(x, y) = (a, b)$, as in Fig. 2. When y is held constant at b, $f(x, y)$ is a function of x with a relative minimum at $x = a$. Therefore, the tangent line to the curve $z = f(x, b)$ is horizontal at $x = a$ and hence has slope 0. That is,

$$\frac{\partial f}{\partial x}(a, b) = 0.$$

Likewise, when x is held constant at a, then $f(x, y)$ is a function of y with a relative minimum at $y = b$. Therefore, its derivative with respect to y is zero at $y = b$. That

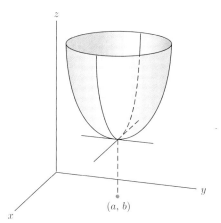

Figure 2. Horizontal tangent lines at a relative minimum.

is,

$$\frac{\partial f}{\partial y}(a,b) = 0.$$

Similar considerations apply when $f(x,y)$ has a relative maximum at $(x,y) = (a,b)$.

First-Derivative Test for Functions of Two Variables   If $f(x,y)$ has either a relative maximum or minimum at $(x,y) = (a,b)$, then

$$\frac{\partial f}{\partial x}(a,b) = 0$$

and

$$\frac{\partial f}{\partial y}(a,b) = 0.$$

A relative maximum or minimum may or may not be an absolute maximum or minimum. However, to simplify matters in this text, the examples and exercises have been chosen so that, if an absolute extremum of $f(x,y)$ exists, it will occur at a point where $f(x,y)$ has a relative extremum.

EXAMPLE 1   The function $f(x,y) = 3x^2 - 4xy + 3y^2 + 8x - 17y + 30$ has the graph pictured in Fig. 2. Find the point (a,b) at which $f(x,y)$ attains its minimum value.

Solution   We look for those values of x and y at which both partial derivatives are zero. The partial derivatives are

$$\frac{\partial f}{\partial x} = 6x - 4y + 8,$$

$$\frac{\partial f}{\partial y} = -4x + 6y - 17.$$

Setting $\frac{\partial f}{\partial x} = 0$ and $\frac{\partial f}{\partial y} = 0$, we obtain

$$6x - 4y + 8 = 0 \quad \text{or} \quad y = \frac{6x+8}{4},$$

$$-4x + 6y - 17 = 0 \quad \text{or} \quad y = \frac{4x+17}{6}.$$

By equating these two expressions for y, we have

$$\frac{6x+8}{4} = \frac{4x+17}{6}.$$

Cross-multiplying, we see that

$$36x + 48 = 16x + 68$$
$$20x = 20$$
$$x = 1.$$

When we substitute this value for x into our first equation for y in terms of x, we obtain

$$y = \frac{6x+8}{4} = \frac{6 \cdot 1 + 8}{4} = \frac{7}{2}.$$

If $f(x,y)$ has a minimum, it must occur where $\frac{\partial f}{\partial x} = 0$ and $\frac{\partial f}{\partial y} = 0$. We have determined that the partial derivatives are zero only when $x = 1$, $y = \frac{7}{2}$. From Fig. 2 we know that $f(x,y)$ has a minimum, so it must be at $(x,y) = (1, \frac{7}{2})$.   ∎

EXAMPLE 2

Price discrimination A monopolist markets a product in two countries and can charge different amounts in each country. Let x be the number of units to be sold in the first country and y the number of units to be sold in the second country. Due to the laws of demand, the monopolist must set the price at $97 - (x/10)$ dollars in the first country and $83 - (y/20)$ dollars in the second country to sell all the units. The cost of producing these units is $20{,}000 + 3(x + y)$. Find the values of x and y that maximize the profit.

Solution Let $f(x, y)$ be the profit derived from selling x units in the first country and y in the second. Then

$$f(x, y) = [\text{revenue from first country}] + [\text{revenue from second country}] - [\text{cost}]$$

$$= \left(97 - \frac{x}{10}\right)x + \left(83 - \frac{y}{20}\right)y - [20{,}000 + 3(x + y)]$$

$$= 97x - \frac{x^2}{10} + 83y - \frac{y^2}{20} - 20{,}000 - 3x - 3y$$

$$= 94x - \frac{x^2}{10} + 80y - \frac{y^2}{20} - 20{,}000.$$

To find where $f(x, y)$ has its maximum value, we look for those values of x and y at which both partial derivatives are zero.

$$\frac{\partial f}{\partial x} = 94 - \frac{x}{5},$$

$$\frac{\partial f}{\partial y} = 80 - \frac{y}{10}.$$

We set $\dfrac{\partial f}{\partial x} = 0$ and $\dfrac{\partial f}{\partial y} = 0$ to obtain

$$94 - \frac{x}{5} = 0 \quad \text{or} \quad x = 470,$$

$$80 - \frac{y}{10} = 0 \quad \text{or} \quad y = 800.$$

Therefore, the firm should adjust its prices to levels where it will sell 470 units in the first country and 800 units in the second country. ▪

EXAMPLE 3

Heat loss Suppose that we want to design a rectangular building having a volume of 147,840 cubic feet. Assuming that the daily loss of heat is given by

$$w = 11xy + 14yz + 15xz,$$

where x, y, and z are, respectively, the length, width, and height of the building, find the dimensions of the building for which the daily heat loss is minimal.

Solution We must minimize the function

$$w = 11xy + 14yz + 15xz, \tag{1}$$

where x, y, z satisfy the constraint equation (refer to Section 2.5)

$$xyz = 147{,}840.$$

For simplicity, let us denote 147,840 by V. Then $xyz = V$, so $z = V/xy$. We substitute this expression for z into the objective function (1) to obtain a heat-loss function $g(x, y)$ of two variables:

$$g(x, y) = 11xy + 14y\frac{V}{xy} + 15x\frac{V}{xy} = 11xy + \frac{14V}{x} + \frac{15V}{y}.$$

To minimize this function, we first compute the partial derivatives with respect to x and y; then we equate them to zero.

$$\frac{\partial g}{\partial x} = 11y - \frac{14V}{x^2} = 0,$$

$$\frac{\partial g}{\partial y} = 11x - \frac{15V}{y^2} = 0.$$

These two equations yield

$$y = \frac{14V}{11x^2}, \tag{2}$$

$$11xy^2 = 15V. \tag{3}$$

If we substitute the value of y from (2) into (3), we see that

$$11x\left(\frac{14V}{11x^2}\right)^2 = 15V$$

$$\frac{14^2V^2}{11x^3} = 15V$$

$$x^3 = \frac{14^2 \cdot V^2}{11 \cdot 15 \cdot V} = \frac{14^2 \cdot V}{11 \cdot 15}$$

$$= \frac{14^2 \cdot 147{,}840}{11 \cdot 15}$$

$$= 175{,}616.$$

Therefore, we see (using a calculator) that

$$x = 56.$$

From equation (2) we find that

$$y = \frac{14 \cdot V}{11x^2} = \frac{14 \cdot 147{,}840}{11 \cdot 56^2} = 60.$$

Finally,

$$z = \frac{V}{xy} = \frac{147{,}840}{56 \cdot 60} = 44.$$

Thus the building should be 56 feet long, 60 feet wide, and 44 feet high to minimize the heat loss.*

---

*For further discussion of this heat-loss problem, as well as other examples of optimization in architectural design, see L. March, "Elementary Models of Built Forms," Chapter 3 in *Urban Space and Structures*, L. Martin and L. March, eds. (New York: Cambridge University Press, 1972).

When considering a function of two variables, we find points (x, y) at which $f(x, y)$ has a potential relative maximum or minimum by setting $\dfrac{\partial f}{\partial x}$ and $\dfrac{\partial f}{\partial y}$ equal to zero and solving for x and y. However, if we are given no additional information about $f(x, y)$, it may be difficult to determine whether we have found a maximum or a minimum (or neither). In the case of functions of one variable, we studied concavity and deduced the second-derivative test. There is an analog of the second derivative test for functions of two variables, but it is much more complicated than the one-variable test. We state it without proof.

Second-Derivative Test for Functions of Two Variables Suppose that $f(x, y)$ is a function and (a, b) is a point at which

$$\frac{\partial f}{\partial x}(a, b) = 0 \quad \text{and} \quad \frac{\partial f}{\partial y}(a, b) = 0,$$

and let

$$D(x, y) = \frac{\partial^2 f}{\partial x^2} \cdot \frac{\partial^2 f}{\partial y^2} - \left(\frac{\partial^2 f}{\partial x \, \partial y} \right)^2.$$

1. If

$$D(a, b) > 0 \quad \text{and} \quad \frac{\partial^2 f}{\partial x^2}(a, b) > 0,$$

then $f(x, y)$ has a relative minimum at (a, b).

2. If

$$D(a, b) > 0 \quad \text{and} \quad \frac{\partial^2 f}{\partial x^2}(a, b) < 0,$$

then $f(x, y)$ has a relative maximum at (a, b).

3. If

$$D(a, b) < 0,$$

then $f(x, y)$ has neither a relative maximum nor a relative minimum at (a, b).

4. If $D(a, b) = 0$, no conclusion can be drawn from this test.

The saddle-shaped graph in Fig. 3 illustrates a function $f(x, y)$ for which $D(a, b) < 0$. Both partial derivatives are zero at $(x, y) = (a, b)$, and yet the function has neither a relative maximum nor a relative minimum there. (Observe that the function has a relative maximum with respect to x when y is held constant and a relative minimum with respect to y when x is held constant.)

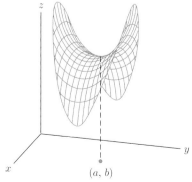

Figure 3

EXAMPLE 4   Let $f(x, y) = x^3 - y^2 - 12x + 6y + 5$. Find all possible relative maximum and minimum points of $f(x, y)$. Use the second-derivative test to determine the nature of each such point.

Solution Since

$$\frac{\partial f}{\partial x} = 3x^2 - 12, \qquad \frac{\partial f}{\partial y} = -2y + 6,$$

we find that $f(x, y)$ has a potential relative extreme point when

$$3x^2 - 12 = 0,$$
$$-2y + 6 = 0.$$

From the first equation, $3x^2 = 12$, $x^2 = 4$, and $x = \pm 2$. From the second equation, $y = 3$. Thus, $\dfrac{\partial f}{\partial x}$ and $\dfrac{\partial f}{\partial y}$ are both zero when $(x, y) = (2, 3)$ and when $(x, y) = (-2, 3)$. To apply the second derivative test, compute

$$\frac{\partial^2 f}{\partial x^2} = 6x, \qquad \frac{\partial^2 f}{\partial y^2} = -2, \qquad \frac{\partial^2 f}{\partial x \, \partial y} = 0,$$

and

$$D(x, y) = \frac{\partial^2 f}{\partial x^2} \cdot \frac{\partial^2 f}{\partial y^2} - \left(\frac{\partial^2 f}{\partial x \, \partial y} \right)^2 = (6x)(-2) - 0^2 = -12x. \tag{4}$$

Since $D(2, 3) = -12(2) = -24$, which is negative, case 3 of the second-derivative test says that $f(x, y)$ has neither a relative maximum nor a relative minimum at $(2, 3)$. However, $D(-2, 3) = -12(-2) = 24$. Since $D(-2, 3)$ is positive, the function $f(x, y)$ has either a relative maximum or a relative minimum at $(-2, 3)$. To determine which, we compute

$$\frac{\partial^2 f}{\partial x^2}(-2, 3) = 6(-2) = -12 < 0.$$

By case 2 of the second-derivative test, the function $f(x, y)$ has a relative maximum at $(-2, 3)$.   ◼

In this section we have restricted ourselves to functions of two variables, but the case of three or more variables is handled in a similar fashion. For instance, here is the first-derivative test for a function of three variables.

If $f(x, y, z)$ has a relative maximum or minimum at $(x, y, z) = (a, b, c)$, then

$$\frac{\partial f}{\partial x}(a, b, c) = 0,$$

$$\frac{\partial f}{\partial y}(a, b, c) = 0,$$

$$\frac{\partial f}{\partial z}(a, b, c) = 0.$$

Practice Problems 7.3

1. Find all points (x, y) where $f(x, y) = x^3 - 3xy + \frac{1}{2}y^2 + 8$ has a possible relative maximum or minimum.

2. Apply the second-derivative test to the function $g(x, y)$ of Example 3 to confirm that a relative minimum actually occurs when $x = 56$ and $y = 60$.

EXERCISES 7.3

Find all points (x, y) where $f(x, y)$ has a possible relative maximum or minimum.

1. $f(x, y) = x^2 - 3y^2 + 4x + 6y + 8$
2. $f(x, y) = \frac{1}{2}x^2 + y^2 - 3x + 2y - 5$
3. $f(x, y) = x^2 - 5xy + 6y^2 + 3x - 2y + 4$
4. $f(x, y) = -3x^2 + 7xy - 4y^2 + x + y$
5. $f(x, y) = x^3 + y^2 - 3x + 6y$
6. $f(x, y) = x^2 - y^3 + 5x + 12y + 1$
7. $f(x, y) = \frac{1}{3}x^3 - 2y^3 - 5x + 6y - 5$
8. $f(x, y) = x^4 - 8xy + 2y^2 - 3$
9. The function $f(x, y) = 2x + 3y + 9 - x^2 - xy - y^2$ has a maximum at some point (x, y). Find the values of x and y where this maximum occurs.
10. The function $f(x, y) = \frac{1}{2}x^2 + 2xy + 3y^2 - x + 2y$ has a minimum at some point (x, y). Find the values of x and y where this minimum occurs.

In Exercises 11–16, both first partial derivatives of the function $f(x, y)$ are zero at the given points. Use the second-derivative test to determine the nature of $f(x, y)$ at each of these points. If the second-derivative test is inconclusive, so state.

11. $f(x, y) = 3x^2 - 6xy + y^3 - 9y; (3, 3), (-1, -1)$
12. $f(x, y) = 6xy^2 - 2x^3 - 3y^4; (0, 0), (1, 1), (1, -1)$
13. $f(x, y) = 2x^2 - x^4 - y^2; (-1, 0), (0, 0), (1, 0)$
14. $f(x, y) = x^4 - 4xy + y^4; (0, 0), (1, 1), (-1, -1)$
15. $f(x, y) = ye^x - 3x - y + 5; (0, 3)$
16. $f(x, y) = \dfrac{1}{x} + \dfrac{1}{y} + xy; (1, 1)$

Find all points (x, y) where $f(x, y)$ has a possible relative maximum or minimum. Then use the second-derivative test to determine, if possible, the nature of $f(x, y)$ at each of these points. If the second-derivative test is inconclusive, so state.

17. $f(x, y) = x^2 - 2xy + 4y^2$
18. $f(x, y) = 2x^2 + 3xy + 5y^2$
19. $f(x, y) = -2x^2 + 2xy - y^2 + 4x - 6y + 5$
20. $f(x, y) = -x^2 - 8xy - y^2$
21. $f(x, y) = x^2 + 2xy + 5y^2 + 2x + 10y - 3$
22. $f(x, y) = x^2 - 2xy + 3y^2 + 4x - 16y + 22$
23. $f(x, y) = x^3 - y^2 - 3x + 4y$
24. $f(x, y) = x^3 - 2xy + 4y$
25. $f(x, y) = 2x^2 + y^3 - x - 12y + 7$
26. $f(x, y) = x^2 + 4xy + 2y^4$
27. Find the possible values of x, y, z at which
$$f(x, y, z) = 2x^2 + 3y^2 + z^2 - 2x - y - z$$
assumes its minimum value.

28. Find the possible values of x, y, z at which
$$f(x, y, z) = 5 + 8x - 4y + x^2 + y^2 + z^2$$
assumes its minimum value.

29. United States postal rules require that the length plus the girth of a package cannot exceed 84 inches. Find the dimensions of the rectangular package of greatest volume that can be mailed. [*Note:* From Fig. 4 we see that $84 = (\text{length}) + (\text{girth}) = l + (2x + 2y)$.]

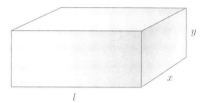

Figure 4

30. Find the dimensions of the rectangular box of least surface area that has a volume of 1000 cubic inches.
31. A company manufactures and sells two products, I and II, that sell for \$10 and \$9 per unit, respectively. The cost of producing x units of product I and y units of product II is
$$400 + 2x + 3y + .01(3x^2 + xy + 3y^2).$$
Find the values of x and y that maximize the company's profits. [*Note:* Profit = (revenue) − (cost).]
32. A monopolist manufactures and sells two competing products, I and II, that cost \$30 and \$20 per unit, respectively, to produce. The revenue from marketing x units of product I and y units of product II is $98x + 112y - .04xy - .1x^2 - .2y^2$. Find the values of x and y that maximize the monopolist's profits.
33. A company manufactures and sells two products, I and II, that sell for \$$p_{\text{I}}$ and \$$p_{\text{II}}$ per unit, respectively. Let $C(x, y)$ be the cost of producing x units of product I and y units of product II. Show that if the company's profit is maximized when $x = a$, $y = b$ then
$$\frac{\partial C}{\partial x}(a, b) = p_{\text{I}} \quad \text{and} \quad \frac{\partial C}{\partial y}(a, b) = p_{\text{II}}.$$
34. A monopolist manufactures and sells two competing products, I and II, that cost \$$p_{\text{I}}$ and \$$p_{\text{II}}$ per unit, respectively, to produce. Let $R(x, y)$ be the revenue from marketing x units of product I and y units of product II. Show that if the monopolist's profit is maximized when $x = a$, $y = b$ then
$$\frac{\partial R}{\partial x}(a, b) = p_{\text{I}} \quad \text{and} \quad \frac{\partial R}{\partial y}(a, b) = p_{\text{II}}.$$

Solutions to Practice Problems 7.3

1. Compute the first partial derivatives of $f(x, y)$ and solve the system of equations that results from setting the partials equal to zero.

$$\frac{\partial f}{\partial x} = 3x^2 - 3y = 0,$$

$$\frac{\partial f}{\partial y} = -3x + y = 0.$$

Solve each equation for y in terms of x.

$$\begin{cases} y = x^2 \\ y = 3x. \end{cases}$$

Equate expressions for y and solve for x.

$$x^2 = 3x$$
$$x^2 - 3x = 0$$
$$x(x - 3) = 0$$
$$x = 0 \quad \text{or} \quad x = 3.$$

When $x = 0$, $y = 0^2 = 0$. When $x = 3$, $y = 3^2 = 9$. Therefore, the possible relative maximum or minimum points are $(0, 0)$ and $(3, 9)$.

2. We have

$$g(x, y) = 11xy + \frac{14V}{x} + \frac{15V}{y},$$

$$\frac{\partial g}{\partial x} = 11y - \frac{14V}{x^2}, \quad \text{and} \quad \frac{\partial g}{\partial y} = 11x - \frac{15V}{y^2}.$$

Now,

$$\frac{\partial^2 g}{\partial x^2} = \frac{28V}{x^3}, \quad \frac{\partial^2 g}{\partial y^2} = \frac{30V}{y^3}, \quad \text{and} \quad \frac{\partial^2 g}{\partial x \, \partial y} = 11.$$

Therefore,

$$D(x, y) = \frac{28V}{x^3} \cdot \frac{30V}{y^3} - (11)^2$$

$$D(56, 60) = \frac{28(147,840)}{(56)^3} \cdot \frac{30(147,840)}{(60)^3} - 121$$

$$= 484 - 121 = 363 > 0,$$

and

$$\frac{\partial^2 g}{\partial x^2}(56, 60) = \frac{28(147,840)}{(56)^3} > 0.$$

It follows that $g(x, y)$ has a relative minimum at $x = 56$, $y = 60$.

7.4 Lagrange Multipliers and Constrained Optimization

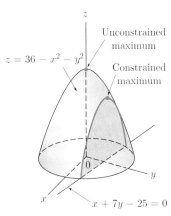

Figure 1. A constrained optimization problem.

We have seen a number of optimization problems in which we were required to minimize (or maximize) an objective function where the variables were subject to a constraint equation. For instance, in Example 4 of Section 2.5, we minimized the cost of a rectangular enclosure by minimizing the objective function $42x + 28y$, where x and y were subject to the constraint equation $600 - xy = 0$. In the preceding section (Example 3) we minimized the daily heat loss from a building by minimizing the objective function $11xy + 14yz + 15xz$, subject to the constraint equation $147,840 - xyz = 0$.

Figure 1 gives a graphical illustration of what happens when an objective function is maximized subject to a constraint. The graph of the objective function is the cone-shaped surface $z = 36 - x^2 - y^2$, and the colored curve on that surface consists of those points whose x- and y-coordinates satisfy the constraint equation $x + 7y - 25 = 0$. The constrained maximum is at the highest point on this curve. Of course, the surface itself has a higher "unconstrained maximum" at $(x, y, z) = (0, 0, 36)$, but these values of x and y do not satisfy the constraint equation.

In this section we introduce a powerful technique for solving problems of this type. Let us begin with the following general problem, which involves two variables.

Problem   Let $f(x, y)$ and $g(x, y)$ be functions of two variables. Find values of x and y that maximize (or minimize) the objective function $f(x, y)$ and that also satisfy the constraint equation $g(x, y) = 0$.

Of course, if we can solve the equation $g(x, y) = 0$ for one variable in terms of the other and substitute the resulting expression into $f(x, y)$, we arrive at a function of a single variable that can be maximized (or minimized) by using the methods of Chapter 2. However, this technique can be unsatisfactory for two reasons. First, it may be difficult to solve the equation $g(x, y) = 0$ for x or for y. For example, if $g(x, y) = x^4 + 5x^3y + 7x^2y^3 + y^5 - 17 = 0$, it is difficult to write y as a function of x or x as a function of y. Second, even if $g(x, y) = 0$ can be solved for one variable in terms of the other, substitution of the result into $f(x, y)$ may yield a complicated function.

One clever idea for handling the preceding problem was discovered by the eighteenth-century mathematician Lagrange, and the technique that he pioneered today bears his name, the method of *Lagrange multipliers*. The basic idea of this method is to replace $f(x, y)$ by an auxiliary function of three variables $F(x, y, \lambda)$, defined as

$$F(x, y, \lambda) = f(x, y) + \lambda g(x, y).$$

The new variable λ (lambda) is called a *Lagrange multiplier* and always multiplies the constraint function $g(x, y)$. The following theorem is stated without proof.

Theorem Suppose that, subject to the constraint $g(x, y) = 0$, the function $f(x, y)$ has a relative maximum or minimum at $(x, y) = (a, b)$. Then there is a value of λ, say $\lambda = c$, such that the partial derivatives of $F(x, y, \lambda)$ all equal zero at $(x, y, \lambda) = (a, b, c)$.

The theorem implies that, if we locate all points (x, y, λ) where the partial derivatives of $F(x, y, \lambda)$ are all zero, among the corresponding points (x, y), we then will find all possible places where $f(x, y)$ may have a constrained relative maximum or minimum. Thus the first step in the method of Lagrange multipliers is to set the partial derivatives of $F(x, y, \lambda)$ equal to zero and solve for x, y, and λ:

$$\frac{\partial F}{\partial x} = 0 \tag{L-1}$$

$$\frac{\partial F}{\partial y} = 0 \tag{L-2}$$

$$\frac{\partial F}{\partial \lambda} = 0. \tag{L-3}$$

From the definition of $F(x, y, \lambda)$, we see that $\dfrac{\partial F}{\partial \lambda} = g(x, y)$. Thus the third equation (L-3) is just the original constraint equation $g(x, y) = 0$. So, when we find a point (x, y, λ) that satisfies (L-1), (L-2), and (L-3), the coordinates x and y will automatically satisfy the constraint equation.

The first example applies this method to the problem described in Fig. 1.

EXAMPLE 1

Maximize $36 - x^2 - y^2$ subject to the constraint $x + 7y - 25 = 0$.

Solution Here $f(x, y) = 36 - x^2 - y^2$, $g(x, y) = x + 7y - 25$, and

$$F(x, y, \lambda) = 36 - x^2 - y^2 + \lambda(x + 7y - 25).$$

Equations (L-1) to (L-3) read

$$\frac{\partial F}{\partial x} = -2x + \lambda = 0, \tag{1}$$

$$\frac{\partial F}{\partial y} = -2y + 7\lambda = 0, \tag{2}$$

$$\frac{\partial F}{\partial \lambda} = x + 7y - 25 = 0. \tag{3}$$

We solve the first two equations for λ:

$$\lambda = 2x$$

$$\lambda = \tfrac{2}{7}y. \tag{4}$$

If we equate these two expressions for λ, we obtain

$$2x = \tfrac{2}{7}y$$

$$x = \tfrac{1}{7}y. \tag{5}$$

Substituting this expression for x into equation (3), we have

$$\tfrac{1}{7}y + 7y - 25 = 0$$

$$\tfrac{50}{7}y = 25$$

$$y = \tfrac{7}{2}.$$

With this value for y, equations (4) and (5) produce the values of x and λ:

$$x = \tfrac{1}{7}y = \tfrac{1}{7}\left(\tfrac{7}{2}\right) = \tfrac{1}{2},$$

$$\lambda = \tfrac{2}{7}y = \tfrac{2}{7}\left(\tfrac{7}{2}\right) = 1.$$

Therefore, the partial derivatives of $F(x, y, \lambda)$ are zero when $x = \tfrac{1}{2}$, $y = \tfrac{7}{2}$, and $\lambda = 1$. So the maximum value of $36 - x^2 - y^2$ subject to the constraint $x + 7y - 25 = 0$ is

$$36 - \left(\tfrac{1}{2}\right)^2 - \left(\tfrac{7}{2}\right)^2 = \tfrac{47}{2}. \qquad \blacksquare$$

The preceding technique for solving three equations in the three variables x, y, and λ can usually be applied to solve Lagrange multiplier problems. Here is the basic procedure.

1. Solve (L-1) and (L-2) for λ in terms of x and y; then equate the resulting expressions for λ.
2. Solve the resulting equation for one of the variables.
3. Substitute the expression so derived into the equation (L-3), and solve the resulting equation of one variable.
4. Use the one known variable and the equations of steps 1 and 2 to determine the other two variables.

In most applications we know that an absolute (constrained) maximum or minimum exists. In the event that the method of Lagrange multipliers produces exactly one possible relative extreme value, we will assume that it is indeed the sought after absolute extreme value. For instance, the statement of Example 1 is meant to imply that there is an absolute maximum value. Since we determined that there was just one possible relative extreme value, we concluded that it was the absolute maximum value.

EXAMPLE 2

Using Lagrange multipliers, minimize $42x + 28y$, subject to the constraint $600 - xy = 0$, where x and y are restricted to positive values. (This problem arose in Example 4 of Section 2.5, where $42x + 28y$ was the cost of building a 600-square-foot enclosure having dimensions x and y.)

Solution We have $f(x, y) = 42x + 28y$, $g(x, y) = 600 - xy$, and

$$F(x, y, \lambda) = 42x + 28y + \lambda(600 - xy).$$

The equations (L-1) to (L-3), in this case, are

$$\frac{\partial F}{\partial x} = 42 - \lambda y = 0,$$

$$\frac{\partial F}{\partial y} = 28 - \lambda x = 0,$$

$$\frac{\partial F}{\partial \lambda} = 600 - xy = 0.$$

From the first two equations we see that

$$\lambda = \frac{42}{y} = \frac{28}{x}. \tag{step 1}$$

Therefore,

$$42x = 28y$$

and

$$x = \frac{2}{3}y. \tag{step 2}$$

Substituting this expression for x into the third equation, we derive

$$600 - \left(\frac{2}{3}y\right)y = 0$$

$$y^2 = \frac{3}{2} \cdot 600 = 900$$

$$y = \pm 30. \tag{step 3}$$

We discard the case $y = -30$ because we are interested only in positive values of x and y. Using $y = 30$, we find that

$$\left.\begin{array}{l} x = \dfrac{2}{3}(30) = 20 \\[2mm] \lambda = \dfrac{28}{20} = \dfrac{7}{5}. \end{array}\right\} \tag{step 4}$$

So the minimum value of $42x + 28y$ with x and y subject to the constraint occurs when $x = 20$, $y = 30$, and $\lambda = \frac{7}{5}$. That minimum value is

$$42 \cdot (20) + 28 \cdot (30) = 1680.$$ ■

EXAMPLE 3

Production Suppose that x units of labor and y units of capital can produce $f(x, y) = 60x^{3/4}y^{1/4}$ units of a certain product. Also suppose that each unit of labor costs \$100, whereas each unit of capital costs \$200. Assume that \$30,000 is available to spend on production. How many units of labor and how many units of capital should be utilized to maximize production?

Solution The cost of x units of labor and y units of capital equals $100x + 200y$. Therefore, since we want to use all the available money ($30,000), we must satisfy the constraint equation

$$100x + 200y = 30{,}000$$

or

$$g(x, y) = 30{,}000 - 100x - 200y = 0.$$

The objective function is $f(x, y) = 60x^{3/4}y^{1/4}$. In this case, we have

$$F(x, y, \lambda) = 60x^{3/4}y^{1/4} + \lambda(30{,}000 - 100x - 200y).$$

The equations (L-1) to (L-3) read

$$\frac{\partial F}{\partial x} = 45x^{-1/4}y^{1/4} - 100\lambda = 0, \tag{L-1}$$

$$\frac{\partial F}{\partial y} = 15x^{3/4}y^{-3/4} - 200\lambda = 0, \tag{L-2}$$

$$\frac{\partial F}{\partial \lambda} = 30{,}000 - 100x - 200y = 0. \tag{L-3}$$

By solving the first two equations for λ, we see that

$$\lambda = \frac{45}{100}x^{-1/4}y^{1/4} = \frac{9}{20}x^{-1/4}y^{1/4},$$

$$\lambda = \frac{15}{200}x^{3/4}y^{-3/4} = \frac{3}{40}x^{3/4}y^{-3/4}.$$

Therefore, we must have

$$\frac{9}{20}x^{-1/4}y^{1/4} = \frac{3}{40}x^{3/4}y^{-3/4}.$$

To solve for y in terms of x, let us multiply both sides of this equation by $x^{1/4}y^{3/4}$:

$$\frac{9}{20}y = \frac{3}{40}x$$

or

$$y = \frac{1}{6}x.$$

Inserting this result in (L-3), we find that

$$100x + 200\left(\frac{1}{6}x\right) = 30{,}000$$

$$\frac{400x}{3} = 30{,}000$$

$$x = 225.$$

Hence

$$y = \frac{225}{6} = 37.5.$$

So maximum production is achieved by using 225 units of labor and 37.5 units of capital.

In Example 3 it turns out that, at the optimum values of x and y,

$$\lambda = \frac{9}{20}x^{-1/4}y^{1/4} = \frac{9}{20}(225)^{-1/4}(37.5)^{1/4} \approx .2875,$$

$$\frac{\partial f}{\partial x} = 45x^{-1/4}y^{1/4} = 45(225)^{-1/4}(37.5)^{1/4}, \tag{6}$$

$$\frac{\partial f}{\partial y} = 15x^{3/4}y^{-3/4} = 15(225)^{3/4}(37.5)^{-3/4}. \tag{7}$$

It can be shown that the Lagrange multiplier λ can be interpreted as the *marginal productivity of money*. That is, if 1 additional dollar is available, approximately .2875 additional units of the product can be produced.

Recall that the partial derivatives $\dfrac{\partial f}{\partial x}$ and $\dfrac{\partial f}{\partial y}$ are called the marginal productivity of labor and capital, respectively. From equations (6) and (7) we have

$$\frac{[\text{marginal productivity of labor}]}{[\text{marginal productivity of capital}]} = \frac{45(225)^{-1/4}(37.5)^{1/4}}{15(225)^{3/4}(37.5)^{-3/4}}$$

$$= \frac{45}{15}(225)^{-1}(37.5)^1$$

$$= \frac{3(37.5)}{225} = \frac{37.5}{75} = \frac{1}{2}.$$

On the other hand,

$$\frac{[\text{cost per unit of labor}]}{[\text{cost per unit of capital}]} = \frac{100}{200} = \frac{1}{2}.$$

This result illustrates the following law of economics. *If labor and capital are at their optimal levels, the ratio of their marginal productivities equals the ratio of their unit costs.*

The method of Lagrange multipliers generalizes to functions of any number of variables. For instance, we can maximize $f(x, y, z)$, subject to the constraint equation $g(x, y, z) = 0$, by considering the Lagrange function

$$F(x, y, z, \lambda) = f(x, y, z) + \lambda g(x, y, z).$$

The analogs of equations (L-1) to (L-3) are

$$\frac{\partial F}{\partial x} = 0, \quad \frac{\partial F}{\partial y} = 0, \quad \frac{\partial F}{\partial z} = 0, \quad \frac{\partial F}{\partial \lambda} = 0.$$

Let us now show how we can solve the heat-loss problem of Section 7.3 by using this method.

EXAMPLE 4   Use Lagrange multipliers to find the values of x, y, z that minimize the objective function

$$f(x, y, z) = 11xy + 14yz + 15xz,$$

subject to the constraint

$$xyz = 147{,}840.$$

Solution The Lagrange function is

$$F(x, y, z, \lambda) = 11xy + 14yz + 15xz + \lambda(147{,}840 - xyz).$$

The conditions for a relative minimum are

$$\frac{\partial F}{\partial x} = 11y + 15z - \lambda yz = 0,$$

$$\frac{\partial F}{\partial y} = 11x + 14z - \lambda xz = 0,$$

$$\frac{\partial F}{\partial z} = 14y + 15x - \lambda xy = 0,$$

$$\frac{\partial F}{\partial \lambda} = 147{,}840 - xyz = 0. \tag{8}$$

From the first three equations we have

$$\left.\begin{array}{l} \lambda = \dfrac{11y + 15z}{yz} = \dfrac{11}{z} + \dfrac{15}{y} \\[2mm] \lambda = \dfrac{11x + 14z}{xz} = \dfrac{11}{z} + \dfrac{14}{x} \\[2mm] \lambda = \dfrac{14y + 15x}{xy} = \dfrac{14}{x} + \dfrac{15}{y} \end{array}\right\}. \tag{9}$$

Let us equate the first two expression for λ:

$$\frac{11}{z} + \frac{15}{y} = \frac{11}{z} + \frac{14}{x}$$

$$\frac{15}{y} = \frac{14}{x}$$

$$x = \frac{14}{15}y.$$

Next, we equate the second and third expressions for λ in (9):

$$\frac{11}{z} + \frac{14}{x} = \frac{14}{x} + \frac{15}{y}$$

$$\frac{11}{z} = \frac{15}{y}$$

$$z = \frac{11}{15}y.$$

We now substitute the expressions for x and z into the constraint equation (8) and obtain

$$\frac{14}{15}y \cdot y \cdot \frac{11}{15}y = 147{,}840$$

$$y^3 = \frac{(147{,}840)(15)^2}{(14)(11)} = 216{,}000$$

$$y = 60.$$

From this, we find that

$$x = \frac{14}{15}(60) = 56 \quad \text{and} \quad z = \frac{11}{15}(60) = 44.$$

We conclude that the heat loss is minimized when $x = 56$, $y = 60$, and $z = 44$. ∎

In the solution of Example 4, we found that, at the optimal values of x, y, and z,

$$\frac{14}{x} = \frac{15}{y} = \frac{11}{z}.$$

Referring to Example 2 of Section 7.1, we see that 14 is the combined heat loss through the east and west sides of the building, 15 is the heat loss through the north and south sides of the building, and 11 is the heat loss through the floor and roof. Thus we have that under optimal conditions

$$\frac{[\text{heat loss through east and west sides}]}{[\text{distance between east and west sides}]}$$

$$= \frac{[\text{heat loss through north and south sides}]}{[\text{distance between north and south sides}]}$$

$$= \frac{[\text{heat loss through floor and roof}]}{[\text{distance between floor and roof}]}.$$

This is a principle of optimal design: Minimal heat loss occurs when the distance between each pair of opposite sides is some fixed constant times the heat loss from the pair of sides.

The value of λ in Example 4 corresponding to the optimal values of x, y, and z is

$$\lambda = \frac{11}{z} + \frac{15}{y} = \frac{11}{44} + \frac{15}{60} = \frac{1}{2}.$$

We can show that the Lagrange multiplier λ is the marginal heat loss with respect to volume. That is, if a building of volume slightly more than 147,840 cubic feet is optimally designed, $\frac{1}{2}$ unit of additional heat will be lost for each additional cubic foot of volume.

Practice Problems 7.4

1. Let $F(x, y, \lambda) = 2x + 3y + \lambda(90 - 6x^{1/3}y^{2/3})$. Find $\dfrac{\partial F}{\partial x}$.

2. Refer to Exercise 29 of Section 7.3. What is the function $F(x, y, l, \lambda)$ when the exercise is solved using the method of Lagrange multipliers?

EXERCISES 7.4

Solve the following exercises by the method of Lagrange multipliers.

1. Minimize $x^2 + 3y^2 + 10$, subject to the constraint $8 - x - y = 0$.

2. Maximize $x^2 - y^2$, subject to the constraint $2x + y - 3 = 0$.

3. Maximize $x^2 + xy - 3y^2$, subject to the constraint $2 - x - 2y = 0$.

4. Minimize $\frac{1}{2}x^2 - 3xy + y^2 + \frac{1}{2}$, subject to the constraint $3x - y - 1 = 0$.

5. Find the values of x, y that maximize

$$-2x^2 - 2xy - \tfrac{3}{2}y^2 + x + 2y,$$

subject to the constraint $x + y - \frac{5}{2} = 0$.

6. Find the values of x, y that minimize

$$x^2 + xy + y^2 - 2x - 5y,$$

subject to the constraint $1 - x + y = 0$.

7. Find the two positive numbers whose product is 25 and whose sum is as small as possible.

8. Four hundred eighty dollars are available to fence in a rectangular garden. The fencing for the north and south sides of the garden costs $10 per foot and the fencing for the east and west sides costs $15 per foot. Find the dimensions of the largest possible garden.

9. Three hundred square inches of material are available to construct an open rectangular box with a square base. Find the dimensions of the box that maximize the volume.

10. The amount of space required by a particular firm is $f(x,y) = 1000\sqrt{6x^2 + y^2}$, where x and y are, respectively, the number of units of labor and capital utilized. Suppose that labor costs \$480 per unit and capital costs \$40 per unit and that the firm has \$5000 to spend. Determine the amounts of labor and capital that should be utilized in order to minimize the amount of space required.

11. Find the dimensions of the rectangle of maximum area that can be inscribed in the unit circle. [See Fig. 2(a).]

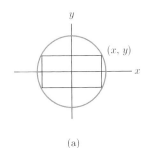

(a)

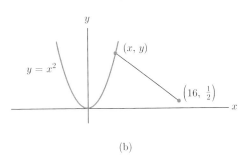

(b)

Figure 2

12. Find the point on the parabola $y = x^2$ that has minimal distance from the point $\left(16, \frac{1}{2}\right)$. [See Fig. 2(b).] [*Suggestion*: If d denotes the distance from (x,y) to $\left(16, \frac{1}{2}\right)$, then $d^2 = (x-16)^2 + (y - \frac{1}{2})^2$. If d^2 is minimized, then d will be minimized.]

13. Suppose that a firm makes two products A and B that use the same raw materials. Given a fixed amount of raw materials and a fixed amount of manpower, the firm must decide how much of its resources should be allocated to the production of A and how much to B. If x units of A and y units of B are produced, suppose that x and y must satisfy

$$9x^2 + 4y^2 = 18{,}000.$$

The graph of this equation (for $x \geq 0$, $y \geq 0$) is called a *production possibilities curve* (Fig. 3). A point (x,y) on this curve represents a *production schedule* for the firm, committing it to produce x units of A and y units of B. The reason for the relationship between x and y

involves the limitations on personnel and raw materials available to the firm. Suppose that each unit of A yields a \$3 profit, whereas each unit of B yields a \$4 profit. Then the profit of the firm is

$$P(x,y) = 3x + 4y.$$

Find the production schedule that maximizes the profit function $P(x,y)$.

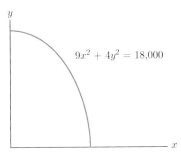

Figure 3. A production possibilities curve.

14. A firm makes x units of product A and y units of product B and has a production possibilities curve given by the equation $4x^2 + 25y^2 = 50{,}000$ for $x \geq 0$, $y \geq 0$. (See Exercise 13.) Suppose profits are \$2 per unit for product A and \$10 per unit for product B. Find the production schedule that maximizes the total profit.

15. The production function for a firm is $f(x,y) = 64x^{3/4}y^{1/4}$, where x and y are the number of units of labor and capital utilized. Suppose that labor costs \$96 per unit and capital costs \$162 per unit and that the firm decides to produce 3456 units of goods.

   (a) Determine the amounts of labor and capital that should be utilized in order to minimize the cost. That is, find the values of x, y that minimize $96x + 162y$, subject to the constraint $3456 - 64x^{3/4}y^{1/4} = 0$.

   (b) Find the value of λ at the optimal level of production.

   (c) Show that, at the optimal level of production, we have

   $$\frac{[\text{marginal productivity of labor}]}{[\text{marginal productivity of capital}]}$$
   $$= \frac{[\text{unit price of labor}]}{[\text{unit price of capital}]}.$$

16. Consider the monopolist of Example 2, Section 7.3, who sells his goods in two countries. Suppose that he must set the same price in each country. That is, $97 - (x/10) = 83 - (y/20)$. Find the values of x and y that maximize profits under this new restriction.

17. Find the values of x, y, and z that maximize xyz subject to the constraint $36 - x - 6y - 3z = 0$.

18. Find the values of x, y, and z that maximize $xy + 3xz + 3yz$ subject to the constraint $9 - xyz = 0$.

19. Find the values of x, y, z that maximize

$$3x + 5y + z - x^2 - y^2 - z^2,$$

subject to the constraint $6 - x - y - z = 0$.

20. Find the values of x, y, z that minimize

$$x^2 + y^2 + z^2 - 3x - 5y - z,$$

subject to the constraint $20 - 2x - y - z = 0$.

21. The material for a closed rectangular box costs $2 per square foot for the top and $1 per square foot for the sides and bottom. Using Lagrange multipliers, find the dimensions for which the volume of the box is 12 cubic feet and the cost of the materials is minimized. [Referring to Fig. 4(a), the cost will be $3xy + 2xz + 2yz$.]

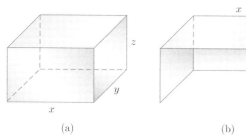

(a)   (b)

Figure 4

22. Use Lagrange multipliers to find the three positive numbers whose sum is 15 and whose product is as large as possible.

23. Find the dimensions of an open rectangular glass tank of volume 32 cubic feet for which the amount of material needed to construct the tank is minimized. [See Fig. 4(a).]

24. A shelter for use at the beach has a back, two sides, and a top made of canvas. [See Fig. 4(b).] Find the dimensions that maximize the volume and require 96 square feet of canvas.

25. Let $f(x, y)$ be any production function where x represents labor (costing $a per unit) and y represents capital (costing $b per unit). Assuming that $c is available, show that, at the values of x, y that maximize production,

$$\frac{\frac{\partial f}{\partial x}}{\frac{\partial f}{\partial y}} = \frac{a}{b}.$$

Note: Let $F(x, y, \lambda) = f(x, y) + \lambda(c - ax - by)$. The result follows from (L-1) and (L-2).

26. By applying the result in Exercise 25 to the production function $f(x, y) = kx^\alpha y^\beta$, show that, for the values of x, y that maximize production, we have

$$\frac{y}{x} = \frac{a\beta}{b\alpha}.$$

(This tells us that the ratio of capital to labor does not depend on the amount of money available nor on the level of production but only on the numbers a, b, α, and β.)

Solutions to Practice Problems 7.4

1. The function can be written as

$$F(x, y, \lambda) = 2x + 3y + \lambda \cdot 90 - \lambda \cdot 6x^{1/3}y^{2/3}.$$

When differentiating with respect to x, both y and λ should be treated as constants (so $\lambda \cdot 90$ and $\lambda \cdot 6$ are also regarded as constants).

$$\frac{\partial F}{\partial x} = 2 - \lambda \cdot 6 \cdot \frac{1}{3} x^{-2/3} \cdot y^{2/3}$$

$$= 2 - 2\lambda x^{-2/3} y^{2/3}.$$

(*Note*: It is not necessary to write out the multiplication by λ as we did. Most people just do this mentally and then differentiate.)

2. The quantity to be maximized is the volume xyl. The constraint is that length plus girth is 84. This translates to $84 = l + 2x + 2y$ or $84 - l - 2x - 2y = 0$. Therefore,

$$F(x, y, l, \lambda) = xyl + \lambda(84 - l - 2x - 2y).$$

7.5 The Method of Least Squares

Today, people can compile graphs of literally thousands of different quantities: the purchasing value of the dollar as a function of time, the pressure of a fixed volume of air as a function of temperature, the average income of people as a function of their years of formal education, or the incidence of strokes as a function of blood pressure. The observed points on such graphs tend to be irregularly distributed due to the complicated nature of the phenomena underlying them, as well as to errors made in observation. (For example, a given procedure for measuring average income may not count certain groups.)

In spite of the imperfect nature of the data, we are often faced with the problem of making assessments and predictions based on them. Roughly speaking, this problem amounts to filtering the sources of errors in the data and isolating the basic underlying trend. Frequently, on the basis of a suspicion or a working hypothesis, we may suspect that the underlying trend is linear; that is, the data should lie on a straight line. But which straight line? This is the problem that the *method of least squares* attempts to answer. To be more specific, let us consider the following problem:

Problem of Fitting a Straight Line to Data   Given observed data points (x_1, y_1), $(x_2, y_2), \ldots, (x_N, y_N)$ on a graph, find the straight line that best fits these points.

To completely understand the statement of the problem being considered, we must define what it means for a line to "best" fit a set of points. If (x_i, y_i) is one of our observed points, we will measure how far it is from a given line $y = Ax + B$ by the vertical distance from the point to the line. Since the point on the line with x-coordinate x_i is $(x_i, Ax_i + B)$, this vertical distance is the distance between the y-coordinates $Ax_i + B$ and y_i. (See Fig. 1.) If $E_i = (Ax_i + B) - y_i$, either E_i or $-E_i$ is the vertical distance from (x_i, y_i) to the line. To avoid this ambiguity, we work with the square of this vertical distance:

$$E_i^2 = (Ax_i + B - y_i)^2.$$

The total error in approximating the data points $(x_1, y_1), \ldots, (x_N, y_N)$ by the line $y = Ax + B$ is usually measured by the sum E of the squares of the vertical distances from the points to the line,

$$E = E_1^2 + E_2^2 + \cdots + E_N^2.$$

E is called the *least-squares error* of the observed points with respect to the line. If all the observed points lie on the line $y = Ax + B$, all E_i are zero and the error E is zero. If a given observed point is far away from the line, the corresponding E_i^2 is large and hence makes a large contribution to the error E.

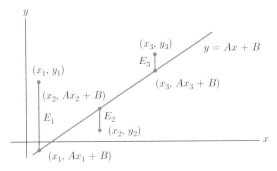

Figure 1. Fitting a line to data points.

In general, we cannot expect to find a line $y = Ax + B$ that fits the observed points so well that the error E is zero. Actually, this situation will occur only if the observed points lie on a straight line. However, we can rephrase our original problem as follows:

Problem   Given observed data points $(x_1, y_1), (x_2, y_2), \ldots, (x_N, y_N)$, find a straight line $y = Ax + B$ for which the error E is as small as possible. This line is called the *least-squares line* or *regression line*.

It turns out that this problem is a minimization problem in the two variables A and B and can be solved by using the methods of Section 7.3. Let us consider an example.

EXAMPLE 1

Find the straight line that minimizes the least-squares error for the points $(1, 4)$, $(2, 5)$, $(3, 8)$.

Solution   Let the straight line be $y = Ax + B$. When $x = 1, 2, 3$, the y-coordinate of the corresponding point of the line is $A+B$, $2A+B$, $3A+B$, respectively. Therefore, the squares of the vertical distances from the points $(1, 4)$, $(2, 5)$, $(3, 8)$ are, respectively,

$$E_1^2 = (A + B - 4)^2,$$
$$E_2^2 = (2A + B - 5)^2,$$
$$E_3^2 = (3A + B - 8)^2.$$

(See Fig. 2.) Thus the least-squares error is

$$E = E_1^2 + E_2^2 + E_3^2 = (A + B - 4)^2 + (2A + B - 5)^2 + (3A + B - 8)^2.$$

This error obviously depends on the choice of A and B. Let $f(A, B)$ denote this least-squares error. We want to find values of A and B that minimize $f(A, B)$. To do so, we take partial derivatives with respect to A and B and set the partial derivatives equal to zero:

$$\frac{\partial f}{\partial A} = 2(A + B - 4) + 2(2A + B - 5) \cdot 2 + 2(3A + B - 8) \cdot 3$$
$$= 28A + 12B - 76 = 0,$$

$$\frac{\partial f}{\partial B} = 2(A + B - 4) + 2(2A + B - 5) + 2(3A + B - 8)$$
$$= 12A + 6B - 34 = 0.$$

To find A and B, we must solve the system of simultaneous linear equations

$$28A + 12B = 76$$
$$12A + 6B = 34.$$

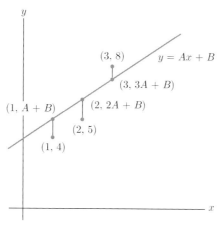

Figure 2

Multiplying the second equation by 2 and subtracting from the first equation, we have $4A = 8$, or $A = 2$. Therefore, $B = \frac{5}{3}$, and the straight line that minimizes the least-squares error is $y = 2x + \frac{5}{3}$. ■

The minimization process used in Example 1 can be applied to a general set of data points $(x_1, y_1), \ldots, (x_N, y_N)$ to obtain the following algebraic formula for A and B:

$$A = \frac{N \cdot \Sigma\, xy - \Sigma\, x \cdot \Sigma\, y}{N \cdot \Sigma\, x^2 - (\Sigma\, x)^2},$$

$$B = \frac{\Sigma\, y - A \cdot \Sigma\, x}{N},$$

where

$\Sigma\, x$ = sum of the x-coordinates of the data points

$\Sigma\, y$ = sum of the y-coordinates of the data points

$\Sigma\, xy$ = sum of the products of the coordinates of the data points

$\Sigma\, x^2$ = sum of the squares of the x-coordinates of the data points

N = number of data points.

That is,

$$\Sigma\, x = x_1 + x_2 + \cdots + x_N$$

$$\Sigma\, y = y_1 + y_2 + \cdots + y_N$$

$$\Sigma\, xy = x_1 \cdot y_1 + x_2 \cdot y_2 + \cdots + x_N \cdot y_N$$

$$\Sigma\, x^2 = x_1^2 + x_2^2 + \cdots + x_N^2.$$

EXAMPLE 2

The following table* gives the crude male death rate for lung cancer in 1950 and the per capita consumption of cigarettes in 1930 in various countries.

Country	Cigarette Consumption (Per Capita)	Lung Cancer Deaths (Per Million Males)
Norway	250	95
Sweden	300	120
Denmark	350	165
Australia	470	170

(a) Use the preceding formulas to obtain the straight line that best fits these data.

(b) In 1930 the per capita cigarette consumption in Finland was 1100. Use the straight line found in part (a) to estimate the male lung cancer death rate in Finland in 1950.

Solution (a) The points are plotted in Fig. 3. The sums are calculated in Table 1 and then used to determine the values of A and B.

---

*These data were obtained from *Smoking and Health*, Report of the Advisory Committee to the Surgeon General of the Public Health Service, U.S. Department of Health, Education, and Welfare, Washington, D.C., Public Health Service Publication No. 1103, p. 176.

Figure 3. Lung cancer data for least-squares analysis.

TABLE 1 Least-Squares Calculation for Smoking Data

x	y	xy	x^2
250	95	23,750	62,500
300	120	36,000	90,000
350	165	57,750	122,500
470	170	79,900	220,900
$\Sigma x = 1370$	$\Sigma y = 550$	$\Sigma xy = 197,400$	$\Sigma x^2 = 495,900$

$$A = \frac{4 \cdot 197,400 - 1370 \cdot 550}{4 \cdot 495,900 - 1370^2} = \frac{36,100}{106,700} = \frac{361}{1067} \approx .338,$$

$$B = \frac{550 - \frac{361}{1067} \cdot 1370}{4} = \frac{1067 \cdot 550 - 361 \cdot 1370}{1067 \cdot 4} = \frac{92,280}{4268} \approx 21.621.$$

Therefore, the equation of the least-squares line is $y = .338x + 21.621$.

(b) We use the straight line to estimate the lung cancer death rate in Finland by setting $x = 1100$. Then we get

$$y = .338(1100) + 21.621 = 393.421 \approx 393.$$

Therefore, we estimate the lung cancer death rate in Finland to be 393 deaths per million males. (*Note*: The actual rate was 350 deaths per million males.)

INCORPORATING TECHNOLOGY

Least Squares Method   To implement the least-squares method on your TI-83/84, select [SELECT] [1] for the EDIT screen to obtain a table used for entering the data. If necessary, clear data from columns L_1 and/or L_2 by moving the cursor to the top of the column and pressing [CLEAR] [ENTER]. [See Fig. 4(a).]

After the x- and y-values are placed into lists on a graphing calculator, we use the statistical routine LinReg to calculate the coefficients of the least-squares line. Now press [STAT] [▷] for the CALC menu, and press [4] to place **LinReg(ax+b)** on the home screen. Press [ENTER] to obtain the slope and y-intercept of the least-squares line. [See Fig. 4(b).]

If desired, the equation for the line can automatically be assigned to a function and graphed along with the original points. First, we assign the equation for the least-squares line to a function. Select [Y=], move to the function, and press [CLEAR] to erase any current expression. Now press [VARS] [5] to select the **Statistics** variables. Move your cursor over to he EQ menu, and press [1] for **RegEQ** (Regression Equation).

To graph this line, press GRAPH. To graph this line along with the original data points, we proceed as follows. From the Y=, and with only the least-squares line selected, press 2nd [STAT PLOT] ENTER to select **Plot1**, and press ENTER to turn **Plot1 ON**. Now select the first plot from the six icons for the plot **Type**. This corresponds to a scatter plot. Finally, press GRAPH. [See Fig. 4(c).] ∎

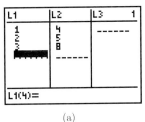
(a)

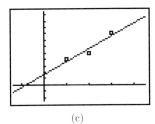
(b)

(c)

Figure 4

Practice Problems 7.5

1. Let $E = (A + B + 2)^2 + (3A + B)^2 + (6A + B - 8)^2$. What is $\dfrac{\partial E}{\partial A}$?

2. Find the formula (of the type in Problem 1) that gives the least-squares error E for the points $(1, 10)$, $(5, 8)$, and $(7, 0)$.

EXERCISES 7.5

1. Find the least-squares error E for the least-squares line fit to the four points in Fig. 5.

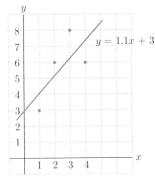
$y = 1.1x + 3$

Figure 5

2. Find the least-squares error E for the least-squares line fit to the five points in Fig. 6.

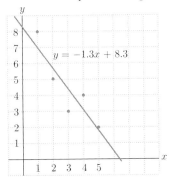
$y = -1.3x + 8.3$

Figure 6

3. Find the formula (of the type in Practice Problem 1) that gives the least-squares error for the points $(2, 6)$, $(5, 10)$, and $(9, 15)$.

4. Find the formula (of the type in Practice Problem 1) that gives the least-squares error for the points $(8, 4)$, $(9, 2)$, and $(10, 3)$.

In Exercises 5–8, use partial derivatives to obtain the formula for the best least-squares fit to the data points.

5. $(1, 2)$, $(2, 5)$, $(3, 11)$

6. $(1, 8)$, $(2, 4)$, $(4, 3)$

7. $(1, 9), (2, 8), (3, 6), (4, 3)$

8. $(1, 5), (2, 7), (3, 6), (4, 10)$

9. Complete Table 2 and find the values of A and B for the straight line that provides the best least-squares fit to the data.

TABLE 2

x	y	xy	x^2
1	7		
2	6		
3	4		
4	3		
$\Sigma x =$	$\Sigma y =$	$\Sigma xy =$	$\Sigma x^2 =$

10. Complete Table 3 and find the values of A and B for the straight line that provides the best least-squares fit to the data.

TABLE 3

x	y	xy	x^2
1	2		
2	4		
3	7		
4	9		
5	12		
$\Sigma x =$	$\Sigma y =$	$\Sigma xy =$	$\Sigma x^2 =$

In the remaining exercises, use one or more of the three methods discussed in this section (partial derivatives, formulas, or graphing utilities) to obtain the formula for the least-squares line.

11. Table 4[*] gives the U.S. per capita health care expenditures for the years 1990–1994.

TABLE 4   U.S. Per Capita Health Care Expenditures

Years (after 1990)	Dollars (in thousands)
0	2.688
1	2.902
2	3.144
3	3.331
4	3.510

(a) Find the least-squares line for these data.

(b) Use the least-squares line to predict the per capita health care expenditures for the year 2000.

(c) Use the least-squares line to predict when per capita health care expenditures will reach $6000.

12. Table 5 shows the 1994 price of a gallon of fuel (in U.S. dollars) and the average miles driven per automobile for several countries.[†]

(a) Find the straight line that provides the best least-squares fit to these data.

(b) In 1994, the price of gas in Japan was $4.14 per gallon. Use the straight line of part (a) to estimate the average number of miles automobiles were driven in Japan.

TABLE 5   Effect of Gas Prices on Miles Driven

Country	Price per Gallon	Average Miles per Auto
Canada	$1.57	10,371
England	$2.86	10,186
France	$3.31	8,740
Germany	$3.34	7,674
Sweden	$3.44	7,456
United States	$1.24	11,099

13. Table 6 gives the percent of persons 25 years and over who have completed four or more years of college.[‡]

TABLE 6   College Completion Rates

Year	1970	1975	1980	1985	1990	1995
Percent	10.7	13.9	16.2	19.4	21.3	23.0

(a) Use the method of least squares to obtain the straight line that best fits these data. [*Hint*: First convert *Year* to *Years after 1970*.]

(b) Estimate the percent for the year 1993.

(c) If the trend determined by the straight line in part (a) continues, when will the percent reach 27.1?

14. Table 7 gives the number of cars (in millions) in use in the United States[§] for certain years.

TABLE 7   Automobile Population

Year	Cars	Year	Cars
1980	104.6	1991	123.3
1985	114.7	1992	120.3
1989	122.8	1993	121.1
1990	123.3	1994	122

(a) Use the method of least squares to obtain the straight line that best fits these data. [*Hint*: First convert *Years* to *Years after 1980*.]

(b) Estimate the number of cars in use in 1983.

(c) If the trend determined by the straight line in part (a) continues, when will the number of cars in use reach 130 million?

---

[*]U.S. Health Care Financing Administration, *Health Care Financing Review*, Spring 1996.

[†]Source: Energy Information Administration, *International Energy Annual*. U.S. Highway Administration, *Highway Statistics*, 1994.

[‡]U.S. Bureau of the Census.

[§]American Automobile Manufacturers Association, Inc., Detroit, Michigan, *Motor Vehicle Facts and Figures*.

15. An ecologist wished to know whether certain species of aquatic insects have their ecological range limited by temperature. He collected the data in Table 8, relating the average daily temperature at different portions of a creek with the elevation (above sea level) of that portion of the creek.[*]

(a) Find the straight line that provides the best least-squares fit to these data.

(b) Use the linear function to estimate the average daily temperature for this creek at altitude 3.2 kilometers.

TABLE 8   Relationship between Elevation and Temperature in a Creek

Elevation (kilometers)	Average Temperature (degrees Celsius)
2.7	11.2
2.8	10
3.0	8.5
3.5	7.5

Solutions to Practice Problems 7.5

1. $\dfrac{\partial E}{\partial A} = 2(A + B + 2) \cdot 1 + 2(3A + B) \cdot 3$
$\qquad + 2(6A + B - 8) \cdot 6$

$\qquad = (2A + 2B + 4) + (18A + 6B)$
$\qquad + (72A + 12B - 96)$

$\qquad = 92A + 20B - 92.$

(Notice that we used the general power rule when differentiating and so had to always multiply by the derivative of the quantity inside the parentheses. Also, you might be tempted to first square the terms in the expression for E and then differentiate. We recommend that you resist this temptation.)

2. $E = (A + B - 10)^2 + (5A + B - 8)^2 + (7A + B)^2.$ In general, E is a sum of squares, one for each point being fitted. The point (a, b) gives rise to the term $(aA + B - b)^2.$

7.6 Double Integrals

Up to this point, our discussion of the calculus of several variables has been confined to the study of differentiation. Let us now take up the topic of the integration of functions of several variables. As has been the case throughout most of this chapter, we restrict our discussion to functions $f(x, y)$ of two variables.

We begin with some motivation. Before we define the concept of an integral for functions of several variables, we review the essential features of the integral in one variable.

Consider the definite integral $\int_a^b f(x)\,dx$. To write down this integral takes two pieces of information. The first is the function $f(x)$. The second is the interval over which the integration is to be performed. In this case, the interval is the portion of the x-axis from $x = a$ to $x = b$. The value of the definite integral is a number. In case the function $f(x)$ is nonnegative throughout the interval from $x = a$ to $x = b$, this number equals the area under the graph of $f(x)$ from $x = a$ to $x = b$. (See Fig. 1.) If $f(x)$ is negative for some values of x in the interval, the integral still equals the area bounded by the graph, but areas below the x-axis are counted as negative.

Let us generalize the foregoing ingredients to a function $f(x, y)$ of two variables. First, we must provide a two-dimensional analog of the interval from $x = a$ to $x = b$. This is easy. We take a two-dimensional region R of the plane, such as the region shown in Fig. 2. As our generalization of $f(x)$, we take a function $f(x, y)$ of two

---

[*]The authors express their thanks to Dr. J. David Allen, formerly of the Department of Zoology at the University of Maryland, for providing the data for this exercise.

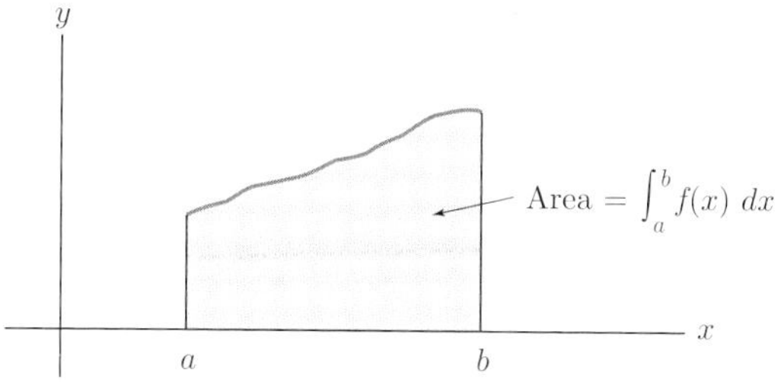

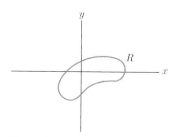

Figure 1

Figure 2. A region in the xy-plane.

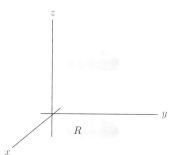

Figure 3. Graph of $f(x, y)$ above the region R.

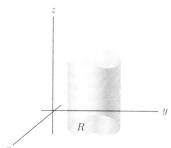

Figure 4. Solid bounded by $f(x, y)$ over R.

variables. Our generalization of the definite integral is denoted

$$\iint\limits_{R} f(x, y)\, dx\, dy$$

and is called the *double integral of $f(x, y)$ over the region R*. The value of the double integral is a number defined as follows. For the sake of simplicity, let us begin by assuming that $f(x, y) \geq 0$ for all points (x, y) in the region R. [This is the analog of the assumption that $f(x) \geq 0$ for all x in the interval from $x = a$ to $x = b$.] This means that the graph of f lies above the region R in three-dimensional space. (See Fig. 3.) The portion of the graph over R determines a solid figure. (See Fig. 4.) This figure is called the *solid bounded by $f(x, y)$ over the region R*. We define the double integral $\iint\limits_{R} f(x, y)\, dx\, dy$ to be the volume of this solid. In case the graph of $f(x, y)$ lies partially above the region R and partially below, we define the double integral to be the volume of the solid above the region minus the volume of the solid below the region. That is, we count volumes below the xy-plane as negative.

Now that we have defined the notion of a double integral, we must learn how to calculate its value. To do so, let us introduce the notion of an iterated integral. Let $f(x, y)$ be a function of two variables, let $g(x)$ and $h(x)$ be two functions of x alone, and let a and b be numbers. Then an *iterated integral* is an expression of the form

$$\int_{a}^{b} \left(\int_{g(x)}^{h(x)} f(x, y)\, dy \right) dx.$$

To explain the meaning of this collection of symbols, we proceed from the inside out. We evaluate the integral

$$\int_{g(x)}^{h(x)} f(x, y)\, dy$$

by considering $f(x, y)$ as a function of y alone. This is indicated by the dy in the inner integral. We treat x as a constant in this integration. So we evaluate the integral by first finding an antiderivative $F(x, y)$ with respect to y. The integral above is then evaluated as

$$F(x, h(x)) - F(x, g(x)).$$

That is, we evaluate the antiderivative between the limits $y = g(x)$ and $y = h(x)$. This gives us a function of x alone. To complete the evaluation of the integral, we integrate this function from $x = a$ to $x = b$. The next two examples illustrate the procedure for evaluating iterated integrals.

EXAMPLE 1 Evaluate the iterated integral

$$\int_1^2 \left(\int_3^4 (y - x)\, dy \right) dx.$$

Solution Here $g(x)$ and $h(x)$ are constant functions: $g(x) = 3$ and $h(x) = 4$. We evaluate the inner integral first. The variable in this integral is y, so we treat x as a constant.

$$\int_3^4 (y - x)\, dy = \left(\frac{1}{2} y^2 - xy \right) \Big|_3^4$$

$$= \left(\frac{1}{2} \cdot 16 - x \cdot 4 \right) - \left(\frac{1}{2} \cdot 9 - x \cdot 3 \right)$$

$$= 8 - 4x - \frac{9}{2} + 3x$$

$$= \frac{7}{2} - x.$$

Now we carry out the integration with respect to x:

$$\int_1^2 \left(\frac{7}{2} - x \right) dx = \frac{7}{2} x - \frac{1}{2} x^2 \Big|_1^2$$

$$= \left(\frac{7}{2} \cdot 2 - \frac{1}{2} \cdot 4 \right) - \left(\frac{7}{2} - \frac{1}{2} \cdot 1 \right)$$

$$= (7 - 2) - (3) = 2.$$

So the value of the iterated integral is 2. ◼

EXAMPLE 2 Evaluate the iterated integral

$$\int_0^1 \left(\int_{\sqrt{x}}^{x+1} 2xy\, dy \right) dx.$$

Solution We evaluate the inner integral first.

$$\int_{\sqrt{x}}^{x+1} 2xy\, dy = xy^2 \Big|_{\sqrt{x}}^{x+1} = x(x+1)^2 - x(\sqrt{x})^2$$

$$= x(x^2 + 2x + 1) - x \cdot x$$

$$= x^3 + 2x^2 + x - x^2$$

$$= x^3 + x^2 + x.$$

Now we evaluate the outer integral.

$$\int_0^1 (x^3 + x^2 + x)\, dx = \frac{1}{4} x^4 + \frac{1}{3} x^3 + \frac{1}{2} x^2 \Big|_0^1 = \frac{1}{4} + \frac{1}{3} + \frac{1}{2} = \frac{13}{12}$$

So the value of the iterated integral is $\frac{13}{12}$. ◼

Let us now return to the discussion of the double integral $\iint\limits_R f(x, y)\, dx\, dy$. When the region R has a special form, the double integral may be expressed as an iterated integral, as follows: Suppose that R is bounded by the graphs of $y = g(x)$, $y = h(x)$ and by the vertical lines $x = a$ and $x = b$. (See Fig. 5.) In this case, we have the following fundamental result, which we cite without proof.

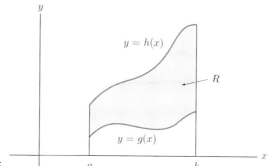

Figure 5

Let R be the region in the xy-plane bounded by the graphs of $y = g(x)$, $y = h(x)$, and the vertical lines $x = a$, $x = b$. Then

$$\iint\limits_{R} f(x, y)\, dx\, dy = \int_a^b \left(\int_{g(x)}^{h(x)} f(x, y)\, dy \right) dx.$$

Since the value of the double integral gives the volume of the solid bounded by the graph of $f(x, y)$ over the region R, the preceding result may be used to calculate volumes, as the next two examples show.

EXAMPLE 3

Calculate the volume of the solid bounded above by the function $f(x, y) = y - x$ and lying over the rectangular region R: $1 \leq x \leq 2$, $3 \leq y \leq 4$. (See Fig. 6.)

Solution The desired volume is given by the double integral $\iint\limits_{R} (y - x)\, dx\, dy$. By the result just cited, this double integral is equal to the iterated integral

$$\int_1^2 \left(\int_3^4 (y - x)\, dy \right) dx.$$

The value of this iterated integral was shown in Example 1 to be 2, so the volume of the solid shown in Fig. 6 is 2. ∎

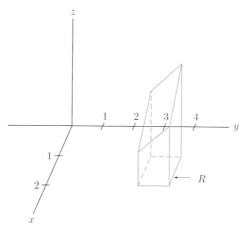

Figure 6

EXAMPLE 4   Calculate $\iint\limits_{R} 2xy\,dx\,dy$, where R is the region shown in Fig. 7.

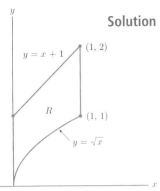

Figure 7

Solution The region R is bounded below by $y = \sqrt{x}$, above by $y = x + 1$, on the left by $x = 0$, and on the right by $x = 1$. Therefore,

$$\iint\limits_{R} 2xy\,dx\,dy = \int_0^1 \left(\int_{\sqrt{x}}^{x+1} 2xy\,dy \right) dx = \frac{13}{12} \quad \text{(by Example 2).}$$

In our discussion, we have confined ourselves to iterated integrals in which the inner integral was with respect to y. In a completely analogous manner, we may treat iterated integrals in which the inner integral is with respect to x. Such iterated integrals may be used to evaluate double integrals over regions R bounded by curves of the form $x = g(y)$, $x = h(y)$, and horizontal lines $y = a$, $y = b$. The computations are analogous to those given in this section.

Practice Problems 7.6

1. Calculate the iterated integral

$$\int_0^2 \left(\int_0^{x/2} e^{2y-x}\,dy \right) dx.$$

2. Calculate

$$\iint\limits_{R} e^{2y-x}\,dx\,dy$$

where R is the region in Fig. 8.

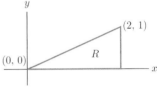

Figure 8

EXERCISES 7.6

Calculate the following iterated integrals.

1. $\int_0^1 \left(\int_0^1 e^{x+y}\,dy \right) dx$ 2. $\int_{-1}^1 \left(\int_{-1}^1 xy\,dx \right) dy$

3. $\int_{-2}^0 \left(\int_{-1}^1 xe^{xy}\,dy \right) dx$ 4. $\int_0^1 \left(\int_{-1}^1 \frac{1}{3}y^3x\,dy \right) dx$

5. $\int_1^4 \left(\int_x^{x^2} xy\,dy \right) dx$ 6. $\int_0^3 \left(\int_x^{2x} y\,dy \right) dx$

7. $\int_{-1}^1 \left(\int_x^{2x} (x+y)\,dy \right) dx$ 8. $\int_0^1 \left(\int_0^x e^{x+y}\,dy \right) dx$

Let R be the rectangle consisting of all points (x, y) such that $0 \le x \le 2$, $2 \le y \le 3$. Calculate the following double integrals. Interpret each as a volume.

9. $\iint\limits_{R} xy^2\,dx\,dy$ 10. $\iint\limits_{R} (xy + y^2)\,dx\,dy$

11. $\iint\limits_{R} e^{-x-y}\,dx\,dy$ 12. $\iint\limits_{R} e^{y-x}\,dx\,dy$

Calculate the volumes over the following regions R bounded above by the graph of $f(x, y) = x^2 + y^2$.

13. R is the rectangle bounded by the lines $x = 1$, $x = 3$, $y = 0$, and $y = 1$.

14. R is the region bounded by the lines $x = 0$, $x = 1$ and the curves $y = 0$ and $y = \sqrt[3]{x}$.

Solutions to Practice Problems 7.6

1. $\int_0^2 \left(\int_0^{x/2} e^{2y-x} \, dy \right) dx = \int_0^2 \left(\frac{1}{2} e^{2y-x} \Big|_0^{x/2} \right) dx$

$= \int_0^2 \left(\frac{1}{2} e^{2(x/2)-x} - \frac{1}{2} e^{2(0)-x} \right) dx$

$= \int_0^2 \left(\frac{1}{2} - \frac{1}{2} e^{-x} \right) dx$

$= \frac{1}{2} x + \frac{1}{2} e^{-x} \Big|_0^2$

$= \frac{1}{2} \cdot 2 + \frac{1}{2} e^{-2} - \left(\frac{1}{2} \cdot 0 + \frac{1}{2} e^{-0} \right)$

$= 1 + \frac{1}{2} e^{-2} - 0 - \frac{1}{2}$

$= \frac{1}{2} + \frac{1}{2} e^{-2}.$

2. The line passing through the points $(0,0)$ and $(2,1)$ has equation $y = x/2$. Hence the region R is bounded below by $y = 0$, above by $y = x/2$, on the left by $x = 0$, and on the right by $x = 2$. Therefore,

$$\iint\limits_R e^{2y-x} \, dx \, dy = \int_0^2 \left(\int_0^{x/2} e^{2y-x} \, dy \right) dx$$

$$= \frac{1}{2} + \frac{1}{2} e^{-2}$$

by Problem 1.

REVIEW OF FUNDAMENTAL CONCEPTS

1. Give an example of a level curve of a function of two variables.

2. Explain how to find a first partial derivative of a function of two variables.

3. Explain how to find a second partial derivative of a function of two variables.

4. What expression involving a partial derivative gives an approximation to $f(a + h, b) - f(a, b)$?

5. Interpret $\dfrac{\partial f}{\partial y}(2, 3)$ as a rate of change.

6. Give an example of a Cobb–Douglas production function. What is the marginal productivity of labor? Of capital?

7. Explain how to find possible relative extreme points for a function of several variables.

8. State the second-derivative test for functions of two variables.

9. Outline how the method of Lagrange multipliers is used to solve an optimization problem.

10. What is the least-squares line approximation to a set of data points? How is the line determined?

11. Give a geometric interpretation for $\iint\limits_R f(x, y) \, dx \, dy$, where $f(x, y) \geq 0$.

12. Give a formula for evaluating a double integral in terms of an iterated integral.

SUPPLEMENTARY EXERCISES

1. Let $f(x, y) = x\sqrt{y}/(1 + x)$. Compute $f(2, 9)$, $f(5, 1)$, and $f(0, 0)$.

2. Let $f(x, y, z) = x^2 e^{y/z}$. Compute $f(-1, 0, 1)$, $f(1, 3, 3)$, and $f(5, -2, 2)$.

3. If A dollars are deposited in a bank at a 6% continuous interest rate, the amount in the account after t years is $f(A, t) = A e^{.06t}$. Find and interpret $f(10, 11.5)$.

4. Let $f(x, y, \lambda) = xy + \lambda(5 - x - y)$. Find $f(1, 2, 3)$.

5. Let $f(x, y) = 3x^2 + xy + 5y^2$. Find $\dfrac{\partial f}{\partial x}$ and $\dfrac{\partial f}{\partial y}$.

6. Let $f(x, y) = 3x - \frac{1}{2} y^4 + 1$. Find $\dfrac{\partial f}{\partial x}$ and $\dfrac{\partial f}{\partial y}$.

7. Let $f(x, y) = e^{x/y}$. Find $\dfrac{\partial f}{\partial x}$ and $\dfrac{\partial f}{\partial y}$.

8. Let $f(x, y) = x/(x - 2y)$. Find $\dfrac{\partial f}{\partial x}$ and $\dfrac{\partial f}{\partial y}$.

9. Let $f(x, y, z) = x^3 - yz^2$. Find $\dfrac{\partial f}{\partial x}$, $\dfrac{\partial f}{\partial y}$, and $\dfrac{\partial f}{\partial z}$.

10. Let $f(x, y, \lambda) = xy + \lambda(5 - x - y)$. Find $\dfrac{\partial f}{\partial x}$, $\dfrac{\partial f}{\partial y}$, and $\dfrac{\partial f}{\partial \lambda}$.

11. Let $f(x, y) = x^3 y + 8$. Compute $\dfrac{\partial f}{\partial x}(1, 2)$ and $\dfrac{\partial f}{\partial y}(1, 2)$.

12. Let $f(x, y, z) = (x + y)z$. Evaluate $\dfrac{\partial f}{\partial y}$ at $(x, y, z) = (2, 3, 4)$.

13. Let $f(x, y) = x^5 - 2x^3y + \frac{1}{2}y^4$. Find $\dfrac{\partial^2 f}{\partial x^2}$, $\dfrac{\partial^2 f}{\partial y^2}$, $\dfrac{\partial^2 f}{\partial x\, \partial y}$, and $\dfrac{\partial^2 f}{\partial y\, \partial x}$.

14. Let $f(x, y) = 2x^3 + x^2y - y^2$. Compute $\dfrac{\partial^2 f}{\partial x^2}$, $\dfrac{\partial^2 f}{\partial y^2}$, and $\dfrac{\partial^2 f}{\partial x\, \partial y}$ at $(x, y) = (1, 2)$.

15. A dealer in a certain brand of electronic calculator finds that (within certain limits) the number of calculators she can sell per week is given by $f(p, t) = -p + 6t - .02pt$, where p is the price of the calculator and t is the number of dollars spent on advertising. Compute $\dfrac{\partial f}{\partial p}(25, 10{,}000)$ and $\dfrac{\partial f}{\partial t}(25, 10{,}000)$ and interpret these numbers.

16. The crime rate in a certain city can be approximated by a function $f(x, y, z)$, where x is the unemployment rate, y is the amount of social services available, and z is the size of the police force. Explain why $\dfrac{\partial f}{\partial x} > 0$, $\dfrac{\partial f}{\partial y} < 0$, and $\dfrac{\partial f}{\partial z} < 0$.

In Exercises 17–20, find all points (x, y) where $f(x, y)$ has a possible relative maximum or minimum.

17. $f(x, y) = -x^2 + 2y^2 + 6x - 8y + 5$

18. $f(x, y) = x^2 + 3xy - y^2 - x - 8y + 4$

19. $f(x, y) = x^3 + 3x^2 + 3y^2 - 6y + 7$

20. $f(x, y) = \frac{1}{2}x^2 + 4xy + y^3 + 8y^2 + 3x + 2$

In Exercises 21–23, find all points (x, y) where $f(x, y)$ has a possible relative maximum or minimum. Then use the second-derivative test to determine, if possible, the nature of $f(x, y)$ at each of these points. If the second-derivative test is inconclusive, so state.

21. $f(x, y) = x^2 + 3xy + 4y^2 - 13x - 30y + 12$

22. $f(x, y) = 7x^2 - 5xy + y^2 + x - y + 6$

23. $f(x, y) = x^3 + y^2 - 3x - 8y + 12$

24. Find the values of x, y, z at which
$$f(x, y, z) = x^2 + 4y^2 + 5z^2 - 6x + 8y + 3$$
assumes its minimum value.

Use the method of Lagrange multipliers to:

25. Maximize $3x^2 + 2xy - y^2$, subject to the constraint $5 - 2x - y = 0$.

26. Find the values of x, y that minimize $-x^2 - 3xy - \frac{1}{2}y^2 + y + 10$, subject to the constraint $10 - x - y = 0$.

27. Find the values of x, y, z that minimize $3x^2 + 2y^2 + z^2 + 4x + y + 3z$, subject to the constraint $4 - x - y - z = 0$.

28. Find the dimensions of a rectangular box of volume 1000 cubic inches for which the sum of the dimensions is minimized.

29. A person wants to plant a rectangular garden along one side of a house and put a fence on the other three sides. (See Fig. 1.) Using the method of Lagrange multipliers, find the dimensions of the garden of greatest area that can be enclosed by using 40 feet of fencing.

Figure 9. A garden.

30. The solution to Exercise 29 is $x = 10$, $y = 20$, $\lambda = 10$. If 1 additional foot of fencing becomes available, compute the new optimal dimensions and the new area. Show that the increase in area (compared with the area in Exercise 29) is approximately equal to 10 (the value of λ).

In Exercises 31–33, find the straight line that best fits the following data points, where "best" is meant in the sense of least squares.

31. $(1, 1)$, $(2, 3)$, $(3, 6)$

32. $(1, 1)$, $(3, 4)$, $(5, 7)$

33. $(0, 1)$, $(1, -1)$, $(2, -3)$, $(3, -5)$

In Exercises 34 and 35, calculate the iterated integral.

34. $\displaystyle \int_0^1 \left(\int_0^4 (x\sqrt{y} + y)\, dy \right) dx$

35. $\displaystyle \int_0^5 \left(\int_1^4 (2xy^4 + 3)\, dy \right) dx$

In Exercises 36 and 37, let R be the rectangle consisting of all points (x, y) such that $0 \le x \le 4$, $1 \le y \le 3$, and calculate the double integral.

36. $\displaystyle \iint_R (2x + 3y)\, dx\, dy$ **37.** $\displaystyle \iint_R 5\, dx\, dy$

38. The present value of y dollars after x years at 15% continuous interest is $f(x, y) = ye^{-.15x}$. Sketch some sample level curves. (Economists call this collection of level curves a *discount system*.)

THE TRIGONOMETRIC FUNCTIONS

In this chapter we expand the collection of functions to which we can apply calculus by introducing the trigonometric functions. As we shall see, these functions are *periodic*. That is, after a certain point their graphs repeat themselves. This repetitive phenomenon is not displayed by any of the functions that we have considered until now. Yet many natural phenomena are repetitive or cyclical, for example, the motion of the planets in our solar system, earthquake vibrations, and the natural rhythm of the heart. Thus the functions introduced in this chapter add considerably to our capacity to describe physical processes.

8.1 Radian Measure of Angles

The ancient Babylonians introduced angle measurement in terms of degrees, minutes, and seconds, and these units are still generally used today for navigation and practical measurements. In calculus, however, it is more convenient to measure angles in terms of *radians*, for in this case the differentiation formulas for the trigonometric functions are easier to remember and use. Also, the radian is becoming more widely used today in scientific work because it is the unit of angle measurement in the international metric system (Système International d'Unités).

To define a radian, we consider a circle of radius 1 and measure angles in terms of distances around the circumference. The central angle determined by an arc of length 1 along the circumference is said to have a measure of 1 *radian*. (See Fig. 1.) Since the circumference of the circle of radius 1 has length 2π, there are 2π radians in one full revolution of the circle. Equivalently,

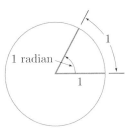

Figure 1

$$360° = 2\pi \text{ radians.} \tag{1}$$

The following important relations should be memorized (see Fig. 2):

$$90° = \frac{\pi}{2} \text{ radians} \qquad \text{(one quarter-revolution)}$$

$$180° = \pi \text{ radians} \qquad \text{(one half-revolution)}$$

$$270° = \frac{3\pi}{2} \text{ radians} \qquad \text{(three quarter-revolutions)}$$

$$360° = 2\pi \text{ radians} \qquad \text{(one full revolution).}$$

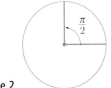

Figure 2

From formula (1) we see that

$$1° = \frac{2\pi}{360} \text{ radians} = \frac{\pi}{180} \text{ radians.}$$

If d is any number, then

$$d° = d \times \frac{\pi}{180} \text{ radians.} \tag{2}$$

That is, to convert degrees to radians, multiply the number of degrees by $\pi/180$.

EXAMPLE 1   Convert $45°$, $60°$, and $135°$ to radians.

Solution
$$45° = \overset{1}{\cancel{45}} \times \frac{\pi}{\underset{4}{\cancel{180}}} \text{ radians} = \frac{\pi}{4} \text{ radians,}$$

$$60° = \overset{1}{\cancel{60}} \times \frac{\pi}{\underset{3}{\cancel{180}}} \text{ radians} = \frac{\pi}{3} \text{ radians,}$$

$$135° = \overset{3}{\cancel{135}} \times \frac{\pi}{\underset{4}{\cancel{180}}} \text{ radians} = \frac{3\pi}{4} \text{ radians.}$$

These three angles are shown in Fig. 3.

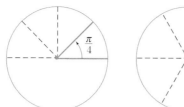 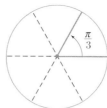 

Figure 3

We usually omit the word "radian" when measuring angles because all our angle measurements will be in radians unless degrees are specifically indicated.

For our purposes, it is important to be able to speak of both negative and positive angles, so let us define what we mean by a negative angle. We shall usually consider angles that are in *standard position* on a coordinate system, with the vertex of the angle at $(0,0)$ and one side, called the "initial side," along the positive x-axis. We measure such an angle from the initial side to the "terminal side," where a *counterclockwise angle is positive* and a *clockwise angle is negative*. Some examples are given in Fig. 4.

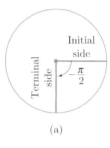 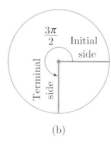 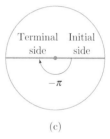

Figure 4   (a)   (b)   (c)

Notice in Figs. 4(a) and (b) how essentially the same picture can describe more than one angle.

By considering angles formed from more than one revolution (in the positive or negative direction), we can construct angles whose measure is of arbitrary size (that is, not necessarily between -2π and 2π). Three examples are illustrated in Fig. 5.

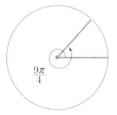 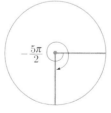 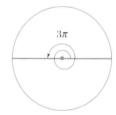

Figure 5

EXAMPLE 2   (a) What is the radian measure of the angle in Fig. 6?

(b) Construct an angle of $5\pi/2$ radians.

Solution   (a) The angle described in Fig. 6 consists of one full revolution (2π radians) plus three quarter-revolutions [$3 \times (\pi/2)$ radians]. That is,

$$t = 2\pi + 3 \times \frac{\pi}{2} = 4 \times \frac{\pi}{2} + 3 \times \frac{\pi}{2} = \frac{7\pi}{2}.$$

(b) Think of $5\pi/2$ radians as $5 \times (\pi/2)$ radians, that is, five quarter-revolutions of the circle. This is one full revolution plus one quarter-revolution. An angle of $5\pi/2$ radians is shown in Fig. 7.

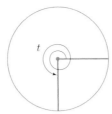

Figure 6

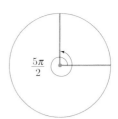

Figure 7

Practice Problems 8.1

1. A right triangle has one angle of $\pi/3$ radians. What are the other angles?

2. How many radians are there in an angle of $-780°$? Draw the angle.

EXERCISES 8.1

Convert the following to radian measure.

1. $30°, 120°, 315°$

2. $18°, 72°, 150°$

3. $450°, -210°, -90°$

4. $990°, -270°, -540°$

Give the radian measure of each angle described.

5.

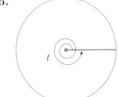

6.

7.

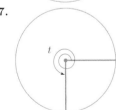

8.

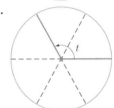

9.

10.

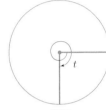

11.

12.

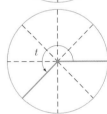

Construct angles with the following radian measure.

13. $3\pi/2, 3\pi/4, 5\pi$

14. $\pi/3, 5\pi/2, 6\pi$

15. $-\pi/3, -3\pi/4, -7\pi/2$

16. $-\pi/4, -3\pi/2, -3\pi$

17. $\pi/6, -2\pi/3, -\pi$

18. $2\pi/3, -\pi/6, 7\pi/2$

Solutions to Practice Problems 8.1

1. The sum of the angles of a triangle is $180°$ or π radians. Since a right angle is $\pi/2$ radians and one angle is $\pi/3$ radians, the remaining angle is $\pi - (\pi/2 + \pi/3) = \pi/6$ radians.

2. $-780° = -780 \times (\pi/180)$ radians

$\qquad = -13\pi/3$ radians.

Since $-13\pi/3 = -4\pi - \pi/3$, we draw the angle by first making two revolutions in the negative direction and then a rotation of $\pi/3$ in the negative direction. (See Fig. 8.)

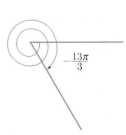

Figure 8

8.2 The Sine and the Cosine

Given a number t, we consider an angle of t radians placed in standard position, as in Fig. 1, and we let P be a point on the terminal side of this angle. Denote the coordinates of P by (x, y) and let r be the length of the segment OP; that is, $r = \sqrt{x^2 + y^2}$. The *sine* and *cosine* of t, denoted by $\sin t$ and $\cos t$, respectively, are defined by the ratios

$$\sin t = \frac{y}{r}$$
$$\cos t = \frac{x}{r}. \tag{1}$$

It does not matter which point on the ray through P we use to define $\sin t$ and $\cos t$. If $P' = (x', y')$ is another point on the same ray and if r' is the length of OP' (Fig. 2), then, by properties of similar triangles, we have

$$\frac{y'}{r'} = \frac{y}{r} = \sin t,$$

$$\frac{x'}{r'} = \frac{x}{r} = \cos t.$$

Three examples that illustrate the definition of $\sin t$ and $\cos t$ are shown in Fig. 3.

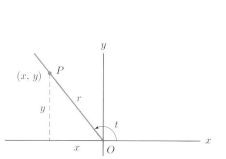

Figure 1. Diagram for the definitions of sine and cosine.

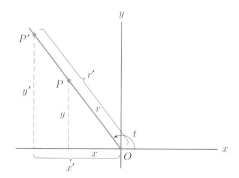

Figure 2

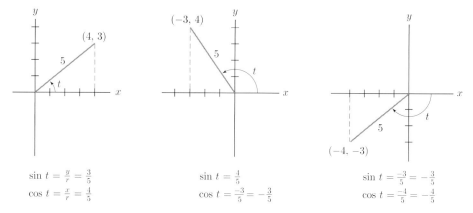

$$\sin t = \frac{y}{r} = \frac{3}{5} \qquad\qquad \sin t = \frac{4}{5} \qquad\qquad \sin t = \frac{-3}{5} = -\frac{3}{5}$$
$$\cos t = \frac{x}{r} = \frac{4}{5} \qquad\qquad \cos t = \frac{-3}{5} = -\frac{3}{5} \qquad\qquad \cos t = \frac{-4}{5} = -\frac{4}{5}$$

Figure 3. Calculation of $\sin t$ and $\cos t$.

When $0 < t < \pi/2$, the values of $\sin t$ and $\cos t$ may be expressed as ratios of the lengths of the sides of a right triangle. Indeed, if we are given the right triangle in Fig. 4, we have

$$\sin t = \frac{\text{opposite}}{\text{hypotenuse}}, \qquad \cos t = \frac{\text{adjacent}}{\text{hypotenuse}}. \qquad (2)$$

A typical application of (2) appears in Example 1.

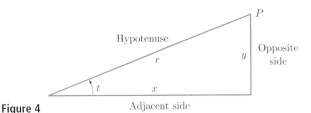

Figure 4

EXAMPLE 1

The hypotenuse of a right triangle is 4 units and one angle is .7 radian. Determine the length of the side opposite this angle.

Solution See Fig. 5. Since $y/4 = \sin .7$, we have

$$y = 4 \sin .7$$
$$\approx 4(.64422) = 2.57688. \qquad \blacksquare$$

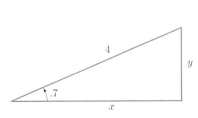

Figure 5

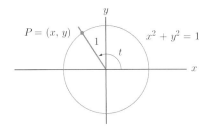

Figure 6

Another way to describe the sine and cosine functions is to choose the point P in Fig. 1 so that $r = 1$. That is, choose P on the unit circle. (See Fig. 6.) In this case

$$\sin t = \frac{y}{1} = y,$$

$$\cos t = \frac{x}{1} = x.$$

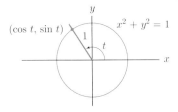

Figure 7

So the y-coordinate of P is $\sin t$, and the x-coordinate of P is $\cos t$. Thus we have the following result:

Alternative Definition of Sine and Cosine Functions   We can think of $\cos t$ and $\sin t$ as the x- and y-coordinates of the point P on the unit circle that is determined by an angle of t radians. (See Fig. 7.)

EXAMPLE 2

Find a value of t such that $0 < t < \pi/2$ and $\cos t = \cos(-\pi/3)$.

Solution On the unit circle we locate the point P that is determined by an angle of $-\pi/3$ radians. The x-coordinate of P is $\cos(-\pi/3)$. There is another point Q on the unit circle with the same x-coordinate. (See Fig. 8.) Let t be the radian measure of the angle determined by Q. Then

$$\cos t = \cos\left(-\frac{\pi}{3}\right)$$

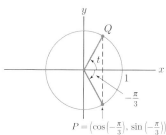

because Q and P have the same x-coordinate. Also, $0 < t < \pi/2$. From the symmetry of the diagram, it is clear that $t = \pi/3$. ∎

Figure 8

Properties of the Sine and Cosine Functions Each number t determines a point $(\cos t, \sin t)$ on the unit circle $x^2 + y^2 = 1$ as in Fig. 7. Therefore, $(\cos t)^2 + (\sin t)^2 = 1$. It is convenient (and traditional) to write $\sin^2 t$ instead of $(\sin t)^2$ and $\cos^2 t$ instead of $(\cos t)^2$. Thus we can write the last formula as follows:

$$\cos^2 t + \sin^2 t = 1. \tag{3}$$

The numbers t and $t \pm 2\pi$ determine the same point on the unit circle (because 2π represents a full revolution of the circle). But $t + 2\pi$ and $t - 2\pi$ correspond to the points $(\cos(t + 2\pi), \sin(t + 2\pi))$ and $(\cos(t - 2\pi), \sin(t - 2\pi))$, respectively. Hence

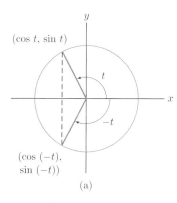

$$\cos(t \pm 2\pi) = \cos t, \qquad \sin(t \pm 2\pi) = \sin t. \tag{4}$$

Figure 9(a) illustrates another property of the sine and cosine:

$$\cos(-t) = \cos t, \qquad \sin(-t) = -\sin t. \tag{5}$$

Figure 9(b) shows that the points P and Q corresponding to t and to $\pi/2 - t$ are reflections of each other through the line $y = x$. Consequently, the coordinates of Q are obtained by interchanging the coordinates of P. This means that

$$\cos\left(\frac{\pi}{2} - t\right) = \sin t, \qquad \sin\left(\frac{\pi}{2} - t\right) = \cos t. \tag{6}$$

The equations in (3) to (6) are called *identities* because they hold for all values of t. Another identity that holds for all numbers s and t is

$$\sin(s + t) = \sin s \, \cos t + \cos s \, \sin t. \tag{7}$$

Figure 9. Diagrams for two identities.

A proof of (7) may be found in any introductory book on trigonometry. There are a number of other identities concerning trigonometric functions, but we shall not need them here.

The Graph of sin t Let us analyze what happens to $\sin t$ as t increases from 0 to π. When $t = 0$, the point $P = (\cos t, \sin t)$ is at $(1, 0)$, as in Fig. 10(a). As t increases, P moves counterclockwise around the unit circle. [See Fig. 10(b).] The y-coordinate of P, that is, $\sin t$, increases until $t = \pi/2$, where $P = (0, 1)$. [See Fig. 10(c).] As t

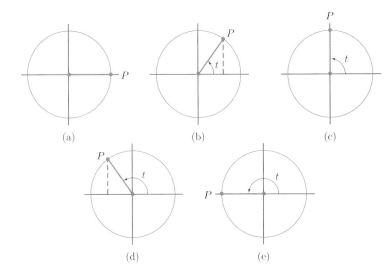

Figure 10. Movement along the unit circle.

increases from $\pi/2$ to π, the y-coordinate of P, that is, $\sin t$, decreases from 1 to 0. [See Figs. 10(d) and (e).]

Part of the graph of $\sin t$ is sketched in Fig. 11. For t between 0 and π, notice that the values of $\sin t$ increase from 0 to 1 and then decrease back to 0, just as we predicted from Fig. 10. For t between π and 2π, the values of $\sin t$ are negative. The graph of $y = \sin t$ for t between 2π and 4π is exactly the same as the graph for t between 0 and 2π. This result follows from formula (4). We say that the sine function is *periodic with period* 2π because the graph repeats itself every 2π units. We can use this fact to make a quick sketch of part of the graph for negative values of t. (See Fig. 12.)

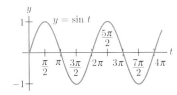

Figure 11

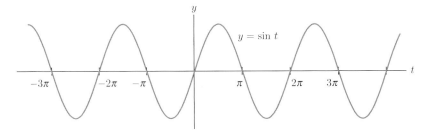

Figure 12. Graph of the sine function.

The Graph of cos *t*   By analyzing what happens to the first coordinate of the point $(\cos t, \sin t)$ as t varies, we obtain the graph of $\cos t$. Note from Fig. 13 that the graph of the cosine function is also periodic with period 2π.

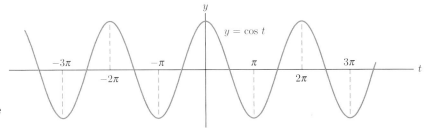

Figure 13. Graph of the cosine function.

REMARK ABOUT NOTATION   The sine and cosine functions assign to each number t the values $\sin t$ and $\cos t$, respectively. There is nothing special, however, about the letter t. Although we chose to use the letters t, x, y, and r in the *definition* of the sine and cosine, other letters could have been used as well. Now that the sine and cosine of every number are defined, we are free to use *any* letter to represent the independent variable. ■

INCORPORATING TECHNOLOGY

Graphing Trigonometric Functions The ZTrig window setting is optimized for displaying graphs of trigonometric functions. This can be accessed via zoom 7, and it sets the window dimensions to $[-2\pi, 2\pi]$ by $[-4, 4]$ with an x-scale of $\pi/2$. Figure 14 is the graph of y = sin x in this setting. ■

Figure 14

Practice Problems 8.2

1. Find $\cos t$, where t is the radian measure of the angle shown in Fig. 15.

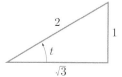

Figure 15

2. Assume that $\cos(1.17) = .390$. Use properties of the cosine and sine to determine $\sin(1.17)$, $\cos(1.17+4\pi)$, $\cos(-1.17)$, and $\sin(-1.17)$.

EXERCISES 8.2

In Exercises 1–12, give the values of $\sin t$ and $\cos t$, where t is the radian measure of the angle shown.

1.
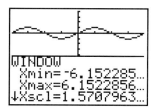

2.

3.
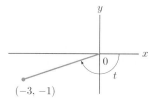

4.
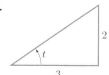

5.
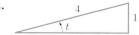

6.

7. $(-2, 1)$
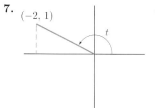

8.
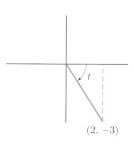
$(2, -3)$

9.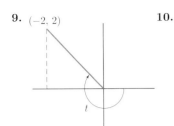
(−2, 2)

10.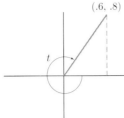
(.6, .8)

11.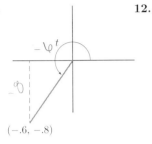
(−.6, −.8)

12.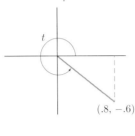
(.8, −.6)

Exercises 13–20 refer to various right triangles whose sides and angles are labeled as in Fig. 16. Round off all lengths of sides to one decimal place.

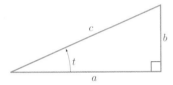

Figure 16

13. Estimate t if $a = 12$, $b = 5$, and $c = 13$.

14. If $t = 1.1$ and $c = 10.0$, find b.

15. If $t = 1.1$ and $b = 3.2$, find c.

16. If $t = .4$ and $c = 5.0$, find a.

17. If $t = .4$ and $a = 10.0$, find c.

18. If $t = .9$ and $c = 20.0$, find a and b.

19. If $t = .5$ and $a = 2.4$, find b and c.

20. If $t = 1.1$ and $b = 3.5$, find a and c.

Find t such that $0 \leq t \leq \pi$ and t satisfy the stated condition.

21. $\cos t = \cos(-\pi/6)$ **22.** $\cos t = \cos(3\pi/2)$

23. $\cos t = \cos(5\pi/4)$ **24.** $\cos t = \cos(-4\pi/6)$

25. $\cos t = \cos(-5\pi/8)$ **26.** $\cos t = \cos(-3\pi/4)$

Find t such that $-\pi/2 \leq t \leq \pi/2$ and t satisfy the stated condition.

27. $\sin t = \sin(3\pi/4)$ **28.** $\sin t = \sin(7\pi/6)$

29. $\sin t = \sin(-4\pi/3)$ **30.** $\sin t = -\sin(3\pi/8)$

31. $\sin t = -\sin(\pi/6)$ **32.** $\sin t = -\sin(-\pi/3)$

33. $\sin t = \cos t$ **34.** $\sin t = -\cos t$

35. Refer to Fig. 10. Describe what happens to $\cos t$ as t increases from 0 to π.

36. Use the unit circle to describe what happens to $\sin t$ as t increases from π to 2π.

37. Determine the value of $\sin t$ when $t = 5\pi$, -2π, $17\pi/2$, $-13\pi/2$.

38. Determine the value of $\cos t$ when $t = 5\pi$, -2π, $17\pi/2$, $-13\pi/2$.

39. Assume that $\cos(.19) = .98$. Use properties of the cosine and sine to determine $\sin(.19)$, $\cos(.19 - 4\pi)$, $\cos(-.19)$, and $\sin(-.19)$.

40. Assume that $\sin(.42) = .41$. Use properties of the cosine and sine to determine $\sin(-.42)$, $\sin(6\pi - .42)$, and $\cos(.42)$.

Technology Exercises

41. In any given locality, tap water temperature varies during the year. In Dallas, Texas, the tap water temperature (in degrees Fahrenheit) t days after the beginning of a year is given approximately by the formula*

$$T = 59 + 14 \cos\left[\frac{2\pi}{365}(t - 208)\right], \qquad 0 \leq t \leq 365.$$

  (a) Graph the function in the window $[0, 365]$ by $[-10, 73]$.

  (b) What is the temperature on February 14, that is, when $t = 45$?

  (c) Use the fact that the value of the cosine function ranges from -1 to 1 to find the coldest and warmest tap water temperatures during the year.

  (d) Use the **TRACE** feature or the **MINIMUM** command to estimate the day during which the tap water temperature is coldest. Find the exact day algebraically by using the fact that $\cos(-\pi) = -1$.

  (e) Use the **TRACE** feature or the **MAXIMUM** command to estimate the day during which the tap water temperature is warmest. Find the exact day algebraically by using the fact that $\cos(0) = 1$.

  (f) The average tap water temperature during the year is $59°$. Find the two days during which the average temperature is achieved. [*Note:* Answer this question both graphically and algebraically.]

42. In any given locality, the length of daylight varies during the year. In Des Moines, Iowa, the number of minutes of daylight in a day t days after the beginning of a year is given approximately by the formula†

$$D = 720 + 200 \sin\left[\frac{2\pi}{365}(t - 79.5)\right], \qquad 0 \leq t \leq 365.$$

*See D. Rapp, *Solar Energy* (Upper Saddle River, NJ: Prentice-Hall, Inc., 1981), p. 171.

†See D. R. Duncan et al., "Climate Curves," *School Science and Mathematics*, Vol. 76 (January 1976), pp. 41–49.

(a) Graph the function in the window $[0, 365]$ by $[-100, 940]$.

(b) How many minutes of daylight are there on February 14, that is, when $t = 45$?

(c) Use the fact that the value of the sine function ranges from -1 to 1 to find the shortest and longest amounts of daylight during the year.

(d) Use the **TRACE** feature or the **MINIMUM** command to estimate the day with the shortest amount of daylight. Find the exact day alge-

braically by using the fact that $\sin(3\pi/2) = -1$.

(e) Use the **TRACE** feature or the **MAXIMUM** command to estimate the day with the longest amount of daylight. Find the exact day algebraically by using the fact that $\sin(\pi/2) = 1$.

(f) Find the two days during which the amount of daylight equals the amount of darkness. (These days are called *equinoxes.*) [*Note*: Answer this question both graphically and algebraically.]

Solutions to Practice Problems 8.2

1. Here $P = (x, y) = (-3, -1)$. The length of the line segment OP is

$$r = \sqrt{x^2 + y^2} = \sqrt{(-3)^2 + (-1)^2} = \sqrt{10}.$$

Then

$$\cos t = \frac{x}{r} = \frac{-3}{\sqrt{10}} \approx -.94868.$$

2. Given $\cos(1.17) = .390$, use the relation $\cos^2 t + \sin^2 t = 1$ with $t = 1.17$ to solve for $\sin(1.17)$:

$$\cos^2(1.17) + \sin^2(1.17) = 1$$

$$\sin^2(1.17) = 1 - \cos^2(1.17)$$

$$= 1 - (.390)^2 = .8479.$$

So

$$\sin(1.17) = \sqrt{.8479} \approx .921.$$

Also, from properties (4) and (5),

$$\cos(1.17 + 4\pi) = \cos(1.17) = .390$$

$$\cos(-1.17) = \cos(1.17) = .390$$

$$\sin(-1.17) = -\sin(1.17) = -.921.$$

8.3 Differentiation and Integration of sin *t* and cos *t*

In this section we study the two differentiation rules

$$\frac{d}{dt} \sin t = \cos t, \tag{1}$$

$$\frac{d}{dt} \cos t = -\sin t. \tag{2}$$

It is not difficult to see why these rules might be true. Formula (1) says that the slope of the curve $y = \sin t$ at a particular value of t is given by the corresponding value of $\cos t$. To check it, we draw a careful graph of $y = \sin t$ and estimate the slope at various points. (See Fig. 1.) Let us plot the slope as a function of t. (See Fig. 2.) As can be seen, the "slope function" (the derivative) of $\sin t$ has a graph similar to the curve $y = \cos t$. Thus formula (1) seems to be reasonable. A similar analysis of the graph of $y = \cos t$ would show why (2) might be true. Proofs of these differentiation rules are outlined in an appendix at the end of this section.

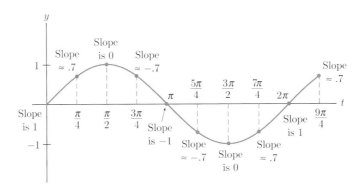

Figure 1. Slope estimates along the graph of $y = \sin t$.

Combining (1), (2), and the chain rule, we obtain the following general rules.

$$\frac{d}{dt}(\sin g(t)) = [\cos g(t)]\, g'(t), \tag{3}$$

$$\frac{d}{dt}(\cos g(t)) = [-\sin g(t)]\, g'(t). \tag{4}$$

EXAMPLE 1   Differentiate
(a) $\sin 3t$ (b) $(t^2 + 3\sin t)^5$.

Solution (a) $\dfrac{d}{dt}(\sin 3t) = (\cos 3t)\dfrac{d}{dt}(3t) = (\cos 3t)\cdot 3 = 3\cos 3t$

(b) $\dfrac{d}{dt}(t^2 + 3\sin t)^5 = 5(t^2 + 3\sin t)^4 \cdot \dfrac{d}{dt}(t^2 + 3\sin t)$

$\qquad\qquad\qquad = 5(t^2 + 3\sin t)^4(2t + 3\cos t).$ ∎

EXAMPLE 2   Differentiate
(a) $\cos(t^2 + 1)$ (b) $\cos^2 t$.

Solution (a) $\dfrac{d}{dt}\cos(t^2 + 1) = -\sin(t^2 + 1)\dfrac{d}{dt}(t^2 + 1) = -\sin(t^2 + 1)\cdot (2t)$

$\qquad\qquad\qquad = -2t\sin(t^2 + 1).$

(b) Recall that the notation $\cos^2 t$ means $(\cos t)^2$.

$$\frac{d}{dt}\cos^2 t = \frac{d}{dt}(\cos t)^2 = 2(\cos t)\frac{d}{dt}\cos t = -2\cos t \sin t.$$ ∎

EXAMPLE 3   Differentiate
(a) $t^2 \cos 3t$ (b) $(\sin 2t)/t$.

Solution (a) From the product rule we have

$$\frac{d}{dt}(t^2 \cos 3t) = t^2 \frac{d}{dt}\cos 3t + (\cos 3t)\frac{d}{dt}t^2$$

$$= t^2(-3\sin 3t) + (\cos 3t)(2t)$$

$$= -3t^2 \sin 3t + 2t\cos 3t.$$

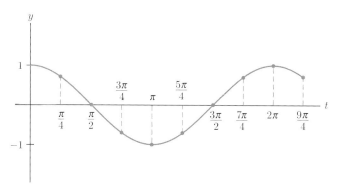

Figure 2. Graph of the slope function for $y = \sin t$.

(b) From the quotient rule we have

$$\frac{d}{dt}\left(\frac{\sin 2t}{t}\right) = \frac{t\dfrac{d}{dt}\sin 2t - (\sin 2t)\cdot 1}{t^2} = \frac{2t\cos 2t - \sin 2t}{t^2}.$$

EXAMPLE 4   A V-shaped trough is to be constructed with sides that are 200 centimeters long and 30 centimeters wide. (See Fig. 3.) Find the angle t between the sides that maximizes the capacity of the trough.

Solution   The volume of the trough is its length times its cross-sectional area. Since the length is constant, it suffices to maximize the cross-sectional area. Let us rotate the diagram of a cross section so that one side is horizontal. (See Fig. 4.) Note that $h/30 = \sin t$, so $h = 30\sin t$. Thus the area A of the cross section is

$$A = \tfrac{1}{2}\cdot\text{base}\cdot\text{height}$$

$$= \tfrac{1}{2}(30)(h) = 15(30\sin t) = 450\sin t.$$

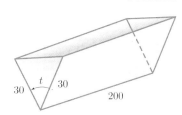

Figure 3

To find where A is a maximum, we set the derivative equal to zero and solve for t.

$$\frac{dA}{dt} = 0$$

$$450\cos t = 0$$

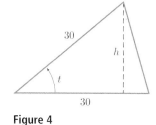

Figure 4

Physical considerations force us to consider only values of t between 0 and π. From the graph of $y = \cos t$ we see that $t = \pi/2$ is the only value of t between 0 and π that makes $\cos t = 0$. So, to maximize the volume of the trough, the two sides should be perpendicular to one another.

EXAMPLE 5   Calculate the following indefinite integrals.

(a) $\displaystyle\int \sin t\, dt$ (b) $\displaystyle\int \sin 3t\, dt$

Solution   (a) Since $\dfrac{d}{dt}(-\cos t) = \sin t$, we have

$$\int \sin t\, dt = -\cos t + C,$$

where C is an arbitrary constant.

(b) From part (a) we guess that an antiderivative of $\sin 3t$ should resemble the function $-\cos 3t$. However, if we differentiate, we find that

$$\frac{d}{dt}(-\cos 3t) = (\sin 3t) \cdot \frac{d}{dt}(3t) = 3\sin 3t,$$

which is three times too much. So we multiply this last equation by $\frac{1}{3}$ to derive that

$$\frac{d}{dt}\left(-\tfrac{1}{3}\cos 3t\right) = \sin 3t,$$

so

$$\int \sin 3t\, dt = -\tfrac{1}{3}\cos 3t + C. \qquad \blacksquare$$

EXAMPLE 6   Find the area under the curve $y = \sin 3t$ from $t = 0$ to $t = \pi/3$.

Solution The area is shaded in Fig. 5.

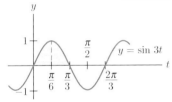

Figure 5

$$[\text{shaded area}] = \int_0^{\pi/3} \sin 3t\, dt$$

$$= -\frac{1}{3}\cos 3t \Big|_0^{\pi/3}$$

$$= -\frac{1}{3}\cos\left(3 \cdot \frac{\pi}{3}\right) - \left(-\frac{1}{3}\cos 0\right)$$

$$= -\frac{1}{3}\cos\pi + \frac{1}{3}\cos 0$$

$$= \frac{1}{3} + \frac{1}{3} = \frac{2}{3}. \qquad \blacksquare$$

As mentioned earlier, the trigonometric functions are required to model situations that are repetitive (or periodic). The next example illustrates such a situation.

EXAMPLE 7   In many mathematical models used to study the interaction between predators and prey, both the number of predators and the number of prey are described by periodic functions. Suppose that in one such model the number of predators (in a particular geographical region) at time t is given by the equation

$$N(t) = 5000 + 2000\cos(2\pi t/36),$$

where t is measured in months from June 1, 1990.

(a) At what rate is the number of predators changing on August 1, 1990?

(b) What is the average number of predators during the time interval from June 1, 1990, to June 1, 2002?

Solution **(a)** The date August 1, 1990, corresponds to $t = 2$. The rate of change of $N(t)$ is given by the derivative $N'(t)$:

$$N'(t) = \frac{d}{dt}\left[5000 + 2000\cos\left(\frac{2\pi t}{36}\right)\right]$$

$$= 2000\left[-\sin\left(\frac{2\pi t}{36}\right)\cdot\left(\frac{2\pi}{36}\right)\right]$$

$$= -\frac{1000\pi}{9}\sin\left(\frac{2\pi t}{36}\right),$$

$$N'(2) = -\frac{1000\pi}{9}\sin\left(\frac{\pi}{9}\right)$$

$$\approx -119.$$

Thus, on August 1, 1990, the number of predators is decreasing at the rate of 119 per month.

(b) The time interval from June 1, 1990, to June 1, 2002, corresponds to $t = 0$ to $t = 144$. (There are 144 months in 12 years!) The average value of $N(t)$ over this interval is

$$\frac{1}{144 - 0}\int_0^{144} N(t)\,dt = \frac{1}{144}\int_0^{144}\left[5000 + 2000\cos\left(\frac{2\pi t}{36}\right)\right]dt$$

$$= \frac{1}{144}\left[5000t + \frac{2000}{2\pi/36}\sin\left(\frac{2\pi t}{36}\right)\right]\Bigg|_0^{144}$$

$$= \frac{1}{144}\left[5000\cdot 144 + \frac{2000}{2\pi/36}\sin(8\pi)\right]$$

$$- \frac{1}{144}\left[5000\cdot 0 + \frac{2000}{2\pi/36}\sin(0)\right]$$

$$= 5000.$$

The graph of $N(t)$ is sketched in Fig. 6. Note how $N(t)$ oscillates around 5000, the average value. ■

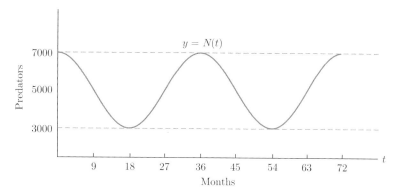

Figure 6. Periodic fluctuation of a predator population.

APPENDIX Informal Justification of the Differentiation Rules for sin *t* and cos *t*

First, let us examine the derivatives of $\cos t$ and $\sin t$ at $t = 0$. The function $\cos t$ has a maximum at $t = 0$; consequently, its derivative there must be zero. [See Fig. 7(a).] If we approximate the tangent line at $t = 0$ by a secant line, as in Fig. 7(b), the slope of the secant line must approach 0 as $h \to 0$. Since the slope of the secant line is $(\cos h - 1)/h$, we conclude that

$$\lim_{h \to 0} \frac{\cos h - 1}{h} = 0. \tag{5}$$

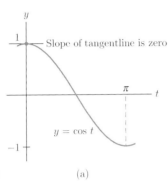

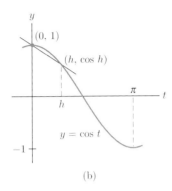

Figure 7   (a)   (b)

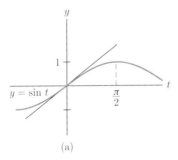

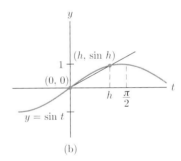

Figure 8.   Slope of $\sin t$ at $t = 0$.

(a)   (b)

It appears from the graph of $y = \sin t$ that the tangent line at $t = 0$ has slope 1. [See Fig. 8(a).] If it does, the slope of the approximating secant line in Fig. 8(b) must approach 1. Since the slope of this line is $(\sin h)/h$, this implies that

$$\lim_{h \to 0} \frac{\sin h}{h} = 1. \tag{6}$$

```
sin(.01)/.01
          .9999833334
sin(.001)/.001
          .999999833
sin(.0001)/.0001
          .9999999983
```

Figure 9

We can evaluate $\sin h/h$ for small values of h with a calculator. (See Fig. 9.) The numerical evidence does not prove (6), but should be sufficiently convincing for our purposes.

To obtain the differentiation formula for $\sin t$, we approximate the slope of a tangent line by the slope of a secant line. (See Fig. 10.) The slope of a secant line is

$$\frac{\sin(t + h) - \sin t}{h}.$$

From formula (7) of Section 8.2, we note that $\sin(t + h) = \sin t \cos h + \cos t \sin h$.

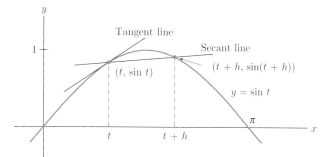

Figure 10. Secant line approximation for $y = \sin t$.

Thus,

$$[\text{slope of secant line}] = \frac{(\sin t \cos h + \cos t \sin h) - \sin t}{h}$$

$$= \frac{\sin t \, (\cos h - 1) + \cos t \sin h}{h}$$

$$= (\sin t)\frac{\cos h - 1}{h} + (\cos t)\frac{\sin h}{h}.$$

From (5) and (6) it follows that

$$\frac{d}{dt}\sin t = \lim_{h \to 0}\left[(\sin t)\frac{\cos h - 1}{h} + (\cos t)\frac{\sin h}{h}\right]$$

$$= (\sin t)\lim_{h \to 0}\frac{\cos h - 1}{h} + (\cos t)\lim_{h \to 0}\frac{\sin h}{h}$$

$$= (\sin t)\cdot 0 + (\cos t)\cdot 1$$

$$= \cos t.$$

A similar argument may be given to verify the formula for the derivative of $\cos t$. Here is a shorter proof that uses the chain rule and the two identities

$$\cos t = \sin\left(\frac{\pi}{2} - t\right), \qquad \sin t = \cos\left(\frac{\pi}{2} - t\right).$$

[See formula (6) of Section 8.2.] We have

$$\frac{d}{dt}\cos t = \frac{d}{dt}\sin\left(\frac{\pi}{2} - t\right)$$

$$= \cos\left(\frac{\pi}{2} - t\right)\cdot\frac{d}{dt}\left(\frac{\pi}{2} - t\right)$$

$$= \cos\left(\frac{\pi}{2} - t\right)\cdot(-1)$$

$$= -\sin t.$$

Practice Problems 8.3

1. Differentiate $y = 2\sin[t^2 + (\pi/6)]$.

2. Differentiate $y = e^t \sin 2t$.

EXERCISES 8.3

Differentiate (with respect to t or x):

1. $y = \sin 4t$ **2.** $y = 2\cos 2t$ **3.** $y = 4\sin t$

4. $y = \cos(-4t)$ **5.** $y = 2\cos 3t$ **6.** $y = -\dfrac{\sin 3t}{3}$

7. $y = t + \cos \pi t$ **8.** $y = t\cos t$ **9.** $y = \sin(\pi - t)$

10. $y = \dfrac{\cos(2x + 2)}{2}$ **11.** $y = \cos^3 t$ **12.** $y = \sin^3 t^2$

13. $y = \sin\sqrt{x-1}$ **14.** $y = \cos(e^x)$

15. $y = \sqrt{\sin(x-1)}$ **16.** $y = e^{\cos x}$

17. $y = (1 + \cos t)^8$ **18.** $y = \sqrt[3]{\sin \pi t}$ **19.** $y = \cos^2 x^3$

20. $y = \cos^2 x + \sin^2 x$ **21.** $y = e^x \sin x$

22. $y = (\cos x + \sin x)^2$ **23.** $y = \sin 2x \cos 3x$

24. $y = \dfrac{1+x}{\cos x}$ **25.** $y = \dfrac{\sin t}{\cos t}$ **26.** $y = \cos\left(e^{2x+3}\right)$

27. $y = \ln(\cos t)$ **28.** $y = \ln(\sin 2t)$

29. $y = \sin(\ln t)$ **30.** $y = (\cos t)\ln t$

31. Find the slope of the line tangent to the graph of $y = \cos 3x$ at $x = 13\pi/6$.

32. Find the slope of the line tangent to the graph of $y = \sin 2x$ at $x = 5\pi/4$.

33. Find the equation of the line tangent to the graph of $y = 3\sin x + \cos 2x$ at $x = \pi/2$.

34. Find the equation of the line tangent to the graph of $y = 3\sin 2x - \cos 2x$ at $x = 3\pi/4$.

Find the following indefinite integrals.

35. $\displaystyle\int \cos 2x\, dx$ **36.** $\displaystyle\int 3\sin 3x\, dx$

37. $\displaystyle\int -\frac{1}{2}\cos\frac{x}{7}\, dx$ **38.** $\displaystyle\int 2\sin\frac{x}{2}\, dx$

39. $\displaystyle\int (\cos x - \sin x)\, dx$ **40.** $\displaystyle\int \left(2\sin 3x + \frac{\cos 2x}{2}\right) dx$

41. $\displaystyle\int (-\sin x + 3\cos(-3x))\, dx$

42. $\displaystyle\int \sin(-2x)\, dx$ **43.** $\displaystyle\int \sin(4x + 1)\, dx$

44. $\displaystyle\int \cos\frac{x-2}{2}\, dx$ **45.** $\displaystyle\int 7\sin(3x - 2)\, dx$

46. $\displaystyle\int (\cos(2x) + 3)\, dx$

47. A person's blood pressure P at time t (in seconds) is given by $P = 100 + 20\cos 6t$.
   (a) Find the maximum value of P (called the systolic pressure) and the minimum value of P (called the diastolic pressure) and give one or two values of t where these maximum and minimum values of P occur.

   (b) If time is measured in seconds, approximately how many heartbeats per minute are predicted by the equation for P?

48. The *basal metabolism* (BM) of an organism over a certain time period may be described as the total amount of heat in kilocalories (kcal) that the organism produces during this period, assuming that the organism is at rest and not subject to stress. The *basal metabolic rate* (BMR) is the rate in kcal per hour at which the organism produces heat. The BMR of an animal such as a desert rat fluctuates in response to changes in temperature and other environmental factors. The BMR generally follows a *diurnal* cycle, rising at night during low temperatures and decreasing during the warmer daytime temperatures. Find the BM for 1 day if $\mathrm{BMR}(t) = .4 + .2\cos(\pi t/12)$ kcal per hour ($t = 0$ corresponds to 3 A.M.). (See Fig. 11.)

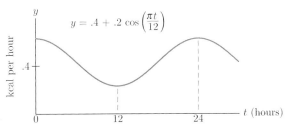

Figure 11. Diurnal cycle of the basal metabolic rate.

49. As h approaches 0, what value is approached by
$$\frac{\sin\left(\frac{\pi}{2} + h\right) - 1}{h}?$$
$\left[Hint: \sin\dfrac{\pi}{2} = 1. \right]$

50. As h approaches 0, what value is approached by
$$\frac{\cos(\pi + h) + 1}{h}?$$
$[Hint: \cos\pi = -1.]$

51. Average Temperature The average weekly temperature in Washington, D.C., t weeks after the beginning of the year is
$$f(t) = 54 + 23\sin\left[\frac{2\pi}{52}(t - 12)\right].$$
The graph of this function is sketched in Fig. 12.
   (a) What is the average weekly temperature at week 18?
   (b) At week 20, how fast is the temperature changing?
   (c) When is the average weekly temperature 39 degrees?
   (d) When is the average weekly temperature falling at the rate of 1 degree per week?

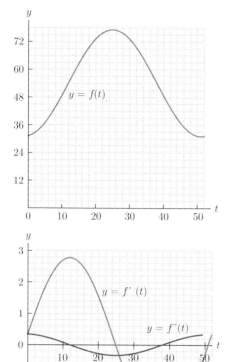

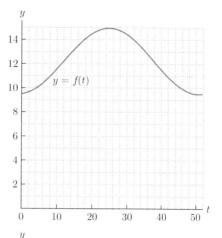

Figure 12

Figure 13

(e) When is the average weekly temperature greatest? Least?

(f) When is the average weekly temperature increasing fastest? Decreasing fastest?

52. Average Daylight Hours The number of hours of daylight per day in Washington, D.C., t weeks after the beginning of the year is

$$f(t) = 12.18 + 2.725 \sin \left[\frac{2\pi}{52}(t - 12) \right].$$

The graph of this function is sketched in Fig. 13.

(a) How many hours of daylight are there after 42 weeks?

(b) After 32 weeks, how fast is the number of hours of daylight decreasing?

(c) When is there 14 hours of daylight per day?

(d) When is the number of hours of daylight increasing at the rate of 15 minutes per week?

(e) When are the days longest? Shortest?

(f) When is the number of hours of daylight increasing fastest? Decreasing fastest?

Solutions to Practice Problems 8.3

1. By the chain rule,

$$y' = 2 \cos \left(t^2 + \frac{\pi}{6} \right) \cdot \frac{d}{dt} \left(t^2 + \frac{\pi}{6} \right)$$

$$= 2 \cos \left(t^2 + \frac{\pi}{6} \right) \cdot 2t$$

$$= 4t \cos \left(t^2 + \frac{\pi}{6} \right).$$

2. By the product rule,

$$y' = e^t \frac{d}{dt}(\sin 2t) + (\sin 2t)\frac{d}{dt}e^t$$

$$= 2e^t \cos 2t + e^t \sin 2t.$$

8.4 The Tangent and Other Trigonometric Functions

Certain functions involving the sine and cosine functions occur so frequently in applications that they have been given special names. The *tangent* (tan), *cotangent* (cot), *secant* (sec), and *cosecant* (csc) are such functions and are defined as follows:

$$\tan t = \frac{\sin t}{\cos t}, \qquad \cot t = \frac{\cos t}{\sin t},$$

$$\sec t = \frac{1}{\cos t}, \qquad \csc t = \frac{1}{\sin t}.$$

They are defined only for t such that the denominators in the preceding quotients are not zero. These four functions, together with the sine and cosine, are called the *trigonometric functions*. Our main interest in this section is with the tangent function. Some properties of the cotangent, secant, and cosecant are developed in the exercises.

Many identities involving the trigonometric functions can be deduced from the identities given in Section 8.2. We shall mention just one:

$$\tan^2 t + 1 = \sec^2 t. \tag{1}$$

[Here $\tan^2 t$ means $(\tan t)^2$ and $\sec^2 t$ means $(\sec t)^2$.] This identity follows from the identity $\sin^2 t + \cos^2 t = 1$ when we divide everything by $\cos^2 t$.

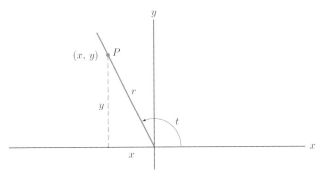

Figure 1

An important interpretation of the tangent function can be given in terms of the diagram used to define the sine and cosine. For a given t, let us construct an angle of t radians. (See Fig. 1.) Since $\sin t = y/r$ and $\cos t = x/r$, we have

$$\frac{\sin t}{\cos t} = \frac{y/r}{x/r} = \frac{y}{x},$$

where this formula holds provided that $x \neq 0$. Thus

$$\tan t = \frac{y}{x}. \tag{2}$$

Three examples that illustrate this property of the tangent appear in Fig. 2.

When $0 < t < \pi/2$, the value of $\tan t$ is a ratio of the lengths of the sides of a right triangle. In other words, if we are given a triangle as in Fig. 3, we would have

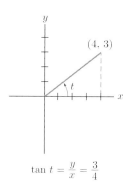

$$\tan t = \frac{y}{x} = \frac{3}{4}$$

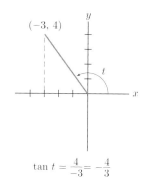

$$\tan t = \frac{4}{-3} = -\frac{4}{3}$$

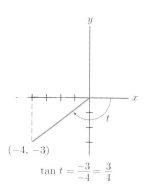

$$\tan t = \frac{-3}{-4} = \frac{3}{4}$$

Figure 2

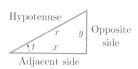

Figure 3

$$\tan t = \frac{\text{opposite}}{\text{adjacent}}. \tag{3}$$

EXAMPLE 1   The angle of elevation from an observer to the top of a building is $29°$. (See Fig. 4.) If the observer is 100 meters from the base of the building, how high is the building?

Solution   Let h denote the height of the building. Then formula (3) implies that

$$\frac{h}{100} = \tan 29°$$

$$h = 100 \tan 29°.$$

We convert $29°$ into radians. We find that $29° = (\pi/180) \cdot 29$ radians $\approx .5$ radian, and $\tan .5 \approx .54630$. Hence

$$h \approx 100(.54630) = 54.63 \text{ meters.} \qquad \blacksquare$$

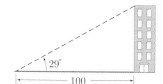

Figure 4

The Derivative of tan t   Since $\tan t$ is defined in terms of $\sin t$ and $\cos t$, we can compute the derivative of $\tan t$ from our rules of differentiation. That is, by applying the quotient rule for differentiation, we have

$$\frac{d}{dt}(\tan t) = \frac{d}{dt}\left(\frac{\sin t}{\cos t}\right) = \frac{(\cos t)(\cos t) - (\sin t)(-\sin t)}{(\cos t)^2}$$

$$= \frac{\cos^2 t + \sin^2 t}{\cos^2 t} = \frac{1}{\cos^2 t}.$$

Now

$$\frac{1}{\cos^2 t} = \frac{1}{(\cos t)^2} = \left(\frac{1}{\cos t}\right)^2 = (\sec t)^2 = \sec^2 t.$$

So the derivative of $\tan t$ can be expressed in two equivalent ways:

$$\frac{d}{dt}(\tan t) = \frac{1}{\cos^2 t} = \sec^2 t. \tag{4}$$

Combining (4) with the chain rule, we have

$$\frac{d}{dt}(\tan g(t)) = [\sec^2 g(t)]g'(t). \tag{5}$$

EXAMPLE 2   Differentiate

(a) $\tan(t^3 + 1)$ (b) $\tan^3 t$.

Solution (a) From (5) we find that

$$\frac{d}{dt}[\tan(t^3 + 1)] = \sec^2(t^3 + 1) \cdot \frac{d}{dt}(t^3 + 1)$$

$$= 3t^2 \sec^2(t^3 + 1).$$

(b) We write $\tan^3 t$ as $(\tan t)^3$ and use the chain rule (in this case, the general power rule):

$$\frac{d}{dt}(\tan t)^3 = (3\tan^2 t) \cdot \frac{d}{dt}\tan t = 3\tan^2 t \sec^2 t.$$ ∎

The Graph of tan t   Recall that $\tan t$ is defined for all t except where $\cos t = 0$. (We cannot have zero in the denominator of $\sin t / \cos t$.) The graph of $\tan t$ is sketched in Fig. 5. Note that $\tan t$ is periodic with period π.

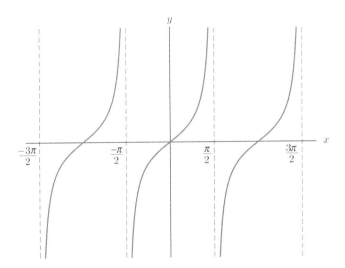

Figure 5.   Graph of the tangent function.

Practice Problems 8.4

1. Show that the slope of a straight line is equal to the tangent of the angle that the line makes with the x-axis.

2. Calculate $\int_0^{\pi/4} \sec^2 t \, dt$.

EXERCISES 8.4

1. If $0 < t < \pi/2$, use Fig. 3 to describe $\sec t$ as a ratio of the lengths of the sides of a right triangle.

2. Describe $\cot t$ for $0 < t < \pi/2$ as a ratio of the lengths of the sides of a right triangle.

In Exercises 3–10, give the values of $\tan t$ and $\sec t$, where t is the radian measure of the angle shown.

3.

4.

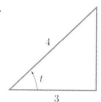

5. $(-2, 1)$

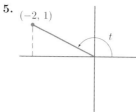

6.

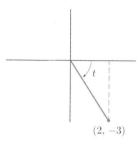

$(2, -3)$

7. $(-2, 2)$

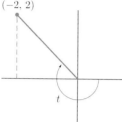

BAC is $90°$, the angle ACB is $40°$, and the distance from A to C is 75 feet. See Fig. 6.

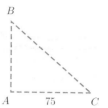

Figure 6

12. The angle of elevation from an observer to the top of a church is .3 radian, while the angle of elevation from the observer to the top of the church spire is .4 radian. If the observer is 70 meters from the church, how tall is the spire on top of the church?

Differentiate (with respect to t or x):

13. $f(t) = \sec t$ **14.** $f(t) = \csc t$

15. $f(t) = \cot t$ **16.** $f(t) = \cot 3t$

17. $f(t) = \tan 4t$ **18.** $f(t) = \tan \pi t$

19. $f(x) = 3\tan(\pi - x)$ **20.** $f(x) = 5\tan(2x + 1)$

21. $f(x) = 4\tan(x^2 + x + 3)$ **22.** $f(x) = 3\tan(1 - x^2)$

23. $y = \tan \sqrt{x}$ **24.** $y = 2\tan \sqrt{x^2 - 4}$

25. $y = x \tan x$ **26.** $y = e^{3x} \tan 2x$

27. $y = \tan^2 x$ **28.** $y = \sqrt{\tan x}$

29. $y = (1 + \tan 2t)^3$ **30.** $y = \tan^4 3t$

31. $y = \ln(\tan t + \sec t)$ **32.** $y = \ln(\tan t)$

33. (a) Find the equation of the tangent line to the graph of $y = \tan x$ at the point $\left(\frac{\pi}{4}, 1\right)$.

    (b) Copy the portion of the graph of $y = \tan x$ for $-\frac{\pi}{2} < x < \frac{\pi}{2}$ from Fig. 5, then draw on this graph the tangent line that you found in part (a).

34. Repeat Exercise 33(a) and (b) using the point $(0, 0)$ on the graph of $y = \tan x$ instead of the point $\left(\frac{\pi}{4}, 1\right)$.

Evaluate the following integrals.

35. $\displaystyle\int \sec^2 3x \, dx$ **36.** $\displaystyle\int \sec^2(2x + 1) \, dx$

37. $\displaystyle\int_{-\pi/4}^{\pi/4} \sec^2 x \, dx$ **38.** $\displaystyle\int_{-\pi/8}^{\pi/8} \sec^2\left(x + \frac{\pi}{8}\right) dx$

8. $(.6, .8)$

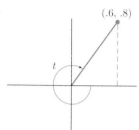

9.

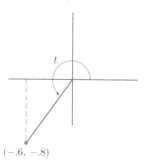

$(-.6, -.8)$

10.

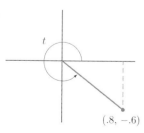

$(.8, -.6)$

11. Find the width of a river at points A and B if the angle

39. $\displaystyle\int \frac{1}{\cos^2 x} \, dx$ **40.** $\displaystyle\int \frac{3}{\cos^2 2x} \, dx$

Solutions to Practice Problems 8.4

1. A line of positive slope m is shown in Fig. 7(a). Here, $\tan\theta = m/1 = m$. Suppose that $y = mx + b$ where the slope m is negative. The line $y = mx$ has the same slope and makes the same angle with the x-axis.

[See Fig. 7(b).] We see that $\tan\theta = -m/-1 = m$.

2. $\displaystyle\int_0^{\pi/4} \sec^2 t\, dt = \tan t \Big|_0^{\pi/4} = \tan\frac{\pi}{4} - \tan 0 = 1 - 0 = 1.$

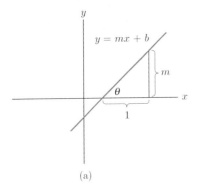

(a)

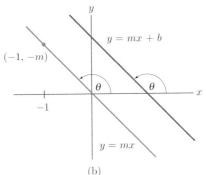

(b)

Figure 7

REVIEW OF FUNDAMENTAL CONCEPTS

1. Explain the radian measure of an angle.

2. Give the formula for converting degree measure to radian measure.

3. Give the triangle interpretation of $\sin t$, $\cos t$, and $\tan t$ for t between 0 and $\pi/2$.

4. Define $\sin t$, $\cos t$, and $\tan t$ for an angle of measure t for any t.

5. What does it mean when we say that the sine and cosine functions are periodic with period 2π?

6. Give verbal descriptions of the graphs of $\sin t$, $\cos t$, and $\tan t$.

7. State as many identities involving the sine and cosine functions as you can recall.

8. Define $\cot t$, $\sec t$, and $\csc t$ for an angle of measure t.

9. State an identity involving $\tan t$ and $\sec t$.

10. What are the derivatives of $\sin g(t)$, $\cos g(t)$, and $\tan g(t)$?

SUPPLEMENTARY EXERCISES

Determine the radian measure of the angles shown in Exercises 1–3.

1.

2.

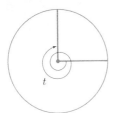

3.

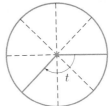

Construct angles with the following radian measure.

4. $-\pi$ 5. $\dfrac{5\pi}{4}$ 6. $-\dfrac{9\pi}{2}$

In Exercises 7–10, the point with the given coordinates determines an angle of t radians, where $0 \le t \le 2\pi$. Find $\sin t$, $\cos t$, and $\tan t$.

7. $(3,4)$

8. $(-.6,.8)$

9. $(-.6,-.8)$

10. $(3,-4)$

11. If $\sin t = \frac{1}{5}$, what are the possible values for $\cos t$?

12. If $\cos t = -\frac{2}{3}$, what are the possible values for $\sin t$?

13. Find the four values of t between -2π and 2π at which $\sin t = \cos t$.

14. Find the four values of t between -2π and 2π at which $\sin t = -\cos t$.

15. When $-\pi/2 < t < 0$, is $\tan t$ positive or negative?

16. When $\pi/2 < t < \pi$, is $\sin t$ positive or negative?

17. A gabled roof is to be built on a house that is 30 feet wide so that the roof rises at a pitch of $23°$. Determine the length of the rafters needed to support the roof.

18. A tree casts a 60-foot shadow when the angle of elevation of the sun (measured from the horizontal) is $53°$. How tall is the tree?

Differentiate (with respect to t or x):

19. $f(t) = 3\sin t$

20. $f(t) = \sin 3t$

21. $f(t) = \sin\sqrt{t}$

22. $f(t) = \cos t^3$

23. $g(x) = x^3 \sin x$

24. $g(x) = \sin(-2x)\cos 5x$

25. $f(x) = \dfrac{\cos 2x}{\sin 3x}$

26. $f(x) = \dfrac{\cos x - 1}{x^3}$

27. $f(x) = \cos^3 4x$

28. $f(x) = \tan^3 2x$

29. $y = \tan(x^4 + x^2)$

30. $y = \tan e^{-2x}$

31. $y = \sin(\tan x)$

32. $y = \tan(\sin x)$

33. $y = \sin x \tan x$

34. $y = \ln x \cos x$

35. $y = \ln(\sin x)$

36. $y = \ln(\cos x)$

37. $y = e^{3x}\sin^4 x$

38. $y = \sin^4 e^{3x}$

39. $f(t) = \dfrac{\sin t}{\tan 3t}$

40. $f(t) = \dfrac{\tan 2t}{\cos t}$

41. $f(t) = e^{\tan t}$

42. $f(t) = e^t \tan t$

43. If $f(t) = \sin^2 t$, find $f''(t)$.

44. Show that $y = 3\sin 2t + \cos 2t$ satisfies the differential equation $y'' = -4y$.

45. If $f(s,t) = \sin s \cos 2t$, find $\dfrac{\partial f}{\partial s}$ and $\dfrac{\partial f}{\partial t}$.

46. If $z = \sin wt$, find $\dfrac{\partial z}{\partial w}$ and $\dfrac{\partial z}{\partial t}$.

47. If $f(s,t) = t\sin st$, find $\dfrac{\partial f}{\partial s}$ and $\dfrac{\partial f}{\partial t}$.

48. The identity

$$\sin(s+t) = \sin s \cos t + \cos s \sin t$$

was given in Section 8.2. Compute the partial derivative of each side with respect to t and obtain an identity involving $\cos(s+t)$.

49. Find the equation of the line tangent to the graph of $y = \tan t$ at $t = \pi/4$.

50. Sketch the graph of $f(t) = \sin t + \cos t$ for $-2\pi \le t \le 2\pi$, using the following steps:

(a) Find all t between -2π and 2π such th Plot the corresponding points on the gr $y = f(t)$.

(b) Check the concavity of $f(t)$ at the points in part (a). Make sketches of the graph near these points.

(c) Determine any inflection points and plot them. Then complete the sketch of the graph.

51. Sketch the graph of $y = t + \sin t$ for $0 \le t \le 2\pi$.

52. Find the area under the curve $y = 2 + \sin 3t$ from $t = 0$ to $t = \pi/2$.

53. Find the area of the region between the curve $y = \sin t$ and the t-axis from $t = 0$ to $t = 2\pi$.

54. Find the area of the region between the curve $y = \cos t$ and the t-axis from $t = 0$ to $t = 3\pi/2$.

55. Find the area of the region bounded by the curves $y = x$ and $y = \sin x$ from $x = 0$ to $x = \pi$.

A spirogram is a device that records on a graph the volume of air in a person's lungs as a function of time. If a person undergoes spontaneous hyperventilation, the spirogram trace will closely approximate a sine curve. A typical trace is given by

$$V(t) = 3 + .05\sin\left(160\pi t - \frac{\pi}{2}\right),$$

where t is measured in minutes and $V(t)$ is the lung volume in liters. (See Fig. 1.) Exercises 56–58 refer to this function.

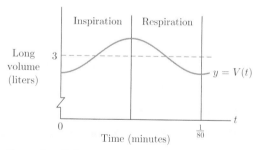

Figure 1. Spirogram trace.

56. (a) Compute $V(0)$, $V(\frac{1}{320})$, $V(\frac{1}{160})$, and $V(\frac{1}{80})$.

(b) What is the maximum lung volume?

57. (a) Find a formula for the rate of flow of air into the lungs at time t.

(b) Find the maximum rate of flow of air during inspiration (breathing in). This is called the *peak inspiratory flow*.

(c) Inspiration occurs during the time from $t = 0$ to $t = 1/160$. Find the average rate of flow of air during inspiration. This quantity is called the *mean inspiratory flow*.

defined to be the total amount
.ed in) during 1 minute. Accord-
.xt on respiratory physiology, when
es spontaneous hyperventilation, the
y flow equals π times the minute vol-
mean inspiratory flow equals twice the
.me.* Verify these assertions using the data
from L rcise 57.

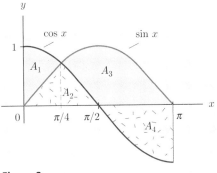

Figure 2

Evaluate the following integrals.

59. $\displaystyle\int \sin(\pi - x)\, dx$

60. $\displaystyle\int (3\cos 3x - 2\sin 2x)\, dx$

61. $\displaystyle\int_0^{\pi/2} \cos 6x\, dx$

62. $\displaystyle\int \cos(6 - 2x)\, dx$

63. $\displaystyle\int_0^{\pi} (x - 2\cos(\pi - 2x))\, dx$

64. $\displaystyle\int_{-\pi}^{\pi} (\cos 3x + 2\sin 7x)\, dx$

65. $\displaystyle\int \sec^2 \frac{x}{2}\, dx$

66. $\displaystyle\int 2\sec^2 2x\, dx$

In Fig. 2:

67. Find shaded area A_1.

68. Find shaded area A_2.

69. Find shaded area A_3.

70. Find shaded area A_4.

*In Exercises 71–74, find the average of the function $f(t)$
over the given interval.*

71. $f(t) = 1 + \sin 2t - \frac{1}{3}\cos 2t,\ 0 \le t \le 2\pi$

72. $f(t) = t - \cos 2t,\ 0 \le t \le \pi$

73. $f(t) = 1000 + 200\sin 2\left(t - \frac{\pi}{4}\right),\ 0 \le t \le \frac{3\pi}{4}$

74. $f(t) = \cos t + \sin t,\ -\pi \le t \le 0$

*Evaluate the given integral. [Hint: Use identity (1), Section
8.4, to transform the integral before evaluating it.]*

75. $\displaystyle\int \tan^2 x\, dx$

76. $\displaystyle\int \tan^2 3x\, dx$

77. $\displaystyle\int (1 + \tan^2 x)\, dx$

78. $\displaystyle\int (2 + \tan^2 x)\, dx$

79. $\displaystyle\int_0^{\pi/4} \tan^2 x\, dx$

80. $\displaystyle\int_0^{\pi/4} (2 + 2\tan^2 x)\, dx$

---

*J. F. Nunn, *Applied Respiratory Physiology*, 2nd ed. (London: Butterworths, 1977), p. 122.

TECHNIQUES OF INTEGRATION

In this chapter we develop techniques for calculating integrals, both indefinite and definite. The need for these techniques has been justified in the preceding chapters. In addition to adding to our fund of applications, we will see even more clearly how the need to calculate integrals arises in physical problems.

Integration is the reverse process of differentiation. However, integration is much harder to carry out. If a function is an expression involving elementary functions (such as x^r, $\sin x$, e^x, ...), so is its derivative. Moreover, we were able to develop methods of calculation that enable us to differentiate, with comparative ease, almost any function that we can write down. Although many integration problems have these characteristics, some do not. For some elementary functions (for example, e^{x^2}), an antiderivative cannot be expressed in terms of elementary functions. Even when an elementary antiderivative exists, the techniques for finding it are often complicated. For this reason, we must be prepared with a broad range of tools to cope with the problem of calculating integrals. Among the ideas to be discussed in this chapter are the following:

1. Techniques for evaluating indefinite integrals. We will concentrate on two methods, integration by substitution and integration by parts.

2. Evaluation of definite integrals.

3. Approximation of definite integrals. We will develop two new techniques for obtaining numerical approximations to $\int_a^b f(x)\,dx$. These techniques are especially useful in those cases in which we cannot find an antiderivative for $f(x)$.

Let us review the most elementary facts about integration. The indefinite integral

$$\int f(x)\,dx$$

is, by definition, a function whose derivative is $f(x)$. If $F(x)$ is one such function, then the most general function whose derivative is $f(x)$ is simply $F(x) + C$, where C is any constant. We write

$$\int f(x)\,dx = F(x) + C$$

to mean that all antiderivatives of $f(x)$ are precisely the functions $F(x) + C$, where C is any constant.

Each time we differentiate a function, we also derive an integration formula. For example, the fact that

$$\frac{d}{dx}(3x^2) = 6x$$

can be turned into the integration formula

$$\int 6x\,dx = 3x^2 + C.$$

Some of the formulas that follow immediately from differentiation formulas are reviewed in the following table.

Differentiation Formula	Corresponding Integration Formula
$\dfrac{d}{dx}(x^r)\,dx = rx^{r-1}$	$\displaystyle\int rx^{r-1}\,dx = x^r + C$ or
	$\displaystyle\int x^r\,dx = \dfrac{x^{r+1}}{r+1} + C,\ r \neq -1$
$\dfrac{d}{dx}(e^x) = e^x$	$\displaystyle\int e^x\,dx = e^x + C$
$\dfrac{d}{dx}(\ln|x|) = \dfrac{1}{x}$	$\displaystyle\int \dfrac{1}{x}\,dx = \ln|x| + C$
$\dfrac{d}{dx}(\sin x) = \cos x$	$\displaystyle\int \cos x\,dx = \sin x + C$
$\dfrac{d}{dx}(\cos x) = -\sin x$	$\displaystyle\int \sin x\,dx = -\cos x + C$
$\dfrac{d}{dx}(\tan x) = \sec^2 x$	$\displaystyle\int \sec^2 x\,dx = \tan x + C$

This table illustrates the need for techniques of integration. For although $\sin x$, $\cos x$, and $\sec^2 x$ occur as derivatives of simple trigonometric functions, the functions $\tan x$ and $\cot x$ are not on our list. In fact, if we experiment with various elementary combinations of the trigonometric functions, it is easy to convince ourselves that antiderivatives of $\tan x$ and $\cot x$ are not easy to compute. In this chapter we develop techniques for calculating such antiderivatives (among others).

9.1 Integration by Substitution

Every differentiation formula can be turned into a corresponding integration formula. This point is true even for the chain rule. The resulting formula is called *integration by substitution* and is often used to transform a complicated integral into a simpler one.

Let $f(x)$ and $g(x)$ be two given functions, and let $F(x)$ be an antiderivative for $f(x)$. The chain rule asserts that

$$\frac{d}{dx}[F(g(x))] = F'(g(x))g'(x)$$
$$= f(g(x))g'(x) \qquad [\text{since } F'(x) = f(x)].$$

Turning this formula into an integration formula, we have

$$\int f(g(x))g'(x)\,dx = F(g(x)) + C, \tag{1}$$

where C is any constant.

EXAMPLE 1   Determine

$$\int (x^2+1)^3 \cdot 2x\,dx.$$

Solution   If we set $f(x) = x^3$, $g(x) = x^2+1$, then $f(g(x)) = (x^2+1)^3$ and $g'(x) = 2x$. Therefore, we can apply formula (1). An antiderivative $F(x)$ of $f(x)$ is given by

$$F(x) = \frac{1}{4}x^4,$$

so that, by formula (1), we have

$$\int (x^2+1)^3 \cdot 2x\,dx = F(g(x)) + C = \frac{1}{4}(x^2+1)^4 + C. \qquad \blacksquare$$

Formula (1) can be elevated from the status of a sometimes-useful formula to a technique of integration by the introduction of a simple mnemonic device. Suppose that we are faced with integrating a function of the form $f(g(x))g'(x)$. Of course, we know the answer from formula (1). However, let us proceed somewhat differently. Replace the expression $g(x)$ by a new variable u, and replace $g'(x)\,dx$ by du. Such a substitution has the advantage that it reduces the generally complex expression $f(g(x))$ to the simpler form $f(u)$. In terms of u, the integration problem may be written

$$\int f(g(x))g'(x)\,dx = \int f(u)\,du.$$

However, the integral on the right is easy to evaluate, since

$$\int f(u)\,du = F(u) + C.$$

Since $u = g(x)$, we obtain

$$\int f(g(x))g'(x)\,dx = F(u) + C = F(g(x)) + C,$$

which is the correct answer by (1). Remember, however, that replacing $g'(x)\,dx$ by du only has status as a correct mathematical statement, because doing so leads to the correct answers. We do not, in this book, seek to explain in any deeper way what this replacement means.

Let us rework Example 1 using this method.

Second Solution of Example 1 Set $u = x^2 + 1$. Then $du = \dfrac{d}{dx}(x^2+1)\, dx = 2x\, dx$, and

$$\int (x^2+1)^3 \cdot 2x\, dx = \int u^3\, du$$

$$= \frac{1}{4}u^4 + C$$

$$= \frac{1}{4}(x^2+1)^4 + C \quad (\text{since } u = x^2 + 1). \quad \blacksquare$$

EXAMPLE 2

Evaluate

$$\int 2xe^{x^2}\, dx.$$

Solution Let $u = x^2$, so $du = \dfrac{d}{dx}(x^2)\, dx = 2x\, dx$. Therefore,

$$\int 2xe^{x^2}\, dx = \int e^{x^2} \cdot 2x\, dx$$

$$= \int e^u\, du$$

$$= e^u + C$$

$$= e^{x^2} + C. \quad \blacksquare$$

From Examples 1 and 2 we can deduce the following method for integration of functions of the form $f'(g(x))g'(x)$.

Integration by Substitution

1. Define a new variable $u = g(x)$, where $g(x)$ is chosen in such a way that, when written in terms of u, the integrand is simpler than when written in terms of x.

2. Transform the integral with respect to x into an integral with respect to u by replacing $g(x)$ everywhere by u and $g'(x)\, dx$ by du.

3. Integrate the resulting function of u.

4. Rewrite the answer in terms of x by replacing u by $g(x)$.

Let us try a few more examples.

EXAMPLE 3

Evaluate

$$\int 3x^2 \sqrt{x^3 + 1}\, dx.$$

Solution The first problem facing us is to find an appropriate substitution that will simplify the integral. An immediate possibility is offered by setting $u = x^3 + 1$. Then $\sqrt{x^3 + 1}$ will become $\sqrt{u}$, a significant simplification. If $u = x^3 + 1$, then

$$du = \frac{d}{dx}(x^3 + 1)\,dx = 3x^2\,dx, \text{ so}$$

$$\int 3x^2 \sqrt{x^3 + 1}\,dx = \int \sqrt{u}\,du$$

$$= \frac{2}{3}u^{3/2} + C$$

$$= \frac{2}{3}(x^3 + 1)^{3/2} + C. \qquad \blacksquare$$

EXAMPLE 4   Find

$$\int \frac{(\ln x)^2}{x}\,dx.$$

Solution   Let $u = \ln x$. Then $du = (1/x)\,dx$ and

$$\int \frac{(\ln x)^2}{x}\,dx = \int (\ln x)^2 \cdot \frac{1}{x}\,dx$$

$$= \int u^2\,du$$

$$= \frac{u^3}{3} + C$$

$$= \frac{(\ln x)^3}{3} + C \quad (\text{since } u = \ln x). \qquad \blacksquare$$

Knowing the correct substitution to make is a skill that develops through practice. Basically, we look for an occurrence of function composition, $f(g(x))$, where $f(x)$ is a function that we know how to integrate and where $g'(x)$ also appears in the integrand. Sometimes $g'(x)$ does not appear exactly, but can be obtained by multiplying by a constant. Such a shortcoming is easily remedied, as is illustrated in Examples 5 and 6.

EXAMPLE 5   Find

$$\int x^2 e^{x^3}\,dx.$$

Solution   Let $u = x^3$; then $du = 3x^2\,dx$. The integrand involves $x^2\,dx$, not $3x^2\,dx$. To introduce the missing factor 3, we write

$$\int x^2 e^{x^3}\,dx = \int \frac{1}{3} \cdot 3x^2 e^{x^3}\,dx = \frac{1}{3}\int e^{x^3} 3x^2\,dx.$$

(Recall from Section 6.1 that constant multiples may be moved through the integral sign.) Substituting, we obtain

$$\int x^2 e^{x^3}\,dx = \frac{1}{3}\int e^u\,du = \frac{1}{3}e^u + C$$

$$= \frac{1}{3}e^{x^3} + C \quad (\text{since } u = x^3).$$

Another way to handle the missing factor 3 is to write

$$u = x^3, \quad du = 3x^2\,dx, \quad \text{and} \quad \frac{1}{3}du = x^2\,dx.$$

Then substitution yields

$$\int x^2 e^{x^3}\, dx = \int e^{x^3} \cdot x^2\, dx = \int e^u \cdot \frac{1}{3}\, du = \frac{1}{3}\int e^u\, du$$

$$= \frac{1}{3}e^u + C = \frac{1}{3}e^{x^3} + C.$$ ∎

EXAMPLE 6

Find

$$\int \frac{2-x}{\sqrt{2x^2 - 8x + 1}}\, dx.$$

Solution Let $u = 2x^2 - 8x + 1$; then $du = (4x - 8)\, dx$. Observe that $4x - 8 = -4(2 - x)$. So we multiply the integrand by -4 and compensate by placing a factor of $-\frac{1}{4}$ in front of the integral.

$$\int \frac{1}{\sqrt{2x^2 - 8x + 1}} \cdot (2 - x)\, dx = -\frac{1}{4}\int \frac{1}{\sqrt{2x^2 - 8x + 1}} \cdot (-4)(2 - x)\, dx$$

$$= -\frac{1}{4}\int \frac{1}{\sqrt{u}}\, du = -\frac{1}{4}\int u^{-1/2}\, du$$

$$= -\frac{1}{4} \cdot 2u^{1/2} + C = -\frac{1}{2}u^{1/2} + C$$

$$= -\frac{1}{2}(2x^2 - 8x + 1)^{1/2} + C.$$ ∎

EXAMPLE 7

Find

$$\int \frac{2x}{x^2 + 1}\, dx.$$

Solution We note that the derivative of $x^2 + 1$ is $2x$. Thus we make the substitution $u = x^2 + 1$, $du = 2x\, dx$ to derive

$$\int \frac{2x}{x^2 + 1}\, dx = \int \frac{1}{u}\, du = \ln|u| + C = \ln(x^2 + 1) + C.$$ ∎

EXAMPLE 8

Evaluate

$$\int \tan x\, dx.$$

Solution Since $\tan x = \dfrac{\sin x}{\cos x}$, we have

$$\int \tan x\, dx = \int \frac{\sin x}{\cos x}\, dx.$$

Let $u = \cos x$, so $du = -\sin x\, dx$. Then

$$\int \frac{\sin x}{\cos x}\, dx = -\int \frac{-\sin x}{\cos x}\, dx$$

$$= -\int \frac{1}{u}\, du$$

$$= -\ln|u| + C$$

$$= -\ln|\cos x| + C.$$

Note that

$$-\ln|\cos x| = \ln\left|\frac{1}{\cos x}\right| = \ln|\sec x|.$$

So the preceding formula can be written

$$\int \tan x \, dx = \ln|\sec x| + C. \qquad \blacksquare$$

Practice Problems 9.1

1. (*Review*) Differentiate the following functions:

   (a) $e^{(2x^3+3x)}$ (b) $\ln x^5$

   (c) $\ln\sqrt{x}$ (d) $\ln 5|x|$

   (e) $x \ln x$ (f) $\ln(x^4 + x^2 + 1)$

   (g) $\sin x^3$ (h) $\tan x$

2. Use the substitution $u = \dfrac{3}{x}$ to determine $\displaystyle\int \frac{e^{3/x}}{x^2}\, dx.$

EXERCISES 9.1

Determine the integrals in Exercises 1–36 by making appropriate substitutions.

1. $\displaystyle\int 2x(x^2+4)^5\, dx$

2. $\displaystyle\int 2(2x-1)^7\, dx$

3. $\displaystyle\int \frac{2x+1}{\sqrt{x^2+x+3}}\, dx$

4. $\displaystyle\int (x^2+2x+3)^6(x+1)\, dx$

5. $\displaystyle\int 3x^2 e^{(x^3-1)}\, dx$

6. $\displaystyle\int 2xe^{-x^2}\, dx$

7. $\displaystyle\int x\sqrt{4-x^2}\, dx$

8. $\displaystyle\int \frac{(1+\ln x)^3}{x}\, dx$

9. $\displaystyle\int \frac{1}{\sqrt{2x+1}}\, dx$

10. $\displaystyle\int (x^3-6x)^7(x^2-2)\, dx$

11. $\displaystyle\int xe^{x^2}\, dx$

12. $\displaystyle\int \frac{e^{\sqrt{x}}}{\sqrt{x}}\, dx$

13. $\displaystyle\int \frac{\ln(2x)}{x}\, dx$

14. $\displaystyle\int \frac{\sqrt{\ln x}}{x}\, dx$

15. $\displaystyle\int \frac{x^4}{x^5+1}\, dx$

16. $\displaystyle\int \frac{x}{\sqrt{x^2+1}}\, dx$

17. $\displaystyle\int \frac{x-3}{(1-6x+x^2)^2}\, dx$

18. $\displaystyle\int x^{-2}\left(\frac{1}{x}+2\right)^5\, dx$

19. $\displaystyle\int \frac{\ln\sqrt{x}}{x}\, dx$

20. $\displaystyle\int \frac{x^2}{3-x^3}\, dx$

21. $\displaystyle\int \frac{x^2-2x}{x^3-3x^2+1}\, dx$

22. $\displaystyle\int \frac{\ln(3x)}{3x}\, dx$

23. $\displaystyle\int \frac{8x}{e^{x^2}}\, dx$

24. $\displaystyle\int \frac{3}{(2x+1)^3}\, dx$

25. $\displaystyle\int \frac{1}{x\ln x^2}\, dx$

26. $\displaystyle\int \frac{2}{x(\ln x)^4}\, dx$

27. $\displaystyle\int (3-x)(x^2-6x)^4\, dx$

28. $\displaystyle\int \frac{dx}{3-5x}$

29. $\displaystyle\int e^x(1+e^x)^5\, dx$

30. $\displaystyle\int e^x\sqrt{1+e^x}\, dx$

31. $\displaystyle\int \frac{e^x}{1+2e^x}\, dx$

32. $\displaystyle\int \frac{e^x+e^{-x}}{e^x-e^{-x}}\, dx$

33. $\displaystyle\int \frac{e^{-x}}{1-e^{-x}}\, dx$

34. $\displaystyle\int \frac{(1+e^{-x})^3}{e^x}\, dx$

[*Hint:* In Exercises 35 and 36, multiply the numerator and denominator by e^{-x}.]

35. $\displaystyle\int \frac{1}{1+e^x}\, dx$

36. $\displaystyle\int \frac{e^{2x}-1}{e^{2x}+1}\, dx$

37. Figure 1 shows graphs of several functions $f(x)$ whose slope at each x is $x/\sqrt{x^2+9}$. Find the expression for the function $f(x)$ whose graph passes through $(4,8)$.

38. Figure 2 shows graphs of several functions $f(x)$ whose slope at each x is $(2\sqrt{x}+1)/\sqrt{x}$. Find the expression for the function $f(x)$ whose graph passes through $(4,15)$.

Determine the following integrals using the indicated substitution.

39. $\displaystyle\int (x+5)^{-1/2}e^{\sqrt{x+5}}\, dx;\ u=\sqrt{x+5}$

40. $\displaystyle\int \frac{x^4}{x^5-7}\ln(x^5-7)\, dx;\ u=\ln(x^5-7)$

41. $\displaystyle\int x\sec^2 x^2\, dx;\ u=x^2$

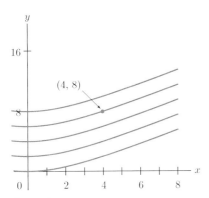

Figure 1

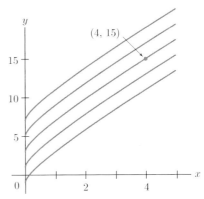

Figure 2

42. $\int (1 + \ln x) \sin(x \ln x)\, dx$; $u = x \ln x$

Determine the following integrals by making an appropriate substitution.

43. $\int \sin x \cos x\, dx$

44. $\int 2x \cos x^2\, dx$

45. $\int \dfrac{\cos \sqrt{x}}{\sqrt{x}}\, dx$

46. $\int \dfrac{\cos x}{(2 + \sin x)^3}\, dx$

47. $\int \cos^3 x \sin x\, dx$

48. $\int (\sin 2x) e^{\cos 2x}\, dx$

49. $\int \dfrac{\cos 3x}{\sqrt{2 - \sin 3x}}\, dx$

50. $\int \cot x\, dx$

51. $\int \dfrac{\sin x + \cos x}{\sin x - \cos x}\, dx$

52. $\int \tan x \sec^2 x\, dx$

53. Determine $\int 2x(x^2 + 5)\, dx$ by making a substitution. Then determine the integral by multiplying out the integrand and antidifferentiating. Account for the difference in the two results.

1. (a) $\dfrac{d}{dx} e^{(2x^3 + 3x)} = e^{(2x^3 + 3x)} \cdot (6x^2 + 3)$ (chain rule)

(b) $\dfrac{d}{dx} \ln x^5 = \dfrac{d}{dx} 5 \ln x = 5 \cdot \dfrac{1}{x}$ (Logarithm Property LIV)

(c) $\dfrac{d}{dx} \ln \sqrt{x} = \dfrac{d}{dx} \dfrac{1}{2} \ln x = \dfrac{1}{2} \cdot \dfrac{1}{x} = \dfrac{1}{2x}$ (Logarithm Property LIV)

(d) $\dfrac{d}{dx} \ln 5|x| = \dfrac{d}{dx}[\ln 5 + \ln |x|] = 0 + \dfrac{1}{x} = \dfrac{1}{x}$ (Logarithm Property LI)

(e) $\dfrac{d}{dx} x \ln x = x \cdot \dfrac{1}{x} + (\ln x) \cdot 1 = 1 + \ln x$ (product rule)

(f) $\dfrac{d}{dx} \ln(x^4 + x^2 + 1) = \dfrac{4x^3 + 2x}{x^4 + x^2 + 1}$ (chain rule)

(g) $\dfrac{d}{dx} \sin x^3 = (\cos x^3) \cdot (3x^2)$ (chain rule)

(h) $\dfrac{d}{dx} \tan x = \sec^2 x$ (formula for the derivative of $\tan x$)

2. Let $u = 3/x$, $du = (-3/x^2)\, dx$. Then

$$\int \dfrac{e^{3/x}}{x^2}\, dx = -\dfrac{1}{3} \int e^{3/x} \cdot \left(-\dfrac{3}{x^2}\right) dx$$

$$= -\dfrac{1}{3} \int e^u\, du = -\dfrac{1}{3} e^u + C = -\dfrac{1}{3} e^{3/x} + C.$$

9.2 Integration by Parts

In the preceding section we developed the method of integration by substitution by turning the chain rule into an integration formula. Let us do the same for the product rule. Let $f(x)$ and $g(x)$ be any two functions, and let $G(x)$ be an

$L \rightarrow \log \ (\ln(x))$

$I \rightarrow$ inverse trig $\sin^{-1}$

$A \rightarrow$ algebraic $x, \ x^3 ...$

$T \rightarrow$ trig

$E \rightarrow$ exponential e^x

antiderivative of $g(x)$. The product rule asserts that

$$\frac{d}{dx}[f(x)G(x)] = f(x)G'(x) + f'(x)G(x)$$

$$= f(x)g(x) + f'(x)G(x) \quad [\text{since } G'(x) = g(x)].$$

Therefore,

$$f(x)G(x) = \int f(x)g(x)\,dx + \int f'(x)G(x)\,dx.$$

This last formula can be rewritten in the following more useful form.

$$\int f(x)g(x)\,dx = f(x)G(x) - \int f'(x)G(x)\,dx. \tag{1}$$

Equation (1) is the principle of *integration by parts* and is one of the most important techniques of integration.

EXAMPLE 1   Evaluate

$$\int xe^x\,dx.$$

Solution   Set $f(x) = x$, $g(x) = e^x$. Then $f'(x) = 1$, $G(x) = e^x$, and equation (1) yields

$$\int xe^x\,dx = xe^x - \int 1 \cdot e^x\,dx = xe^x - e^x + C.$$ ■

The following principles underlie Example 1 and also illustrate general features of situations to which integration by parts may be applied:

1. The integrand is the product of two functions $f(x) = x$ and $g(x) = e^x$.

2. It is easy to compute $f'(x)$ and $G(x)$. That is, we can differentiate $f(x)$ and integrate $g(x)$.

3. The integral $\int f'(x)G(x)\,dx$ can be calculated.

Let us consider another example to see how these three principles work.

EXAMPLE 2   Evaluate

$$\int x(x+5)^8\,dx.$$

Solution   Our calculations can be set up as follows:

$$f(x) = x, \qquad g(x) = (x+5)^8,$$

$$f'(x) = 1, \qquad G(x) = \frac{1}{9}(x+5)^9.$$

Then

$$\int x(x+5)^8 \, dx = x \cdot \frac{1}{9}(x+5)^9 - \int 1 \cdot \frac{1}{9}(x+5)^9 \, dx$$

$$= \frac{1}{9}x(x+5)^9 - \frac{1}{9}\int (x+5)^9 \, dx$$

$$= \frac{1}{9}x(x+5)^9 - \frac{1}{9} \cdot \frac{1}{10}(x+5)^{10} + C$$

$$= \frac{1}{9}x(x+5)^9 - \frac{1}{90}(x+5)^{10} + C. \qquad \blacksquare$$

We were led to try integration by parts because our integrand is the product of two functions. We choose $f(x) = x$ [and not $(x+5)^8$] because $f'(x) = 1$, so the new integrand has only the factor $x + 5$, thereby simplifying the integral.

EXAMPLE 3

Evaluate

$$\int x \sin x \, dx.$$

Solution Let us set

$$f(x) = x, \qquad g(x) = \sin x,$$
$$f'(x) = 1, \qquad G(x) = -\cos x.$$

Then

$$\int x \sin x \, dx = -x \cos x - \int 1 \cdot (-\cos x) \, dx$$

$$= -x \cos x + \int \cos x \, dx$$

$$= -x \cos x + \sin x + C. \qquad \blacksquare$$

EXAMPLE 4

Evaluate

$$\int x^2 \ln x \, dx.$$

Solution Set

$$f(x) = \ln x, \qquad g(x) = x^2$$
$$f'(x) = \frac{1}{x}, \qquad G(x) = \frac{x^3}{3}.$$

Then

$$\int x^2 \ln x \, dx = \frac{x^3}{3} \ln x - \int \frac{1}{x} \cdot \frac{x^3}{3} \, dx$$

$$= \frac{x^3}{3} \ln x - \frac{1}{3} \int x^2 \, dx$$

$$= \frac{x^3}{3} \ln x - \frac{1}{9}x^3 + C. \qquad \blacksquare$$

The next example shows how integration by parts can be used to compute a reasonably complicated integral.

EXAMPLE 5

Find

$$\int \frac{xe^x}{(x+1)^2}\,dx.$$

Solution Let $f(x) = xe^x$, $g(x) = \dfrac{1}{(x+1)^2}$. Then

$$f'(x) = xe^x + e^x\cdot 1 = (x+1)e^x, \qquad G(x) = \frac{-1}{x+1}.$$

As a result, we have

$$\int \frac{xe^x}{(x+1)^2}\,dx = xe^x\cdot\frac{-1}{x+1} - \int (x+1)e^x\cdot\frac{-1}{x+1}\,dx$$

$$= -\frac{xe^x}{x+1} + \int e^x\,dx$$

$$= -\frac{xe^x}{x+1} + e^x + C = \frac{e^x}{x+1} + C. \qquad \blacksquare$$

Sometimes we must use integration by parts more than once.

EXAMPLE 6

Find

$$\int x^2\sin x\,dx.$$

Solution Let $f(x) = x^2$, $g(x) = \sin x$. Then $f'(x) = 2x$ and $G(x) = -\cos x$. Applying our formula for integration by parts, we have

$$\int x^2\sin x\,dx = -x^2\cos x - \int 2x\cdot(-\cos x)\,dx$$

$$= -x^2\cos x + 2\int x\cos x\,dx. \qquad (2)$$

The integral $\int x\cos x\,dx$ can itself be handled by integration by parts. Let $f(x) = x$, $g(x) = \cos x$. Then $f'(x) = 1$ and $G(x) = \sin x$, so

$$\int x\cos x\,dx = x\sin x - \int 1\cdot\sin x\,dx$$

$$= x\sin x + \cos x + C. \qquad (3)$$

Combining (2) and (3), we see that

$$\int x^2\sin x\,dx = -x^2\cos x + 2(x\sin x + \cos x) + C$$

$$= -x^2\cos x + 2x\sin x + 2\cos x + C. \qquad \blacksquare$$

EXAMPLE 7

Evaluate

$$\int \ln x\,dx.$$

Solution Since $\ln x = 1\cdot\ln x$, we may view $\ln x$ as a product $f(x)g(x)$, where $f(x) = \ln x$, $g(x) = 1$. Then

$$f'(x) = \frac{1}{x}, \qquad G(x) = x.$$

Finally,

$$\int \ln x \, dx = x \ln x - \int \frac{1}{x} \cdot x \, dx$$

$$= x \ln x - \int 1 \, dx$$

$$= x \ln x - x + C.$$

Practice Problems 9.2

Evaluate the following integrals.

1. $\displaystyle\int \frac{x}{e^{3x}} \, dx$

2. $\displaystyle\int \ln \sqrt{x} \, dx$

EXERCISES 9.2

Evaluate the following integrals:

1. $\displaystyle\int xe^{5x} \, dx$

2. $\displaystyle\int xe^{x/2} \, dx$

3. $\displaystyle\int x(x+7)^4 \, dx$

4. $\displaystyle\int x(2x-3)^3 \, dx$

5. $\displaystyle\int \frac{x}{e^x} \, dx$

6. $\displaystyle\int x^2 e^x \, dx$

7. $\displaystyle\int \frac{x}{\sqrt{x+1}} \, dx$

8. $\displaystyle\int \frac{x}{\sqrt{3+2x}} \, dx$

9. $\displaystyle\int e^{2x}(1-3x) \, dx$

10. $\displaystyle\int (1+x)^2 e^{2x} \, dx$

11. $\displaystyle\int \frac{6x}{e^{3x}} \, dx$

12. $\displaystyle\int \frac{x+2}{e^{2x}} \, dx$

13. $\displaystyle\int x\sqrt{x+1} \, dx$

14. $\displaystyle\int x\sqrt{2-x} \, dx$

15. $\displaystyle\int \sqrt{x} \ln \sqrt{x} \, dx$

16. $\displaystyle\int x^5 \ln x \, dx$

17. $\displaystyle\int x \cos x \, dx$

18. $\displaystyle\int x \sin 8x \, dx$

19. $\displaystyle\int x \ln 5x \, dx$

20. $\displaystyle\int x^{-3} \ln x \, dx$

21. $\displaystyle\int \ln x^4 \, dx$

22. $\displaystyle\int \frac{\ln(\ln x)}{x} \, dx$

23. $\displaystyle\int x^2 e^{-x} \, dx$

24. $\displaystyle\int \ln \sqrt{x+1} \, dx$

Evaluate the following integrals using techniques studied thus far.

25. $\displaystyle\int x(x+5)^4 \, dx$

26. $\displaystyle\int 4x \cos(x^2+1) \, dx$

27. $\displaystyle\int x(x^2+5)^4 \, dx$

28. $\displaystyle\int 4x \cos(x+1) \, dx$

29. $\displaystyle\int (3x+1)e^{x/3} \, dx$

30. $\displaystyle\int \frac{(\ln x)^5}{x} \, dx$

31. $\displaystyle\int x \sec^2(x^2+1) \, dx$

32. $\displaystyle\int \frac{\ln x}{x^5} \, dx$

33. $\displaystyle\int (xe^{2x}+x^2) \, dx$

34. $\displaystyle\int (x^{3/2}+\ln 2x) \, dx$

35. $\displaystyle\int (xe^{x^2}-2x) \, dx$

36. $\displaystyle\int (x^2-x\sin 2x) \, dx$

37. Figure 1 shows graphs of several functions $f(x)$ whose slope at each x is $x/\sqrt{x+9}$. Find the expression for the function $f(x)$ whose graph passes through $(0,2)$.

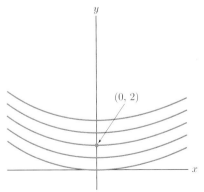

Figure 1

38. Figure 2 shows graphs of several functions $f(x)$ whose slope at each x is $\dfrac{x}{e^{x/3}}$. Find the expression for the function $f(x)$ whose graph passes through $(0,6)$.

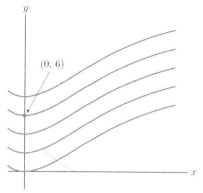

(0, 6)

Figure 2

Solutions to Practice Problems 9.2

1. $\dfrac{x}{e^{3x}}$ is the same as xe^{-3x}, a product of two familiar functions. Set $f(x) = x$, $g(x) = e^{-3x}$. Then

$$f'(x) = 1, \qquad G(x) = -\frac{1}{3}e^{-3x},$$

so

$$\int \frac{x}{e^{3x}}\,dx = x \cdot \left(-\frac{1}{3}e^{-3x}\right) - \int 1 \cdot \left(-\frac{1}{3}e^{-3x}\right) dx$$

$$= -\frac{1}{3}xe^{-3x} + \frac{1}{3}\int e^{-3x}\,dx$$

$$= -\frac{1}{3}xe^{-3x} + \frac{1}{3}\left[-\frac{1}{3}e^{-3x}\right] + C$$

$$= -\frac{1}{3}xe^{-3x} - \frac{1}{9}e^{-3x} + C.$$

2. This problem is similar to Example 7, which asks for $\int \ln x\,dx$, and can be approached in the same way

by letting $f(x) = \ln\sqrt{x}$ and $g(x) = 1$. Another approach is to use a property of logarithms to simplify the integrand.

$$\int \ln\sqrt{x}\,dx = \int \ln(x)^{1/2}\,dx$$

$$= \int \frac{1}{2}\ln x\,dx$$

$$= \frac{1}{2}\int \ln x\,dx.$$

Since we know $\int \ln x\,dx$ from Example 7,

$$\int \ln\sqrt{x}\,dx = \frac{1}{2}\int \ln x\,dx = \frac{1}{2}(x\ln x - x) + C.$$

9.3 Evaluation of Definite Integrals

Earlier we discussed techniques for determining antiderivatives (indefinite integrals). One of the most important applications of such techniques concerns the computation of definite integrals. For if $F(x)$ is an antiderivative of $f(x)$, then

$$\int_a^b f(x)\,dx = F(b) - F(a).$$

Thus the techniques of the previous sections can be used to evaluate definite integrals. Here we will simplify the method of evaluating definite integrals in those cases where the antiderivative is found by integration by substitution or parts.

EXAMPLE 1   Evaluate

$$\int_0^1 2x(x^2+1)^5\,dx.$$

Solution—First Method Let $u = x^2 + 1$, $du = 2x\,dx$. Then

$$\int 2x(x^2+1)^5\,dx = \int u^5\,du = \frac{u^6}{6} + C = \frac{(x^2+1)^6}{6} + C.$$

Consequently,

$$\int_0^1 2x(x^2+1)^5\,dx = \frac{(x^2+1)^6}{6}\bigg|_0^1 = \frac{2^6}{6} - \frac{1^6}{6} = \frac{21}{2}.$$

Solution—Second Method Again we make the substitution $u = x^2 + 1$, $du = 2x\,dx$; however, we also apply the substitution to the limits of integration. When $x = 0$ (the lower limit of integration), we have $u = 0^2 + 1 = 1$; and when $x = 1$ (the upper limit of integration), we have $u = 1^2 + 1 = 2$. Therefore,

$$\int_0^1 2x(x^2+1)^5\,dx = \int_1^2 u^5\,du = \frac{u^6}{6}\bigg|_1^2 = \frac{2^6}{6} - \frac{1^6}{6} = \frac{21}{2}.$$

In utilizing the second method, notice that we did not need to re-express the function $u^6/6$ in terms of x.

The foregoing computation is an example of a general computational method, which can be expressed as follows:

Change of Limits Rule Suppose that the integral $\int f(g(x))g'(x)\,dx$ is subjected to the substitution $u = g(x)$ so that $\int f(g(x))g'(x)\,dx$ becomes $\int f(u)\,du$. Then

$$\int_a^b f(g(x))g'(x)\,dx = \int_{g(a)}^{g(b)} f(u)\,du.$$

Justification of Change of Limits Rule If $F(x)$ is an antiderivative of $f(x)$, then

$$\frac{d}{dx}[F(g(x))] = F'(g(x))g'(x) = f(g(x))g'(x).$$

Therefore,

$$\int_a^b f(g(x))g'(x)\,dx = F(g(x))\bigg|_a^b = F(g(b)) - F(g(a)) = \int_{g(a)}^{g(b)} f(u)\,du.$$

EXAMPLE 2   Evaluate

$$\int_3^5 x\sqrt{x^2-9}\,dx.$$

Solution Let $u = x^2 - 9$; then $du = 2x\,dx$. When $x = 3$, we have $u = 3^2 - 9 = 0$. When

$x = 5$, we have $u = 5^2 - 9 = 16$. Thus

$$\int_3^5 x\sqrt{x^2 - 9}\,dx = \frac{1}{2}\int_3^5 2x\sqrt{x^2 - 9}\,dx$$

$$= \frac{1}{2}\int_0^{16} \sqrt{u}\,du$$

$$= \frac{1}{2}\cdot\frac{2}{3}u^{3/2}\Big|_0^{16}$$

$$= \frac{1}{3}\cdot\left[16^{3/2} - 0\right] = \frac{1}{3}\cdot 16^{3/2}$$

$$= \frac{1}{3}\cdot 64 = \frac{64}{3}.$$

EXAMPLE 3

Determine the area of the ellipse $x^2/a^2 + y^2/b^2 = 1$. (See Fig. 1.)

Solution Owing to the symmetry of the ellipse, the area is equal to twice the area of the upper half of the ellipse. Solving for y,

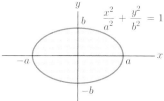

Figure 1

$$\frac{y^2}{b^2} = 1 - \frac{x^2}{a^2}$$

$$\frac{y}{b} = \pm\sqrt{1 - \left(\frac{x}{a}\right)^2}$$

$$y = \pm b\sqrt{1 - \left(\frac{x}{a}\right)^2}.$$

Since the area of the upper half-ellipse is the area under the curve

$$y = b\sqrt{1 - \left(\frac{x}{a}\right)^2},$$

the area of the ellipse is given by the integral

$$2\int_{-a}^a b\sqrt{1 - \left(\frac{x}{a}\right)^2}\,dx.$$

Let $u = x/a$; then $du = 1/a\,dx$. When $x = -a$, we have $u = -a/a = -1$. When $x = a$, we have $u = a/a = 1$. So

$$2\int_{-a}^a b\sqrt{1 - \left(\frac{x}{a}\right)^2}\,dx = 2b\cdot a\int_{-a}^a \frac{1}{a}\sqrt{1 - \left(\frac{x}{a}\right)^2}\,dx$$

$$= 2ba\int_{-1}^1 \sqrt{1 - u^2}\,du.$$

We cannot evaluate this integral using our existing techniques; we obtain its value immediately by recognizing that, since the area under the curve $y = \sqrt{1 - x^2}$ from $x = -1$ to $x = 1$ is the top half of a unit circle and since we know that the area of a unit circle is π, the area of the ellipse is $2ba\cdot(\pi/2) = \pi ab$.

Integration by Parts in Definite Integrals

EXAMPLE 4　　　Evaluate

$$\int_0^{\pi/2} x \cos x \, dx.$$

Solution　We use integration by parts to find an antiderivative of $x \cos x$. Let $f(x) = x$, $g(x) = \cos x$, $f'(x) = 1$, and $G(x) = \sin x$. Then

$$\int x \cos x \, dx = x \sin x - \int 1 \cdot \sin x \, dx = x \sin x + \cos x + C.$$

Hence

$$\int_0^{\pi/2} x \cos x \, dx = (x \sin x + \cos x) \Big|_0^{\pi/2}$$

$$= \left(\frac{\pi}{2} \sin \frac{\pi}{2} + \cos \frac{\pi}{2} \right) - (0 + \cos 0)$$

$$= \frac{\pi}{2} - 1. \qquad \blacksquare$$

EXAMPLE 5　　　Evaluate

$$\int_0^5 \frac{x}{\sqrt{x+4}} \, dx.$$

Solution　Let $f(x) = x$, $g(x) = (x+4)^{-1/2}$, $f'(x) = 1$, and $G(x) = 2(x+4)^{1/2}$. Then

$$\int_0^5 \frac{x}{\sqrt{x+4}} \, dx = 2x(x+4)^{1/2} \Big|_0^5 - \int_0^5 1 \cdot 2(x+4)^{1/2} \, dx$$

$$= 2x(x+4)^{1/2} \Big|_0^5 - \frac{4}{3}(x+4)^{3/2} \Big|_0^5$$

$$= \left[10(9)^{1/2} - 0 \right] - \left[\frac{4}{3}(9)^{3/2} - \frac{4}{3}(4)^{3/2} \right]$$

$$= [30] - \left[36 - \frac{32}{3} \right] = 4\frac{2}{3}. \qquad \blacksquare$$

Practice Problems 9.3

Evaluate the following definite integrals:

1. $\displaystyle\int_0^1 (2x + 3)e^{x^2+3x+6} \, dx$

2. $\displaystyle\int_e^{e^{\pi/2}} \frac{\sin(\ln x)}{x} \, dx$

EXERCISES 9.3

Evaluate the following definite integrals:

1. $\displaystyle\int_{5/2}^3 2(2x - 5)^{14} \, dx$　　**2.** $\displaystyle\int_2^6 \frac{1}{\sqrt{4x+1}} \, dx$

3. $\displaystyle\int_0^2 4x(1 + x^2)^3 \, dx$　　**4.** $\displaystyle\int_0^1 \frac{2x}{\sqrt{x^2+1}} \, dx$

5. $\displaystyle\int_0^3 \frac{x}{\sqrt{x+1}} \, dx$　　**6.** $\displaystyle\int_0^1 x(3 + x)^5 \, dx$

7. $\displaystyle\int_3^5 x\sqrt{x^2-9}\,dx$ **8.** $\displaystyle\int_0^1 \frac{1}{(1+2x)^4}\,dx$

9. $\displaystyle\int_{-1}^2 (x^2-1)(x^3-3x)^4\,dx$

10. $\displaystyle\int_0^1 (2x-1)(x^2-x)^{10}\,dx$

11. $\displaystyle\int_0^1 \frac{x}{x^2+3}\,dx$ **12.** $\displaystyle\int_0^4 8x(x+4)^{-3}\,dx$

13. $\displaystyle\int_1^3 x^2 e^{x^3}\,dx$ **14.** $\displaystyle\int_{-1}^1 2xe^x\,dx$

15. $\displaystyle\int_1^e \frac{\ln x}{x}\,dx$ **16.** $\displaystyle\int_1^e \ln x\,dx$

17. $\displaystyle\int_0^\pi e^{\sin x}\cos x\,dx$ **18.** $\displaystyle\int_0^{\pi/4} \tan x\,dx$

19. $\displaystyle\int_0^1 x\sin\pi x\,dx$ **20.** $\displaystyle\int_0^{\pi/2} \sin\left(2x-\frac{\pi}{2}\right)dx$

Use substitutions and the fact that a circle of radius r has area πr^2 to evaluate the following integrals:

21. $\displaystyle\int_{-\pi/2}^{\pi/2} \sqrt{1-\sin^2 x}\,\cos x\,dx$

22. $\displaystyle\int_0^{\sqrt2} \sqrt{4-x^4}\cdot 2x\,dx$

23. $\displaystyle\int_{-6}^0 \sqrt{-x^2-6x}\,dx$ [Complete the square: $-x^2-6x = 9-(x+3)^2$]

In Exercises 24 and 25, find the area of the shaded regions.

24.

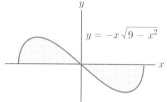

$y = -x\sqrt{9-x^2}$

25.

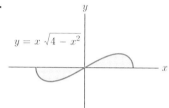

$y = x\sqrt{4-x^2}$

---

1. Let $u = x^2+3x+6$, so $du = (2x+3)\,dx$. When $x=0$, $u=6$; when $x=1$, $u=10$. Thus

$$\int_0^1 (2x+3)e^{x^2+3x+6}\,dx = \int_6^{10} e^u\,du = e^u\Big|_6^{10}$$

$$= e^{10}-e^6.$$

2. Let $u = \ln x$, $du = (1/x)\,dx$. When $x=e$, $u=\ln e = $

1; when $x = e^{\pi/2}$, $u = \ln e^{\pi/2} = \pi/2$. Thus

$$\int_e^{e^{\pi/2}} \frac{\sin(\ln x)}{x}\,dx = \int_1^{\pi/2} \sin u\,du = -\cos u\Big|_1^{\pi/2}$$

$$= -\cos\frac{\pi}{2} + \cos 1 \approx .54030.$$

9.4 Approximation of Definite Integrals

The definite integrals that arise in practical problems cannot always be evaluated by computing the net change in an antiderivative, as we did in the preceding section. Mathematicians have compiled extensive tables of antiderivatives. Moreover, many excellent software programs can be used to determine antiderivatives. However, the form of an antiderivative may be quite complex, and in some cases there may actually be no way to express an antiderivative in terms of elementary functions. In this section we discuss three methods for approximating the numerical value of the definite integral,

$$\int_a^b f(x)\,dx$$

without computing an antiderivative.

Given a positive integer n, divide the interval $a \leq x \leq b$ into n equal subintervals, each of length $\Delta x = (b - a)/n$. Denote the endpoints of the subintervals by $a_0, a_1, \ldots, a_n$, and denote the midpoints of the subintervals by $x_1, x_2, \ldots, x_n$. (See Fig. 1.) Recall from Chapter 6 that the definite integral is the limit of Riemann sums. When the midpoints of the subintervals in Fig. 1 are used to construct a Riemann sum, the resulting approximation to $\int_a^b f(x)\,dx$ is called the *midpoint rule*.

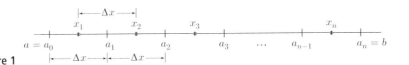

Figure 1

Midpoint Rule

$$\int_a^b f(x)\,dx \approx f(x_1)\Delta x + f(x_2)\Delta x + \cdots + f(x_n)\Delta x \qquad (1)$$
$$= [f(x_1) + f(x_2) + \cdots + f(x_n)]\Delta x.$$

EXAMPLE 1   Use the midpoint rule with $n = 4$ to approximate

$$\int_0^2 \frac{1}{1 + e^x}\,dx.$$

Solution   We have $\Delta x = (b - a)/n = (2 - 0)/4 = .5$. The endpoints of the four subintervals begin at $a = 0$ and are spaced .5 unit apart. The first midpoint is at $a + \Delta x/2 = .25$.

The midpoints are also spaced .5 unit apart. According to the midpoint rule, the integral is approximately equal to

$$\left[\frac{1}{1 + e^{.25}} + \frac{1}{1 + e^{.75}} + \frac{1}{1 + e^{1.25}} + \frac{1}{1 + e^{1.75}} \right](.5)$$

$$\approx .5646961 \quad \text{(to seven decimal places).} \quad \blacksquare$$

A second method of approximation, the *trapezoidal rule*, uses the values of $f(x)$ at the endpoints of the subintervals of the interval $a \leq x \leq b$.

Trapezoidal Rule

$$\int_a^b f(x)\,dx \approx [f(a_0) + 2f(a_1) + \cdots + 2f(a_{n-1}) + f(a_n)]\frac{\Delta x}{2}. \qquad (2)$$

We will discuss the origin of the trapezoidal rule and why we call it by that name later in this section.

EXAMPLE 2   Use the trapezoidal rule with $n = 4$ to approximate

$$\int_0^2 \frac{1}{1 + e^x}\,dx.$$

Solution As in Example 1, $\Delta x = .5$ and the endpoints of the subintervals are $a_0 = 0$, $a_1 = .5$, $a_2 = 1$, $a_3 = 1.5$, and $a_4 = 2$. The trapezoidal rule gives

$$\left[\frac{1}{1+e^0} + 2 \cdot \frac{1}{1+e^{.5}} + 2 \cdot \frac{1}{1+e^1} + 2 \cdot \frac{1}{1+e^{1.5}} + \frac{1}{1+e^2}\right]\frac{.5}{2}$$

$$\approx .5692545 \quad \text{(to seven decimal places)}. \quad \blacksquare$$

When the function $f(x)$ is given explicitly, either the midpoint rule or the trapezoidal rule may be used to approximate the definite integral. However, occasionally the values of $f(x)$ may be known only at the endpoints of the subintervals. This may happen, for instance, when the values of $f(x)$ are obtained from experimental data. In this case, the midpoint rule cannot be used.

EXAMPLE 3

Measuring cardiac output[*] Five milligrams of dye is injected into a vein leading to the heart. The concentration of the dye in the aorta, an artery leading from the heart, is determined every 2 seconds for 22 seconds. (See Table 1.) Let $c(t)$ be the concentration in the aorta after t seconds. Use the trapezoidal rule to estimate $\int_0^{22} c(t)\, dt$.

TABLE 1 Concentration of Dye in the Aorta

Seconds after injection	0	2	4	6	8	10	12	14	16	18	20	22
Concentration (mg/liter)	0	0	.6	1.4	2.7	3.7	4.1	3.8	2.9	1.5	.9	.5

Solution Let $n = 11$. Then $a = 0$, $b = 22$, and $\Delta t = (22-0)/11 = 2$. The endpoints of the subintervals are $a_0 = 0, a_1 = 2, a_2 = 4, \ldots, a_{10} = 20$, and $a_{11} = 22$. By the trapezoidal rule,

$$\int_0^{22} c(t)\, dt \approx [c(0) + 2c(2) + 2c(4) + 2c(6) + \cdots + 2c(20) + c(22)]\left(\frac{2}{2}\right)$$

$$= [0 + 2(0) + 2(.6) + 2(1.4) + \cdots + 2(.9) + .5](1)$$

$$\approx 43.7 \text{ liters}.$$

Note that cardiac output is the rate (usually measured in liters per minute) at which the heart pumps blood, and it may be computed by the formula

$$R = \frac{60D}{\int_0^{22} c(t)\, dt},$$

where D is the quantity of dye injected. For the preceding data, $R = 60(5)/43.7 \approx 6.9$ liters per minute. $\quad \blacksquare$

Let us return to the approximations to $\int_0^2 \frac{1}{1+e^x}\, dx$ found in Examples 1 and 2. These numbers are shown in Fig. 2 along with the exact value of the definite

---

[*]Data from B. Horelick and S. Koont, Project UMAP, *Measuring Cardiac Output* (Newton, MA: Educational Development Center, Inc., 1978).

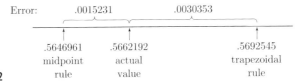

Figure 2

integral to seven decimal places and the error of the two approximations. [The scale is greatly enlarged. The exact value of the integral is $\ln 2 - \ln(1 + e^{-2}) \approx .5662192$. To find it, see Exercise 35, Section 9.1.] It can be shown that, in general, the error from the midpoint rule is about one-half the error from the trapezoidal rule, and the estimates from these two rules are usually on opposite sides of the actual value of the definite integral. These observations suggest that we might improve our estimate of the value of a definite integral by using a "weighted average" of these two estimates. Let M and T denote the estimates from the midpoint and trapezoidal rules, respectively, and define

$$S = \frac{2}{3}M + \frac{1}{3}T = \frac{2M + T}{3}. \tag{3}$$

The use of S as an estimate of the value of a definite integral is called *Simpson's rule*. If we use Simpson's rule to estimate the definite integral in Example 1, we find that

$$S = \frac{2(.5646961) + .5692545}{3} \approx .5662156.$$

The error here is only .0000036. The error from the trapezoidal rule, in this example, is over 800 times as large!

As the number n of subintervals increases, Simpson's rule becomes more accurate than both the midpoint rule and the trapezoidal rule. For a given definite integral, the error in the midpoint and trapezoidal rules is proportional to $1/n^2$, so doubling n will divide the error by 4. However, the error in Simpson's rule is proportional to $1/n^4$, so doubling n will divide the error by 16, and multiplying n by a factor of 10 will divide the error by 10,000.

It is possible to combine the formulas for the midpoint and trapezoidal rules into a single formula for Simpson's rule by using the fact that $S = (4M + 2T)/6$.

Simpson's Rule

$$\int_a^b f(x)\,dx \approx [f(a_0) + 4f(x_1) + 2f(a_1) + 4f(x_2) + 2f(a_2)$$
$$+ \cdots + 2f(a_{n-1}) + 4f(x_n) + f(a_n)]\frac{\Delta x}{6}. \tag{4}$$

Distribution of IQs Psychologists use various standardized tests to measure intelligence. The method most commonly used to describe the results of such tests is an intelligence quotient (or IQ). An IQ is a positive number that, in theory, indicates how a person's mental age compares with the person's chronological age. The median IQ is arbitrarily set at 100, so half the population has an IQ less than 100 and half greater. IQs are distributed according to a bell-shaped curve called a *normal curve*, pictured in Fig. 3. The proportion of all people having IQs between A and

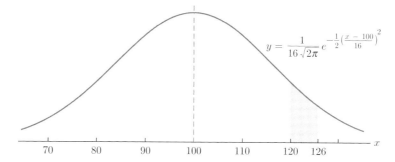

Figure 3. Proportion of IQs between 120 and 126.

B is given by the area under the curve from A to B, that is, by the integral

$$\frac{1}{16\sqrt{2\pi}} \int_A^B e^{-(1/2)[(x-100)/16]^2} \, dx.$$

EXAMPLE 4 Estimate the proportion of all people having IQs between 120 and 126.

Solution We have seen that this proportion is given by

$$\frac{1}{16\sqrt{2\pi}} \int_{120}^{126} f(x) \, dx, \quad \text{where } f(x) = e^{-(1/2)[(x-100)/16]^2}.$$

Let us approximate the definite integral by Simpson's rule with $n = 3$. Then $\Delta x = (126 - 120)/3 = 2$. The endpoints of the subintervals are 120, 122, 124, and 126; the midpoints of these subintervals are 121, 123, and 125. Simpson's rule gives

$$[f(120) + 4f(121) + 2f(122) + 4f(123) + 2f(124) + 4f(125) + f(126)]\frac{\Delta x}{6}$$

$$\approx [.4578 + 1.6904 + .7771 + 1.4235 + .6493 + 1.1801 + .2671]\left(\frac{2}{6}\right)$$

$$\approx 2.1484.$$

Multiplying this estimate by $1/(16\sqrt{2\pi})$, the constant in front of the integral, we get .0536. Thus approximately 5.36% of the population have IQs between 120 and 126.

Geometric Interpretation of the Approximation Rules Let $f(x)$ be a continuous nonnegative function on $a \leq x \leq b$. The approximation rules discussed previously may be interpreted as methods for estimating the area under the graph of $f(x)$. The midpoint rule arises from replacing this area by a collection of n rectangles, one lying over each subinterval, the first of height $f(x_1)$, the second of height $f(x_2)$, and so on. (See Fig. 4.)

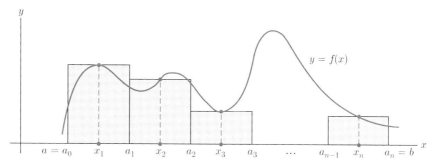

Figure 4. Approximation by rectangles.

If we approximate the area under the graph of $f(x)$ by trapezoids, as in Fig. 5, the total area of these trapezoids turns out to be the number given by the trapezoidal rule (hence the name of the rule).

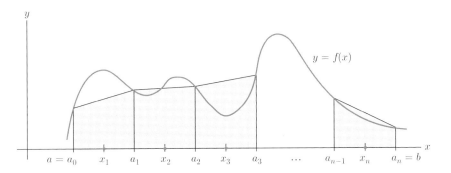

Figure 5. Approximation by trapezoids.

Simpson's rule corresponds to approximating the graph of $f(x)$ on each subinterval by a parabola instead of a straight line, as in the midpoint and trapezoidal rules. On each subinterval, the parabola is chosen so that it intersects the graph of $f(x)$ at the midpoint and both endpoints of the subinterval. (See Fig. 6.) It can be shown that the sum of the areas under these parabolas is the number given by Simpson's rule. Even more powerful approximation rules may be obtained by approximating the graph of $f(x)$ on each subinterval by cubic curves, or graphs of higher-order polynomials.

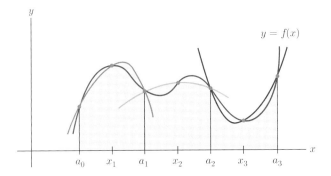

Figure 6. Approximation by parabolas.

Error Analysis A simple measure of the error of an approximation to a definite integral is the quantity

$$\big|[\text{approximate value}] - [\text{actual value}]\big|.$$

The following theorem gives an idea of how small this error must be for the various approximation rules. In a concrete example, the actual error of an approximation may be even substantially less than the "error bound" given in the theorem.

Error of Approximation Theorem Let n be the number of subintervals used in an approximation of the definite integral

$$\int_a^b f(x)\,dx.$$

1. The error for the midpoint rule is at most $\dfrac{A(b-a)^3}{24n^2}$, where A is a number such that $|f''(x)| \le A$ for all x satisfying $a \le x \le b$.

2. The error for the trapezoidal rule is at most $\dfrac{A(b-a)^3}{12n^2}$, where A is a number such that $|f''(x)| \leq A$ for all x satisfying $a \leq x \leq b$.

3. The error for Simpson's rule is at most $\dfrac{A(b-a)^5}{2880n^4}$, where A is a number such that $|f''''(x)| \leq A$ for all x satisfying $a \leq x \leq b$.

EXAMPLE 5

Obtain a bound on the error of using the trapezoidal rule with $n = 20$ to approximate

$$\int_0^1 e^{x^2}\, dx.$$

Solution Here $a = 0$, $b = 1$, and $f(x) = e^{x^2}$. Differentiating twice, we find that

$$f''(x) = (4x^2 + 2)e^{x^2}.$$

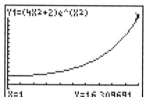

How large could $|f''(x)|$ be if x satisfies $0 \leq x \leq 1$? Since the function $(4x^2 + 2)e^{x^2}$ is clearly increasing on the interval from 0 to 1, its greatest value occurs at $x = 1$. (See Fig. 7.) Therefore, its greatest value is

$$(4 \cdot 1^2 + 2)e^{1^2} = 6e,$$

so we may take $A = 6e$ in the preceding theorem. The error of approximation using the trapezoidal rule is at most

Figure 7

$$\frac{6e(1-0)^3}{12(20)^2} = \frac{e}{800} \approx \frac{2.71828}{800} \approx .003398.$$ ∎

INCORPORATING TECHNOLOGY

Approximating Integrals   In the Incorporating Technology part of Section 6.2 we showed how to use the TI-83/84's **sum** and **seq** functions to evaluate Riemann sums. Here we use that technique to demonstrate how to implement the approximations discussed in this section. In Fig. 8 we use the Midpoint Rule as in Example 1 and store the result in a variable M.

In Fig. 9 we implement the Trapezoidal Rule and store the result in a variable T. Here we calculate the first term separately, use **sum(seq** to total the middle three terms, and then we calculate the last term separately.

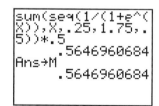

Figure 8. Calculation for Example 1.

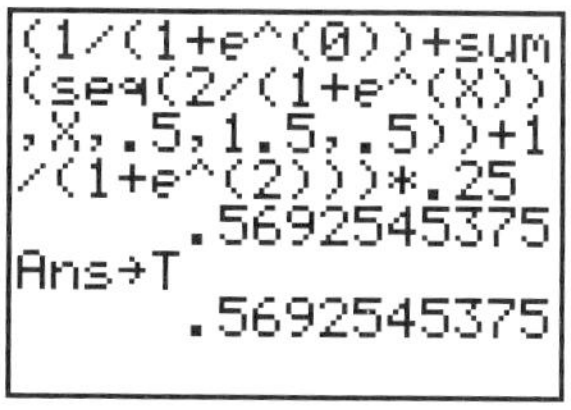

Figure 9. Calculation for Example 2.

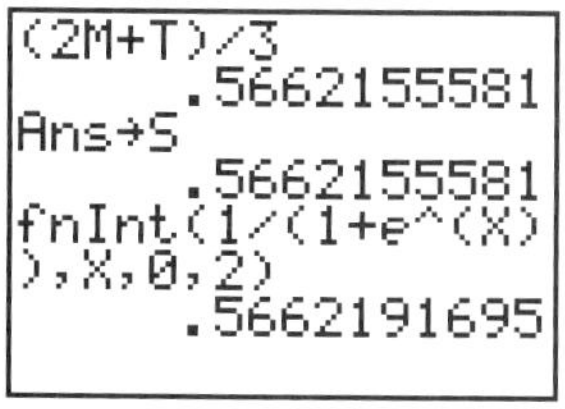

Figure 10. Simpson's rule.

Figure 10 applies Simpson's rule to the same function and shows that it is very close to the highly accurate value given by **fnInt**.

We can also use our TI-83/84 to determine a suitable value for A in the error approximation theorem by finding the greatest value of either $f''(x)$ or $f''''(x)$. Graphing derivatives is explained in the Incorporating Technology section of Section 2.2. The method demonstrated there can be easily extended to graph the second and fourth derivatives of a function.   ∎

Practice Problems 9.4

Consider $\int_{1}^{3.4} (5x-9)^2\, dx.$

1. Divide the interval $1 \le x \le 3.4$ into three subintervals. List Δx and the endpoints and midpoints of the subintervals.

2. Approximate the integral by the midpoint rule with $n = 3$.

3. Approximate the integral by the trapezoidal rule with $n = 3$.

4. Approximate the integral by Simpson's rule with $n = 3$.

5. Find the exact value of the integral by integration.

EXERCISES 9.4

In Exercises 1 and 2, divide the given interval into n subintervals and list the value of Δx and the endpoints $a_0, a_1, \ldots, a_n$ of the subintervals.

1. $3 \le x \le 5;\ n = 5$ 2. $-1 \le x \le 2;\ n = 5$

In Exercises 3 and 4, divide the interval into n subintervals and list the value of Δx and the midpoints $x_1, \ldots, x_n$ of the subintervals.

3. $-1 \le x \le 1;\ n = 4$ 4. $0 \le x \le 3;\ n = 6$

5. Refer to the graph in Fig. 11. Draw the rectangles that approximate the area under the curve from 0 to 8 when using the midpoint rule with $n = 4$.

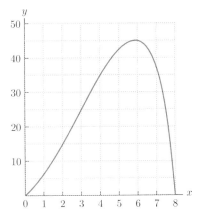

Figure 11

6. Refer to the graph in Fig. 11. Apply the trapezoidal rule with $n = 4$ to estimate the area under the curve.

Approximate the following integrals by the midpoint rule; then find the exact value by integration. Express your answers to five decimal places.

7. $\int_0^4 (x^2+5)\, dx;\ n = 2, 4$

8. $\int_1^5 (x-1)^2\, dx;\ n = 2, 4$

9. $\int_0^1 e^{-x}\, dx;\ n = 5$ 10. $\int_1^2 \frac{1}{x+1}\, dx;\ n = 5$

Approximate the following integrals by the trapezoidal rule; then find the exact value by integration. Express your answers to five decimal places.

11. $\int_0^1 \left(x - \tfrac{1}{2}\right)^2\, dx;\ n = 4$ 12. $\int_4^9 \frac{1}{x-3}\, dx;\ n = 5$

13. $\int_1^5 \frac{1}{x^2}\, dx;\ n = 3$ 14. $\int_{-1}^1 e^{2x}\, dx;\ n = 2, 4$

Approximate the following integrals by the midpoint rule, the trapezoidal rule, and Simpson's rule. Then find the exact value by integration. Express your answers to five decimal places.

15. $\int_1^4 (2x-3)^3\, dx;\ n = 3$ 16. $\int_{10}^{20} \frac{\ln x}{x}\, dx;\ n = 5$

17. $\int_0^2 2xe^{x^2}\, dx;\ n = 4$ 18. $\int_0^3 x\sqrt{4-x}\, dx;\ n = 5$

19. $\int_2^5 xe^x\, dx;\ n = 5$ 20. $\int_1^5 (4x^3 - 3x^2)\, dx;\ n = 2$

The following integrals cannot be evaluated in terms of elementary antiderivatives. Find an approximate value by Simpson's rule. Express your answers to five decimal places.

21. $\int_0^2 \sqrt{1+x^3}\, dx;\ n = 4$ 22. $\int_0^1 \frac{1}{x^3+1}\, dx;\ n = 2$

23. $\int_0^2 \sqrt{\sin x}\, dx;\ n = 5$ 24. $\int_{-1}^1 \sqrt{1+x^4}\, dx;\ n = 4$

25. **Area** In a survey of a piece of oceanfront property, measurements of the distance to the water were made every 50 feet along a 200-foot side. (See Fig. 12.) Use the trapezoidal rule to estimate the area of the property.

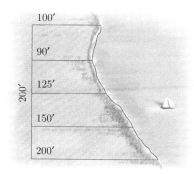

Figure 12. Survey of an oceanfront property.

26. Area To determine the amount of water flowing down a certain 100-yard-wide river, engineers need to know the area of a vertical cross section of the river. Measurements of the depth of the river were made every 20 yards from one bank to the other. The readings in fathoms were 0, 1, 2, 3, 1, 0. (One fathom equals 2 yards.) Use the trapezoidal rule to estimate the area of the cross section.

27. Distance Traveled Upon takeoff, the velocity readings of a rocket noted every second for 10 seconds were 0, 30, 75, 115, 155, 200, 250, 300, 360, 420, and 490 feet per second. Use the trapezoidal rule to estimate the distance the rocket traveled during the first 10 seconds. [*Hint*: If $s(t)$ is the distance traveled by time t and $v(t)$ is the velocity at time t, then $s(10) = \int_0^{10} v(t)\,dt$.]

28. Distance Traveled In a drive along a country road, the speedometer readings are recorded each minute during a 5-minute interval.

Time (minutes)	0	1	2	3	4	5
Velocity (mph)	33	32	28	30	32	35

Use the trapezoidal rule to estimate the distance traveled during the 5 minutes. [*Hint*: If time is measured in minutes, velocity should be expressed in distance per minute. For example, 35 mph is $\frac{35}{60}$ miles per minute. Also, see the hint for Exercise 27.]

29. Consider $\int_0^2 f(x)\,dx$, where $f(x) = \frac{1}{12}x^4 + 3x^2$.
   (a) Make a rough sketch of the graph of $f''(x)$ for $0 \le x \le 2$.
   (b) Find a number A such that $|f''(x)| \le A$ for all x satisfying $0 \le x \le 2$.
   (c) Obtain a bound on the error of using the midpoint rule with $n = 10$ to approximate the definite integral.
   (d) The exact value of the definite integral (to four decimal places) is 8.5333, and the midpoint rule with $n = 10$ gives 8.5089. What is the error for the midpoint approximation? Does this error satisfy the bound obtained in part (c)?

(e) Redo part (c) with the number of intervals doubled to $n = 20$. Is the bound on the error halved? Quartered?

30. Consider $\int_1^2 f(x)\,dx$, where $f(x) = 3\ln x$.
   (a) Make a rough sketch of the graph of the fourth derivative of $f(x)$ for $1 \le x \le 2$.
   (b) Find a number A such that $|f''''(x)| \le A$ for all x satisfying $1 \le x \le 2$.
   (c) Obtain a bound on the error of using Simpson's rule with $n = 2$ to approximate the definite integral.
   (d) The exact value of the definite integral (to four decimal places) is 1.1589, and Simpson's rule with $n = 2$ gives 1.1588. What is the error for the approximation by Simpson's rule? Does this error satisfy the bound obtained in part (c)?
   (e) Redo part (c) with the number of intervals tripled to $n = 6$. Is the bound on the error divided by three?

31. (a) Show that the area of the trapezoid in Fig. 13(a) is $\frac{1}{2}(h + k)l$. [*Hint*: Divide the trapezoid into a rectangle and a triangle.]
   (b) Show that the area of the first trapezoid on the left in Fig. 13(b) is $\frac{1}{2}[f(a_0) + f(a_1)]\Delta x$.
   (c) Derive the trapezoidal rule for the case $n = 4$.

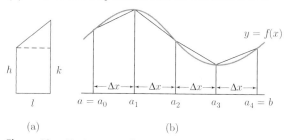

(a)   (b)

Figure 13. Derivation of the trapezoidal rule.

32. Approximate the value of $\int_a^b f(x)\,dx$, where $f(x) \ge 0$, by dividing the interval $a \le x \le b$ into four subintervals and constructing five rectangles. (See Fig. 14.) Note that the width of the three inside rectangles is Δx, while the width of the two outside rectangles is $\Delta x/2$. Compute the sum of the areas of these five rectangles and compare this sum with the trapezoidal rule for $n = 4$.

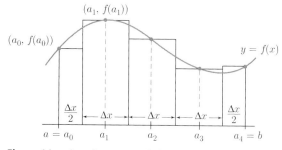

Figure 14. Another view of the trapezoidal rule.

33. (a) Suppose that the graph of $f(x)$ is above the x-axis and concave down on the interval $a_0 \leq x \leq a_1$. Let x_1 be the midpoint of this interval, let $\Delta x = a_1 - a_0$, and construct the line tangent to the graph of $f(x)$ at $(x_1, f(x_1))$, as in Fig. 15(a). Show that the area of the shaded trapezoid in Fig. 15(a) is the same as the area of the shaded rectangle in Fig. 15(c), that is, $f(x_1)\Delta x$. [*Hint:* Look at Fig. 15(b).] This shows that the area of the rectangle in Fig. 15(c) exceeds the area under the graph of $f(x)$ on the interval $a_0 \leq x \leq a_1$.

(b) Suppose that the graph of $f(x)$ is above the x-axis and concave down for all x in the interval $a \leq x \leq b$. Explain why $T \leq \int_a^b f(x)\,dx \leq M$, where T and M are the approximations given by the trapezoidal and midpoint rules, respectively.

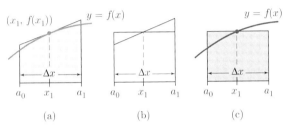

Figure 15

34. Riemann Sum Derivation of Formula for Cardiac Output; see Example 3. Subdivide the interval $0 \leq t \leq 22$ into n subintervals of length $\Delta t = 22/n$ seconds. Let t_i be a point in the ith subinterval.

(a) Show that $(R/60)\Delta t \approx$ [number of liters of blood flowing past the monitoring point during the ith time interval].

(b) Show that $c(t_i)(R/60)\Delta t \approx$ [quantity of dye flowing past the monitoring point during the ith time interval].

(c) Assume that basically all the dye will have flowed past the monitoring point during the 22 seconds. Explain why $D \approx (R/60)[c(t_1) + c(t_2) + \cdots + c(t_n)]\Delta t$, where the approximation improves as n gets large.

(d) Conclude that $D = \int_0^{22} (R/60)c(t)\,dt$, and solve for R.

Technology Exercises

35. In Fig. 16 a definite integral of the form $\int_a^b f(x)\,dx$ is approximated by the midpoint rule. Determine $f(x)$, a, b, and n.

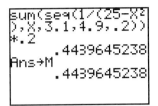

Figure 16

36. In Fig. 17 a definite integral of the form $\int_a^b f(x)\,dx$ is approximated by the trapezoidal rule. Determine $f(x)$, a, b, and n.

Figure 17

In Exercises 37–40, approximate the integrals by the midpoint rule, the trapezoidal rule, and Simpson's rule with $n = 10$. Then find the exact value by integration and give the error for each approximation. Express your answers to the full accuracy given by the calculator or computer.

37. $\displaystyle\int_1^{11} \frac{1}{x}\,dx$

38. $\displaystyle\int_0^{\pi/2} \cos x\,dx$

39. $\displaystyle\int_0^{\pi/4} \sec^2 x\,dx$

40. $\displaystyle\int_0^1 2xe^{x^2}\,dx$

In Exercises 41 and 42, consider the definite integral $\int_0^1 \dfrac{4}{1+x^2}\,dx$, which has the value π.

41. Suppose the midpoint rule with $n = 20$ is used to estimate π. Graph the second derivative of the function in the window $[0, 1]$ by $[-10, 10]$ and then use the graph to obtain a bound on the error of the estimate.

42. Suppose the trapezoidal rule with $n = 15$ is used to estimate π. Graph the second derivative of the function in the window $[0, 1]$ by $[-10, 10]$ and then use the graph to obtain a bound on the error of the estimate.

Solutions to Practice Problems 9.4

1. $\Delta x = (3.4 - 1)/3 = 2.4/3 = .8$. Each subinterval will have length .8. A good way to proceed is first to draw two hatchmarks that subdivide the interval into three equal subintervals. [See Fig. 18(a).] Then label the hatchmarks by successively adding .8 to the left endpoint. [See Fig. 18(b).] The first midpoint can be obtained by adding one-half of .8 to the left endpoint. Then add .8 to get the next midpoint, and so on. [See Fig. 18(c).]

2. The midpoint rule uses only the midpoints of the subintervals:

$$\int_1^{3.4} (5x - 9)^2 \, dx \approx \left\{ (5[1.4] - 9)^2 + (5[2.2] - 9)^2 \right.$$
$$\left. + (5[3] - 9)^2 \right\} (.8)$$
$$= \left\{ (-2)^2 + 2^2 + 6^2 \right\} (.8)$$
$$= 35.2.$$

3. The trapezoidal rule uses only the endpoints of the subintervals:

$$\int_1^{3.4} (5x - 9)^2 \, dx \approx \left\{ (5[1] - 9)^2 + 2(5[1.8] - 9)^2 \right.$$
$$+ 2(5[2.6] - 9)^2$$
$$\left. + (5[3.4] - 9)^2 \right\} \left(\frac{.8}{2} \right)$$
$$= \left\{ (-4)^2 + 2(0)^2 + 2(4)^2 + 8^2 \right\} (.4)$$
$$= 44.8.$$

4. Using the formula $S = \dfrac{2M + T}{3}$, we obtain

$$\int_1^{3.4} (5x - 9)^2 \, dx \approx \frac{2(35.2) + 44.8}{3} = \frac{115.2}{3} = 38.4.$$

This approximation may also be obtained directly with formula (4), but the arithmetic requires about the same effort as calculating the midpoint and trapezoidal approximations separately and then combining them, as we do here.

5. $\displaystyle \int_1^{3.4} (5x - 9)^2 \, dx = \frac{1}{15} (5x - 9)^3 \Big|_1^{3.4}$

$$= \frac{1}{15} \left[8^3 - (-4)^3 \right]$$
$$= 38.4.$$

(Notice that here Simpson's rule gives the exact answer. This is so since the function to be integrated is a quadratic polynomial. Actually, Simpson's rule gives the exact value of the definite integral of any polynomial of degree 3 or less. The reason for this can be discovered from the **error of approximation theorem**.)

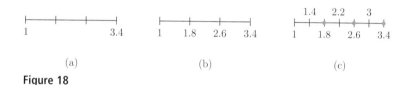

(a)   (b)   (c)

Figure 18

9.5 Some Applications of the Integral

Recall that the integral

$$\int_a^b f(t) \, dt$$

can be approximated by a Riemann sum as follows: We divide the t-axis from a to b into n subintervals by adding intermediate points $t_0 = a, t_1, \ldots, t_{n-1}, t_n = b$.

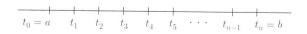

We assume that the points are equally spaced so that each subinterval has length $\Delta t = (b - a)/n$. For large n, the integral is very closely approximated by the

Riemann sum

$$\int_a^b f(t)\,dt \approx f(t_1)\Delta t + f(t_2)\Delta t + \cdots + f(t_n)\Delta t. \tag{1}$$

The approximation in (1) works both ways. If we encounter a Riemann sum like that in (1), we can approximate it by the corresponding integral. The approximation becomes better as the number of subintervals increases, that is, as n gets large. Thus, as n gets large, the sum approaches the value of the integral. This will be our approach in the examples that follow.

Our first two examples involve the concept of the present value of money. Suppose that we make an investment that promises to repay A dollars at time t (measuring the present as time 0). How much should we be willing to pay for such an investment? Clearly, we would not want to pay as much as A dollars. For if we had A dollars now, we could invest it at the current rate of interest and, at time t, we would get back our original A dollars plus the accrued interest. Instead, we should only be willing to pay an amount P that, if invested for t years, would yield A dollars. We call P the *present value of A dollars in t years*. We shall assume continuous compounding of interest. If the current (annual) rate of interest is r, then P dollars invested for t years will yield Pe^{rt} dollars (see Section 5.2). That is,

$$Pe^{rt} = A.$$

Thus the formula for the present value of A dollars in t years at interest rate r is

$$P = Ae^{-rt}.$$

EXAMPLE 1

Present value of an income stream Consider a small printing company that does most of its work on one printing press. The firm's profits are directly influenced by the amount of material that the press can produce (assuming that other factors, such as wages, are held constant). We may say that the press is producing a continuous stream of income for the company. Of course, the efficiency of the press may decline as it gets older. At time t, let $K(t)$ be the annual rate of income from the press. [This means that the press is producing $K(t) \cdot \frac{1}{365}$ dollars per day at time t.] Find a model for the present value of the income generated by the printing press over the next T years, assuming an interest rate r (with interest compounded continuously).

Solution We will divide the T-year period into n small subintervals of time, each of duration Δt years. (If each subinterval were 1 day, for example, Δt would equal $\frac{1}{365}$.)

We now consider the income produced by the printing press during a small time interval from t_{j-1} to t_j. Since Δt is small, the rate $K(t)$ of income production changes by only a negligible amount in that interval and can be considered approximately equal to $K(t_j)$. Since $K(t_j)$ gives an annual rate of income, the actual income produced during the period of Δt years is $K(t_j)\Delta t$. This income will be produced at approximately time t_j (t_j years from $t = 0$), so its present value is

$$[K(t_j)\Delta t]e^{-rt_j}.$$

The present value of the total income produced over the T-year period is the sum of the present values of the amounts produced during each time subinterval; that is,

$$K(t_1)e^{-rt_1}\Delta t + K(t_2)e^{-rt_2}\Delta t + \cdots + K(t_n)e^{-rt_n}\Delta t. \tag{2}$$

As the number of subintervals gets large, the length Δt of each subinterval becomes small, and the sum in (2) approaches the integral

$$\int_0^T K(t)e^{-rt}\,dt. \tag{3}$$

We call this quantity the *present value of the stream of income* produced by the printing press over the period from $t = 0$ to $t = T$ years. (The interest rate r used to compute present value is often called the company's *internal rate of return*.) ■

   The concept of the present value of a continuous stream of income is an important tool in management decision processes involving the selection or replacement of equipment. It is also useful when analyzing various investment opportunities. Even when $K(t)$ is a simple function, the evaluation of the integral in (3) usually requires special techniques, such as integration by parts, as we see in the next example.

EXAMPLE 2   A company estimates that the rate of revenue produced by a machine at time t will be $5000 - 100t$ dollars per year. Find the present value of this continuous stream of income over the next 4 years at a 16% interest rate.

Solution   We use formula (3) with $K(t) = 5000 - 100t$, $T = 4$, and $r = .16$. The present value of this income stream is

$$\int_0^4 (5000 - 100t)e^{-.16t}\,dt.$$

Using integration by parts, with $f(t) = 5000 - 100t$ and $g(t) = e^{-.16t}$, we find that the preceding integral equals

$$(5000 - 100t)\,\frac{1}{-.16}e^{-.16t}\Big|_0^4 - \int_0^4 (-100)\frac{1}{-.16}e^{-.16t}\,dt$$

$$\approx 16{,}090 - \frac{100}{.16}\cdot\frac{1}{-.16}e^{-.16t}\Big|_0^4$$

$$\approx 16{,}090 - 1847 = \$14{,}243. \qquad\blacksquare$$

   A slight modification of the discussion in Example 1 gives the following general result.

Present Value of a Continuous Stream of Income

$$[\text{present value}] = \int_{T_1}^{T_2} K(t)e^{-rt}\,dt,$$

where
   1. $K(t)$ dollars per year is the annual rate of income at time t,
   2. r is the annual interest rate of invested money,
   3. T_1 to T_2 (years) is the time period of the income stream.

EXAMPLE 3   **A demographic model** It has been determined* that in 1940 the population density t miles from the center of New York City was approximately $120e^{-.2t}$ thousand

---

*C. Clark, "Urban Population Densities," *Journal of the Royal Statistical Society*, Series A, 114 (1951), 490–496. See also M. J. White, "On Cumulative Urban Growth and Urban Density Functions," *Journal of Urban Economics*, 4 (1977), 104–112.

people per square mile. Estimate the number of people who lived within 2 miles of the center of New York in 1940.

Solution Choose a fixed line emanating from the center of the city along which to measure distance. Subdivide this line from $t = 0$ to $t = 2$ into a large number of subintervals, each of length Δt. Each subinterval determines a ring. (See Fig. 1.)

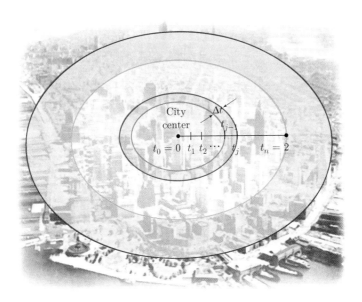

Figure 1. A ring around the city center.

We will estimate the population of each ring and then add these populations together to obtain the total population. Suppose that j is an index ranging from 1 to n. If the outer circle of the jth ring is at a distance t_j from the center, the inner circle of this ring is at a distance $t_{j-1} = t_j - \Delta t$ from the center. The area of the jth ring is

$$\pi t_j^2 - \pi t_{j-1}^2 = \pi t_j^2 - \pi(t_j - \Delta t)^2$$
$$= \pi t_j^2 - \pi[t_j^2 - 2t_j\Delta t + (\Delta t)^2]$$
$$= 2\pi t_j \Delta t - \pi(\Delta t)^2.$$

Assume that Δt is very small. Then $\pi(\Delta t)^2$ is much smaller than $2\pi t_j\Delta t$. Hence the area of this ring is very close to $2\pi t_j\Delta t$.

Within the jth ring, the density of people is about $120e^{-.2t_j}$ thousand people per square mile. So the number of people in this ring is approximately

$$[\text{population density}] \cdot [\text{area of ring}] \approx 120e^{-.2t_j} \cdot 2\pi t_j\Delta t$$
$$= 240\pi t_j e^{-.2t_j}\Delta t.$$

Adding up the populations of all the rings, we obtain a total of

$$240\pi t_1 e^{-.2t_1}\Delta t + 240\pi t_2 e^{-.2t_2}\Delta t + \cdots + 240\pi t_n e^{-.2t_n}\Delta t,$$

which is a Riemann sum for the function $f(t) = 240t\pi e^{-.2t}$ over the interval from $t = 0$ to $t = 2$. This approximation to the population improves as the number n increases. Thus, the number of people (in thousands) who lived within 2 miles of the center of the city was

$$\int_0^2 240\pi t e^{-.2t}\,dt = 240\pi \int_0^2 t e^{-.2t}\,dt.$$

The last integral can be computed using integration by parts to obtain

$$240\pi \int_0^2 te^{-.2t}\, dt = 240\pi \frac{te^{-.2t}}{-.2}\Big|_0^2 - 240\pi \int_0^2 \frac{e^{-.2t}}{-.2}\, dt$$

$$= -2400\pi e^{-.4} + 1200\pi \left(\frac{e^{-.2t}}{-.2}\right)\Big|_0^2$$

$$= -2400\pi e^{-.4} + (-6000\pi e^{-.4} + 6000\pi)$$

$$\approx 1160.$$

Thus, in 1940, approximately 1,160,000 people lived within 2 miles of the center of the city.

An argument analogous to that in Example 3 leads to the following result.

Total Population in a Ring around the City Center

$$[\text{population}] = \int_a^b 2\pi t D(t)\, dt,$$

where

1. $D(t)$ is the density of population (in persons per square mile) at distance t miles from city center,
2. Ring includes all persons who live between a and b miles from the city center.

EXERCISES 9.5

1. Find the present value of a continuous stream of income over 5 years when the rate of income is constant at $35,000 per year and the interest rate is 7%.

2. A continuous stream of income is being produced at the constant rate of $60,000 per year. Find the present value of the income generated during the time from $t = 2$ to $t = 6$ years, with a 6% interest rate.

3. Find the present value of a continuous stream of income over the time from $t = 1$ to $t = 5$ years when the interest rate is 10% and the income is produced at the rate of $12,000 per year.

4. Find the present value of a continuous stream of income over 4 years if the rate of income is $25e^{-.02t}$ thousand dollars per year at time t and the interest rate is 8%.

5. Find the present value of a continuous stream of income over 3 years if the rate of income is $80e^{-.08t}$ thousand dollars per year at time t and the interest rate is 11%.

6. A continuous stream of income is produced at the rate of $20e^{1-.09t}$ thousand dollars per year at time t, and invested money earns 6% interest.
   (a) Write a definite integral that gives the present value of this stream of income over the time from $t = 2$ to $t = 5$ years.
   (b) Compute the present value described in part (a).

7. A growth company is one whose net earnings tend to increase each year. Suppose that the net earnings of a company at time t are being generated at the rate of $30 + 5t$ million dollars per year.
   (a) Write a definite integral that gives the present value of the company's earnings over the next 2 years using a 10% interest rate.
   (b) Compute the present value described in part (a).

8. Find the present value of a stream of earnings generated over the next 2 years at the rate of $50 + 7t$ thousand dollars per year at time t assuming a 10% interest rate.

9. **Demographic Model** In 1900 the population density of Philadelphia t miles from the city center was $120e^{-.65t}$ thousand people per square mile.
   (a) Write a definite integral whose value equals the number of people (in thousands) who lived within 5 miles of the city center.
   (b) Calculate the definite integral in part (a).

10. Use the population density from Exercise 9 to calculate the number of people who lived between 3 and 5 miles of the city center.

11. The population density of Philadelphia in 1940 was given by the function $60e^{-.4t}$. Calculate the number of people who lived within 5 miles of the city center. Sketch the graphs of the population densities for 1900 and 1940 (see Exercise 9) on a common graph. What trend do the graphs exhibit?

12. **Ecological Model** A volcano erupts and spreads lava in all directions. The density of the deposits at a distance t kilometers from the center is $D(t)$ thousand tons per square kilometer, where $D(t) = 11(t^2 + 10)^{-2}$. Find the tonnage of lava deposited between the distances of 1 and 10 kilometers from the center.

13. Suppose that the population density function for a city is $40e^{-.5t}$ thousand people per square mile. Let $P(t)$ be the total population that lives within t miles of the city center, and let Δt be a small positive number.

    (a) Consider the ring about the city whose inner circle is at t miles and outer circle is at $t + \Delta t$ miles. The text shows that the area of this ring is approximately $2\pi t \Delta t$ square miles. Approximately how many people live within this ring? (Your answer will involve t and Δt.)

    (b) What does
    $$\frac{P(t + \Delta t) - P(t)}{\Delta t}$$

    approach as Δt tends to zero?

    (c) What does the quantity $P(5 + \Delta t) - P(5)$ represent?

    (d) Use parts (a) and (c) to find a formula for
    $$\frac{P(t + \Delta t) - P(t)}{\Delta t}$$
    and from that obtain an approximate formula for the derivative $P'(t)$. This formula gives the rate of change of total population with respect to the distance t from the city center.

    (e) Given two positive numbers a and b, find a formula involving a definite integral, for the number of people who live in the city between a miles and b miles of the city center. [*Hint*: Use part (d) and the fundamental theorem of calculus to compute $P(b) - P(a)$.]

9.6 Improper Integrals

In applications of calculus, especially to statistics, it is often necessary to consider the area of a region that extends infinitely far to the right or left along the x-axis. We have drawn several such regions in Fig. 1. Note that the area under a curve that extends infinitely far along the x-axis is not necessarily infinite itself. The areas of such "infinite" regions may be computed using *improper integrals*.

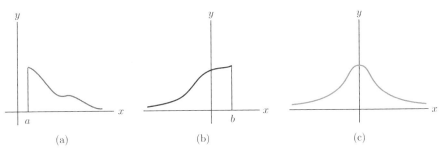

(a)   (b)   (c)

Figure 1

To motivate the idea of an improper integral, let us attempt to calculate the area under the curve $y = 3/x^2$ to the right of $x = 1$. (See Fig. 2.)

First, we compute the area under the graph of this function from $x = 1$ to $x = b$, where b is some number greater than 1. [See Fig. 3(a).] Then we examine how the area increases as we let b get larger. [See Figs. 3(b) and 3(c).] The area from 1 to b is given by

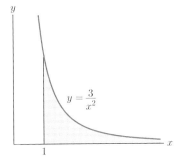

$y = \dfrac{3}{x^2}$

Figure 2

$$\int_1^b \frac{3}{x^2}\, dx = -\frac{3}{x}\Big|_1^b = \left(-\frac{3}{b}\right) - \left(-\frac{3}{1}\right) = 3 - \frac{3}{b}.$$

When b is large, $3/b$ is small and the integral nearly equals 3. That is, the area under the curve from 1 to b nearly equals 3. (See Table 1.) In fact, the area gets arbitrarily close to 3 as b gets larger. Thus it is reasonable to say that the region under the curve $y = 3/x^2$ for $x \geq 1$ has area 3.

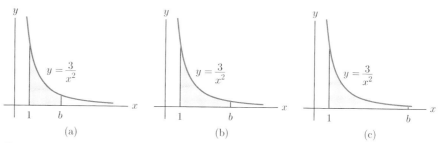

Figure 3

b	$Area = \int_1^b \dfrac{3}{x^2}\, dx = 3 - \dfrac{3}{b}$
TABLE 1 Value of an "Infinitely Long" Area as a Limit	
10	2.7000
100	2.9700
1,000	2.9970
10,000	2.9997

Recall from Chapter 1 that we write $b \to \infty$ as shorthand for "b gets arbitrarily large, without bound." Then, to express the fact that the value of

$$\int_1^b \frac{3}{x^2}\, dx$$

approaches 3 as $b \to \infty$, we write

$$\int_1^\infty \frac{3}{x^2}\, dx = \lim_{b\to\infty} \int_1^b \frac{3}{x^2}\, dx = 3.$$

We call $\int_1^\infty \dfrac{3}{x^2}\, dx$ an *improper* integral because the upper limit of the integral is ∞ (infinity), rather than a finite number.

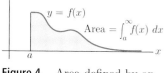

Figure 4. Area defined by an improper integral.

DEFINITION Let a be fixed and suppose that $f(x)$ is a nonnegative function for $x \geq a$. If $\lim\limits_{b\to\infty} \int_a^b f(x)\, dx = L$, we define

$$\int_a^\infty f(x)\, dx = \lim_{b\to\infty} \int_a^b f(x)\, dx = L.$$

We say that the improper integral $\int_a^\infty f(x)\, dx$ is *convergent* and that the region under the curve $y = f(x)$ for $x \geq a$ has area L. (See Fig. 4.)

It is possible to consider improper integrals in which $f(x)$ is both positive and negative. However, we shall consider only nonnegative functions, since this is the case occurring in most applications.

EXAMPLE 1

Find the area under the curve $y = e^{-x}$ for $x \geq 0$. (See Fig. 5.)

Solution   We must calculate the improper integral

$$\int_0^\infty e^{-x}\, dx.$$

We take $b > 0$ and compute

$$\int_0^b e^{-x}\, dx = -e^{-x}\Big|_0^b = (-e^{-b}) - (-e^0) = 1 - e^{-b} = 1 - \frac{1}{e^b}.$$

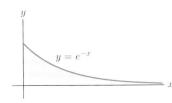

Figure 5

We now consider the limit as $b \to \infty$ and note that $1/e^b$ approaches zero. Thus

$$\int_0^\infty e^{-x}\, dx = \lim_{b\to\infty} \int_0^b e^{-x}\, dx = \lim_{b\to\infty}\left(1 - \frac{1}{e^b}\right) = 1.$$

Therefore, the region in Fig. 5 has area 1.   ■

EXAMPLE 2

Evaluate the improper integral

$$\int_7^\infty \frac{1}{(x-5)^2}\, dx.$$

Solution $\displaystyle \int_7^b \frac{1}{(x-5)^2}\, dx = -\frac{1}{x-5}\Big|_7^b = -\frac{1}{b-5} - \left(-\frac{1}{7-5}\right) = \frac{1}{2} - \frac{1}{b-5}.$

As $b \to \infty$, the fraction $1/(b-5)$ approaches zero, so

$$\int_7^\infty \frac{1}{(x-5)^2}\, dx = \lim_{b\to\infty} \int_7^b \frac{1}{(x-5)^2}\, dx = \lim_{b\to\infty}\left(\frac{1}{2} - \frac{1}{b-5}\right) = \frac{1}{2}.$$ ■

Not every improper integral is convergent. If the value $\int_a^b f(x)\, dx$ does not have a limit as $b \to \infty$, we cannot assign any numerical value to $\int_a^\infty f(x)\, dx$, and we say that the improper integral $\int_a^\infty f(x)\, dx$ is *divergent*.

EXAMPLE 3

Show that

$$\int_1^\infty \frac{1}{\sqrt{x}}\, dx$$

is divergent.

Solution   For $b > 1$ we have

$$\int_1^b \frac{1}{\sqrt{x}}\, dx = 2\sqrt{x}\Big|_1^b = 2\sqrt{b} - 2.$$

As $b \to \infty$, the quantity $2\sqrt{b} - 2$ increases without bound. That is, $2\sqrt{b} - 2$ can be made larger than any specific number. Therefore, $\int_1^b \frac{1}{\sqrt{x}}\, dx$ has no limit as $b \to \infty$, so $\int_1^\infty \frac{1}{\sqrt{x}}\, dx$ is divergent.   ■

In some cases it is necessary to consider improper integrals of the form

$$\int_{-\infty}^{b} f(x)\, dx.$$

Let b be fixed and examine the value of $\int_{a}^{b} f(x)\, dx$ as $a \to -\infty$, that is, as a moves arbitrarily far to the left on the number line. If $\lim_{a \to -\infty} \int_{a}^{b} f(x)\, dx = L$, we say that the improper integral $\int_{-\infty}^{b} f(x)\, dx$ is *convergent*, and we write

$$\int_{-\infty}^{b} f(x)\, dx = L.$$

Otherwise, the improper integral is divergent. An integral of the form $\int_{-\infty}^{b} f(x)\, dx$ may be used to compute the area of a region such as that shown in Fig. 1(b).

EXAMPLE 4

Determine if $\int_{-\infty}^{0} e^{5x}\, dx$ is convergent. If convergent, find its value.

Solution

$$\int_{-\infty}^{0} e^{5x}\, dx = \lim_{a \to -\infty} \int_{a}^{0} e^{5x}\, dx = \lim_{a \to -\infty} \frac{1}{5} e^{5x}\Big|_{a}^{0} = \lim_{a \to -\infty}\left(\frac{1}{5} - \frac{1}{5} e^{5a} \right).$$

As $a \to -\infty$, e^{5a} approaches 0, so $\frac{1}{5} - \frac{1}{5} e^{5a}$ approaches $\frac{1}{5}$. Thus the improper integral converges and has value $\frac{1}{5}$. ∎

Areas of regions that extend infinitely far to the left *and* right, such as the region in Fig. 1(c), are calculated using improper integrals of the form

$$\int_{-\infty}^{\infty} f(x)\, dx.$$

We define such an integral to have the value

$$\int_{-\infty}^{0} f(x)\, dx + \int_{0}^{\infty} f(x)\, dx,$$

provided that both of the latter improper integrals are convergent.

An important area that arises in probability theory is the area under the so-called normal curve, whose equation is

$$y = \frac{1}{\sqrt{2\pi}} e^{-x^2/2}.$$

(See Fig. 6.) It is of fundamental importance for probability theory that this area be 1. In terms of an improper integral, this fact may be written as

$$\int_{-\infty}^{\infty} \frac{1}{\sqrt{2\pi}} e^{-x^2/2}\, dx = 1.$$

The proof of this result is beyond the scope of this book.

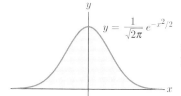

$y = \frac{1}{\sqrt{2\pi}} e^{-x^2/2}$

Figure 6. The standard normal curve.

INCORPORATING TECHNOLOGY

Improper Integrals   Although graphing calculators cannot tell you whether an improper integral converges, you can use the calculator to obtain a reliable indication of the behavior of the integral. Just look at values of $\int_{a}^{b} f(x)\, dx$ as b increases. Figures 7(a) and 7(b), which were created by setting $\mathbf{Y_1} = \mathbf{fnInt(e^\wedge(-X), X, 0, X)}$, give convincing evidence that the value of the improper integral in Example 1 is 1. The final $\mathbf{X}$ in $\mathbf{fnInt(e^\wedge(-X), X, 0, X)}$ is the upper limit of integration, that is, b. ∎

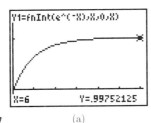

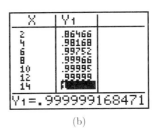

Figure 7   (a)   (b)

Practice Problems 9.6

1. Does $1 - 2(1 - 3b)^{-4}$ approach a limit as $b \to \infty$?

2. Evaluate $\int_1^\infty \frac{x^2}{x^3 + 8}\, dx$.

3. Evaluate $\int_{-\infty}^{-2} \frac{1}{x^4}\, dx$.

EXERCISES 9.6

In Exercises 1–12, determine if the given expression approaches a limit as $b \to \infty$, and find that number when it does.

1. $\dfrac{5}{b}$

2. b^2

3. $-3e^{2b}$

4. $\dfrac{1}{b} + \dfrac{1}{3}$

5. $\dfrac{1}{4} - \dfrac{1}{b^2}$

6. $\dfrac{1}{2}\sqrt{b}$

7. $2 - (b+1)^{-1/2}$

8. $5 - (b-1)^{-1}$

9. $5(b^2 + 3)^{-1}$

10. $4(1 - b^{-3/4})$

11. $e^{-b/2} + 5$

12. $2 - e^{-3b}$

13. Find the area under the graph of $y = 1/x^2$ for $x \geq 2$.

14. Find the area under the graph of $y = (x+1)^{-2}$ for $x \geq 0$.

15. Find the area under the graph of $y = e^{-x/2}$ for $x \geq 0$.

16. Find the area under the graph of $y = 4e^{-4x}$ for $x \geq 0$.

17. Find the area under the graph of $y = (x+1)^{-3/2}$ for $x \geq 3$.

18. Find the area under the graph of $y = (2x + 6)^{-4/3}$ for $x \geq 1$. (See Fig. 8.)

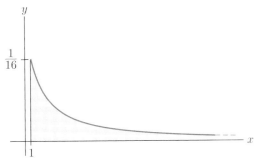

Figure 8

19. Show that the region under the graph of $y = (14x + 18)^{-4/5}$ for $x \geq 1$ cannot be assigned any finite number as its area. (See Fig. 9.)

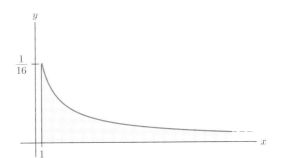

Figure 9

20. Show that the region under the graph of $y = (x-1)^{-1/3}$ for $x \geq 2$ cannot be assigned any finite number as its area.

Evaluate the following improper integrals whenever they are convergent.

21. $\int_1^\infty \frac{1}{x^3}\, dx$

22. $\int_1^\infty \frac{2}{x^{3/2}}\, dx$

23. $\int_0^\infty \frac{1}{(2x+3)^2}\, dx$

24. $\int_0^\infty e^{-3x}\, dx$

25. $\int_0^\infty e^{2x}\, dx$

26. $\int_0^\infty (x^2 + 1)\, dx$

27. $\int_2^\infty \frac{1}{(x-1)^{5/2}}\, dx$

28. $\int_2^\infty e^{2-x}\, dx$

29. $\int_0^\infty .01e^{-.01x}\, dx$

30. $\int_0^\infty \frac{4}{(2x+1)^3}\, dx$

31. $\int_0^\infty 6e^{1-3x}\, dx$

32. $\int_1^\infty e^{-.2x}\, dx$

33. $\int_3^\infty \frac{x^2}{\sqrt{x^3 - 1}}\, dx$

34. $\int_2^\infty \frac{1}{x \ln x}\, dx$

35. $\int_0^\infty xe^{-x^2}\, dx$

36. $\int_0^\infty \frac{x}{x^2 + 1}\, dx$

37. $\displaystyle\int_0^\infty 2x(x^2+1)^{-3/2}\,dx$

38. $\displaystyle\int_1^\infty (5x+1)^{-4}\,dx$

39. $\displaystyle\int_{-\infty}^0 e^{4x}\,dx$

40. $\displaystyle\int_{-\infty}^0 \frac{8}{(x-5)^2}\,dx$

41. $\displaystyle\int_{-\infty}^0 \frac{6}{(1-3x)^2}\,dx$

42. $\displaystyle\int_{-\infty}^0 \frac{1}{\sqrt{4-x}}\,dx$

43. $\displaystyle\int_0^\infty \frac{e^{-x}}{(e^{-x}+2)^2}\,dx$

44. $\displaystyle\int_{-\infty}^\infty \frac{e^{-x}}{(e^{-x}+2)^2}\,dx$

45. If $k>0$, show that $\displaystyle\int_0^\infty ke^{-kx}\,dx=1$.

46. If $k>0$, show that $\displaystyle\int_1^\infty \frac{k}{x^{k+1}}\,dx=1$.

47. If $k>0$, show that $\displaystyle\int_e^\infty \frac{k}{x(\ln x)^{k+1}}\,dx=1$.

The capital value of an asset such as a machine is sometimes defined as the present value of all future net earnings. (See Section 9.5.) The actual lifetime of the asset may not be known, and since some assets may last indefinitely, the capital value of the asset may be written in the form

$$[\text{capital value}]=\int_0^\infty K(t)e^{-rt}\,dt,$$

where r is the annual rate of interest compounded continuously.

48. Find the capital value of an asset that generates income at the rate of $5000 per year, assuming an interest rate of 10%.

49. Construct a formula for the capital value of a rental property that will generate a fixed income at the rate of K dollars per year indefinitely, assuming an annual interest rate of r.

50. Suppose that a large farm with a known reservoir of gas beneath the ground sells the gas rights to a company for a guaranteed payment at the rate of $10{,}000e^{.04t}$ dollars per year. Find the present value of this perpetual stream of income, assuming an interest rate of 12%, compounded continuously.

Solutions to Practice Problems 9.6

1. The expression $1-2(1-3b)^{-4}$ may also be written in the form
$$1-\frac{2}{(1-3b)^4}.$$
When b is large, $(1-3b)^4$ is very large, so $2/(1-3b)^4$ is very small. Thus $1-2(1-3b)^{-4}$ approaches 1 as $b\to\infty$.

2. The first step is to find an antiderivative of $x^2/(x^3+8)$. Using the substitution $u=x^3+8$, $du=3x^2\,dx$, we obtain
$$\int\frac{x^2}{x^3+8}\,dx=\frac13\int\frac1u\,du$$
$$=\frac13\ln|u|+C$$
$$=\frac13\ln|x^3+8|+C.$$
Now
$$\int_1^b\frac{x^2}{x^3+8}\,dx=\frac13\ln|x^3+8|\,\Big|_1^b$$
$$=\frac13\ln(b^3+8)-\frac13\ln 9.$$
Finally, we examine what happens as $b\to\infty$. Certainly, b^3+8 gets arbitrarily large, so $\ln(b^3+8)$ must

also get arbitrarily large. Hence
$$\int_1^b\frac{x^2}{x^3+8}\,dx$$
has no limit as $b\to\infty$; so the improper integral
$$\int_1^\infty\frac{x^2}{x^3+8}\,dx$$
is divergent.

3. $\displaystyle\int_a^{-2}\frac{1}{x^4}\,dx=\int_a^{-2}x^{-4}\,dx$
$$=\frac{x^{-3}}{-3}\Big|_a^{-2}=\frac{1}{-3x^3}\Big|_a^{-2}$$
$$=\frac{1}{-3(-2)^3}-\left(\frac{1}{-3\cdot a^3}\right)$$
$$=\frac{1}{24}+\frac{1}{3a^3}$$
$$\int_{-\infty}^{-2}\frac{1}{x^4}\,dx=\lim_{a\to-\infty}\int_a^{-2}\frac{1}{x^4}\,dx$$
$$=\lim_{a\to-\infty}\left(\frac{1}{24}+\frac{1}{3a^3}\right)=\frac{1}{24}$$

REVIEW OF FUNDAMENTAL CONCEPTS

1. Describe integration by substitution in your own words.
2. Describe integration by parts in your own words.
3. Describe the change of limits rule for the integration by substitution of a definite integral.
4. State the formula for the integration by parts of a definite integral.
5. State the midpoint rule. (Include the meaning of all symbols used.)
6. State the trapezoidal rule. (Include the meaning of all symbols used.)

7. Explain the formula $S = \dfrac{2M + T}{3}$.
8. State the error of approximation theorem for each of the three approximation rules.
9. State the formula for each of the following quantities:
   (a) Present value of a continuous stream of income
   (b) Total population in a ring around the center of a city
10. How do you determine whether an improper integral is convergent?

SUPPLEMENTARY EXERCISES

Determine the following indefinite integrals:

1. $\displaystyle\int x \sin 3x^2 \, dx$

2. $\displaystyle\int \sqrt{2x + 1} \, dx$

3. $\displaystyle\int x(1 - 3x^2)^5 \, dx$

4. $\displaystyle\int \frac{(\ln x)^5}{x} \, dx$

5. $\displaystyle\int \frac{(\ln x)^2}{x} \, dx$

6. $\displaystyle\int \frac{1}{\sqrt{4x + 3}} \, dx$

7. $\displaystyle\int x\sqrt{4 - x^2} \, dx$

8. $\displaystyle\int x \sin 3x \, dx$

9. $\displaystyle\int x^2 e^{-x^3} \, dx$

10. $\displaystyle\int \frac{x \ln(x^2 + 1)}{x^2 + 1} \, dx$

11. $\displaystyle\int x^2 \cos 3x \, dx$

12. $\displaystyle\int \frac{\ln(\ln x)}{x \ln x} \, dx$

13. $\displaystyle\int \ln x^2 \, dx$

14. $\displaystyle\int x\sqrt{x + 1} \, dx$

15. $\displaystyle\int \frac{x}{\sqrt{3x - 1}} \, dx$

16. $\displaystyle\int x^2 \ln x^2 \, dx$

17. $\displaystyle\int \frac{x}{(1 - x)^5} \, dx$

18. $\displaystyle\int x(\ln x)^2 \, dx$

In Exercises 19–36, decide whether integration by parts or a substitution should be used to compute the indefinite integral. If substitution, indicate the substitution to be made. If by parts, indicate the functions $f(x)$ and $g(x)$ to be used in formula (1) of Section 9.2.

19. $\displaystyle\int xe^{2x} \, dx$

20. $\displaystyle\int (x - 3)e^{-x} \, dx$

21. $\displaystyle\int (x + 1)^{-1/2} e^{\sqrt{x+1}} \, dx$

22. $\displaystyle\int x^2 \sin(x^3 - 1) \, dx$

23. $\displaystyle\int \frac{x - 2x^3}{x^4 - x^2 + 4} \, dx$

24. $\displaystyle\int \ln\sqrt{5 - x} \, dx$

25. $\displaystyle\int e^{-x}(3x - 1)^2 \, dx$

26. $\displaystyle\int xe^{3 - x^2} \, dx$

27. $\displaystyle\int (500 - 4x)e^{-x/2} \, dx$

28. $\displaystyle\int x^{5/2} \ln x \, dx$

29. $\displaystyle\int \sqrt{x + 2} \ln(x + 2) \, dx$

30. $\displaystyle\int (x + 1)^2 e^{3x} \, dx$

31. $\displaystyle\int (x + 3)e^{x^2 + 6x} \, dx$

32. $\displaystyle\int \sin^2 x \cos x \, dx$

33. $\displaystyle\int x \cos(x^2 - 9) \, dx$

34. $\displaystyle\int (3 - x) \sin 3x \, dx$

35. $\displaystyle\int \frac{2 - x^2}{x^3 - 6x} \, dx$

36. $\displaystyle\int \frac{1}{x(\ln x)^{3/2}} \, dx$

Evaluate the following definite integrals:

37. $\displaystyle\int_0^1 \frac{2x}{(x^2 + 1)^3} \, dx$

38. $\displaystyle\int_0^{\pi/2} x \sin 8x \, dx$

39. $\displaystyle\int_0^2 xe^{-(1/2)x^2} \, dx$

40. $\displaystyle\int_{1/2}^1 \frac{\ln(2x + 3)}{2x + 3} \, dx$

41. $\displaystyle\int_1^2 xe^{-2x} \, dx$

42. $\displaystyle\int_1^2 x^{-3/2} \ln x \, dx$

Approximate the following definite integrals by the midpoint rule, the trapezoidal rule, and Simpson's rule.

43. $\displaystyle\int_1^9 \frac{1}{\sqrt{x}} \, dx; \; n = 4$

44. $\displaystyle\int_0^{10} e^{\sqrt{x}} \, dx; \; n = 5$

45. $\displaystyle\int_1^4 \frac{e^x}{x + 1} \, dx; \; n = 5$

46. $\displaystyle\int_{-1}^1 \frac{1}{1 + x^2} \, dx; \; n = 5$

Evaluate the following improper integrals whenever they are convergent.

47. $\displaystyle\int_0^\infty e^{6 - 3x} \, dx$

48. $\displaystyle\int_1^\infty x^{-2/3} \, dx$

49. $\int_1^\infty \dfrac{x+2}{x^2+4x-2}\,dx$ **50.** $\int_0^\infty x^2 e^{-x^3}\,dx$

51. $\int_{-1}^\infty (x+3)^{-5/4}\,dx$ **52.** $\int_{-\infty}^0 \dfrac{8}{(5-2x)^3}\,dx$

53. It can be shown that $\lim\limits_{b\to\infty} be^{-b}=0$. Use this fact to compute $\int_1^\infty xe^{-x}\,dx$.

54. Let k be a positive number. It can be shown that $\lim\limits_{b\to\infty} be^{-kb}=0$. Use this fact to compute $\int_0^\infty xe^{-kx}\,dx$.

55. Find the present value of a continuous stream of income over the next 4 years, where the rate of income is $50e^{-.08t}$ thousand dollars per year at time t, and the interest rate is 12%.

56. Suppose that t miles from the center of a certain city the property tax revenue is approximately $R(t)$ thousand dollars per square mile, where $R(t)=50e^{-t/20}$. Use this model to predict the total property tax revenue that will be generated by property within 10 miles of the city center.

57. Suppose that a machine requires daily maintenance, and let $M(t)$ be the *annual* rate of maintenance expense at time t. Suppose that the interval $0\le t\le 2$ is divided into n subintervals, with endpoints $t_0=0, t_1,\ldots, t_n=2$.

(a) Give a Riemann sum that approximates the total maintenance expense over the next 2 years. Then write the integral that the Riemann sum approximates for large values of n.

(b) Give a Riemann sum that approximates the present value of the total maintenance expense over the next 2 years using a 10% annual interest rate compounded continuously. Then write the integral that the Riemann sum approximates for large values of n.

58. The *capitalized cost* of an asset is the total of the original cost and the present value of all future "renewals" or replacements. This concept is useful, for example, when selecting equipment that is manufactured by several different companies. Suppose that a corporation computes the present value of future expenditures using an annual interest rate r, with continuous compounding of interest. Assume that the original cost of an asset is $80,000 and the annual renewal expense will be $50,000, spread more or less evenly throughout each year, for a large but indefinite number of years. Find a formula involving an integral that gives the capitalized cost of the asset.

DIFFERENTIAL EQUATIONS

A *differential equation* is an equation in which derivatives of an unknown function $y = f(t)$ occur. Examples of such equations are

$$y' = 6t + 3, \quad y' = 6y, \quad y'' = 3y' - x, \quad \text{and} \quad y' + 3y + t = 0.$$

As we shall see, many physical processes can be described by differential equations. In this chapter we explore some topics in differential equations and use our resulting knowledge to study problems from many different fields, including business, genetics, and ecology.

10.1 Solutions of Differential Equations

A differential equation is an equation involving an unknown function y and one or more of the derivatives y', y'', y''', and so on. Suppose that y is a function of the variable t. A *solution* of a differential equation is any function $f(t)$ such that the differential equation becomes a true statement when y is replaced by $f(t)$, y' by $f'(t)$, y'' by $f''(t)$, and so forth.

EXAMPLE 1   Show that the function $f(t) = 5e^{-2t}$ is a solution of the differential equation

$$y' + 2y = 0. \tag{1}$$

Solution   The differential equation (1) says that $y' + 2y$ equals zero for all values of t. We must show that this result holds if y is replaced by $5e^{-2t}$ and y' is replaced by $(5e^{-2t})' = -10e^{-2t}$. Now

$$\overbrace{(5e^{-2t})'}^{y'} + 2\overbrace{(5e^{-2t})}^{y} = -10e^{-2t} + 10e^{-2t} = 0.$$

Therefore, $y = 5e^{-2t}$ is a solution of the differential equation (1).   ■

EXAMPLE 2   Show that the function $f(t) = \frac{1}{9}t + \sin 3t$ is a solution of the differential equation

$$y'' + 9y = t. \tag{2}$$

Solution   If $f(t) = \frac{1}{9}t + \sin 3t$, then

$$f'(t) = \frac{1}{9} + 3\cos 3t,$$

$$f''(t) = -9\sin 3t.$$

Substituting $f(t)$ for y and $f''(t)$ for y'' in the left side of (2), we obtain

$$\overbrace{-9\sin 3t}^{y''} + 9\overbrace{\left(\frac{1}{9}t + \sin 3t\right)}^{y} = -9\sin 3t + t + 9\sin 3t = t.$$

Therefore, $y'' + 9y = t$ if $y = \frac{1}{9}t + \sin 3t$, and hence $y = \frac{1}{9}t + \sin 3t$ is a solution to $y'' + 9y = t$.   ■

The differential equation in Example 1 is said to be of *first order*, since it involves the first derivative of the unknown function y. The differential equation in Example 2 is of *second order*, since it involves the second derivative of y. In general, the *order* of a differential equation is the order of the highest derivative that appears in the equation.

The process of determining all the functions that are solutions of a differential equation is called *solving the differential equation*. The process of antidifferentiation amounts to solving a simple type of differential equation. For example, a solution of the differential equation

$$y' = 3t^2 - 4 \tag{3}$$

is a function y whose derivative is $3t^2 - 4$. Thus, solving (3) consists of finding all antiderivatives of $3t^2 - 4$. Clearly, y must be of the form $y = t^3 - 4t + C$, where C is a constant. The solutions of (3) corresponding to several values of C are sketched in Fig. 1. Each graph is called a *solution curve*.

We encountered differential equations such as

$$y' = 2y \tag{4}$$

in our discussion of exponential functions. Unlike (3), equation (4) does not give a specific formula for y', but instead describes a property of y': y' is proportional to y (with 2 as the constant of proportionality). At the moment, the only way we can "solve" (4) is simply to know in advance what the solutions are. Recall from Chapter 4 that the solutions of (4) have the form $y = Ce^{2t}$ for any constant C. Some typical solutions of (4) are sketched in Fig. 2. In the next section we shall discuss a method for solving a class of differential equations that includes both (3) and (4) as special cases.

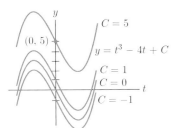

Figure 1.   Typical solutions of $y' = 3t^2 - 4$.

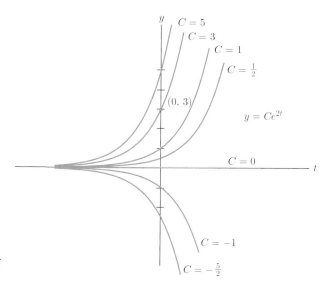

Figure 2. Typical solutions of $y' = 2y$.

Figures 1 and 2 illustrate two important differences between differential equations and algebraic equations (such as $ax^2 + bx + c = 0$). First, a solution of a differential equation is a *function* rather than a number. Second, a differential equation usually has infinitely many solutions.

Sometimes we want to find a particular solution that satisfies certain additional conditions called *initial conditions*. Initial conditions specify the values of a solution and a certain number of its derivatives at some specific value of t, often $t = 0$. If the solution to a differential equation is $y = f(t)$, we often write $y(0)$ for $f(0)$, $y'(0)$ for $f'(0)$, and so on. The problem of determining a solution of a differential equation that satisfies given initial conditions is called an *initial-value problem*.

EXAMPLE 3

(a) Solve the initial value problem $y' = 3t^2 - 4$, $y(0) = 5$.

(b) Solve the initial value problem $y' = 2y$, $y(0) = 3$.

Solution (a) We have already noted that the general solution of $y' = 3t^2 - 4$ is $f(t) = t^3 - 4t + C$. We want the particular solution that satisfies $f(0) = 5$. Geometrically, we are looking for the curve in Fig. 1 that passes through the point $(0, 5)$. Using the general formula for $f(t)$, we have

$$5 = f(0) = (0)^3 - 4(0) + C = C$$
$$C = 5.$$

Thus $f(t) = t^3 - 4t + 5$ is the desired solution.

(b) The general solution of $y' = 2y$ is $y = Ce^{2t}$. The condition $y(0) = 3$ means that y must be 3 when $t = 0$; that is, the point $(0, 3)$ must be on the graph of the solution to $y' = 2y$. (See Fig. 2.) We have

$$3 = y(0) = Ce^{2(0)} = C \cdot 1 = C$$
$$C = 3.$$

Thus $y = 3e^{2t}$ is the desired solution. ∎

A constant function that satisfies a differential equation is called a *constant solution* of the differential equation. Constant solutions occur in many of the applied problems considered later in the chapter.

EXAMPLE 4   Find a constant solution of $y' = 3y - 12$.

Solution   Let $f(t) = c$ for all t. Then $f'(t)$ is zero for all t. If $f(t)$ satisfies the differential equation

$$f'(t) = 3 \cdot f(t) - 12,$$

then

$$0 = 3 \cdot c - 12,$$

and so $c = 4$. This is the only possible value for a constant solution. Substitution shows that the function $f(t) = 4$ is indeed a solution of the differential equation. ∎

Modeling with Differential Equations

Equations describing conditions in a physical process are often referred to as *mathematical models* and discovering these equations is called *modeling*. In our next example, we show how we can use a differential equation to model a physical process. The example should be studied carefully, for it contains the key to understanding many similar problems that will appear in exercises and in later sections.

EXAMPLE 5   **Newton's law of cooling**   Suppose that a red-hot steel rod is plunged into a bath of cool water. Let $f(t)$ be the temperature of the rod at time t, and suppose that the water is maintained at a constant temperature of $10°$C. According to Newton's law of cooling, the rate of change of $f(t)$ is proportional to the difference between the two temperatures $10°$ and $f(t)$. Find a differential equation that describes this physical law.

Solution   The two key ideas are "rate of change" and "proportional." The rate of change of $f(t)$ is the derivative $f'(t)$. Since this is proportional to the difference $10 - f(t)$, there exists a constant k such that

$$f'(t) = k[10 - f(t)]. \tag{5}$$

The term "proportional" does not tell us whether k is positive or negative (or zero). We must decide this, if possible, from the context of the problem. In the present situation, the steel rod is hotter than the water, so $10 - f(t)$ is negative. Also, $f(t)$ will decrease as time passes, so $f'(t)$ should be negative. Thus, to make $f'(t)$ negative in equation (5), k must be a positive number. From (5) we see that $y = f(t)$ satisfies a differential equation of the form

$$y' = k(10 - y), \quad k \text{ a positive constant.} \qquad ∎$$

EXAMPLE 6   Suppose that the constant of proportionality in Example 5 is $k = .2$ and time is measured in seconds. How fast is the temperature of the steel rod changing when the temperature is $110°$C?

Solution   The relationship between the temperature and the rate of change of the temperature is given by the differential equation $y' = .2(10 - y)$, where $y = f(t)$ is the temperature after t seconds. When $y = 110$, the rate of change is

$$y' = .2(10 - 110) = .2(-100) = -20.$$

The temperature is decreasing at the rate of 20 degrees per second. ∎

The differential equation in Examples 5 and 6 is a special case of the differential equation

$$y' = k(M - y).$$

Differential equations of this type describe not only cooling, but also many important applications in economics, medicine, population dynamics, and engineering. Some of these applications are discussed in the exercises and in Sections 10.4 and 10.6.

Geometric Meaning of a Differential Equation: Slope Fields

As observed earlier, a differential equation such as

$$y' = t - y \qquad (6)$$

does not give a specific formula for y' in terms of the variable t; instead, it describes a property of y'. The key to understanding this property is to remember the geometric interpretation of the derivative as a slope formula. So, if $y = f(t)$ is a solution of (6) and (t, y) is a point on the graph of this solution, equation (6) is telling us that the slope of the graph at the point (t, y) (that is, $y'(t)$) is just $t - y$. For example, if a solution curve goes through the point $(1, 2)$, without knowing the formula for this solution, we can say that the slope of the solution through the point $(1, 2)$ is

$$y'(1) = 1 - 2 = -1.$$

This information gives us the direction of the solution curve through the point $(1, 2)$. Figure 3 shows a portion of the solution curve through the point $(1, 2)$, along with the tangent line at that point. Note how the slope of the tangent lines matches with the value $y'(1) = -1$.

Imagine now repeating the previous construction of the tangent line at many points in the ty-plane, not just the point $(1, 2)$. This laborious process is usually done with the help of a computer or a graphing calculator that can generate a collection of small line segments, called a *slope field* or *direction field* of the differential equation. [See Fig. 4(a).] Since each line segment in the slope field is tangent to a solution curve, we can visualize a solution curve by following the flow of the slope field. [See Fig. 4(b).]

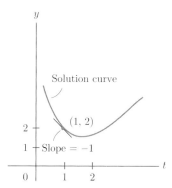

Figure 3. Solution curve of $y' = t - y$ and a tangent line through the point $(1, 2)$.

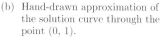

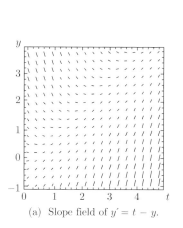

(a) Slope field of $y' = t - y$.

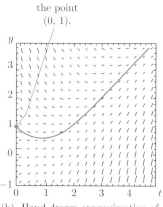

(b) Hand-drawn approximation of the solution curve through the point $(0, 1)$.

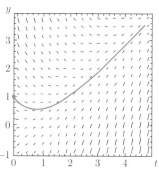

(c) Exact portion of the solution curve through $(0, 1)$.

Figure 4

EXAMPLE 7   Use the slope field of the differential equation $y' = t - y$, shown in Fig. 4(a), to draw by hand a portion of the solution curve that passes through the point $(0, 1)$.

Solution   We are given one point on the solution curve and the slope field. To draw the desired curve, we start at the point $(0, 1)$ and trace a curve in the ty-plane tangent to the line segments in the slope field. The result is the curve shown in Fig. 4(b). Figure 4(c) shows a portion of the exact solution curve for the purpose of comparison. As you can see, the hand-drawn curve in Fig. 4(b) is a pretty good approximation of the exact solution curve. ∎

In general, we can construct a slope field for any first-order differential equation of the form

$$y' = g(t, y), \tag{7}$$

where $g(t, y)$ is a function of t and y. The idea is that at any given point (a, b) of a solution curve the slope $y'(a)$ is given by $g(a, b)$.

As our next example shows, slope fields are useful in deriving qualitative properties of solutions.

EXAMPLE 8   Let $f(t)$ denote the number of people who have contracted a certain strain of flu after t days. The function $f(t)$ satisfies the initial-value problem $y' = .0002y(5000 - y)$, $y(0) = 1000$. A slope field of the differential equation is shown in Fig. 5(a). Based on the slope field, do you think that the number of infected people will ever exceed 5000?

Solution   The initial condition $f(0) = 1000$ tells us that the point $(0, 1000)$ is on the graph of the solution curve $y = f(t)$. Starting at this point in the ty-plane and tracing a curve tangent to the line segments in the slope field, we obtain an approximation to a portion of the solution curve through the point $(0, 1000)$. [See Fig. 5(b).] According to this curve, we can conclude that the solution curve will come very close to but will not exceed the value 5000. Hence the number of infected people will not exceed 5000. ∎

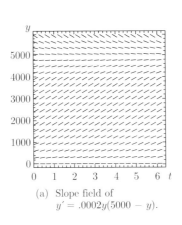

(a) Slope field of
$y' = .0002y(5000 - y)$.

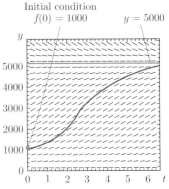

(b) Slope field and hand-drawn approximation of the solution of $y' = .0002y(5000 - y)$, $y(0) = 1000$

Figure 5

The differential equation in Example 8 is a special case of the logistic differential equation, which arises frequently in the study of population growth in a restricted environment. This important equation will be studied in greater detail in later sections.

Throughout this section we have assumed that our solution functions y are functions of the variable t, which in applications usually stands for time. In most of this chapter we will continue to use the variable t. However, if we use another variable occasionally, such as x, we will make the variable explicit by writing $\frac{dy}{dx}$ instead of y'.

INCORPORATING TECHNOLOGY

Slope Fields Drawing slope fields with your TI-83/84 Plus calculator requires a program that is freely available from the Texas Instruments website education.ti.com. Point your web browser to education.ti.com and search for SLPFLD.8xp. Download this file to your computer, connect your calculator to your computer, and use the TI-Connect© program to transfer the file to the calculator.

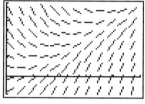

To demonstrate the usage of the SLPFLD prograqm, we consider the differential equation $y' = t - y$. The SLPFLD program requires that the independent variable be X (rather than t), so we begin by pressing $\boxed{Y=}$ and setting $Y_1 = X - Y$. Now return to the home screen and press $\boxed{\text{PRGM}}$. From the **EXEC** menu, scroll down to **SLPFLD** and press $\boxed{\text{ENTER}}$. You will then see **prgmSLPFLD** on the home screen. Press $\boxed{\text{ENTER}}$. Figure 6 shows the result. ∎

Figure 6

Practice Problems 10.1

1. Show that any function of the form $y = Ae^{t^3/3}$, where A is a constant, is a solution of the differential equation $y' - t^2 y = 0$.

2. If the function $f(t)$ is a solution of the initial-value problem $y' = (t+2)y$, $y(0) = 3$, find $f(0)$ and $f'(0)$.

3. Let $f(t)$ be the size of a population after t days. Suppose that $y = f(t)$ satisfies $y' = .06y$, $y(0) = 1000$. Describe this initial-value problem in words. (Include the phrase "is proportional to.") How fast is the population growing when it contains 3000 members?

EXERCISES 10.1

1. Show that the function $f(t) = \frac{3}{2}e^{t^2} - \frac{1}{2}$ is a solution of the differential equation $y' - 2ty = t$.

2. Show that the function $f(t) = t^2 - \frac{1}{2}$ is a solution of the differential equation $(y')^2 - 4y = 2$.

3. Show that the function $f(t) = (e^{-t} + 1)^{-1}$ satisfies $y' + y^2 = y$, $y(0) = \frac{1}{2}$.

4. Show that the function $f(t) = 5e^{2t}$ satisfies $y'' - 3y' + 2y = 0$, $y(0) = 5$, $y'(0) = 10$.

In Exercises 5 and 6, state the order of the differential equation and verify that the given function is a solution.

5. $(1 - t^2)y'' - 2ty' + 2y = 0$, $y(t) = t$

6. $(1 - t^2)y'' - 2ty' + 6y = 0$, $y(t) = \frac{1}{2}(3t^2 - 1)$

7. Is the constant function $f(t) = 3$ a solution of the differential equation $y' = 6 - 2y$?

8. Is the constant function $f(t) = -4$ a solution of the differential equation $y' = t^2(y + 4)$?

9. Find a constant solution of $y' = t^2 y - 5t^2$.

10. Find two constant solutions of $y' = 4y(y - 7)$.

11. If the function $f(t)$ is a solution of the initial-value problem $y' = 2y - 3$, $y(0) = 4$, find $f(0)$ and $f'(0)$.

12. If the function $f(t)$ is a solution of the initial-value problem $y' = e^t + y$, $y(0) = 0$, find $f(0)$ and $f'(0)$.

13. Let $y = v(t)$ be the downward speed (in feet per second) of a skydiver after t seconds of free fall. This function satisfies the differential equation $y' = .2(160 - y)$, $y(0) = 0$. What is the skydiver's acceleration when her downward speed is 60 feet per second? [*Note*: Acceleration is the derivative of speed.]

14. A lake is stocked with 100 fish. Let $f(t)$ be the number of fish after t months, and suppose that $y = f(t)$ satisfies the differential equation $y' = .0004y(1000 - y)$. Figure 7 shows the graph of the solution to this differential equation. The graph is asymptotic to the line $y = 1000$, the maximum number of fish that the lake can support. How fast is the fish population growing when it reaches one-half of its maximum population?

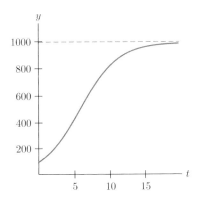

Figure 7. Growth of a fish population.

15. Let $f(t)$ be the balance in a savings account at the end of t years, and suppose that $y = f(t)$ satisfies the differential equation $y' = .05y - 10{,}000$.

(a) If after 1 year the balance is \$150,000, is it increasing or decreasing at that time? At what rate is it increasing or decreasing at that time?

(b) Write the differential equation in the form $y' = k(y - M)$.

(c) Describe this differential equation in words.

16. Let $f(t)$ be the balance in a savings account at the end of t years. Suppose that $y = f(t)$ satisfies the differential equation $y' = .04y + 2000$.

(a) If after 1 year the balance is \$10,000, is it increasing or decreasing at that time? At what rate is it increasing or decreasing at that time?

(b) Write the differential equation in the form $y' = k(y + M)$.

(c) Describe this differential equation in words.

17. A certain piece of news is being broadcast to a potential audience of 200,000 people. Let $f(t)$ be the number of people who have heard the news after t hours. Suppose that $y = f(t)$ satisfies

$$y' = .07(200{,}000 - y), \qquad y(0) = 10.$$

Describe this initial-value problem in words.

18. Let $f(t)$ be the size of a paramecium population after t days. Suppose that $y = f(t)$ satisfies the differential equation

$$y' = .003y(500 - y), \qquad y(0) = 20.$$

Describe this initial-value problem in words.

19. Let $f(t)$ denote the amount of capital invested by a certain business firm at time t. The rate of change of invested capital, $f'(t)$, is sometimes called the *rate of net investment*. The management of the firm decides that the optimum level of investment should be C dollars and that, at any time, the rate of net investment should be proportional to the difference between C and the total capital invested. Construct a differential equation that describes this situation.

20. A cool object is placed in a room that is maintained at a constant temperature of $20°C$. The rate at which the temperature of the object rises is proportional to the difference between the room temperature and the temperature of the object. Let $y = f(t)$ be the temperature of the object at time t, and give a differential equation that describes the rate of change of $f(t)$.

21. Carbon Dioxide Diffusion in Lungs during Breath Holding When the breath is held, carbon dioxide (CO_2) diffuses from the blood into the lungs at a steadily decreasing rate. Let P_0 and P_b denote the pressure of CO_2 in the lungs, respectively, in the blood at the moment when the breath is held. Suppose that P_b is constant during breath holding, and let $P(t)$ denote the pressure of CO_2 in the lungs at time $t > 0$. Experiments show that the rate of change of $P(t)$ is proportional to the difference between the two pressures $P(t)$ and P_b. Find an initial-value problem that describes the diffusion of CO_2 in the lungs during breath holding.

22. The slope field in Fig. 4(a) suggests that the solution curve of the differential equation $y' = t - y$ through the point $(0, -1)$ is a straight line.

(a) Assuming that this is true, find the equation of the line. [*Hint*: Use the differential equation to get the slope of the line through the point $(0, -1)$.]

(b) Verify that the function that you found in part (a) is a solution by plugging its formula into the differential equation.

23. Verify that the function $f(t) = 2e^{-t} + t - 1$ is a solution of the initial-value problem $y' = t - y$, $y(0) = 1$. [This is the function shown in Fig. 4(c). In Section 10.3, you will learn how to derive this solution.]

24. On the slope field in Fig. 5(a) or a copy of it, draw the solution of the initial-value problem $y' = .0002y(5000 - y)$, $y(0) = 500$.

25. The health officials that studied the flu epidemic in Example 8 made an error in counting the initial number of infected people. They are now claiming that $f(t)$ (the number of infected people after t days) is a solution of the initial-value problem $y' = .0002y(5000 - y)$, $y(0) = 1500$. Under this new assumption, can $f(t)$ exceed 5000? [*Hint*: Since the differential equation is the same as the one in Example 8, you can use the slope field in Fig. 5(a) to answer the question.]

26. On the slope field in Fig. 4(a) or a copy of it, draw an approximation of a portion of the solution curve of the differential equation $y' = t - y$ that goes through the point $(0, 2)$. In your opinion, based on the slope field, can this solution pass through the point $(.5, 2.2)$?

27. Figure 8 shows a slope field of the differential equation $y' = 2y(1 - y)$. With the help of this figure, determine the constant solutions, if any, of the differential equation. Verify your answer by substituting back into the equation.

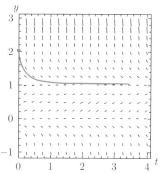

Figure 8. Slope field of
$y' = 2y(1 - y)$.

28. Figure 8 shows a portion of the solution curve of the differential equation $y' = 2y(1 - y)$ through the point $(0, 2)$. On Fig. 8 or a copy of it, draw an approximation of the solution curve of the differential equation $y' = 2y(1 - y)$ through the point $(0, 3)$. Use the slope field to guide your graph.

29. If $y_0 > 1$, is the solution $y = f(t)$ of the initial-value problem $y' = 2y(1 - y)$, $y(0) = y_0$, decreasing for all $t > 0$? Answer this question based on the slope field

shown in Fig. 8.

30. Answer the question in Exercise 29 by using the differential equation to determine the sign of $f'(t)$.

Technology Exercises

31. Consider the differential equation $y' = .2(10 - y)$ from Example 6. If the initial temperature of the steel rod is $510°$, the function $f(t) = 10 + 500e^{-.2t}$ is the solution of the differential equation.

    (a) Graph the function in the window $[0, 30]$ by $[-75, 550]$.

    (b) In the home screen, compute $.2(10 - f(5))$ and compare this value with $f'(5)$.

32. The function $f(t) = \dfrac{5000}{1 + 49e^{-t}}$ is the solution of the differential equation $y' = .0002y(5000 - y)$ from Example 8.

    (a) Graph the function in the window $[0, 10]$ by $[-750, 5750]$

    (b) In the home screen, compute $.0002f(3)(5000 - f(3))$ and compare this value with $f'(3)$.

Solutions to Practice Problems 10.1

1. If $y = Ae^{t^3/3}$, then

$$\overbrace{(Ae^{t^3/3})'}^{y'} - t^2 \overbrace{(Ae^{t^3/3})}^{y} = At^2e^{t^3/3} - t^2 Ae^{t^3/3} = 0.$$

Therefore, $y' - t^2y = 0$ if $y = Ae^{t^3/3}$.

2. The initial condition $y(0) = 3$ says that $f(0) = 3$. Since $f(t)$ is a solution to $y' = (t + 2)y$,

$$f'(t) = (t + 2)f(t)$$

and hence

$$f'(0) = (0 + 2)f(0) = 2 \cdot 3 = 6.$$

3. Initially the population has 1000 members. At any time the rate of growth of the population is proportional to the size of the population at that time, and the constant of proportionality is .06. When $y = 3000$,

$$y' = .06y = .06 \cdot 3000 = 180.$$

Therefore, the population is growing at the rate of 180 members per day.

10.2 Separation of Variables

Here we describe a technique for solving an important class of differential equations, those of the form

$$y' = p(t)q(y),$$

where $p(t)$ is a function of t only and $q(y)$ is a function of y only. Two equations of this type are

$$y' = \frac{3t^2}{y^2} \qquad \left[p(t) = 3t^2, \, q(y) = \frac{1}{y^2} \right], \tag{1}$$

$$y' = e^{-y}(2t + 1) \qquad \left[p(t) = 2t + 1, \, q(y) = e^{-y} \right]. \tag{2}$$

The main feature of such equations is that we may *separate the variables*; that is, we may rewrite the equations so that y occurs only on one side of the equation and t on the other. For example, if we multiply both sides of equation (1) by y^2, the equation becomes

$$y^2 y' = 3t^2;$$

if we multiply both sides of equation (2) by e^y, the equation becomes

$$e^y y' = 2t + 1.$$

It should be pointed out that the differential equation

$$y' = 3t^2 - 4$$

is of the preceding type. Here $p(t) = 3t^2 - 4$ and $q(y) = 1$. The variables are already separated, however. Similarly, the differential equation

$$y' = 5y$$

is of the preceding type, with $p(t) = 5$, $q(y) = y$. We can separate the variables by writing the equation as

$$\frac{1}{y} y' = 5.$$

In the next example we present a procedure for solving differential equations in which the variables are separated.

EXAMPLE 1   Find all solutions of the differential equation $y^2 y' = 3t^2$.

Solution (a) Write y' as $\dfrac{dy}{dt}$:

$$y^2 \frac{dy}{dt} = 3t^2.$$

(b) Integrate both sides with respect to t:

$$\int y^2 \frac{dy}{dt}\, dt = \int 3t^2\, dt.$$

(c) Rewrite the left side, "canceling the dt":

$$\int y^2\, dy = \int 3t^2\, dt.$$

(See the following discussion for an explanation of exactly what this means.)

(d) Calculate the antiderivatives:

$$\frac{1}{3} y^3 + C_1 = t^3 + C_2.$$

(e) Solve for y in terms of t:

$$y^3 = 3(t^3 + C_2 - C_1)$$

$$y = \sqrt[3]{3t^3 + C}, \quad C \text{ a constant.}$$

We can check that this method works by showing that $y = \sqrt[3]{3t^3 + C}$ is a solution to $y^2 y' = 3t^2$. Since $y = (3t^3 + C)^{1/3}$, we have

$$y' = \frac{1}{3}(3t^3 + C)^{-2/3} \cdot 3 \cdot 3t^2 = 3t^2 (3t^3 + C)^{-2/3}$$

$$y^2 y' = \left[(3t^3 + C)^{1/3} \right]^2 \cdot 3t^2 (3t^3 + C)^{-2/3}$$

$$= 3t^2.$$

Figure 1 shows solution curves for various values of C. Note the linear solution that corresponds to $C = 0$.

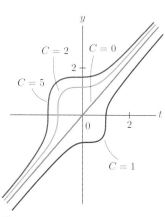

Figure 1. Solution curves in Example 1.

Discussion of Step (c) Suppose that $y = f(t)$ is a solution of the differential equation $y^2 y' = 3t^2$. Then

$$[f(t)]^2 f'(t) = 3t^2.$$

Integrating, we have

$$\int [f(t)]^2 f'(t)\, dt = \int 3t^2\, dt.$$

Make the substitution $y = f(t)$, $dy = f'(t)\, dt$ in the left side to get

$$\int y^2\, dy = \int 3t^2\, dt.$$

This is just the result of step (c). The process of "canceling the dt" and integrating with respect to y is just equivalent to making the substitution $y = f(t)$, $dy = f'(t)\, dt$. ∎

The technique used in Example 1 can be used for any differential equation with separated variables. Suppose that we are given such an equation:

$$h(y)y' = p(t),$$

where $h(y)$ is a function of y only and $p(t)$ is a function of t only. Our method of solution can be summarized as follows:

a. Write y' as $\dfrac{dy}{dt}$:

$$h(y)\frac{dy}{dt} = p(t).$$

b. Integrate both sides with respect to t:

$$\int h(y)\frac{dy}{dt}\, dt = \int p(t)\, dt.$$

c. Rewrite the left side by "canceling the dt":

$$\int h(y)\, dy = \int p(t)\, dt.$$

d. Calculate the antiderivatives $H(y)$ for $h(y)$ and $P(t)$ for $p(t)$:

$$H(y) = P(t) + C.$$

e. Solve for y in terms of t:

$$y = \dots .$$

NOTE In step (d) there is no need to write two constants of integration (as we did in Example 1), since they will be combined into one in step (e). ∎

EXAMPLE 2   Solve $e^y y' = 2t + 1$, $y(0) = 1$.

Solution (a) $e^y \dfrac{dy}{dt} = 2t + 1$

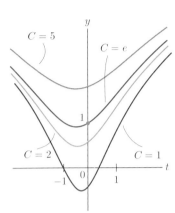

(b) $\displaystyle\int e^y \dfrac{dy}{dt}\, dt = \int (2t+1)\, dt$

(c) $\displaystyle\int e^y\, dy = \int (2t+1)\, dt$

(d) $e^y = t^2 + t + C$

(e) $y = \ln(t^2 + t + C)$ [Take logarithms of both sides of the equation in step (d).]

If $y = \ln(t^2 + t + C)$ is to satisfy the initial condition $y(0) = 1$, then

$$1 = y(0) = \ln(0^2 + 0 + C) = \ln C,$$

Figure 2. Solution curves and the solution of the initial value problem in Example 2.

so that $C = e$ and $y = \ln(t^2 + t + e)$. Figure 2 shows solutions of the differential equation for various values of C. The curve that goes through the point $(0,1)$ is the solution of the initial-value problem. ∎

EXAMPLE 3   Solve $y' = t^3 y^2 + y^2$.

Solution As the equation is given, the right side is not in the form $p(t)q(y)$. However, we may rewrite the equation in the form $y' = (t^3 + 1)y^2$. Now we may separate the variables, dividing both sides by y^2, to get

$$\frac{1}{y^2}\, y' = t^3 + 1. \tag{3}$$

Then we apply our method of solution:

(a) $\dfrac{1}{y^2} \dfrac{dy}{dt} = t^3 + 1$

(b) $\displaystyle\int \frac{1}{y^2} \frac{dy}{dt}\, dt = \int (t^3 + 1)\, dt$

(c) $\displaystyle\int \frac{1}{y^2}\, dy = \int (t^3 + 1)\, dt$

(d) $-\dfrac{1}{y} = \dfrac{1}{4}t^4 + t + C$, C a constant

(e) $y = -\dfrac{1}{\frac{1}{4}t^4 + t + C}$

Our method yields all the solutions of equation (3). However, we have ignored an important point. We wish to solve $y' = y^2(t^3 + 1)$ and not equation (3). Do the two equations have precisely the same solutions? We obtained (3) from the given equation by dividing by y^2. This is a permissible operation, provided that y is not equal to zero for all t. (Of course, if y is zero for some t, the resulting differential equation is understood to hold only for some limited range of t.) Thus, in dividing by y^2, we must assume that y is not the zero function. However, note that $y = 0$ is a solution of the original equation because

$$0 = (0)' = t^3 \cdot 0^2 + 0^2.$$

So, when we divided by y^2, we "lost" the solution $y = 0$. Finally, we see that the solutions of the differential equation $y' = t^3 y^2 + y^2$ are

$$y = -\frac{1}{\frac{1}{4}t^4 + t + C}, \quad C \text{ a constant}$$

and

$$y = 0.$$

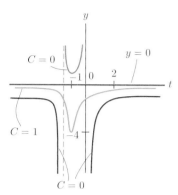

Figure 3. Solution curves in Example 3.

Figure 3 shows two solutions corresponding to different values of the constant C, and the solution $y = 0$. It is interesting to note how a great diversity of solutions arises from a relatively simple differential equation. ∎

WARNING If the equation in Example 3 had been

$$y' = t^3 y^2 + 1,$$

we would not have been able to use the method of separation of variables, because the expression $t^3 y^2 + 1$ cannot be written in the form $p(t)q(y)$. ∎

EXAMPLE 4   Solve the initial-value problem $3y' + y^4 \cos t = 0$, $y(\frac{\pi}{2}) = \frac{1}{2}$.

Solution   Write the equation in the form

$$3y' = -y^4 \cos t. \tag{4}$$

Clearly, the constant function $y = 0$ is a solution of the differential equation because it makes both sides of (4) zero for all t. Now, supposing that $y \neq 0$, we may divide by y^4 and get

$$\frac{3}{y^4} y' = -\cos t$$

$$\int \frac{3}{y^4} \frac{dy}{dt} \, dt = -\int \cos t \, dt$$

$$-y^{-3} = -\sin t + C, \quad C \text{ a constant}$$

$$y^{-3} = \sin t + C.$$

In the last step, there is no need to change the sign of C, since it stands for an arbitrary constant. Solving for y in terms of t, we find

$$y^3 = \frac{1}{\sin t + C}$$

$$y = \frac{1}{\sqrt[3]{\sin t + C}}.$$

If y is to satisfy the initial condition $y(\frac{\pi}{2}) = \frac{1}{2}$, we must have

$$\frac{1}{2} = y\left(\frac{\pi}{2}\right) = \frac{1}{\sqrt[3]{\sin(\frac{\pi}{2}) + C}} = \frac{1}{\sqrt[3]{1 + C}} \quad \text{[Recall that } \sin(\frac{\pi}{2}) = 1.\text{]}$$

$$2 = \sqrt[3]{1 + C} \qquad\qquad \text{[Take inverses.]}$$

$$2^3 = 1 + C$$

$$C = 7.$$

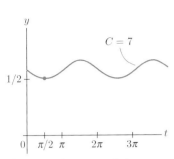

Figure 4.   Solution of the initial-value problem in Example 4.

Hence the desired solution is

$$y = \frac{1}{\sqrt[3]{\sin t + 7}}.$$

The graph of y in Fig. 4 goes through the point $(\frac{\pi}{2}, \frac{1}{2})$. ∎

EXAMPLE 5

Solve $y' = te^t/y$, $y(0) = -5$.

Solution Separating the variables, we have

$$yy' = te^t$$

$$\int y\,\frac{dy}{dt}\,dt = \int te^t\,dt$$

$$\int y\,dy = \int te^t\,dt.$$

The integral $\int te^t\,dt$ may be found by integration by parts:

$$\int te^t\,dt = te^t - \int 1 \cdot e^t\,dt = te^t - e^t + C.$$

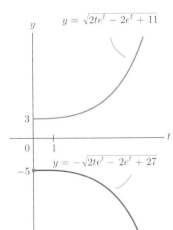

Figure 5.   Solution curves in Example 5.

Therefore,

$$\tfrac{1}{2}y^2 = te^t - e^t + C$$

$$y^2 = 2te^t - 2e^t + C_1$$

$$y = \pm\sqrt{2te^t - 2e^t + C_1}.$$

Note that the $\pm$ appears because there are two square roots of $2te^t - 2e^t + C_1$ that differ from one another by a minus sign. Thus the solutions are of two sorts:

$$y = +\sqrt{2te^t - 2e^t + C_1}$$

$$y = -\sqrt{2te^t - 2e^t + C_1}.$$

Two of these solutions are shown in Fig. 5 with different signs in front of the square root. We must choose C_1 so that $y(0) = -5$. Since the values of y for the first solution are always positive, the given initial condition must correspond to the second solution, and we must have

$$-5 = y(0) = -\sqrt{2 \cdot 0 \cdot e^0 - 2e^0 + C_1} = -\sqrt{-2 + C_1}$$

$$-2 + C_1 = 25$$

$$C_1 = 27.$$

Hence the desired solution is

$$y = -\sqrt{2te^t - 2e^t + 27}.$$

Its graph goes through the point $(0, -5)$ in Fig. 5.   ■

When working the exercises at the end of the section, it is a good practice first to find the constant solution(s), if any. A constant function $y = c$ is a solution of $y' = p(t)q(y)$ if and only if $q(c) = 0$. [For $y = c$ implies that $y' = (c)' = 0$, and $p(t)q(y)$ will be zero for all t if and only if $q(y) = 0$—that is, $q(c) = 0$.] After listing the constant solutions, one may assume that $q(y) \neq 0$ and go on to divide both sides of the equation $y' = p(t)q(y)$ by $q(y)$ to separate the variables.

Practice Problems 10.2

1. Solve the initial-value problem $y' = 5y$, $y(0) = 2$, by separation of variables.

2. Solve $y' = \sqrt{ty}$, $y(1) = 4$.

EXERCISES 10.2

Solve the following differential equations:

1. $\dfrac{dy}{dt} = \dfrac{5 - t}{y^2}$

2. $\dfrac{dy}{dt} = te^{2y}$

3. $\dfrac{dy}{dt} = \dfrac{e^t}{e^y}$

4. $\dfrac{dy}{dt} = -\dfrac{1}{t^2 y^2}$

5. $\dfrac{dy}{dt} = t^{1/2} y^2$

6. $\dfrac{dy}{dt} = \dfrac{t^2 y^2}{t^3 + 8}$

7. $y' = \left(\dfrac{t}{y}\right)^2 e^{t^3}$

8. $y' = e^{4y} t^3 - e^{4y}$

9. $y' = \sqrt{\dfrac{y}{t}}$

10. $y' = \left(\dfrac{e^t}{y}\right)^2$

11. $y' = 3t^2 y^2$

12. $(1 + t^2)y' = ty^2$

13. $y' e^y = te^{t^2}$

14. $y' = \dfrac{1}{ty + y}$

15. $y' = \dfrac{\ln t}{ty}$

16. $y^2 y' = \tan t$

17. $y' = (y - 3)^2 \ln t$

18. $yy' = t \sin(t^2 + 1)$

Solve the following differential equations with the given initial conditions.

19. $y' = 2te^{-2y} - e^{-2y}$, $y(0) = 3$

20. $y' = y^2 - e^{3t} y^2$, $y(0) = 1$

21. $y^2 y' = t \cos t$, $y(0) = 2$

22. $y' = t^2 e^{-3y}$, $y(0) = 2$

23. $3y^2 y' = -\sin t$, $y(\frac{\pi}{2}) = 1$

24. $y' = -y^2 \sin t$, $y(\frac{\pi}{2}) = 1$

25. $\dfrac{dy}{dt} = \dfrac{t + 1}{ty}$, $t > 0$, $y(1) = -3$

26. $\dfrac{dy}{dt} = \left(\dfrac{1 + t}{1 + y}\right)^2$, $y(0) = 2$

27. $y' = 5ty - 2t$, $y(0) = 1$

28. $y' = \dfrac{t^2}{y}$, $y(0) = -5$

29. $\dfrac{dy}{dx} = \dfrac{\ln x}{\sqrt{xy}}$, $y(1) = 4$

30. $\dfrac{dN}{dt} = 2tN^2$, $N(0) = 5$

31. A model that describes the relationship between the price and the weekly sales of a product might have a form such as

$$\frac{dy}{dp} = -\frac{1}{2}\left(\frac{y}{p + 3}\right),$$

where y is the volume of sales and p is the price per unit. That is, at any time the rate of decrease of sales with respect to price is directly proportional to the sales level and inversely proportional to the sales price plus a constant. Solve this differential equation. (Figure 6 shows several typical solutions.)

32. One problem in psychology is to determine the relation between some physical stimulus and the corresponding sensation or reaction produced in a subject. Suppose that, measured in appropriate units, the strength of a stimulus is s and the intensity of the corresponding sensation is some function of s, say $f(s)$. Some experimental data suggest that the rate of change of intensity

Figure 6. Demand curves.

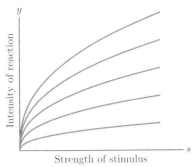

Figure 7. Reaction to stimuli.

of the sensation with respect to the stimulus is directly proportional to the intensity of the sensation and inversely proportional to the strength of the stimulus; that is, $f(s)$ satisfies the differential equation

$$\frac{dy}{ds} = k\frac{y}{s}$$

for some positive constant k. Solve this differential equation. (Figure 7 shows several solutions corresponding to $k = .4$.)

33. Let t represent the total number of hours that a truck driver spends during a year driving on a certain highway connecting two cities, and let $p(t)$ represent the probability that the driver will have at least one accident during these t hours. Then $0 \le p(t) \le 1$, and $1 - p(t)$ represents the probability of not having an accident. Under ordinary conditions, the rate of increase in the probability of an accident (as a function of t) is proportional to the probability of not having an accident. Construct and solve a differential equation for this situation.

34. In certain learning situations a maximum amount, M, of information can be learned, and at any time the rate of learning is proportional to the amount yet to be learned. Let $y = f(t)$ be the amount of information learned up to time t. Construct and solve a differential equation that is satisfied by $f(t)$.

35. Mothballs tend to evaporate at a rate proportional to their surface area. If V is the volume of a mothball, then its surface area is roughly a constant times $V^{2/3}$. So the mothball's volume decreases at a rate proportional to $V^{2/3}$. Suppose that initially a mothball has a volume of 27 cubic centimeters and 4 weeks later has a volume of 15.625 cubic centimeters. Construct and solve a differential equation satisfied by the volume at time t. Then determine if and when the mothball will vanish ($V = 0$).

36. Some homeowner's insurance policies include automatic inflation coverage based on the U.S. Commerce Department's construction cost index (CCI). Each year

the property insurance coverage is increased by an amount based on the change in the CCI. Let $f(t)$ be the CCI at time t years since January 1, 1990, and let $f(0) = 100$. Suppose that the construction cost index is rising at a rate proportional to the CCI and the index was 115 on January 1, 1992. Construct and solve a differential equation satisfied by $f(t)$. Then determine when the CCI will reach 200.

37. The Gompertz growth equation is

$$\frac{dy}{dt} = -ay \ln \frac{y}{b},$$

where a and b are positive constants. This equation is used in biology to describe the growth of certain populations. Find the general form of solutions to this differential equation. (Figure 8 shows several solutions corresponding to $a = .04$ and $b = 90$.)

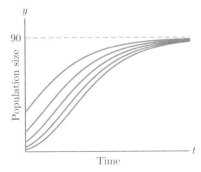

Figure 8. Gompertz growth curves.

38. When a certain liquid substance A is heated in a flask, it decomposes into a substance B at a rate (measured in units of A per hour) that at any time t is proportional to the square of the amount of substance A present. Let $y = f(t)$ be the amount of substance A present at time t. Construct and solve a differential equation that is satisfied by $f(t)$.

39. Let $f(t)$ denote the number (in thousands) of fish in a lake after t years, and suppose that $f(t)$ satisfies the differential equation

$$y' = 0.1y(5 - y).$$

The slope field for this equation is shown in Fig. 9.

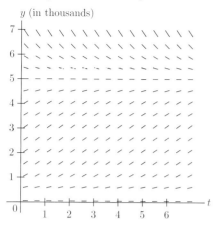

Figure 9

(a) With the help of the slope field, discuss what happens to an initial population of 6000 fish. Does it increase or decrease?

(b) How about an initial population of 1000 fish? Does it increase or decrease?

(c) On the slope field in Fig. 9 or a copy of it, draw the solution of the initial-value problem

$$y' = 0.1y(5 - y), \quad y(0) = 1.$$

What does this solution represent?

40. Refer to the differential equation in Exercise 39.

(a) Obviously, if you start with zero fish, $f(t) = 0$ for all t. Confirm this on the slope field. Are there any other constant solutions?

(b) Describe the population of fish if the initial population is greater than 5000; less than 5000. On the slope field in Fig. 9 or a copy of it, draw solution curves to illustrate your description.

Solutions to Practice Problems 10.2

1. The constant function $y = 0$ is a solution of $y' = 5y$. If $y \neq 0$, we may divide by y and obtain

$$\frac{1}{y} y' = 5$$

$$\int \frac{1}{y} \frac{dy}{dt} \, dt = \int 5 \, dt$$

$$\int \frac{1}{y} \, dy = \int 5 \, dt$$

$$\ln |y| = 5t + C$$

$$|y| = e^{5t+C} = e^C \cdot e^{5t}$$

$$y = \pm e^C \cdot e^{5t}.$$

These two types of solutions and the constant solution may all be written in the form

$$y = Ae^{5t},$$

where A is an arbitrary constant (positive, negative, or zero). The initial condition $y(0) = 2$ implies that

$$2 = y(0) = Ae^{5(0)} = A.$$

Hence the solution of the initial-value problem is $y = 2e^{5t}$.

2. We rewrite $y' = \sqrt{ty}$ as $y' = \sqrt{t} \cdot \sqrt{y}$. The constant function $y = 0$ is one solution. To find the others, we suppose that $y \neq 0$ and divide by $\sqrt{y}$ to obtain

$$\frac{1}{\sqrt{y}} y' = \sqrt{t}$$

$$\int y^{-1/2} \frac{dy}{dt} \, dt = \int t^{1/2} \, dt$$

$$\int y^{-1/2} \, dy = \int t^{1/2} \, dt$$

$$2y^{1/2} = \frac{2}{3} t^{3/2} + C$$

$$y^{1/2} = \frac{1}{3} t^{3/2} + C_1 \qquad (5)$$

$$y = \left(\frac{1}{3} t^{3/2} + C_1 \right)^2. \qquad (6)$$

We must choose C_1 so that $y(1) = 4$. The quickest method is to use (5) instead of (6). We have $y = 4$ when $t = 1$, so

$$4^{1/2} = \frac{1}{3}(1)^{3/2} + C_1$$

$$2 = \frac{1}{3} + C_1$$

$$C_1 = \frac{5}{3}.$$

Hence the desired solution is

$$y = \left(\frac{1}{3} t^{3/2} + \frac{5}{3} \right)^2.$$

10.3 First-Order Linear Differential Equations

In this section we study first-order differential equations of the form

$$y' + a(t)y = b(t), \tag{1}$$

where $a(t)$ and $b(t)$ are continuous functions on a given interval. Equation (1) is called a *first-order linear* differential equation in *standard form.*

The following are examples of first-order linear differential equations:

$$y' - 2ty = 0 \qquad [a(t) = -2t, \, b(t) = 0]$$

$$y' + y = 2 \qquad [a(t) = 1, \, b(t) = 2]$$

$$ty' = ty + t^2 + 1 \qquad \left[y' - y = \frac{t^2 + 1}{t}, \, a(t) = -1, \, b(t) = \frac{t^2 + 1}{t} \right]$$

$$e^t y' + e^t y = 5 \qquad \left[y' + y = 5e^{-t}, \, a(t) = 1, \, b(t) = 5e^{-t} \right]$$

In the last two examples, we first put the equation in standard form $y' + a(t)y = b(t)$ before determining the functions $a(t)$ and $b(t)$.

Given equation (1), form the function $e^{A(t)}$, called an *integrating factor*, where $A(t) = \int a(t)\, dt$. Observe that, as a consequence of the chain rule and the product rule,

$$\frac{d}{dt}\left[e^{A(t)} \right] = e^{A(t)} \frac{d}{dt} A(t) = e^{A(t)} a(t) = a(t) e^{A(t)},$$

and

$$\frac{d}{dt}\left[e^{A(t)} y \right] = e^{A(t)} y' + a(t) e^{A(t)} y$$

$$= e^{A(t)} [\, \overbrace{y' + a(t)y}^{\text{left side of (1)}} \,]. \tag{2}$$

Returning to equation (1), multiply both sides by $e^{A(t)}$, and then simplify the resulting equation with the help of (2) as follows:

$$e^{A(t)} [y' + a(t)y] = e^{A(t)} b(t)$$

$$\frac{d}{dt}\left[e^{A(t)} y \right] = e^{A(t)} b(t) \quad \text{[by (2)]}. \tag{3}$$

Equation (3) is equivalent to equation (1). Integrate both sides to get rid of the derivative on the left side of (3) and get

$$e^{A(t)} y = \int e^{A(t)} b(t) \, dt + C.$$

Solve for y by multiplying both sides by $e^{-A(t)}$:

$$y = e^{-A(t)} \left[\int e^{A(t)} b(t) \, dt + C \right], \quad C \text{ a constant.} \tag{4}$$

This formula gives all the solutions of equation (1). It is called the *general solution* of (1). As our next examples illustrate, to solve a first-order linear differential equation, you can appeal directly to (4), or you can use an integrating factor and repeat the steps leading to (4).

EXAMPLE 1   Solve $y' = 3 - 2y$.

Solution *Step 1* Put the equation in standard form: $y' + 2y = 3$.

Step 2 Find an integrating factor $e^{A(t)}$. We have $a(t) = 2$, so

$$A(t) = \int a(t) \, dt = \int 2 \, dt = 2t.$$

Note how we picked one antiderivative of $a(t)$ by setting the constant of integration equal to zero. Hence the integrating factor is $e^{A(t)} = e^{2t}$.

Step 3 Multiply both sides of the differential equation by the integrating factor e^{2t}:

$$\overbrace{e^{2t}y' + 2e^{2t}y}^{\frac{d}{dt}[e^{2t}y]} = 3e^{2t}.$$

Recognizing the terms on the left side as a derivative of the product $e^{2t}y$, we get

$$\frac{d}{dt}\left[e^{2t}y\right] = 3e^{2t}.$$

Step 4 Integrating both sides and solving for y, we obtain

$$e^{2t}y = \int 3e^{2t} \, dt = \frac{3}{2}e^{2t} + C$$

$$y = e^{-2t}\left[\frac{3}{2}e^{2t} + C\right] = \frac{3}{2} + Ce^{-2t}.$$

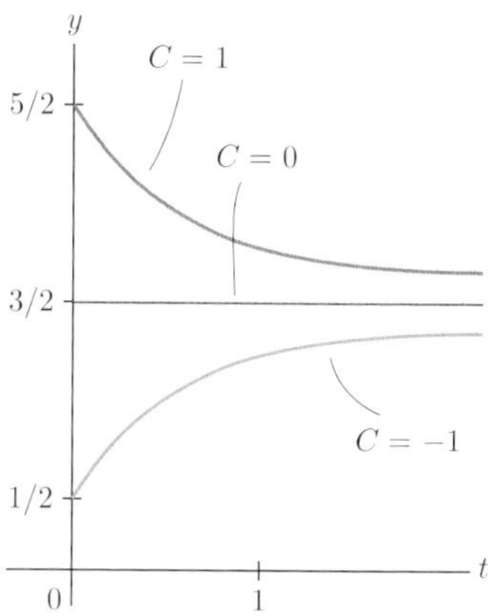

Figure 1. Typical solutions of the differential equation in Example 1: $y' + 2y = 3$.

Figure 1 shows solution curves for various values of C. Note the constant solution, $y = \frac{3}{2}$, corresponding to $C = 0$. ∎

From the preceding example, we can state a step-by-step process for solving a first-order linear differential equation.

Solving a First-Order Linear Differential Equation

Step 1 Put the equation in the standard form $y' + a(t)y = b(t)$.

Step 2 Compute an antiderivative of $a(t)$, $A(t) = \int a(t) \, dt$. [When evaluating $\int a(t) \, dt$, it is customary to choose 0 for the constant of integration.] Form the integrating factor $e^{A(t)}$.

Step 3 Multiply the differential equation by the integrating factor $e^{A(t)}$. This transforms the terms on the left side of the equation into the derivative of a product, $\frac{d}{dt}\left[e^{A(t)}y\right]$, as in equation (3).

Step 4 Integrate to get rid of the derivative and then solve for y.

EXAMPLE 2 Solve

$$\frac{1}{3t^2}y' + y = 4, \quad t > 0.$$

Solution *Step 1* Multiply through by $3t^2$ and get

$$y' + 3t^2y = 12t^2.$$

Hence $a(t) = 3t^2$.

Step 2 An antiderivative of $a(t)$ is

$$A(t) = \int a(t) \, dt = \int 3t^2 \, dt = t^3.$$

So the integrating factor is $e^{A(t)} = e^{t^3}$.

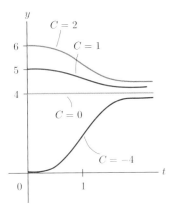

Figure 2. Typical solutions of the differential equation in Example 2.

Step 3   Multiply both sides of the differential equation by e^{t^3} and get

$$e^{t^3} y' + 3t^2 e^{t^3} y = 12t^2 e^{t^3}$$

$$\frac{d}{dt}\left[e^{t^3} y\right] = 12t^2 e^{t^3}.$$

Step 4   Integrating both sides, we obtain

$$e^{t^3} y = \int 12t^2 e^{t^3}\, dt = 4e^{t^3} + C$$

$$y = e^{-t^3}\left[4e^{t^3} + C\right] = 4 + Ce^{-t^3}.$$

In evaluating the integral $\int 12t^2 e^{t^3}\, dt$, we used integration by substitution (Section 9.1): Let $u = t^3$, $du = 3t^2\, dt$. Then

$$\int 12t^2 e^{t^3}\, dt = 4\int \overbrace{e^{t^3}}^{e^u} \overbrace{3t^2\, dt}^{du} = 4\int e^u\, du = 4e^u + C = 4e^{t^3} + C.$$

Figure 2 shows solution curves for various values of C. Note the constant solution, $y = 4$, which corresponds to $C = 0$. ∎

EXAMPLE 3

Solve the initial-value problem $t^2 y' + ty = 2$, $y(1) = 1$, $t > 0$.

Solution ***Step 1***   Divide by t^2 to put the equation in standard form:

$$y' + \frac{1}{t}y = \frac{2}{t^2}.$$

Step 2   An antiderivative of $a(t) = \frac{1}{t}$ is

$$A(t) = \int \frac{1}{t}\, dt = \ln t.$$

Hence the integrating factor is $e^{A(t)} = e^{\ln t} = t$.

Step 3   Multiply both sides of the differential equation by t and get

$$ty' + y = \frac{2}{t}$$

$$\frac{d}{dt}[ty] = \frac{2}{t}.$$

Step 4   Integrating both sides and solving for y, we obtain

$$ty = \int \frac{2}{t}\, dt = 2\ln t + C$$

$$y = \frac{2\ln t + C}{t}.$$

To satisfy the initial condition, we must have

$$1 = y(1) = \frac{2\ln(1) + C}{1} = C \quad [\ln(1) = 0].$$

Hence the solution of the initial value problem is

$$y = \frac{2\ln t + 1}{t}, \quad t > 0.$$

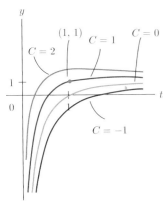

Figure 3. Solution of the initial-value problem $t^2 y' + ty = 2$, $y(1) = 1$, $t > 0$.

Among all the solution curves that are shown in Fig. 3, the solution of the initial-value problem is the curve that goes through the point $(1, 1)$. ∎

In the following section we present several interesting applications of first-order linear differential equations.

Practice Problems 10.3

1. Using an integrating factor, solve $y' + y = 1 + e^{-t}$.

2. Find an integrating factor for the differential equation $y' = -\dfrac{y}{1+t} + 1$, $t \geq 0$.

EXERCISES 10.3

In Exercises 1–6, find an integrating factor for each equation. Take $t > 0$.

1. $y' - 2y = t$

2. $y' + ty = 6t$

3. $t^3 y' + y = 0$

4. $y' + \sqrt{t}\, y = 2(t + 1)$

5. $y' - \dfrac{y}{10 + t} = 2$

6. $y' = t^2(y + 1)$

In Exercises 7–20, solve the given equation using an integrating factor. Take $t > 0$.

7. $y' + y = 1$

8. $y' + 2ty = 0$

9. $y' - 2ty = -4t$

10. $y' = 2(20 - y)$

11. $y' = .5(35 - y)$

12. $y' + y = e^{-t} + 1$

13. $y' + \dfrac{y}{10 + t} = 0$

14. $y' - 2y = e^{2t}$

15. $(1 + t)y' + y = -1$

16. $y' = e^{-t}(y + 1)$

17. $6y' + ty = t$

18. $e^t y' + y = 1$

19. $y' + y = 2 - e^t$

20. $\dfrac{1}{\sqrt{t+1}} y' + y = 1$

In Exercises 21–28, solve the initial-value problem.

21. $y' + 2y = 1$, $y(0) = 1$

22. $ty' + y = \ln t$, $y(e) = 0$, $t > 0$

23. $y' + \dfrac{y}{1+t} = 20$, $y(0) = 10$, $t \geq 0$

24. $y' = 2(10 - y)$, $y(0) = 1$

25. $y' + y = e^{2t}$, $y(0) = -1$

26. $ty' - y = -1$, $y(1) = 1$, $t > 0$

27. $y' + 2y \cos(2t) = 2\cos(2t)$, $y(\frac{\pi}{2}) = 0$

28. $ty' + y = \sin t$, $y(\frac{\pi}{2}) = 0$, $t > 0$

Technology Exercises

29. Consider the initial-value problem

$$y' = -\frac{y}{1+t} + 10, \quad y(0) = 50.$$

(a) Is the solution increasing or decreasing when $t = 0$? [*Hint:* Compute $y'(0)$.]

(b) Find the solution and plot it for $0 \leq t \leq 4$.

Solutions to Practice Problems 10.3

1. We follow the step-by-step method outlined in this section. The equation $y' + y = 1 + e^{-t}$ is already in standard form. We have $a(t) = 1$, $A(t) = \int 1\, dt = t$, and so the integrating factor is $e^{A(t)} = e^t$. Multiplying the equation by the integrating factor, we transform the terms on its left side into the derivative of a product, as follows:

$e^t(y' + y) = e^t(1 + e^{-t})$ [Multiply the equation by the integrating factor e^t.]

$e^t y' + e^t y = e^t + 1$ [The left side is the derivative of the product $e^t y$.]

$\dfrac{d}{dt}\left[e^t y\right] = e^t + 1$

Integrating both sides, we get rid of the derivative and obtain

$$e^t y = \int (e^t + 1)\, dt = e^t + t + C.$$

To solve for y, we multiply both sides by e^{-t} and get

$$y = e^{-t}(e^t + t + C) = 1 + te^{-t} + Ce^{-t}.$$

2. In standard form, the equation becomes

$$y' + \frac{y}{1+t} = 1.$$

We have $a(t) = \dfrac{1}{1+t}$. An antiderivative of $a(t)$ is

$$A(t) = \int \frac{1}{1+t}\, dt = \ln|1+t|.$$

But since $t \geq 0$, it follows that $1 + t \geq 0$; hence $\ln|1+t| = \ln(1+t)$. So the integrating factor is

$$e^{A(t)} = e^{\ln(1+t)} = 1 + t.$$

10.4 Applications of First-Order Linear Differential Equations

This section discusses several interesting applications that lead to first-order linear differential equations. Modeling or setting up the mathematical equations is a crucial part of the solution. You can develop your modeling skills by studying carefully the details leading to the mathematical equations in each of the following examples. Look for the key expression "rate of change" and translate it as a derivative. Then continue your description of the rate of change to obtain a differential equation.

Our first examples are related to the topics of compound interest from Section 5.2 and future value of an income stream from Section 6.5.

EXAMPLE 1   **A retirement account**   You invest in a retirement account that pays 6% interest per year. You make an initial deposit of $1000 and plan on making future deposits at the rate of $2400 per year. Assume that the deposits are made continuously and that interest is compounded continuously. Let $P(t)$ denote the amount of money in the account t years after the initial deposit.

(a) Set up an initial-value problem that is satisfied by $P(t)$.

(b) Find $P(t)$.

Solution (a) If no deposits or withdrawals are made, only interest is being added to the account at a rate proportional to the amount in the account with constant of proportionality $k = .06$ or 6%. Since in this case the growth of $P(t)$ comes from interest only, it follows that $P(t)$ satisfies the equation

$$y' \qquad = \qquad .06 \qquad \times \qquad y$$

$$\begin{bmatrix} \text{rate of} \\ \text{change of } y \end{bmatrix} = \begin{bmatrix} \text{constant of} \\ \text{proportionality} \end{bmatrix} \times \begin{bmatrix} \text{amount in} \\ \text{the account} \end{bmatrix}.$$

Taking into consideration the deposits, which are adding money to the account at the rate of $2400 per year, we see that there are two influences on the way the amount of money in the account changes: the rate at which interest is added and the rate at which deposits are made. The rate of change of $P(t)$ is the *net effect* of these two influences. That is, $P(t)$ now satisfies the first-order linear differential equation

$$y' \qquad = \qquad .06y \qquad + \qquad 2400$$

$$\begin{bmatrix} \text{rate of} \\ \text{change of } y \end{bmatrix} = \begin{bmatrix} \text{rate at which} \\ \text{interest is added} \end{bmatrix} + \begin{bmatrix} \text{rate at which} \\ \text{money is deposited} \end{bmatrix}.$$

Since the initial deposit in the account was $1000, it follows that $P(t)$ satisfies the initial condition $y(0) = 1000$. Putting the equation in standard form [see Section 10.3, equation (1)], we conclude that $P(t)$ satisfies the initial-value problem

$$y' - .06y = 2400, \quad y(0) = 1000.$$

(b) To solve the equation, use the step-by-step method from the previous section. We have $a(t) = -.06$. So $A(t) = -\int .06 \, dt = -.06t$; hence the integrating factor is $e^{A(t)} = e^{-.06t}$. Multiplying both sides of the equation by the integrating factor, we obtain

$$e^{-.06t}[y' - .06y] = 2400e^{-.06t}$$

$$e^{-.06t}y' - .06e^{-.06t}y = 2400e^{-.06t} \quad \text{[The left side is a derivative of a product.]}$$

$$\frac{d}{dt}\left[e^{-.06t}y\right] = 2400e^{-.06t}.$$

Integrating both sides and solving for y, we get

$$e^{-.06t}y = \int 2400e^{-.06t}\,dt$$

$$e^{-.06t}y = -40,000e^{-.06t} + C \qquad \left[\int 2400e^{-.06t}\,dt = -\frac{2400}{.06}e^{-.06t} + C\right]$$

$$y = e^{.06t}\left[-40,000e^{-.06t} + C\right] \quad \text{[Solve for } y.\text{]}$$

$$y = -40,000 + Ce^{.06t} \qquad \text{[Simplify.]}$$

Thus the solution is $P(t) = -40,000 + Ce^{.06t}$. To satisfy the initial condition, we must have

$$1000 = P(0) = -40,000 + Ce^{.06\cdot(0)} = -40,000 + C$$

$$C = 41,000$$

Hence the amount of money in the account at time t is given by

$$P(t) = -40,000 + 41,000e^{.06t}.$$

The graph of $P(t)$ is shown in Fig. 1.

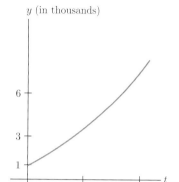

Figure 1. The account $P(t)$ in Example 1.

Let us quickly examine the modeling ideas in Example 1. The quantity that we were looking for was the amount of money in the account at time t. Its rate of change was affected by two influences: the interest rate and the rate at which money was deposited. To describe the rate of change of the money in the account, we added both rates of change and obtained the differential equation $y' = .06y + 2400$.

Many interesting situations can be modeled by refining these ideas. First identify the quantity of concern (amount of money in the account). Then identify the various influences that affect the rate of change of this quantity (interest rate, rate of deposits). Finally, derive a differential equation by expressing the rate of change of the quantity of interest in terms of the rates of change of the various influences. In Example 1, we added two rates of change to describe y'. As our next example illustrates, to model problems involving amortization of consumer loans and mortgages, you may have to subtract two rates of change.

EXAMPLE 2

Paying off a car loan   You took a loan of $25,000 to pay for a new car. The interest rate on the loan is 5%. You arranged through your online banking to make daily payments totaling $4800 per year. This allows you to assume that your payments are flowing continuously into your account. Let $P(t)$ denote the amount that you owe on the loan at time t (in years). Assume that interest is compounded continuously. Set up an initial-value problem that is satisfied by $P(t)$.

Solution   As in Example 1, there are two influences on the way the amount of money owed changes: the rate at which interest is added to the amount owed and the rate at which payments are subtracted from the amount owed. We know that interest is being added at a rate proportional to the amount owed, with constant of proportionality $k = .05$. The effect of the payments is to subtract from the amount owed at the rate of $4800 per year. Since the rate of change of $P(t)$ is the *net effect* of these two influences, we see that $P(t)$ satisfies the first-order linear differential equation

$$y' \qquad = \qquad .05y \qquad - \qquad 4800$$

$$\begin{bmatrix}\text{rate of}\\\text{change of } y\end{bmatrix} = \begin{bmatrix}\text{rate at which}\\\text{interest is added}\end{bmatrix} - \begin{bmatrix}\text{rate of}\\\text{payments}\end{bmatrix}.$$

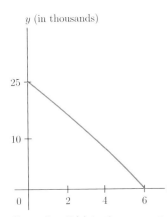

Figure 2. $P(t)$ is the amount owed at time t. The loan is paid off in approximately 6 years.

Recalling the initial condition and rewriting the equation in standard form, we find that $P(t)$ satisfies the initial-value problem

$$y' - .05y = -4800, \quad y(0) = 25{,}000.$$

Using an integrating factor and proceeding in a manner very similar to Example 1, we find the solution of the initial-value problem in Example 2 to be

$$P(t) = 96{,}000 - 71{,}000e^{.05t}.$$

The graph of $P(t)$ is shown in Fig. 2. From the graph, we see that $P(t) = 0$ when $t \approx 6$ years. This is how long it will take to pay off the entire loan.

In the previous examples, the annual rates of deposits or loan payments were constant. If you expect your annual income to increase (which is a reasonable expectation), you may want to increase the rate of your savings deposits or you may consider paying off your loan at a faster rate. The modeling involved in these situations is similar to the previous examples, but may lead to more complicated differential equations. See the exercises for several illustrations.

In Chapter 5 we learned that simple population models are based on the assumption that the growth rate of a population is proportional to the size of the population at time t. The constant of proportionality is called the growth constant and is specific to the population. In reality, the rate of growth of a population may be affected by several other factors. In the next example, we consider the effect of emigration on the size of a population.

EXAMPLE 3   **A population model with emigration** In 1995, people from a country suffering from serious economical problems started to emigrate to other countries in search of work and better living conditions. Let $P(t)$ denote the population of the country in millions t years after 1995. Sociologists studying this population determined that for the next 30 years the number of people emigrating will gradually increase as the news of better prospects outside the country spreads. Suppose that the rate of emigration is given by $.004e^{.04t} + .04$ millions per year t years after 1995. Suppose further that the growth constant of the population is $\frac{3}{125}$. Find a differential equation satisfied by $P(t)$.

Solution In our model, for the next 30 years (from 1995), the rate of growth of the population is affected by two influences: the rate at which the population is growing and the rate at which the population is emigrating. The rate of change of the population is the net effect of these two influences. Thus $P(t)$ satisfies the differential equation

$$y' \quad = \quad \tfrac{3}{125}y \quad - \quad (.004e^{.04t} + .04)$$

$$\begin{bmatrix} \text{rate of} \\ \text{change of } y \end{bmatrix} = \begin{bmatrix} \text{rate at which} \\ \text{population is growing} \end{bmatrix} - \begin{bmatrix} \text{rate at which} \\ \text{population is emigrating} \end{bmatrix}.$$

Putting the equation in standard form, we obtain

$$y' - \frac{3}{125}y = -.004e^{.04t} - .04.$$

To obtain a formula for the population in Example 3, you need to know the initial population. For example, if in 1995 the size of the population was 2 million, then $P(0) = 2$. Solving the differential equation, subject to this initial condition, we obtain

$$P(t) = \frac{7}{12}e^{\frac{3}{125}t} - \frac{1}{4}e^{\frac{t}{25}} + \frac{5}{3}.$$

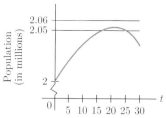

Figure 3. Population with emigration.

(The details are straightforward and are left to Exercise 16.) Figure 3 shows the size of the population since 1995. Starting in 1995, the population continued to grow at a decreasing rate. According to our model, and assuming that the economical conditions remain the same, the population will peak at about 2.055 million between the years 2015 and 2020, and then it will start to decrease.

Our final topic deals with Newton's law of cooling from Example 5, Section 10.1. The modeling ideas involved are useful in many interesting applications, such as determining the time of death of a person and the study of the concentration of waste products in the body and their clearance by artificial kidneys (dialysis).

EXAMPLE 4

Newton's law of cooling   A hungry college student, in a rush to eat, turns the oven on and puts a frozen pizza in it without preheating the oven. Let $f(t)$ denote the temperature of the pizza and $T(t)$ the oven's temperature t minutes after the oven was turned on. According to Newton's law of cooling, the rate of change of $f(t)$ is proportional to the difference between the oven's temperature and the temperature of the pizza. Find a differential equation that is satisfied by $f(t)$.

Solution   We reason as we did in Example 5, Section 10.1. The rate of change of the temperature of the pizza is the derivative of $f(t)$. This derivative is proportional to the difference $T(t) - f(t)$. Thus, there exists a constant k such that

$$f'(t) = k[T(t) - f(t)].$$

Is k positive or negative? While the pizza is heating, its temperature is rising. So $f'(t)$ is positive. Also, the temperature of the oven is always higher than the temperature of the pizza. So $T(t) - f(t)$ is positive. Thus, to make $f'(t)$ positive, k must be a positive number. Consequently, the differential equation satisfied by $f(t)$ is

$$y' = k[T(t) - y],$$

where k is a positive constant.

Example 5 treats an interesting case of the model in Example 4. In the solution, we will appeal to the integral

$$\int (at + b)e^{ct}\, dt = \frac{1}{c^2}e^{ct}(act + bc - a) + C \quad (c \neq 0). \tag{1}$$

You do not need to memorize this formula, but you should be able to evaluate integrals of this form by using integration by parts, as we now illustrate. Set $f(t) = at + b$ and $g(t) = e^{ct}$. Then, $f'(t) = a$ and $G(t) = \frac{1}{c}e^{ct}$. Integrating by parts, we get

$$\int (at + b)e^{ct}\, dt = \frac{1}{c}(at + b)e^{ct} - \int \frac{a}{c}e^{ct}\, dt$$

$$= \frac{1}{c}(at + b)e^{ct} - \frac{a}{c^2}e^{ct} + C$$

$$= \frac{1}{c^2}e^{ct}(c(at + b) - a) + C,$$

and equation (1) follows upon simplifying.

EXAMPLE 5   Suppose that the oven's temperature in Example 4 is given by $T(t) = 70 + 50t$ for $0 \le t \le 8$. [So when the student turned on the oven ($t = 0$), the oven's temperature was $70°$, and then it started to rise at the rate of $50°$ per minute for the next 8 minutes. Presumably, the student set the oven's temperature at $470°$.] Suppose further that the constant of proportionality is $k = .1$ and that the initial temperature of the frozen pizza was $27°$. Determine the temperature of the pizza during the first 8 minutes of heating. What is the temperature of the pizza after 8 minutes of heating?

Solution   Substituting $T(t) = 70 + 50t$ and $k = .1$ into the differential equation in Example 4, we see that $f(t)$ satisfies

$$y' = .1[70 + 50t - y].$$

Putting the equation in standard form and recalling the initial condition $f(0) = 27$, we obtain the initial-value problem

$$y' + .1y = 5t + 7, \quad y(0) = 27.$$

Multiplying both sides of the equation by the integrating factor $e^{.1t}$ and combining terms, we obtain

$$\frac{d}{dt}\left[e^{.1t}y\right] = (5t + 7)e^{.1t}.$$

Integrating both sides, we get

$$e^{.1t}y = \int (5t + 7)e^{.1t}\, dt$$

$$= 100e^{.1t}(.5t + .7 - 5) + C,$$

where we have used equation (1) with $a = 5$, $b = 7$, and $c = .1$. Multiplying both sides by $e^{-.1t}$, we find

$$y = 100(.5t - 4.3) + Ce^{-.1t} = 50t - 430 + Ce^{-.1t}.$$

To satisfy the initial condition, we must have

$$f(0) = 27 = -430 + C.$$

Hence $C = 457$, and so the temperature of the pizza at time t is

$$f(t) = 50t - 430 + 457e^{-.1t}.$$

After 8 minutes of heating, the temperature of the pizza is

$$f(8) = 50(8) - 430 + 457e^{-.1(8)} = -30 + 457e^{-.8} \approx 175°. \qquad \blacksquare$$

     The modeling techniques of this section have many interesting applications in finance, biology, medicine, and sociology. Some of these applications are presented in the exercises.

Practice Problems 10.4

1. A savings account earns 4% interest per year, compounded continuously, and continuous withdrawals are made from the account at the rate of $1200 per year. Set up a differential equation that is satisfied by the amount $f(t)$ of money in the account at time t.

EXERCISES 10.4

1. Refer to Example 1.
   (a) How fast was the amount in the account growing when it reached $30,000?
   (b) How much money was in the account when it was growing at twice the rate of your annual contribution?
   (c) How long do you have to wait for the money in the account to reach $40,000?

2. Refer to Example 2. Answer questions (a) and (b) in Exercise 1 if the interest rate is 7%. How long will it take to pay off the $25,000 loan in this case?

3. A person planning for her retirement arranges to make continuous deposits into a savings account at the rate of $3600 per year. The savings account earns 5% interest compounded continuously.
   (a) Set up a differential equation that is satisfied by $f(t)$, the amount of money in the account at time t.
   (b) Solve the differential equation in part (a), assuming that $f(0) = 0$, and determine how much money will be in the account at the end of 25 years.

4. A person deposits $10,000 in a bank account and decides to make additional deposits at the rate of A dollars per year. The bank compounds interest continuously at the annual rate of 6% and the deposits are made continuously into the account.
   (a) Set up a differential equation that is satisfied by the amount $f(t)$ in the account at time t.
   (b) Determine $f(t)$ (as a function of A).
   (c) Determine A if the initial deposit is to double in 5 years.

5. Twenty years ahead of her retirement, Kelly opened a savings account that earns 5% interest rate compounded continuously and contributed to this account at the annual rate of $1200 per year for 20 years. Ten years ahead of his retirement, John opened a similar savings account that earns 5% interest rate compounded continuously and decided to double the annual rate of contribution to $2400 per year for 10 years. Who has more money in his or her savings account at retirement? (Assume that the contributions are made continuously into the accounts.)

6. Answer the question in Exercise 5 if John contributed to his savings account at the annual rate of $3000 per year for 10 years.

7. A person took out a loan of $100,000 from a bank that charges 7.5% interest compounded continuously. What should be the annual rate of payments if the loan is to be paid in full in exactly 10 years? (Assume that the payments are made continuously throughout the year.)

8. **Car Prices in 2001** The National Automobile Dealers Association reported that the average retail selling price of a new vehicle[*] was $25,800 in 2001. A person purchased a new car at the average price and financed the entire amount. Suppose that the person can only afford to pay $500 per month. Assume that the payments are made at a continuous annual rate and that interest is compounded continuously at the rate of 3.5%.
   (a) Set up a differential equation that is satisfied by the amount $f(t)$ of money owed on the car loan at time t.
   (b) How long will it take to pay off the car loan?

9. **Home Prices in 2001** The Federal Housing Finance Board reported that the national average one-family house[†] purchase price in October 2001 was $219,600. At the same time, the average interest rate on a conventional 30-year fixed-rate mortgage was 6.76%. A person purchased a home at the average price, paid a down payment equal to 10% of the purchase price, and financed the remaining balance with a 30-year fixed-rate mortgage. Assume that the person makes payments continuously at a constant annual rate A and that interest is compounded continuously at the rate of 6.76%.
   (a) Set up a differential equation that is satisfied by the amount $f(t)$ of money owed on the mortgage at time t.
   (b) Determine A, the rate of annual payments, that is required to pay off the loan in 30 years. What will the monthly payments be?
   (c) Determine the total interest paid during the 30-year term mortgage.

10. Answer parts (a), (b), and (c) of Exercise 9 if the person takes a 15-year fixed-rate mortgage with a 6% interest rate and intends to pay off the entire loan in 15 years.

11. **Elasticity of Demand** Let $q = f(p)$ be the demand function for a certain commodity, where q is the demand quantity and p the price of 1 unit. In Section 5.3 we defined the elasticity of demand to be

$$E(p) = \frac{-pf'(p)}{f(p)}.$$

   (a) Find a differential equation satisfied by the demand function if the elasticity of demand is a linear function of price given by $E(p) = p + 1$.
   (b) Find the demand function in part (a), given $f(1) = 100$.

---
[*]Data obtained from the website of the National Automobile Dealers Association, www.nada.com.
[†]Data obtained from the website of the Federal Housing Finance Board, www.fhfb.gov.

12. Find the demand function if the elasticity of demand is a linear function of price given by $E(p) = ap + b$, where a and b are constants.

13. When a red-hot steel rod is plunged in a bath of water that is kept at a constant temperature $10°C$, the temperature of the rod at time t, $f(t)$, satisfies the differential equation

$$y' = k[10 - y],$$

where $k > 0$ is a constant of proportionality. Determine $f(t)$ if the initial temperature of the rod is $f(0) = 350°C$ and $k = .1$.

14. Rework Exercise 13 for a metal with a constant of proportionality $k = .2$. Which rod cools faster, the rod with a constant of proportionality $k = .1$ or the rod with a constant of proportionality $k = .2$? What can you say about the effect of varying the constant of proportionality in a cooling problem?

15. **Determining the Time of Death** A body was found in a room when the room's temperature was $70°F$. Let $f(t)$ denote the temperature of the body t hours from the time of death. According to Newton's law of cooling, f satisfies a differential equation of the form

$$y' = k(T - y).$$

(a) Find T.

(b) After several measurements of the body's temperature, it was determined that when the temperature of the body was 80 degrees it was decreasing at the rate of 5 degrees per hour. Find k.

(c) Suppose that at the time of death the body's temperature was about normal, say $98°F$. Determine $f(t)$.

(d) When the body was discovered, its temperature was $85°F$. Determine how long ago the person died.

16. Derive the formula for the population in Example 3, if the population in 1995 was 2 million. (The formula is given following the solution of Example 3.)

17. In an experiment, a certain type of bacteria was being added to a culture at the rate of $e^{.03t} + 2$ thousand bacteria per hour. Suppose that the bacteria grows at a rate proportional to the size of the culture at time t, with constant of proportionality $k = .45$. Let $P(t)$ denote the number of bacteria in the culture at time t. Find a differential equation satisfied by $P(t)$.

18. Find a formula for $P(t)$ in Exercise 17 if, initially, 10,000 bacteria were present in the culture.

19. **Dialysis and Creatinine Clearance** According to the National Kidney Foundation, in 1997 more than 260,000 Americans suffered from chronic kidney failure and needed an artificial kidney (dialysis) to stay alive.[‡] When the kidneys fail, toxic waste products such as creatinine and urea build up in the blood. One way to remove these wastes is to use a process known as peritoneal dialysis, in which the patient's peritonium, or lining of the abdomen, is used as a filter. When the abdominal cavity is filled with a certain dialysate solution, the waste products in the blood filter through the peritonium into the solution. After a waiting period of several hours, the dialysate solution is drained out of the body along with the waste products.

In one dialysis session, the abdomen of a patient with an elevated concentration of creatinine in the blood equal to 110 grams per liter was filled with two liters of a dialysate (containing no creatinine). Let $f(t)$ denote the concentration of creatinine in the dialysate at time t. The rate of change of $f(t)$ is proportional to the difference between 110 (the maximum concentration that can be attained in the dialysate) and $f(t)$. Thus $f(t)$ satisfies the differential equation

$$y' = k(110 - y).$$

(a) Suppose that at the end of a 4-hour dialysis session the concentration in the dialysate was 75 grams per liter and it was rising at the rate of 10 grams per liter per hour. Find k.

(b) What is the rate of change of the concentration at the beginning of the dialysis session? By comparing with the rate at the end of the session, can you give a (simplistic) justification for draining and replacing the dialysate with a fresh solution after 4 hours of dialysis? [*Hint:* You do not need to solve the differential equation.]

20. Radium 226 is a radioactive substance with a decay constant .00043. Suppose that radium 226 is being continuously added to an initially empty container at a constant rate of 3 milligrams per year. Let $P(t)$ denote the number of grams of radium 226 remaining in the container after t years.

(a) Find an initial-value problem satisfied by $P(t)$.

(b) Solve the initial-value problem for $P(t)$.

(c) What is the limit of the amount of radium 226 in the container as t tends to infinity?

In Exercises 21–25, solving the differential equations that arise from modeling may require using integration by parts. [See formula (1).]

21. A person deposits an inheritance of $100,000 in a savings account that earns 4% interest compounded continuously. This person intends to make withdrawals that will increase gradually in size with time. Suppose that the annual rate of withdrawals is $2000 + 500t$ dol-

---

[‡]Data obtained from the website of the National Kidney Foundation, www.kidney.org.

lars per year, t years from the time the account was opened.

(a) Assume that the withdrawals are made at a continuous rate. Set up a differential equation that is satisfied by the amount $f(t)$ in the account at time t.

(b) Determine $f(t)$.

(c) With the help of your calculator, plot $f(t)$ and approximate the time it will take before the account is depleted.

22. You make an initial deposit of $500 in a savings account and plan on making future deposits at a gradually increasing annual rate given by $90t + 810$ dollars per year, t years after the initial deposit. Assume that the deposits are made continuously and that interest is compounded continuously at the rate of 6%. Let $P(t)$ denote the amount of money in the account.

(a) Set up an initial-value problem that is satisfied by $P(t)$.

(b) Find $P(t)$.

23. After depositing an initial amount of $10,000 in a savings account that earns 4% interest compounded continuously, a person continued to make deposits for a certain period of time and then started to make withdrawals from the account. The annual rate of deposits was given by $3000 - 500t$ dollars per year, t years from the time the account was opened. (Here negative rates of deposits correspond to withdrawals.)

(a) How many years did the person contribute to the account before starting to withdraw money from it?

(b) Let $P(t)$ denote the amount of money in the account, t years after the initial deposit. Find an initial-value problem satisfied by $P(t)$. (Assume that the deposits and withdrawals were made continuously.)

24. Figure 4 contains the solution of the initial-value problem in Exercise 23.

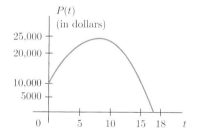

Figure 4

(a) With the help of the graph, approximate how long it will take before the account is depleted.

(b) Solve the initial-value problem to determine $P(t)$.

(c) Use the formula for $P(t)$ to verify your answer in part (a) with the help of a calculator.

25. **Morphine Infusion** Morphine is a drug that is widely used for pain management. However, morphine can be fatal by causing respiratory arrest. Since pain perception and drug tolerance vary with patients, morphine is gradually administered with small increments until pain is controlled or side effects begin to appear.

In one intravenous infusion, morphine was injected continuously at an increasing rate of t milligrams per hour. Suppose that the body removes the drug at a rate proportional to the amount of the drug present in the body, with constant of proportionality $k = .35$. Let $f(t)$ denote the amount of morphine in the body, t hours from the beginning of the infusion.

(a) Find a differential equation satisfied by $f(t)$.

(b) Assuming that the infusion lasted 8 hours, determine the amount of morphine in the body during the infusion if at the beginning of the infusion the body was free of morphine.

Technology Exercises

26. **Therapeutic Level of a Drug** A certain drug is administered intravenously to a patient at the continuous rate of r milligrams per hour. The patient's body removes the drug from the bloodstream at a rate proportional to the amount of the drug in the blood, with constant of proportionality $k = .5$.

(a) Write a differential equation that is satisfied by the amount $f(t)$ of the drug in the blood at time t (in hours).

(b) Find $f(t)$ assuming that $f(0) = 0$. (Give your answer in terms of r.)

(c) In a therapeutic 2-hour infusion, the amount of drug in the body should reach 1 milligram within 1 hour of administration and stay above this level for another hour. However, to avoid toxicity, the amount of drug in the body should not exceed 2 milligrams at any time. Plot the graph of $f(t)$ on the interval $1 \leq t \leq 2$, as r varies between 1 and 2 by increments of .1. That is, plot $f(t)$ for $r = 1, 1.1, 1.2, 1.3, \ldots, 2$. By looking at the graphs, pick the values of r that yield a therapeutic and nontoxic 2-hour infusion.

Solutions to Practice Problems 10.4

1. We reason as in Example 1. There are two influences on the way the savings account changes: the rate at which interest is added to the account and the rate at which money is withdrawn from the account. We know that interest is being added at a rate proportional to the amount in the account and that withdrawals are made at a rate of $1200 per year. Since the rate of change of $f(t)$ is the net effect of these two influences, we see that $f(t)$ satisfies the first-order differential equation

$$y' = .04y - 1200$$

$$\begin{bmatrix} \text{rate of} \\ \text{change of } y \end{bmatrix} = \begin{bmatrix} \text{rate at which} \\ \text{interest is added} \end{bmatrix} - \begin{bmatrix} \text{rate at which} \\ \text{money is withdrawn} \end{bmatrix}.$$

The standard form of this first-order equation is $y' - .04y = -1200$.

10.5 Graphing Solutions of Differential Equations

In this section we present a technique for sketching solutions to differential equations of the form $y' = g(y)$ *without having to solve the differential equation.* This technique is based on the geometric interpretation of a differential equation that we introduced in Section 10.1 and used to construct slope fields. The technique is valuable for three reasons. First, for many differential equations explicit solutions cannot be written down. Second, even when an explicit solution is available, we still face the problem of determining its behavior. For example, does the solution increase or decrease? If it increases, does it approach an asymptote or does it grow arbitrarily large? Third, and probably most significant, in many applications the explicit formula for a solution is unnecessary; only a general knowledge of the behavior of the solution is needed. That is, a qualitative understanding of the solution is sufficient.

The theory introduced in this section is part of what is called the *qualitative theory of differential equations.* We limit our attention to differential equations of the form $y' = g(y)$. Such differential equations are called *autonomous.* The term "autonomous" here means "independent of time" and refers to the fact that the right side of $y' = g(y)$ depends only on y and not on t. All applications studied in the next section involve autonomous differential equations.

Throughout this section we consider the values of each solution $y = f(t)$ only for $t \geq 0$. To introduce the qualitative theory, let us examine the graphs of the various typical solutions of the differential equation $y' = \frac{1}{2}(1 - y)(4 - y)$. The solution curves in Fig. 1 illustrate the following properties.

Property I Corresponding to each zero of $g(y)$ there is a constant solution of the differential equation. Specifically, if $g(c) = 0$, the constant function $y = c$ is a solution. (The constant solutions in Fig. 1 are $y = 1$ and $y = 4$.)

Property II The constant solutions divide the ty-plane into horizontal strips. Each nonconstant solution lies completely in one strip.

Property III Each nonconstant solution is either strictly increasing or decreasing.

Property IV Each nonconstant solution either is asymptotic to a constant solution or else increases or decreases without bound.

It can be shown that Properties I through IV are valid for the solutions of any autonomous differential equation $y' = g(y)$ provided that $g(y)$ is a "sufficiently well-behaved" function. We shall assume these properties in this chapter.

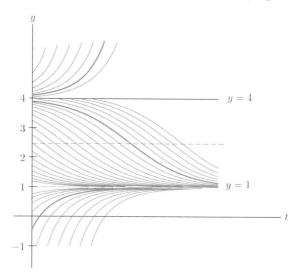

Figure 1. Solutions of $y' = \frac{1}{2}(1 - y)(4 - y)$.

Using Properties I through IV, we can sketch the general shape of any solution curve by looking at the graph of the function $g(y)$ and the behavior of that graph near $y(0)$. The procedure for doing this is illustrated in the following example.

EXAMPLE 1   Sketch the solution to $y' = e^{-y} - 1$ that satisfies $y(0) = -2$.

Solution   Here $g(y) = e^{-y} - 1$. On a yz-coordinate system we draw the graph of the function $z = g(y) = e^{-y} - 1$. [See Fig. 2(a).] The function $g(y) = e^{-y} - 1$ has a zero when $y = 0$. Therefore, the differential equation $y' = e^{-y} - 1$ has the constant solution $y = 0$. We indicate this constant solution on a ty-coordinate system in Fig. 2(b). To begin the sketch of the solution satisfying $y(0) = -2$, we locate this initial value of y on the (horizontal) y-axis in Fig. 2(a) and on the (vertical) y-axis in Fig. 2(b).

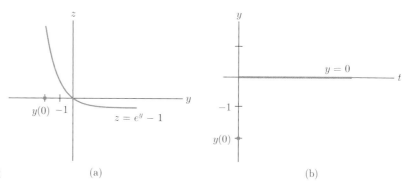

Figure 2   (a)   (b)

To determine whether the solution increases or decreases when it leaves the initial point $y(0)$ on the ty-graph, we look at the yz-graph and note that $z = g(y)$ is positive at $y = -2$. [See Fig. 3(a).] Consequently, since $y' = g(y)$, the derivative of the solution is positive, which implies that the solution is increasing. We indicate this by an arrow at the initial point in Fig. 3(b). Moreover, the solution y will increase asymptotically to the constant solution $y = 0$, by Properties III and IV of autonomous differential equations.

Next, we place an arrow in Fig. 4(a) to remind us that y will move from $y = -2$ toward $y = 0$. As y moves to the right toward $y = 0$ in Fig. 4(a), the z-coordinate of points on the graph of $g(y)$ becomes less positive; that is, $g(y)$ becomes less positive.

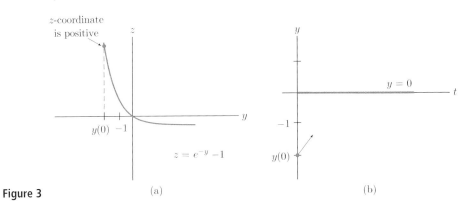

Figure 3   (a)   (b)

Consequently, since $y' = g(y)$, the slope of the solution curve becomes less positive. Thus the solution curve is concave down. [See Fig. 4(b).]

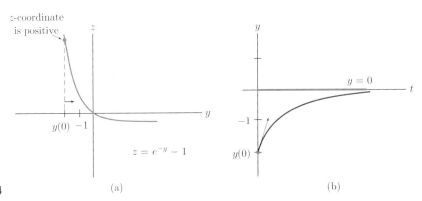

Figure 4   (a)   (b)

An important point to remember when sketching solutions is that z-coordinates on the yz-graph are values of $g(y)$, and since $y' = g(y)$, a z-coordinate gives the *slope* of the solution curve at the corresponding point on the ty-graph.

EXAMPLE 2   Sketch the graphs of the solutions to $y' = y + 2$ satisfying

(a) $y(0) = 1$ (b) $y(0) = -3$

Solution Here $g(y) = y + 2$. The graph of $z = g(y)$ is a straight line of slope 1 and z-intercept 2. [See Fig. 5(a).] This line crosses the y-axis only where $y = -2$. Thus the differential equation $y' = y + 2$ has one constant solution, $y = -2$. [See Fig. 5(b).]

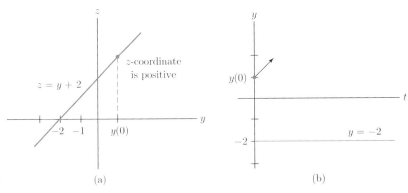

Figure 5   (a)   (b)

(a) We locate the initial value $y(0) = 1$ on the y-axes of both graphs in Fig. 5. The corresponding z-coordinate on the yz-graph is positive; therefore, the solution on the ty-graph has positive slope and is increasing as it leaves the initial point. We indicate this by an arrow in Fig. 5(b). Now, Property IV of autonomous differential equations implies that y will increase without bound from its initial value. As we let y increase from 1 in Fig. 6(a), we see that the z-coordinates [the values of $g(y)$] increase. Consequently, y' is increasing, so the graph of the solution must be concave up. We have sketched the solution in Fig. 6(b).

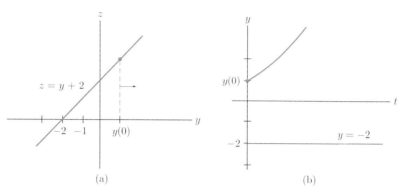

Figure 6   (a)   (b)

(b) Next we graph the solution for which $y(0) = -3$. From the graph of $z = y + 2$, we see that z is negative when $y = -3$. This implies that the solution is decreasing as it leaves the initial point. (See Fig. 7.) It follows that the values of y will continue to decrease without bound and become more and more negative. This means that on the yz-graph y must move to the *left*. [See Fig. 8(a).] We now examine what happens to $g(y)$ as y moves to the left. (This is the opposite

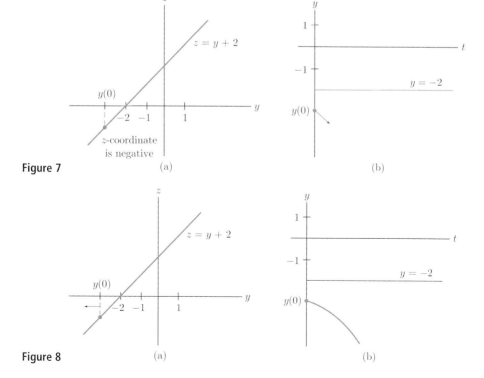

Figure 7   (a)   (b)

Figure 8   (a)   (b)

of the ordinary way to read a graph.) The z-coordinate becomes more negative; hence the slopes on the solution curve will become more negative. Thus the solution curve must be concave down, as in Fig. 8(b).   ■

From the preceding examples we can state a few rules for sketching a solution to $y' = g(y)$ with $y(0)$ given:

1. Sketch the graph of $z = g(y)$ on a yz-coordinate system. Find and label the zeros of $g(y)$.

2. For each zero c of $g(y)$, draw the constant solution $y = c$ on the ty-coordinate system.

3. Plot $y(0)$ on the y-axes of the two coordinate systems.

4. Determine whether the value of $g(y)$ is positive or negative when $y = y(0)$. This tells us whether the solution is increasing or decreasing. On the ty-graph, indicate the direction of the solution through $y(0)$.

5. On the yz-graph, indicate in which direction y should move. (*Note:* If y is moving *down* on the ty-graph, y moves to the *left* on the yz-graph.) As y moves in the proper direction on the yz-graph, determine whether $g(y)$ becomes more positive, less positive, more negative, or less negative. This tells us the concavity of the solution.

6. Beginning at $y(0)$ on the ty-graph, sketch the solution, being guided by the principle that the solution will grow (positively or negatively) without bound unless it encounters a constant solution. In this case, it will approach the constant solution asymptotically.

EXAMPLE 3   Sketch the solutions to $y' = y^2 - 4y$ satisfying $y(0) = 4.5$ and $y(0) = 3$.

Solution   Refer to Fig. 9. Since $g(y) = y^2 - 4y = y(y-4)$, the zeros of $g(y)$ are 0 and 4; hence the constant solutions are $y = 0$ and $y = 4$. The solution satisfying $y(0) = 4.5$ is increasing, because the z-coordinate is positive when $y = 4.5$ on the yz-graph. This solution continues to increase without bound. The solution satisfying $y(0) = 3$ is decreasing because the z-coordinate is negative when $y = 3$ on the yz-graph. This solution will decrease and approach asymptotically the constant solution $y = 0$.

An additional piece of information about the solution satisfying $y(0) = 3$ may be obtained from the graph of $z = g(y)$. We know that y decreases from 3 and approaches 0. From the graph of $z = g(y)$ in Fig. 9 it appears that at first the z-coordinates become more negative until y reaches 2 and then become less negative

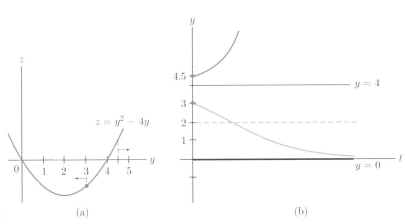

Figure 9   (a)   (b)

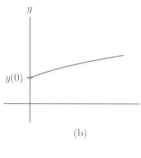

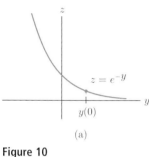

Figure 10

as y moves on toward 0. Since these z-coordinates are slopes on the solution curve, we conclude that, as the solution moves downward from its initial point on the ty-coordinate system, its slope becomes more negative until the y-coordinate is 2, and then the slope becomes less negative as the y-coordinate approaches 0. Hence the solution is concave down until $y = 2$ and then is concave up. Thus there is an inflection point at $y = 2$, where the concavity changes. ∎

We saw in Example 3 that the inflection point at $y = 2$ was produced by the fact that $g(y)$ had a minimum at $y = 2$. A generalization of the argument in Example 3 shows that inflection points of solution curves occur at each value of y where $g(y)$ has a nonzero relative maximum or minimum point. Thus we may formulate an additional rule for sketching a solution of $y' = g(y)$.

7. On the ty-coordinate system, draw dashed horizontal lines at all values of y at which $g(y)$ has a *nonzero* relative maximum or minimum point. A solution curve will have an inflection point whenever it crosses such a dashed line.

It is useful to note that when $g(y)$ is a quadratic function, as in Example 3, its maximum or minimum point occurs at a value of y halfway between the zeros of $g(y)$. This is because the graph of a quadratic function is a parabola, which is symmetric about a vertical line through its vertex.

EXAMPLE 4   Sketch a solution to $y' = e^{-y}$ with $y(0) > 0$.

Solution   Refer to Fig. 10. Since $g(y) = e^{-y}$ is always positive, there are no constant solutions to the differential equation and every solution will increase without bound. When drawing solutions that asymptotically approach a horizontal line, we have no choice as to whether to draw it concave up or concave down. This decision will be obvious from its increasing or decreasing nature and from knowledge of inflection points. However, for solutions that grow without bound, we must look at $g(y)$ to determine concavity. In this example, as t increases, the values of y increase. As y increases, $g(y)$ becomes less positive. Since $g(y) = y'$, we deduce that the slope of the solution curve becomes less positive; therefore, the solution curve is concave down. ∎

Practice Problems 10.5

Consider the differential equation $y' = g(y)$, where $g(y)$ is the function whose graph is drawn in Fig. 11.

1. How many constant solutions are there to the differential equation $y' = g(y)$?

2. For what initial values $y(0)$ will the corresponding solution of the differential equation be an increasing function?

3. If the initial value $y(0)$ is near 4, will the corresponding solution be asymptotic to the constant solution $y = 4$?

4. For what initial values $y(0)$ will the corresponding solution of the differential equation have an inflection point?

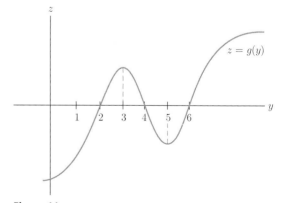

Figure 11

EXERCISES 10.5

Exercises 1–6 review concepts that are important in this section. In each exercise, sketch the graph of a function with the stated properties.

1. Domain: $0 \le t \le 3$; $(0,1)$ is on the graph; the slope is always positive, and the slope becomes less positive (as t increases).

2. Domain: $0 \le t \le 4$; $(0,2)$ is on the graph; the slope is always positive, and the slope becomes more positive (as t increases).

3. Domain: $0 \le t \le 5$; $(0,3)$ is on the graph; the slope is always negative, and the slope becomes less negative.

4. Domain: $0 \le t \le 6$; $(0,4)$ is on the graph; the slope is always negative, and the slope becomes more negative.

5. Domain: $0 \le t \le 7$; $(0,2)$ is on the graph; the slope is always positive, the slope becomes more positive as t increases from 0 to 3, and the slope becomes less positive as t increases from 3 to 7.

6. Domain: $0 \le t \le 8$; $(0,6)$ is on the graph; the slope is always negative, the slope becomes more negative as t increases from 0 to 3, and the slope becomes less negative as t increases from 3 to 8.

One or more initial conditions are given for each differential equation in the following exercises. Use the qualitative theory of autonomous differential equations to sketch the graphs of the corresponding solutions. Include a yz-graph if one is not already provided. Always indicate the constant solutions on the ty-graph whether they are mentioned or not.

7. $y' = 3 - \frac{1}{2}y$, $y(0) = 4$, $y(0) = 8$. [The graph of $z = g(y)$ is drawn in Fig. 12.]

8. $y' = \frac{2}{3}y - 3$, $y(0) = 3$, $y(0) = 6$. (See Fig. 13.)

9. $y' = y^2 - 5$, $y(0) = -4$, $y(0) = 2$, $y(0) = 3$. (See Fig. 14.)

10. $y' = 6 - y^2$, $y(0) = -3$, $y(0) = 3$. (See Fig. 15.)

11. $y' = -\frac{1}{3}(y+2)(y-4)$, $y(0) = -3$, $y(0) = -1$, $y(0) = 6$. (See Fig. 16.)

12. $y' = y^2 - 6y + 5$ or $y' = (y-1)(y-5)$, $y(0) = -2$, $y(0) = 2$, $y(0) = 4$, $y(0) = 6$. (See Fig. 17.)

13. $y' = y^3 - 9y$ or $y' = y(y^2 - 9)$, $y(0) = -4$, $y(0) = -1$, $y(0) = 2$, $y(0) = 4$. (See Fig. 18.)

14. $y' = 9y - y^3$, $y(0) = -4$, $y(0) = -1$, $y(0) = 2$, $y(0) = 4$. (See Fig. 19.)

15. Use the graph in Fig. 20 to sketch the solutions to the Gompertz growth equation

$$\frac{dy}{dt} = -\frac{1}{10}y \ln \frac{y}{100}$$

satisfying $y(0) = 10$ and $y(0) = 150$.

16. The graph of $z = -\frac{1}{2}y \ln(y/30)$ has the same general shape as the graph in Fig. 20 with relative maximum point at $y \approx 11.0364$ and y-intercept at $y = 30$; $y(0) = 1$, $y(0) = 20$, and $y(0) = 40$. Sketch the solutions to the Gompertz growth equation

$$\frac{dy}{dt} = -\frac{1}{2}y \ln \frac{y}{30}.$$

17. $y' = g(y)$, $y(0) = -.5$, $y(0) = .5$, where $g(y)$ is the function whose graph is given in Fig. 21.

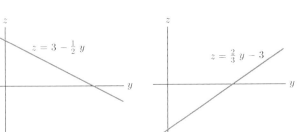

Figure 12

Figure 13

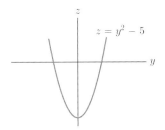

Figure 14

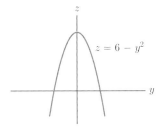

Figure 15

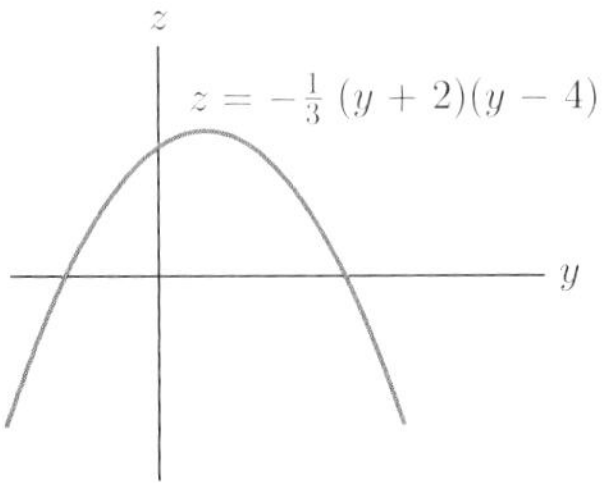

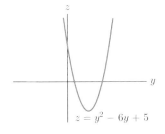

Figure 16

Figure 17

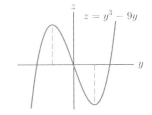

Figure 18

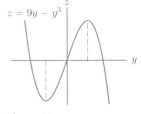

Figure 19

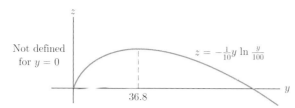

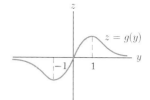

Figure 20

Figure 21

18. $y' = g(y)$, $y(0) = 0$, $y(0) = 4$, where the graph of $g(y)$ is given in Fig. 22.

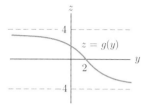

Figure 22

19. $y' = g(y)$, $y(0) = 0$, $y(0) = 1.2$, $y(0) = 5$, $y(0) = 7$, where the graph of $g(y)$ is given in Fig. 23.

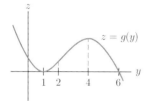

Figure 23

20. $y' = g(y)$, $y(0) = 1$, $y(0) = 3$, $y(0) = 11$, where the graph of $g(y)$ is given in Fig. 24.

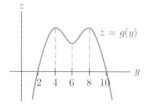

Figure 24

21. $y' = \frac{3}{4}y - 3$, $y(0) = 2$, $y(0) = 4$, $y(0) = 6$

22. $y' = -\frac{1}{2}y$, $y(0) = -2$, $y(0) = 0$, $y(0) = 2$

23. $y' = 5y - y^2$, $y(0) = 1$, $y(0) = 7$

24. $y' = -y^2 + 10y - 21$, $y(0) = 1$, $y(0) = 4$

Refer to Fig. 20 for Exercises 25–36.

25. $y' = y^2 - 3y - 4$, $y(0) = 0$, $y(0) = 3$

26. $y' = \frac{1}{2}y^2 - 3y$, $y(0) = 3$, $y(0) = 6$, $y(0) = 9$

27. $y' = y^2 + 2$, $y(0) = -1$, $y(0) = 1$

28. $y' = y - \frac{1}{4}y^2$, $y(0) = -1$, $y(0) = 1$

29. $y' = \sin y$, $y(0) = -\pi/6$, $y(0) = \pi/6$, $y(0) = 7\pi/4$

30. $y' = 1 + \sin y$, $y(0) = 0$, $y(0) = \pi$

31. $y' = 1/y$, $y(0) = -1$, $y(0) = 1$

32. $y' = y^3$, $y(0) = -1$, $y(0) = 1$

33. $y' = ky^2$, where k is a negative constant, $y(0) = -2$, $y(0) = 2$

34. $y' = ky(M - y)$, where $k > 0$, $M > 10$, and $y(0) = 1$

35. $y' = ky - A$, where k and A are positive constants. Sketch solutions where $0 < y(0) < A/k$ and $y(0) > A/k$.

36. $y' = k(y - A)$, where $k < 0$ and $A > 0$. Sketch solutions where $y(0) < A$ and $y(0) > A$.

37. Suppose that once a sunflower plant has started growing the rate of growth at any time is proportional to the product of its height and the difference between its height at maturity and its current height. Give a differential equation that is satisfied by $f(t)$, the height at time t, and sketch the solution.

38. A parachutist has a terminal velocity of -176 feet per second. That is, no matter how long a person falls, his or her speed will not exceed 176 feet per second, but it will get arbitrarily close to that value. The velocity in feet per second, $v(t)$, after t seconds satisfies the differential equation $v'(t) = 32 - k \cdot v(t)$. What is the value of k?

Technology Exercises

39. Draw the graph of $g(x) = (x - 2)^2(x - 6)^2$ and use the graph to sketch the solutions of the differential equation $y' = (y - 2)^2(y - 6)^2$ with initial conditions $y(0) = 1$, $y(0) = 3$, $y(0) = 5$, and $y(0) = 7$ on a ty-coordinate system.

40. Draw the graph of $g(x) = e^x - 100x^2 - 1$ and use the graph to sketch the solution of the differential equation $y' = e^y - 100y^2 - 1$ with initial condition $y(0) = 4$ on a ty-coordinate system.

Solutions to Practice Problems 10.5

1. Three. The function $g(y)$ has zeros when y is 2, 4, and 6. Therefore, $y' = g(y)$ has the constant functions $y = 2$, $y = 4$, and $y = 6$ as solutions.

2. For $2 < y(0) < 4$ and $y(0) > 6$. Since nonconstant solutions are either strictly increasing or strictly decreasing, a solution is an increasing function provided that it is increasing at time $t = 0$. This is the case when the first derivative is positive at $t = 0$. When $t = 0$, $y' = g(y(0))$. Therefore, the solution corresponding to $y(0)$ is increasing whenever $g(y(0))$ is positive.

3. Yes. If $y(0)$ is slightly to the right of 4, then $g(y(0))$ is negative, so the corresponding solution will be a decreasing function with values moving to the left closer and closer to 4. If $y(0)$ is slightly to the left of 4, then $g(y(0))$ is positive, so the corresponding solution will

be an increasing function with values moving to the right closer and closer to 4. (The constant solution $y = 4$ is referred to as a *stable* constant solution. The solution with initial value 4 stays at 4, and solutions with initial values near 4 move toward 4. The constant solution $y = 2$ is *unstable*. Solutions with initial values near 2 move away from 2.)

4. For $2 < y(0) < 3$ and $5 < y(0) < 6$. Inflection points of solutions correspond to relative maximum and relative minimum points of the function $g(y)$. If $2 < y(0) < 3$, the corresponding solution will be an increasing function. The values of y will move to the right (toward 4) and therefore will cross 3, a place at which $g(y)$ has a relative maximum point. Similarly, if $5 < y(0) < 6$, the corresponding solution will be decreasing. The values of y on the yz-graph will move to the left and cross 5.

10.6 Applications of Differential Equations

In this section we study real-life situations that may be modeled by an autonomous differential equation $y' = g(y)$. Here y will represent some quantity that is changing with time, and the equation $y' = g(y)$ will be obtained from a description of the rate of change of y.

We have already encountered many situations where the rate of change of y is *proportional* to some quantity. For example,

1. $y' = ky$: "the rate of change of y is proportional to y" (exponential growth or decay).

2. $y' = k(M - y)$: "the rate of change of y is proportional to the difference between M and y" (Newton's law of cooling, for example).

Both situations involve *linear* first-order differential equations. The following example gives rise to an equation that is not linear. It concerns the rate at which a technological innovation may spread through an industry, a subject of interest to both sociologists and economists.

EXAMPLE 1

The by-product coke oven was first introduced into the iron and steel industry in 1894. It took about 30 years before all the major steel producers had adopted this innovation. Let $f(t)$ be the percentage of the producers that had installed the new coke ovens by time t. Then a reasonable model* for the way $f(t)$ increased is given by the assumption that the rate of change of $f(t)$ at time t was proportional to the product of $f(t)$ and the percentage of firms that had not yet installed the new coke ovens at time t. Write a differential equation that is satisfied by $f(t)$.

Solution Since $f(t)$ is the *percentage* of firms that have the new coke oven, $100 - f(t)$ is the percentage of firms that still have not installed any new coke ovens. We are told that the rate of change of $f(t)$ is proportional to the product of $f(t)$ and $100 - f(t)$.

---

*See E. Mansfield, "Technical Change and the Rate of Imitation," *Econometrica*, 29 (1961), 741–766.

Hence there is a constant of proportionality k such that

$$f'(t) = kf(t)[100 - f(t)].$$

Replacing $f(t)$ by y and $f'(t)$ by y', we obtain the desired differential equation,

$$y' = ky(100 - y).$$

Note that both y and $100 - y$ are nonnegative quantities. Clearly, y' must be positive, because $y = f(t)$ is an increasing function. Hence the constant k must be positive. ∎

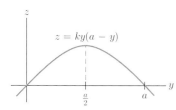

Figure 1. yz-graph for a logistic differential equation.

The differential equation obtained in Example 1 is a special case of the *logistic differential equation*,

$$y' = ky(a - y), \tag{1}$$

where k and a are positive constants. This equation is used as a simple mathematical model of a wide variety of physical phenomena. In Section 5.4, we described applications of the logistic equation to restricted population growth and to the spread of an epidemic. Let us use the qualitative theory of differential equations to gain more insight into this important equation.

The first step in sketching solutions of (1) is to draw the yz-graph. Rewriting the equation $z = ky(a - y)$ in the form

$$z = -ky^2 + kay,$$

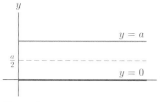

Figure 2

we see that the equation is quadratic in y and hence its graph will be a parabola. The parabola is concave down because the coefficient of y^2 is negative (since k is a positive constant). The zeros of the quadratic expression $ky(a - y)$ occur where $y = 0$ and $y = a$. Since a represents some positive constant, we select an arbitrary point on the positive y-axis and label it "a." With this information we can sketch a representative graph. (See Fig. 1.) Note that the vertex of the parabola occurs at $y = a/2$, halfway between the y-intercepts. (You should review how we obtained this graph, given only that k and a are positive constants. Similar situations will arise in the exercises.)

We begin the ty-graph showing the constant solutions and placing a dashed line at $y = a/2$, where certain solution curves will have an inflection point. (See Fig. 2.) On either side of the constant solutions we choose initial values for y—say, y_1, y_2, y_3, y_4. Then we use the yz-graph to sketch the corresponding solution curves. (See Fig. 3.)

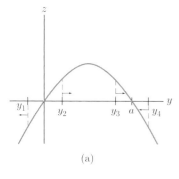

(a)

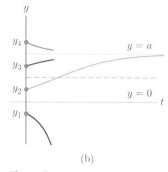

(b)

Figure 3

The solution in Fig. 3(b) beginning at y_2 has the general shape usually referred to as a *logistic curve*. This is the type of solution that would model the situation described in Example 1. The solution in Fig. 3(b) beginning at y_1 usually has no physical significance. The other solutions shown in Fig. 3(b) can occur in practice, particularly in the study of population growth.

In ecology, the growth of a population is often described by a logistic equation written in the form

$$\frac{dN}{dt} = rN\frac{K - N}{K} \tag{2}$$

or, equivalently,

$$\frac{dN}{dt} = \frac{r}{K}N(K - N),$$

where N is used instead of y to denote the size of the population at time t. Typical solutions of this equation are sketched in Fig. 4. The constant K is called the *carrying capacity* of the environment. When the initial population is close to zero, the population curve has the typical S-shaped appearance, and N approaches the

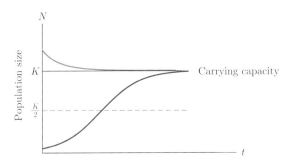

Figure 4. A logistic model for population change.

carrying capacity asymptotically. When the initial population is greater than K, the population decreases in size, again asymptotically approaching the carrying capacity.

The quantity $(K - N)/K$ in equation (2) is a fraction between 0 and 1. It reflects the limiting effect of the environment on the population and is close to 1 when N is close to 0. If this fraction were replaced by the constant 1, then (2) would become

$$\frac{dN}{dt} = rN.$$

This is the equation for ordinary exponential growth, where r is the growth rate. For this reason the parameter r in (2) is called the *intrinsic rate of growth* of the population. It expresses how the population would grow if the environment were to permit unrestricted exponential growth.

We now consider a concrete situation that gives rise to a logistic equation.

EXAMPLE 2

A fish population A pond on a fish farm has a carrying capacity of 1000 fish. The pond was originally stocked with 100 fish. Let $N(t)$ denote the number of fish in the pond after t months.

(a) Set up a logistic differential equation satisfied by $N(t)$ and plot an approximate graph of the fish population.

(b) Find the size of the population of fish with the highest rate of growth. Find this rate, given that the intrinsic rate of growth is .3.

Solution (a) We are told that the equation is a logistic equation with carrying capacity $K = 1000$. Hence, from (2), the equation is

$$\frac{dN}{dt} = rN\frac{1000 - N}{1000} = \frac{r}{1000}N(1000 - N).$$

The fish population at time t is given by the solution of this differential equation with the initial condition $N(0) = 100$. Even though we do not have a numerical value for the intrinsic rate r, we can still estimate the shape of the solution by using qualitative techniques. First sketch the constant solutions, $N = 0$ and $N = 1000$; then place a dashed line at $N = 500$, where certain solutions will have inflection points. The solution starting at $N = 100$ is a typical logistic curve. It is increasing, with a horizontal asymptote $N = 1000$ and inflection point at $N = 500$, where the graph changes concavity. A solution curve satisfying these properties is shown in Fig. 5(b).

(b) Since the question concerns the rate of growth, we should look at the equation itself for answers. The equation tells us that the rate of growth is given by the quadratic function

$$\frac{dN}{dt} = \frac{r}{1000}N(1000 - N),$$

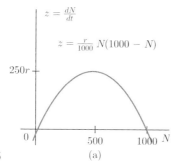

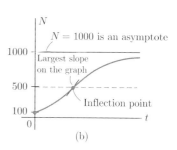

Figure 5

(a)

(b)

whose graph is an inverted parabola with intercepts at $N = 0$ and $N = 1000$. [See Fig. 5(a).] Since the parabola is concave down, it has a maximum at $N = 500$, halfway between 0 and 1000. Thus the size of the population with the highest rate of growth is 500. To find the numerical value of the fastest growth rate, given that $r = .3$, we substitute $r = .3$ and $N = 500$ into the equation and get

$$\left. \frac{dN}{dt} \right|_{N=500} = \frac{.3}{1000}(500)(1000 - 500) = 75 \text{ fish per month.}$$

This is the maximum rate of growth of the fish population. It is attained when 500 fish are in the pond. Note that 500 is not the maximum size of the population. In fact, we know that the fish population will approach 1000 asymptotically. [See Fig. 5(b).] ■

We now turn to applications that involve a different sort of autonomous differential equation. The main idea is illustrated in the following familiar example of the savings account that we discussed in Section 10.4.

EXAMPLE 3   A savings account earns 6% interest per year, compounded continuously, and continuous withdrawals are made from the account at the rate of $900 per year. Set up a differential equation that is satisfied by the amount $f(t)$ of money in the account at time t. Sketch typical solutions of the differential equation.

Solution   At first, let us ignore the withdrawals from the account. In Section 5.2 we discussed continuous compounding of interest and showed that, if no deposits or withdrawals are made, $f(t)$ satisfies the equation

$$y' = .06y.$$

That is, the savings account grows at a rate proportional to the size of the account. Since this growth comes from the interest, we conclude that *interest is being added to the account at a rate proportional to the amount in the account.*

Now suppose that continuous withdrawals are made from this same account at the rate of $900 per year. Then there are two influences on the way the amount of money in the account changes: the rate at which interest is added and the rate at which money is withdrawn. The rate of change of $f(t)$ is the *net effect* of these two influences. That is, $f(t)$ now satisfies the equation

$$y' \qquad = \qquad .06y \qquad - \qquad 900$$

$$\begin{bmatrix} \text{rate of} \\ \text{change of } y \end{bmatrix} = \begin{bmatrix} \text{rate at which} \\ \text{interest is added} \end{bmatrix} - \begin{bmatrix} \text{rate at which} \\ \text{money is withdrawn} \end{bmatrix}.$$

The qualitative sketches for this differential equation are given in Fig. 6. The constant solution is found by solving $.06y - 900 = 0$, which gives $y = 900/.06 = 15,000$. If the initial amount $y(0)$ in the account is \$15,000, the balance in the account will always be \$15,000. If the initial amount is greater than \$15,000, the savings account will accumulate money without bound. If the initial amount is less than \$15,000, the account balance will decrease. Presumably, the bank will stop withdrawals when the account balance reaches zero. ■

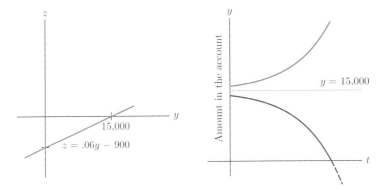

Figure 6. A differential equation model for a savings account: $y' = .06y - 900$.

We may think of the savings account in Example 3 as a compartment or container into which money (interest) is being steadily added and also from which money is being steadily withdrawn. (See Fig. 7.)

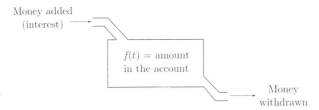

Figure 7. A one-compartment model in economics.

A similar situation arises frequently in physiology in what are called "one-compartment problems."* Typical examples of a compartment are a person's lungs, the digestive system, and the cardiovascular system. A common problem is to study the rate at which the amount of some substance in the compartment is changing when two or more processes act on the substance in the compartment. In many important cases, each of these processes changes the substance, either at a constant rate or at a rate proportional to the amount in the compartment.

An earlier example of such a one-compartment problem, discussed in Section 5.4, concerned the continuous infusion of glucose into a patient's bloodstream. A similar situation is discussed in the next example.

EXAMPLE 4

A one-compartment mixing process Consider a flask that contains 3 liters of salt water. Suppose that water containing 25 grams per liter of salt is pumped into the flask at the rate of 2 liters per hour, and the mixture, being steadily stirred, is pumped out of the flask at the same rate. Find a differential equation satisfied by the amount of salt $f(t)$ in the flask at time t.

---

*See William Simon, *Mathematical Techniques for Physiology and Medicine* (New York: Academic Press, 1972), Chap. 5.

Solution Let $f(t)$ be the amount of salt measured in grams. Since the volume of the mixture in the flask is being held constant at 3 liters, the concentration of salt in the flask at time t is

$$[\text{concentration}] = \frac{[\text{amount of salt}]}{[\text{volume of mixture}]} = \frac{f(t)\ \text{grams}}{3\ \text{liters}} = \frac{1}{3}f(t)\frac{\text{grams}}{\text{liter}}.$$

Next we compute the rates at which salt enters and leaves the flask at time t:

$$[\text{rate of salt entering}] = [\text{entering concentration}] \times [\text{flow rate}]$$

$$= \left[25\ \frac{\text{grams}}{\text{liter}}\right] \times \left[2\ \frac{\text{liters}}{\text{hour}}\right]$$

$$= 50\ \frac{\text{grams}}{\text{hour}}.$$

$$[\text{rate of salt leaving}] = [\text{concentration}] \times [\text{flow rate}]$$

$$= \left[\frac{1}{3}f(t)\ \frac{\text{grams}}{\text{liter}}\right] \times \left[2\ \frac{\text{liters}}{\text{hour}}\right]$$

$$= \frac{2}{3}f(t)\ \frac{\text{grams}}{\text{hour}}.$$

The *net* rate of change of salt (in grams per hour) at time t is $f'(t) = 50 - \frac{2}{3}f(t)$. Hence the desired differential equation is

$$y' = 50 - \tfrac{2}{3}y.$$

Differential Equations in Population Genetics In population genetics, hereditary phenomena are studied on a populational level, rather than on an individual level. Consider a particular hereditary feature of an animal, such as the length of the hair. Suppose that basically there are two types of hair for a certain animal, long hair and short hair. Also suppose that long hair is the dominant type. Let A denote the gene responsible for long hair and a the gene responsible for short hair. Each animal has a pair of these genes, either AA ("dominant" individuals), or aa ("recessive" individuals), or Aa ("hybrid" individuals). If there are N animals in the population, there are $2N$ genes in the population controlling hair length. Each Aa individual has one a gene, and each aa individual has two a genes. The total number of a genes in the population divided by $2N$ gives the fraction of a genes. This fraction is called the *gene frequency of a* in the population. Similarly, the fraction of A genes is called the gene frequency of A. Note that

$$\begin{bmatrix}\text{gene}\\\text{frequency}\\\text{of }a\end{bmatrix} + \begin{bmatrix}\text{gene}\\\text{frequency}\\\text{of }A\end{bmatrix} = \frac{[\text{number of }a\text{ genes}]}{2N} + \frac{[\text{number of }A\text{ genes}]}{2N}$$

$$= \frac{2N}{2N} = 1. \tag{3}$$

We shall denote the gene frequency of a by q. From (3) it follows that the gene frequency of A is $1 - q$.

An important problem in population genetics involves the way the gene frequency q changes as the animals in the population reproduce. If each unit on the time axis represents one "generation," we can consider q as a function of time t. (See Fig. 8.) In general, many hundreds or thousands of generations are studied, so the time for one generation is small compared with the overall time period. For

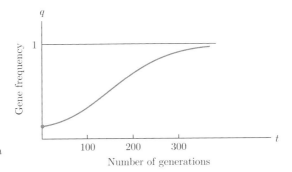

Figure 8. Gene frequency in a population.

many purposes, q is considered to be a differentiable function of t. In what follows we assume that the population mates at random and that the distribution of a and A genes is the same for males and females. In this case, we can show from elementary probability theory that the gene frequency is essentially constant from one generation to the next when no "disturbing factors" are present, such as mutation or external influences on the population. We shall discuss differential equations that describe the effect of such disturbing factors on $q(t)$.[*]

Suppose that in every generation a fraction ν of the a genes mutate and become A genes. Then the rate of change of the gene frequency q due to this mutation is

$$\frac{dq}{dt} = -\nu q. \tag{4}$$

To understand this equation, think of q as a measure of the number of a genes, and think of the a genes as a population that is losing members at a constant percentage rate of $100\nu\%$ per generation (that is, per unit time). This is an exponential decay process, so q satisfies the exponential decay equation (4). Now suppose, instead, that in every generation a fraction μ of the A genes mutate into a genes. Since the gene frequency of A is $1 - q$, the decrease in the gene frequency of A due to mutation will be $\mu(1 - q)$ per generation. But this must match the increase in the gene frequency of a, since from (3) the sum of the two gene frequencies is constant. Thus the rate of change of the gene frequency of a per generation, due to the mutation from A to a, is given by

$$\frac{dq}{dt} = \mu(1 - q).$$

When mutation occurs, it frequently happens that in each generation a fraction μ of A mutate to a and at the same time a fraction ν of a mutate to A. The *net effect* of these two influences on the gene frequency q is described by the equation

$$\frac{dq}{dt} = \mu(1 - q) - \nu q. \tag{5}$$

(The situation here is analogous to the one-compartment problems discussed earlier.)

Let us make a qualitative analysis of equation (5). To be specific, we take $\mu = .00003$ and $\nu = .00001$. Then

$$\frac{dq}{dt} = .00003(1 - q) - .00001q = .00003 - .00004q$$

---

[*]See C. C. Li, *Population Genetics* (Chicago: University of Chicago Press, 1955), pp. 240–263, 283–286.

or

$$\frac{dq}{dt} = -.00004(q - .75). \tag{6}$$

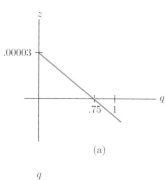

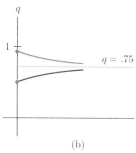

(a)

(b)

Figure 9

Figure 9(a) shows the graph of $z = -.00004(q - .75)$ with the z-axis scale greatly enlarged. Typical solution curves are sketched in Fig. 9(b). We see that the gene frequency $q = .75$ is an equilibrium value. If the initial value of q is smaller than .75, the value of q will rise under the effect of the mutations; after many generations, it will be approximately .75. If the initial value of q is between .75 and 1.00, then q will eventually decrease to .75. The equilibrium value is completely determined by the magnitudes of the two opposing rates of mutation μ and ν. From (6) we see that the rate of change of gene frequency is proportional to the difference between q and the equilibrium value .75.

In the study of how a population adapts to an environment over a long period, geneticists assume that some hereditary types have an advantage over others in survival and reproduction. Suppose that the adaptive ability of the hybrid (Aa) individuals is slightly greater than that of both the dominant (AA) and the recessive (aa) individuals. In this case it turns out that the rate of change of gene frequency due to this "selection pressure" is

$$\frac{dq}{dt} = q(1 - q)(c - dq), \tag{7}$$

where c and d are positive constants with $c < d$. On the other hand, if the adaptive ability of the hybrid individuals is slightly less than that of both the dominant and the recessive individuals, it can be shown that

$$\frac{dq}{dt} = kq(1 - q)(2q - 1), \tag{8}$$

where k is a constant between 0 and 1, called the *coefficient of selection against hybrids*.

It is possible to consider the joint effects of mutation and natural selection. Suppose that mutations from A to a occur at a rate μ per generation and from a to A at a rate ν per generation. Suppose also that selection is against recessive individuals (that is, recessives do not adapt as well as the rest of the population). Then the net rate of change in gene frequency turns out to be

$$\frac{dq}{dt} = \mu(1 - q) - \nu q - kq^2(1 - q).$$

Here $\mu(1 - q)$ represents the gain in a genes from mutations $A \rightarrow a$, the term νq is the loss in a genes from mutations $a \rightarrow A$, and the term $kq^2(1 - q)$ represents the loss in a genes due to natural selection pressures.

Practice Problems 10.6

1. Refer to Example 4, involving the flow of salt water through a flask. Will $f(t)$ be an increasing or a decreasing function?

2. **Rate of Litter Accumulation** In a certain tropical forest, litter (mainly dead vegetation such as leaves and vines) forms on the ground at the rate of 10 grams per square centimeter per year. At the same time, however, the litter is decomposing at the rate of 80% per year. Let $f(t)$ be the amount of litter (in grams per square centimeter) present at time t. Find a differential equation satisfied by $f(t)$.

EXERCISES 10.6

In Exercises 1–4, you are given a logistic equation with one or more initial conditions. (a) Determine the carrying capacity and intrinsic rate. (b) Sketch the graph of $\frac{dN}{dt}$ versus N in an Nz-plane. (c) In the tN-plane, plot the constant solutions and place a dashed line where the concavity of certain solutions may change. (d) Sketch the solution curve corresponding to each given initial condition.

1. $dN/dt = N(1 - N)$, $N(0) = .75$
2. $dN/dt = .3N(100 - N)$, $N(0) = 25$
3. $dN/dt = -.01N^2 + N$, $N(0) = 5$
4. $dN/dt = -N^2 + N$, $N(0) = .5$

5. Answer part (a) in Example 2 if the pond was originally stocked with 600 fish and all other data are unchanged. How does the graph of the fish population in this case differ from the one in Example 2?

6. Answer parts (a) and (b) in Example 2 if the pond has a carrying capacity of 2000 fish and all other data are unchanged.

7. **Social Diffusion** For information being spread by mass media, rather than through individual contact, the rate of spread of the information at any time is proportional to the percentage of the population not having the information at that time. Give the differential equation that is satisfied by $y = f(t)$, the percentage of the population having the information at time t. Assume that $f(0) = 1$. Sketch the solution.

8. **Gravity** At one point in his study of a falling body starting from rest, Galileo conjectured that its velocity at any time is proportional to the distance it has dropped. Using this hypothesis, set up the differential equation whose solution is $y = f(t)$, the distance fallen by time t. By making use of the initial value, show why Galileo's original conjecture is invalid.

9. **Autocatalytic Reaction** In an autocatalytic reaction, one substance is converted into a second substance in such a way that the second substance catalyzes its own formation. This is the process by which trypsinogen is converted into the enzyme trypsin. The reaction starts only in the presence of some trypsin, and each molecule of trypsinogen yields one molecule of trypsin. The rate of formation of trypsin is proportional to the product of the amounts of the two substances present. Set up the differential equation that is satisfied by $y = f(t)$, the amount (number of molecules) of trypsin present at time t. Sketch the solution. For what value of y is the reaction proceeding the fastest? [*Note:* Letting M be the total amount of the two substances, the amount of trypsinogen present at time t is $M - f(t)$.]

10. **Drying** A porous material dries outdoors at a rate that is proportional to the moisture content. Set up the differential equation whose solution is $y = f(t)$, the amount of water at time t in a towel on a clothesline. Sketch the solution.

11. **Movement of Solutes through a Cell Membrane** Let c be the concentration of a solute outside a cell that we assume to be constant throughout the process, that is, unaffected by the small influx of the solute across the membrane due to a difference in concentration. The rate of change of the concentration of the solute inside the cell at any time t is proportional to the difference between the outside concentration and the inside concentration. Set up the differential equation whose solution is $y = f(t)$, the concentration of the solute inside the cell at time t. Sketch a solution.

12. An experimenter reports that a certain strain of bacteria grows at a rate proportional to the square of the size of the population. Set up a differential equation that describes the growth of the population. Sketch a solution.

13. **Chemical Reaction** Suppose that substance A is converted into substance B at a rate that, at any time t, is proportional to the square of the amount of A. This situation occurs, for instance, when it is necessary for two molecules of A to collide to create one molecule of B. Set up the differential equation that is satisfied by $y = f(t)$, the amount of substance A at time t. Sketch a solution.

14. **War Fever** L. F. Richardson proposed the following model to describe the spread of war fever.[*] If $y = f(t)$ is the percent of the population advocating war at time t, the rate of change of $f(t)$ at any time is proportional to the product of the percentage of the population advocating war and the percentage not advocating war. Set up a differential equation that is satisfied by $y = f(t)$ and sketch a solution.

15. **Capital Investment Model** In economic theory, the following model is used to describe a possible capital investment policy. Let $f(t)$ represent the total invested capital of a company at time t. Additional capital is invested whenever $f(t)$ is below a certain equilibrium value E, and capital is withdrawn whenever $f(t)$ exceeds E. The rate of investment is proportional to the difference between $f(t)$ and E. Construct a differential equation whose solution is $f(t)$ and sketch two or three typical solution curves.

16. **Evans Price Adjustment Model** Consider a certain commodity that is produced by many companies and purchased by many other firms. Over a relatively short period there tends to be an equilibrium price p_0 per unit of the commodity that balances the supply and the demand. Suppose that, for some reason, the price is different from the equilibrium price. The Evans price

---

[*]See L. F. Richardson, "War Moods I," *Psychometrica*, 1948, p. 13.

adjustment model says that the rate of change of price with respect to time is proportional to the difference between the actual market price p and the equilibrium price. Write a differential equation that expresses this relation. Sketch two or more solution curves.

17. **Continuous Annuity** A *continuous annuity* is a steady stream of money that is paid to some person. Such an annuity may be established, for example, by making an initial deposit in a savings account and then making steady withdrawals to pay the continuous annuity. Suppose that an initial deposit of $5400 is made into a savings account that earns $5\frac{1}{2}\%$ interest compounded continuously, and immediately continuous withdrawals are begun at the rate of $300 per year. Set up the differential equation that is satisfied by the amount $f(t)$ of money in the account at time t. Sketch the solution.

18. **A Fish Population with Harvesting** The fish population in a pond with carrying capacity 1000 is modeled by the logistic equation

$$\frac{dN}{dt} = \frac{.4}{1000} N(1000 - N).$$

Here $N(t)$ denotes the number of fish at time t in years. When the number of fish reached 250, the owner of the pond decided to remove 50 fish per year.

(a) Modify the differential equation to model the population of fish from the time it reached 250.

(b) Plot several solution curves of the new equation, including the solution curve with $N(0) = 250$.

(c) Is the practice of catching 50 fish per year sustainable or will it deplete the fish population in the pond? Will the size of the fish population ever come close to the carrying capacity of the pond?

19. A company wishes to set aside funds for future expansion and so arranges to make continuous *deposits* into a savings account at the rate of $10,000 per year. The savings account earns 5% interest compounded continuously.

(a) Set up the differential equation that is satisfied by the amount $f(t)$ of money in the account at time t.

(b) Solve the differential equation in part (a), assuming that $f(0) = 0$, and determine how much money will be in the account at the end of 5 years.

20. A company arranges to make continuous deposits into a savings account at the rate of P dollars per year. The savings account earns 5% interest compounded continuously. Find the approximate value of P that will make the savings account balance amount to $50,000 in 4 years.

21. The air in a crowded room full of people contains .25% carbon dioxide (CO_2). An air conditioner is turned on that blows fresh air into the room at the rate of 500 cubic feet per minute. The fresh air mixes with the stale air, and the mixture leaves the room at the rate

of 500 cubic feet per minute. The fresh air contains .01% CO_2, and the room has a volume of 2500 cubic feet.

(a) Find a differential equation satisfied by the amount $f(t)$ of CO_2 in the room at time t.

(b) The model developed in part (a) ignores the CO_2 produced by the respiration of the people in the room. Suppose that the people generate .08 cubic foot of CO_2 per minute. Modify the differential equation in part (a) to take into account this additional source of CO_2.

22. A certain drug is administered intravenously to a patient at the continuous rate of 5 milligrams per hour. The patient's body removes the drug from the bloodstream at a rate proportional to the amount of the drug in the blood. Write a differential equation that is satisfied by the amount $f(t)$ of the drug in the blood at time t. Sketch a typical solution.

23. A single dose of iodine is injected intravenously into a patient. The iodine mixes thoroughly in the blood before any is lost as a result of metabolic processes (ignore the time required for this mixing process). Iodine will leave the blood and enter the thyroid gland at a rate proportional to the amount of iodine in the blood. Also, iodine will leave the blood and pass into the urine at a (different) rate proportional to the amount of iodine in the blood. Suppose that the iodine enters the thyroid at the rate of 4% per hour, and the iodine enters the urine at the rate of 10% per hour. Let $f(t)$ denote the amount of iodine in the blood at time t. Write a differential equation satisfied by $f(t)$.

24. Show that the mathematical model in Practice Problem 2 predicts that the amount of litter in the forest will eventually stabilize. What is the "equilibrium level" of litter in that problem? [*Note*: Today most forests are close to their equilibrium levels. This was not so during the Carboniferous Period when the great coal deposits were formed.]

25. In the study of the effect of natural selection on a population, we encounter the differential equation

$$\frac{dq}{dt} = -.0001q^2(1 - q),$$

where q is the frequency of a gene a and the selection pressure is against the recessive genotype aa. Sketch a solution of this equation when $q(0)$ is close to but slightly less than 1.

26. Typical values of c and d in equation (7) are $c = .15$, $d = .50$, and a typical value of k in equation (8) is $k = .05$. Sketch representative solutions for the equations

(a) $dq/dt = q(1 - q)(.15 - .50q)$ (selection favoring hybrids),

(b) $dq/dt = .05q(1 - q)(2q - 1)$ (selection against hybrids).

Consider various initial conditions with $q(0)$ between 0 and 1. Discuss possible genetic interpretations of these curves; that is, describe the effect of selection on the gene frequency q in terms of the various initial conditions.

Solutions to Practice Problems 10.6

1. The nature of the function $f(t)$ depends on the initial amount of salt water in the flask. Figure 10 contains solutions for three different initial amounts, $y(0)$. If the initial amount is less than 75 grams, the amount of salt in the flask will increase asymptotically to 75. If the initial concentration is greater than 75 grams, the amount of salt in the flask will decrease asymptotically to 75. Of course, if the initial concentration is exactly 75 grams, the amount of salt in the flask will remain constant.

2. This problem resembles a one-compartment problem, where the forest floor is the compartment. We have

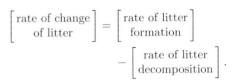

If $f(t)$ is the amount of litter (in grams per square centimeter) at time t, the 80% decomposition rate means that at time t the litter is decaying at the rate of $.80f(t)$ grams per square centimeter per year. Thus the net rate of change of litter is $f'(t) = 10 - .80f(t)$. The desired differential equation is $y' = 10 - .80y$.

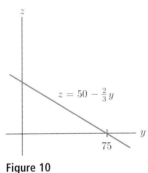

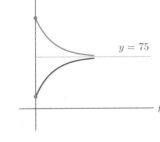

Figure 10

10.7 Numerical Solution of Differential Equations

Many differential equations that arise in real-life applications cannot be solved by *any* known method. However, approximate solutions may be obtained by several different numerical techniques. In this section we describe what is known as *Euler's method* for approximating solutions to initial-value problems of the form

$$y' = g(t, y), \qquad y(a) = y_0 \qquad (1)$$

for values of t in some interval $a \le t \le b$. Here $g(t, y)$ is some reasonably well behaved function of two variables. Equations of the form $y' = p(t)q(y)$ (studied in Section 10.2) and linear equations of the form $y' = -a(t)y + b(t)$ (studied in Sections 10.3 and 10.4) are special cases of equation (1).

In the following discussion we assume that $f(t)$ is a solution of (1) for $a \le t \le b$. The basic idea on which Euler's method rests is the following: *If the graph of $y = f(t)$ passes through some given point (t, y), the slope of the graph (that is, the value of y') at that point is just $g(t, y)$, because $y' = g(t, y)$.* This is the same idea that we used in Section 10.1 in our discussion of slope fields. Euler's method uses this observation to approximate the graph of $f(t)$ by a polygonal path. (See Fig. 1.)

The t-axis from a to b is subdivided by the equally spaced points $t_0, t_1, \ldots, t_n$. Each n subinterval has length $h = (b - a)/n$. The initial condition $y(a) = y_0$

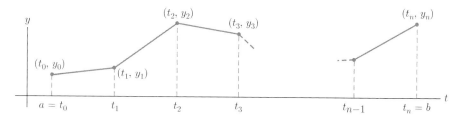

Figure 1. A polygonal path.

in (1) implies that the graph of the solution $f(t)$ passes through the point (t_0, y_0). As noted previously, the slope of this graph at (t_0, y_0) must be $g(t_0, y_0)$. Thus, on the first subinterval, Euler's method approximates the graph of $f(t)$ by the straight line

$$y = y_0 + g(t_0, y_0) \cdot (t - t_0),$$

which passes through (t_0, y_0) and has slope $g(t_0, y_0)$. (See Fig. 2.) When $t = t_1$, the y-coordinate on this line is

$$y_1 = y_0 + g(t_0, y_0) \cdot (t_1 - t_0) = y_0 + g(t_0, y_0) \cdot h.$$

Since the graph of $f(t)$ is close to the point (t_1, y_1) on the line, the slope of the graph of $f(t)$ when $t = t_1$ will be close to $g(t_1, y_1)$. So we draw the straight line

$$y = y_1 + g(t_1, y_1) \cdot (t - t_1) \qquad (2)$$

through (t_1, y_1) with slope $g(t_1, y_1)$, and we use this line to approximate $f(t)$ on the second subinterval. From (2) we determine an estimate y_2 for the value of $f(t)$ at $t = t_2$:

$$y_2 = y_1 + g(t_1, y_1) \cdot h.$$

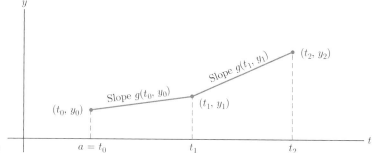

Figure 2

The slope of the graph of $f(t)$ at t_2 is now estimated by $g(t_2, y_2)$, and so on. Let us summarize this procedure:

Euler's Method   The endpoints $(t_0, y_0), \ldots, (t_n, y_n)$ of the line segments approximating the solution of equation (1) on the interval $a \leq t \leq b$ are given by the following formulas, where $h = (b - a)/n$:

$$t_0 = a \ (\text{given}), \qquad y_0 \ (\text{given})$$
$$t_1 = t_0 + h, \qquad y_1 = y_0 + g(t_0, y_0) \cdot h,$$
$$t_2 = t_1 + h, \qquad y_2 = y_1 + g(t_1, y_1) \cdot h,$$
$$\vdots \qquad\qquad \vdots$$
$$t_n = t_{n-1} + h. \qquad y_n = y_{n-1} + g(t_{n-1}, y_{n-1}) \cdot h.$$

EXAMPLE 1   Use Euler's method with $n = 4$ to approximate the solution $f(t)$ to $y' = 2t - 3y$, $y(0) = 4$, for t in the interval $0 \leq t \leq 2$. In particular, estimate $f(2)$.

Solution   Here $g(t, y) = 2t - 3y$, $a = 0$, $b = 2$, $y_0 = 4$ and $h = (2 - 0)/4 = \frac{1}{2}$. Starting with $(t_0, y_0) = (0, 4)$, we find that $g(0, 4) = -12$. Thus

$$t_1 = \frac{1}{2}, \qquad y_1 = 4 + (-12) \cdot \frac{1}{2} = -2.$$

Next $g(\frac{1}{2}, -2) = 7$, so

$$t_2 = 1, \qquad y_2 = -2 + 7 \cdot \frac{1}{2} = \frac{3}{2}.$$

Next $g(1, \frac{3}{2}) = -\frac{5}{2}$, so

$$t_3 = \frac{3}{2}, \qquad y_3 = \frac{3}{2} + \left(-\frac{5}{2}\right) \cdot \frac{1}{2} = \frac{1}{4}.$$

Finally, $g(\frac{3}{2}, \frac{1}{4}) = \frac{9}{4}$, so

$$t_4 = 2, \qquad y_4 = \frac{1}{4} + \frac{9}{4} \cdot \frac{1}{2} = \frac{11}{8}.$$

Thus the approximation to the solution $f(t)$ is given by the polygonal path shown in Fig. 3. The last point $(2, \frac{11}{8})$ is close to the graph of $f(t)$ at $t = 2$, so $f(2) \approx \frac{11}{8}$. ◼

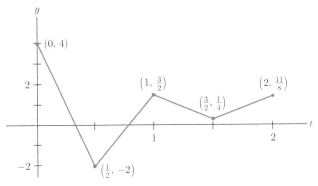

Figure 3

Actually, this polygonal path is somewhat misleading. The accuracy can be improved dramatically by increasing the value of n. Figure 4 shows the Euler approximations for $n = 8$ and $n = 20$. The graph of the exact solution is shown for comparison.

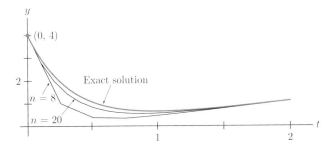

Figure 4. Approximating an exact solution by polygonal paths.

For many purposes, satisfactory graphs can be obtained by running Euler's method on a computer with large values of n. There is a limit to the accuracy obtainable, however, because each computer calculation involves a slight round-off error. When n is very large, the cumulative round-off error can become significant.

INCORPORATING TECHNOLOGY

Euler's Method   Here we demonstrate how to implement Euler's method on a TI-83/84 to approximate the solution to the differential equation from Example 1. In particular, we will approximate the solution to $y' = 2t - 3y$ with $y(0) = 4$ for t in the interval $0 \leq t \leq 2$. As indicated in Example 1, the accuracy of the approximation obtained from Euler's method can be improved by using large values of n, and for this a computer or calculator is necessary. In this example, we will implement Euler's method with $n = 100$.

The method we are demonstrating requires that the calculator be in sequence mode. To invoke the sequence mode, press $\boxed{\text{MODE}}$, move the cursor down to the fourth line, move the cursor right to **Seq**, and press $\boxed{\text{ENTER}}$. Now press $\boxed{\text{Y=}}$ to obtain the sequence editor.

With the calculator in sequence mode, the values for $t_0, t_1, t_2, \ldots$ are stored as the sequence values $u(0), u(1), u(2), \ldots$, and the values for $y_0, y_1, y_2, \ldots$ are stored as the sequence values $v(0), v(1), v(2), \ldots$.

We begin counting our sequences with $n = 0$, so cursor up and set nMin = 0.

Recall that in Euler's method each successive value of t is obtained by adding the step size h to the previous value of t. To implement this, we set $u(n) = u(n-1) + 0.02$. [In Seq mode, pressing $\boxed{\text{2nd}}$ [u] (the second function of the $\boxed{7}$ key) generates u, and pressing $\boxed{\text{X,T,}\Theta,n}$ generates n. In this example, $h = (2-0)/100 = 0.02$.]

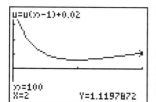

In our example we have $t_0 = 0$, so we set $u(\text{nMin}) = 0$.

In Euler's method the formula for computing successive values of the dependent variable is $y_n = y_{n-1} + g(t_{n-1}, y_{n-1})h$, and in our example, $g(t, y) = 2t - 3y$. To implement this, we set $v(n) = v(n-1) + (2u(n-1) - 3v(n-1))0.02$. [In Seq mode, pressing $\boxed{\text{2nd}}$ [v] (the second function of the $\boxed{8}$ key) generates v.]

In our example, we have $y_0 = 4$, so we set $v(\text{nMin}) = 4$.

We are now nearly ready to graph the approximation, but first we must set up the calculator to display the graph properly. To begin, we set up the calculator to graph u on the horizontal axis and v on the vertical axis. Press $\boxed{\text{2nd}}$ [FORMAT], move on the first row to **uv**, and press $\boxed{\text{ENTER}}$.

Figure 5

Now press $\boxed{\text{WINDOW}}$ and set nMin = 0, nMax = 100. Our variable t is in $[0, 2]$, so we set Xmin = 0 and Xmax = 2. Finally, set Ymin = 0 and Ymax = 4, and leave Xscl, Yscl, PlotStart, and PlotStep set at their default values of 1.

Now, to display a graph of the solution, press $\boxed{\text{GRAPH}}$. (See Fig. 5.)

To display a table of the points on the solution given by Euler's method, first press $\boxed{\text{2nd}}$ [TBLSET], and set TblStart = 0, ΔTbl = 1, and the other items to Auto. Then press $\boxed{\text{2nd}}$ [TABLE]. The successive values of t and y are contained in the $u(n)$ and $v(n)$ columns, respectively. (See Fig. 6.)

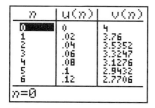

Note: After using Euler's method, reset the calculator to function mode by pressing $\boxed{\text{MODE}}$, moving to **Func** in the fourth line, and pressing $\boxed{\text{ENTER}}$. ■

Figure 6

Practice Problems 10.7

Let $f(t)$ be the solution of $y' = \sqrt{ty}$, $y(1) = 4$.

1. Use Euler's method with $n = 2$ on the interval $1 \leq t \leq 2$ to estimate $f(2)$.

2. Draw the polygonal path corresponding to the application of Euler's method in Problem 1.

EXERCISES 10.7

1. Suppose that $f(t)$ is a solution of the differential equation $y' = ty - 5$ and the graph of $f(t)$ passes through the point $(2, 4)$. What is the slope of the graph at this point?

2. Suppose that $f(t)$ is a solution of $y' = t^2 - y^2$ and the graph of $f(t)$ passes through the point $(2, 3)$. Find the slope of the graph when $t = 2$.

3. Suppose that $f(t)$ satisfies the initial-value problem $y' = y^2 + ty - 7$, $y(0) = 3$. Is $f(t)$ increasing or decreasing at $t = 0$?

4. Suppose that $f(t)$ satisfies the initial-value problem $y' = y^2 + ty - 7$, $y(0) = 2$. Is the graph of $f(t)$ increasing or decreasing at $t = 0$?

5. Use Euler's method with $n = 2$ on the interval $0 \leq t \leq 1$ to approximate the solution $f(t)$ to $y' = t^2y$, $y(0) = -2$. In particular, estimate $f(1)$.

6. Use Euler's method with $n = 2$ on the interval $2 \leq t \leq 3$ to approximate the solution $f(t)$ to $y' = t - 2y$, $y(2) = 3$. Estimate $f(3)$.

7. Use Euler's method with $n = 4$ to approximate the solution $f(t)$ to $y' = 2t - y + 1$, $y(0) = 5$ for $0 \leq t \leq 2$. Estimate $f(2)$.

8. Let $f(t)$ be the solution of $y' = y(2t - 1)$, $y(0) = 8$. Use Euler's method with $n = 4$ to estimate $f(1)$.

9. Let $f(t)$ be the solution of $y' = -(t + 1)y^2$, $y(0) = 1$. Use Euler's method with $n = 5$ to estimate $f(1)$. Then solve the differential equation, find an explicit formula for $f(t)$, and compute $f(1)$. How accurate is the estimated value of $f(1)$?

10. Let $f(t)$ be the solution of $y' = 10 - y$, $y(0) = 1$. Use Euler's method with $n = 5$ to estimate $f(1)$. Then solve the differential equation and find the exact value of $f(1)$.

11. Suppose that the Consumer Products Safety Commission issues new regulations that affect the toy manufacturing industry. Every toy manufacturer will have to make certain changes in its manufacturing process. Let $f(t)$ be the fraction of manufacturers that have complied with the regulations within t months. Note that $0 \leq f(t) \leq 1$. Suppose that the rate at which new companies comply with the regulations is proportional to the fraction of companies who have not yet complied, with constant of proportionality $k = .1$.

   (a) Construct a differential equation satisfied by $f(t)$.

   (b) Use Euler's method with $n = 3$ to estimate the fraction of companies that comply with the regulations within the first 3 months.

   (c) Solve the differential equation in part (a) and compute $f(3)$.

   (d) Compare the answers in parts (b) and (c) and approximate the error in using Euler's method.

12. The Los Angeles Zoo plans to transport a California sea lion to the San Diego Zoo. The animal will be wrapped in a wet blanket during the trip. At any time t the blanket will lose water (due to evaporation) at a rate proportional to the amount $f(t)$ of water in the blanket, with constant of proportionality $k = -.3$. Initially, the blanket will contain 2 gallons of seawater.

   (a) Set up the differential equation satisfied by $f(t)$.

   (b) Use Euler's method with $n = 2$ to estimate the amount of moisture in the blanket after 1 hour.

   (c) Solve the differential equation in part (a) and compute $f(1)$.

   (d) Compare the answers in parts (b) and (c) and approximate the error in using Euler's method.

Technology Exercises

13. The differential equation $y' = .5(1 - y)(4 - y)$ has five types of solutions labeled A–E. For each of the following initial values, graph the solution of the differential equation and identify the type of solution. Use a small value of h, let t range from 0 to 4, and let y range from -1 to 5. Use the technique of Section 10.6 to verify your answer.

   (a) $y(0) = -1$ (b) $y(0) = 1$ (c) $y(0) = 2$

   (d) $y(0) = 3.9$ (e) $y(0) = 4.1$

   A. Constant solution

   B. Decreasing, has an inflection point, and asymptotic to the line $y = 1$

   C. Increasing, concave down, and asymptotic to the line $y = 1$

   D. Concave up and increasing indefinitely

   E. Decreasing, concave up, and asymptotic to the line $y = 1$

14. The differential equation $y' = .5(y - 1)(4 - y)$ has five types of solutions labeled A–E. For each of the following initial values, graph the solution of the differential equation and identify the type of solution. Use a small value of h, let t range from 0 to 4, and let y range from -1 to 5. Use the technique of Section 10.6 to verify your answer.

   (a) $y(0) = .9$ (b) $y(0) = 1.1$ (c) $y(0) = 3$

   (d) $y(0) = 4$ (e) $y(0) = 5$

   A. Constant solution

   B. Decreasing, concave up, and asymptotic to the line $y = 4$

   C. Increasing, has an inflection point, and asymptotic to the line $y = 4$

   D. Increasing, concave down, and asymptotic to the line $y = 4$

   E. Concave down and decreasing indefinitely

15. The differential equation $y' = e^t - 2y$, $y(0) = 1$, has solution $y = \frac{1}{3}(2e^{-2t} + e^t)$. In the following table, fill in the second row with the values obtained from the use of a numerical method and the third row with the actual values calculated from the solution. What is the greatest difference between corresponding values in the second and third rows?

t_i	0	.25	.50	.75	1	1.25	1.5	1.75	2
y_i	1								
y	1	.8324							2.4752

16. The differential equation $y' = 2ty + e^{t^2}$, $y(0) = 5$, has solution $y = (t+5)e^{t^2}$. In the following table, fill in the second row with the values obtained from the use of a numerical method and the third row with the actual values calculated from the solution. What is the greatest difference between corresponding values in the second and third rows?

t_i	0	.2	.4	.6	.8	1	1.2	1.4	1.6	1.8	2
y_i	5										
y	5	5.412									382.2

Solutions to Practice Problems 10.7

1. Here $g(t, y) = \sqrt{ty}$, $a = 1$, $b = 2$, $y_0 = 4$, and $h = (2-1)/2 = \frac{1}{2}$. We have

$$t_0 = 1, \quad y_0 = 4, \qquad\qquad g(1, 4) = \sqrt{1 \cdot 4}$$
$$= 2,$$

$$t_1 = \frac{3}{2}, \quad y_1 = 4 + 2\left(\frac{1}{2}\right) = 5, \quad g\left(\frac{3}{2}, 5\right) = \sqrt{\frac{3}{2} \cdot 5}$$
$$\approx 2.7386,$$

$$t_2 = 2, \quad y_2 = 5 + \left(2.7386\right)\left(\frac{1}{2}\right) = 6.3693.$$

Hence $f(2) \approx y_2 = 6.3693$. [In Practice Problems 10.2, we found the solution of $y' = \sqrt{ty}$, $y(1) = 4$, to be $f(t) = \left(\frac{1}{3}t^{3/2} + \frac{5}{3}\right)^2$. We find that $f(2) = 6.8094$ (to four decimal places). The error $6.8094 - 6.3693 = .4401$ in the preceding approximation is about 6.5%.]

2. To find the polygonal path, plot the points (t_0, y_0), (t_1, y_1), and (t_2, y_2) and join them by line segments. See Fig. 7.

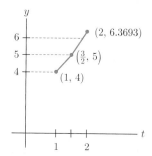

Figure 7

REVIEW OF FUNDAMENTAL CONCEPTS

1. What is a differential equation?

2. What does it mean for a function to be a solution to a differential equation?

3. What is a solution curve?

4. What is a constant solution to a differential equation?

5. What is the slope field?

6. Describe the separation of variables technique for obtaining the solution to a differential equation.

7. What is a first-order linear differential equation?

8. What is an integrating factor and how does it help you solve a first-order linear differential equation?

9. What is an autonomous differential equation?

10. How do you recognize an autonomous differential equation from its slope field?

11. Outline the procedure for sketching a solution of an autonomous differential equation.

12. What is the logistic differential equation?

13. Describe Euler's method for approximating the solution of a differential equation.

SUPPLEMENTARY EXERCISES

Solve the differential equations in Exercises 1–10.

1. $y^2 y' = 4t^3 - 3t^2 + 2$ **2.** $\dfrac{y'}{t+1} = y + 1$

3. $y' = \dfrac{y}{t} - 3y,\ t > 0$ **4.** $(y')^2 = t$

5. $y = 7y' + ty',\ y(0) = 3$ **6.** $y' = te^{t+y},\ y(0) = 0$

7. $yy' + t = 6t^2,\ y(0) = 7$ **8.** $y' = 5 - 8y,\ y(0) = 1$

9. $y' - \dfrac{2}{1-t}y = (1-t)^4$

10. $y' - \dfrac{1}{2(1+t)}y = 1 + t,\ t \ge 0$

11. Find a curve in the xy-plane passing through the origin and whose slope at the point (x, y) is $x + y$.

12. Let $P(t)$ denote the price in dollars of a certain commodity at time t in days. Suppose that the rate of change of P is proportional to the difference $D - S$ of the demand D and supply S at any time t. Suppose further that the demand and supply are related to the price by $D = 10 - .3P$ and $S = -2 + 3P$.

   (a) Find a differential equation that is satisfied by P, given that the price was falling at the rate of one dollar a day when $D = 10$ and $S = 20$.

   (b) Find P given that $P(0) = 1$.

13. If $f(t)$ is a solution of $y' = (2-y)e^{-y}$, is $f(t)$ increasing or decreasing at some value of t where $f(t) = 3$?

14. Solve the initial-value problem

$$y' = e^{y^2}(\cos y)(1 - e^{y-1}), \qquad y(0) = 1.$$

Sketch the solutions of the differential equations in Exercises 15–24. In each case, also indicate the constant solutions.

15. $y' = 2\cos y,\ y(0) = 0$

16. $y' = 5 + 4y - y^2,\ y(0) = 1$

17. $y' = y^2 + y,\ y(0) = -\frac{1}{3}$

18. $y' = y^2 - 2y + 1,\ y(0) = -1$

19. $y' = \ln y,\ y(0) = 2$

20. $y' = 1 + \cos y,\ y(0) = -\frac{3}{4}$

21. $y' = \dfrac{1}{y^2+1},\ y(0) = -1$

22. $y' = \dfrac{3}{y+3},\ y(0) = 2$

23. $y' = .4y^2(1-y),\ y(0) = -1,\ y(0) = .1,\ y(0) = 2$

24. $y' = y^3 - 6y^2 + 9y,\ y(0) = -\frac{1}{4},\ y(0) = \frac{1}{4},\ y(0) = 4$

25. The birth rate in a certain city is 3.5% per year and the death rate is 2% per year. Also, there is a net movement of population out of the city at a steady rate of 3000 people per year. Let $N = f(t)$ be the city's population at time t.

   (a) Write a differential equation satisfied by N.

   (b) Use a qualitative analysis of the equation to determine if there is a size at which the population would remain constant. Is it likely that a city would have such a constant population?

26. Suppose that in a chemical reaction, each gram of substance A combines with 3 grams of substance B to form 4 grams of substance C. The reaction begins with 10 grams of A, 15 grams of B, and 0 grams of C present. Let $y = f(t)$ be the amount of C present at time t. The rate at which substance C is formed is proportional to the product of the unreacted amounts of A and B present. That is, $f(t)$ satisfies the differential equation

$$y' = k\left(10 - \tfrac{1}{4}y\right)\left(15 - \tfrac{3}{4}y\right), \qquad y(0) = 0,$$

where k is a constant.

   (a) What do the quantities $10 - \frac{1}{4}f(t)$ and $15 - \frac{3}{4}f(t)$ represent?

   (b) Should the constant k be positive or negative?

   (c) Make a qualitative sketch of the solution of the preceding differential equation.

27. A bank account has $20,000 earning 5% interest compounded continuously. A pensioner uses the account to pay himself an annuity, drawing continuously at a $2000 annual rate. How long will it take for the balance in the account to drop to zero?

28. A continuous annuity of $12,000 per year is to be funded by steady withdrawals from a savings account that earns 6% interest compounded continuously.

   (a) What is the smallest initial amount in the account that will fund such an annuity forever?

   (b) What initial amount will fund such an annuity for exactly 20 years (at which time the savings account balance will be zero)?

29. Let $f(t)$ be the solution to $y' = 2e^{2t-y},\ y(0) = 0$. Use Euler's method with $n = 4$ on $0 \le t \le 2$ to estimate $f(2)$. Then show that Euler's method gives the exact value of $f(2)$ by solving the differential equation.

30. Let $f(t)$ be the solution to $y' = (t+1)/y,\ y(0) = 1$. Use Euler's method with $n = 3$ on $0 \le t \le 1$ to estimate $f(1)$. Then show that Euler's method gives the exact value of $f(1)$ by solving the differential equation.

31. Use Euler's method with $n = 6$ on the interval $0 \le t \le 3$ to approximate the solution $f(t)$ to

$$y' = .1y(20 - y), \quad y(0) = 2.$$

32. Use Euler's method with $n = 5$ on the interval $0 \le t \le 1$ to approximate the solution $f(t)$ to

$$y' = \frac{1}{2}y(y - 10), \quad y(0) = 9.$$

TAYLOR POLYNOMIALS AND INFINITE SERIES

In earlier chapters we introduced the functions e^x, $\ln x$, $\sin x$, $\cos x$, and $\tan x$. Whenever we needed the value of one of these functions for a particular value of x, such as $e^{.023}$, $\ln 5.8$, or $\sin .25$, we had to use a calculator. Now we shall take up the problem of numerically computing the values of such functions for particular choices of the variable x. The computational methods developed have many applications, for example, to differential equations and probability theory.

11.1 Taylor Polynomials

A polynomial of degree n is a function of the form

$$p(x) = a_0 + a_1 x + \cdots + a_n x^n$$

where $a_0, a_1, \ldots, a_n$ are given numbers and $a_n \neq 0$. In many instances in mathematics and its applications, calculations are much simpler for polynomials than for other functions. In this section we show how to approximate a given function $f(x)$ by a polynomial $p(x)$ for all values of x near some specified number, say $x = a$. To simplify matters, we begin by considering values of x near $x = 0$.

Figure 1 shows the graph of the function $f(x) = e^x$ together with the tangent line through $(0, f(0)) = (0, 1)$. The slope of the tangent line is $f'(0) = 1$.

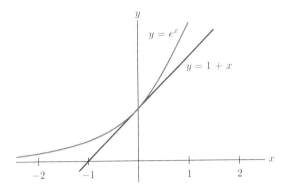

Figure 1.   A linear approximation of e^x at $x = 0$.

So the equation of the tangent line is

$$y - f(0) = f'(0)(x - 0)$$
$$y = f(0) + f'(0)x$$
$$y = 1 + x.$$

From our discussion of the derivative, we know that the tangent line at $x = 0$ closely approximates the graph of $y = e^x$ for values of x near 0. Thus, if we let $p_1(x) = 1 + x$, the values of $p_1(x)$ are close to the corresponding values of $f(x) = e^x$ for x near 0.

In general, a given function $f(x)$ may be approximated for values of x near 0 by the polynomial

$$p_1(x) = f(0) + f'(0)x,$$

which is called the *first Taylor polynomial of $f(x)$ at $x = 0$.* The graph of $p_1(x)$ is just the tangent line to $y = f(x)$ at $x = 0$.

The first Taylor polynomial "resembles" $f(x)$ near $x = 0$ in the sense that

$$p_1(0) = f(0) \qquad \text{(both graphs go through the same point at } x = 0\text{)},$$
$$p_1'(0) = f'(0) \qquad \text{(both graphs have the same slope at } x = 0\text{)}.$$

That is, $p_1(x)$ coincides with $f(x)$ in both its value at $x = 0$ and the value of its first derivative at $x = 0$. This suggests that to approximate $f(x)$ even more closely at $x = 0$ we look for a polynomial that coincides with $f(x)$ in its value at $x = 0$ and in the values of its first *and* second derivatives at $x = 0$. A further approximation can be obtained by going out to the third derivative, and so on.

EXAMPLE 1

Given a function $f(x)$, suppose that $f(0) = 1$, $f'(0) = -2$, $f''(0) = 7$, and $f'''(0) = -5$. Find a polynomial of degree 3,

$$p(x) = a_0 + a_1 x + a_2 x^2 + a_3 x^3,$$

such that $p(x)$ coincides with $f(x)$ up to the third derivative at $x = 0$; that is,

$$p(0) = f(0) = 1 \qquad \text{(same value at } x = 0\text{)},$$
$$p'(0) = f'(0) = -2 \qquad \text{(same first derivative at } x = 0\text{)},$$
$$p''(0) = f''(0) = 7 \qquad \text{(same second derivative at } x = 0\text{)},$$
$$p'''(0) = f'''(0) = -5 \qquad \text{(same third derivative at } x = 0\text{)}.$$

Solution To find the coefficients $a_0, \ldots, a_3$ of $p(x)$, we first compute the values of $p(x)$ and its derivatives at $x = 0$:

$$p(x) = a_0 + a_1 x + a_2 x^2 + a_3 x^3, \qquad p(0) = a_0,$$
$$p'(x) = 0 + a_1 + 2a_2 x + 3a_3 x^2, \qquad p'(0) = a_1,$$
$$p''(x) = 0 + 0 + 2a_2 + 2 \cdot 3a_3 x, \qquad p''(0) = 2a_2,$$
$$p'''(x) = 0 + 0 + 0 + 2 \cdot 3a_3 \qquad p'''(0) = 2 \cdot 3a_3.$$

Since we want $p(x)$ and its derivatives to coincide with the given values of $f(x)$ and its derivatives, we must have

$$a_0 = 1, \quad a_1 = -2, \quad 2a_2 = 7, \quad \text{and} \quad 2 \cdot 3a_3 = -5.$$

So

$$a_0 = 1, \quad a_1 = -2, \quad a_2 = \frac{7}{2}, \quad \text{and} \quad a_3 = \frac{-5}{2 \cdot 3}.$$

Rewriting the coefficients slightly, we have

$$p(x) = 1 + \frac{(-2)}{1} x + \frac{7}{1 \cdot 2} x^2 + \frac{-5}{1 \cdot 2 \cdot 3} x^3.$$

The form in which we have written $p(x)$ clearly exhibits the values $1, -2, 7, -5$ of $f(x)$ and its derivatives at $x = 0$. In fact, we could also write this formula for $p(x)$ in the form

$$p(x) = f(0) + \frac{f'(0)}{1} x + \frac{f''(0)}{1 \cdot 2} x^2 + \frac{f'''(0)}{1 \cdot 2 \cdot 3} x^3. \qquad \blacksquare$$

Given a function $f(x)$, we may use the formula in Example 1 to find a polynomial that coincides with $f(x)$ up to the third derivative at $x = 0$. To describe the general formula for higher-order polynomials, we let $f^{(n)}(x)$ denote the nth derivative of $f(x)$, and we let $n!$ (read "n factorial") denote the product of all the integers from 1 to n, so that $n! = 1 \cdot 2 \cdot \cdots \cdot (n-1) \cdot n$. (Thus, $1! = 1$, $2! = 1 \cdot 2$, $3! = 1 \cdot 2 \cdot 3$, and so forth.)

Given a function $f(x)$, the nth *Taylor polynomial of $f(x)$* at $x = 0$ is the polynomial $p_n(x)$ defined by

$$p_n(x) = f(0) + \frac{f'(0)}{1!} x + \frac{f''(0)}{2!} x^2 + \cdots + \frac{f^{(n)}(0)}{n!} x^n.$$

This polynomial coincides with $f(x)$ up to the nth derivative at $x = 0$ in the sense that

$$p_n(0) = f(0), \quad p_n'(0) = f'(0), \ldots, \; p_n^{(n)}(0) = f^{(n)}(0).$$

The next example shows how Taylor polynomials are used to approximate values of e^x for x near 0. The choice of which polynomial to use depends on how accurate we want the values of e^x to be.

EXAMPLE 2

Determine the first three Taylor polynomials of $f(x) = e^x$ at $x = 0$ and sketch their graphs.

Solution Since all derivatives of e^x are e^x, we see that

$$f(0) = f'(0) = f''(0) = f'''(0) = e^0 = 1.$$

Thus the desired Taylor polynomials are

$$p_1(x) = 1 + \frac{1}{1!} \cdot x = 1 + x,$$

$$p_2(x) = 1 + \frac{1}{1!}x + \frac{1}{2!}x^2 = 1 + x + \frac{1}{2}x^2,$$

$$p_3(x) = 1 + \frac{1}{1!}x + \frac{1}{2!}x^2 + \frac{1}{3!}x^3 = 1 + x + \frac{1}{2}x^2 + \frac{1}{6}x^3.$$

The relative accuracy of these approximations to e^x may be seen from the graphs in Fig. 2.

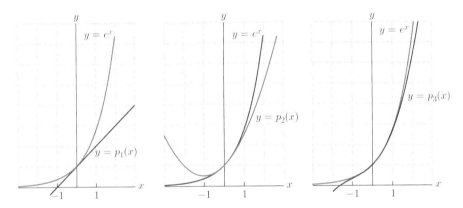

Figure 2.   Taylor polynomials of e^x at $x = 0$.

EXAMPLE 3

Determine the nth Taylor polynomial of

$$f(x) = \frac{1}{1-x}$$

at $x = 0$.

Solution

$$f(x) = (1-x)^{-1}, \qquad\qquad f(0) = 1,$$
$$f'(x) = 1(1-x)^{-2}, \qquad\qquad f'(0) = 1,$$
$$f''(x) = 1 \cdot 2(1-x)^{-3} = 2!(1-x)^{-3}, \qquad f''(0) = 2!,$$
$$f'''(x) = 1 \cdot 2 \cdot 3(1-x)^{-4} = 3!(1-x)^{-4}, \qquad f'''(0) = 3!,$$
$$f^{(4)}(x) = 1 \cdot 2 \cdot 3 \cdot 4(1-x)^{-5} = 4!(1-x)^{-5}, \qquad f^{(4)}(0) = 4!.$$

From the pattern of calculations, it is clear that $f^{(k)}(0) = k!$ for each k. Therefore,

$$p_n(x) = 1 + \frac{1}{1!}x + \frac{2!}{2!}x^2 + \frac{3!}{3!}x^3 + \cdots + \frac{n!}{n!}x^n$$

$$= 1 + x + x^2 + x^3 + \cdots + x^n.$$

We have already mentioned the possibility of using a polynomial to approximate the values of a function near $x = 0$. Here is another way to use a polynomial approximation.

EXAMPLE 4

It can be shown that the second Taylor polynomial of $\sin x^2$ at $x = 0$ is $p_2(x) = x^2$. Use this polynomial to approximate the area under the graph of $y = \sin x^2$ from $x = 0$ to $x = 1$. (See Fig. 3.)

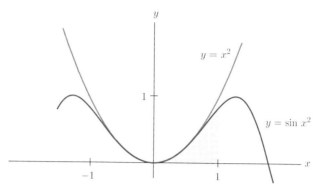

Figure 3. The second Taylor polynomial of $\sin x^2$ at $x = 0$.

Solution   Since the graph of $p_2(x)$ is very close to the graph of $\sin x^2$ for x near 0, the areas under the two graphs should be almost the same. The area under the graph of $p_2(x)$ is

$$\int_0^1 p_2(x)\, dx = \int_0^1 x^2\, dx = \left.\tfrac{1}{3}x^3\right|_0^1 = \tfrac{1}{3}.$$ ■

In Example 4, the exact area under the graph of $\sin x^2$ is given by

$$\int_0^1 \sin x^2\, dx.$$

However, this integral cannot be computed by the usual method because there is no way to construct an antiderivative of $\sin x^2$ consisting of elementary functions. Using an approximation technique from Chapter 9, we can find that the value of the integral is .3103 to four decimal places. Thus the error in using $p_2(x)$ as an approximation for $\sin x^2$ is about .023. (The error can be reduced further by using a Taylor polynomial of higher degree. In this particular example, the effort involved is far less than that required by the approximation methods of Chapter 9.)

Taylor Polynomials at *x = a*   Suppose now that we wish to approximate a given function $f(x)$ by a polynomial for values of x near some number a. Since the behavior of $f(x)$ near $x = a$ is determined by the values of $f(x)$ and its derivatives at $x = a$, we should try to approximate $f(x)$ by a polynomial $p(x)$ for which the values of $p(x)$ and its derivatives at $x = a$ are the same as those of $f(x)$. This is easily done if we use a polynomial that has the form

$$p(x) = a_0 + a_1(x - a) + a_2(x - a)^2 + \cdots + a_n(x - a)^n.$$

We call this a *polynomial in* $x - a$. In this form it is easy to compute $p(a)$, $p'(a)$, and so on, because setting $x = a$ in $p(x)$ or one of its derivatives makes most of the terms equal to zero. The following result is easily verified.

Given a function $f(x)$, the nth *Taylor polynomial of $f(x)$ at $x = a$* is the polynomial $p_n(x)$ defined by

$$p_n(x) = f(a) + \frac{f'(a)}{1!}(x - a) + \frac{f''(a)}{2!}(x - a)^2 + \cdots + \frac{f^{(n)}(a)}{n!}(x - a)^n.$$

This polynomial coincides with $f(x)$ up to the nth derivative at $x = a$ in the sense that

$$p_n(a) = f(a), \quad p'_n(a) = f'(a), \ldots, p_n^{(n)}(a) = f^{(n)}(a).$$

When $a = 0$, of course, these Taylor polynomials are just the same as those introduced earlier.

EXAMPLE 5   Calculate the second Taylor polynomial of $f(x) = \sqrt{x}$ at $x = 1$ and use this polynomial to estimate $\sqrt{1.02}$.

Solution   Here $a = 1$. Since we want the second Taylor polynomial, we must calculate the values of $f(x)$ and of its first two derivatives at $x = 1$.

$$f(x) = x^{1/2}, \qquad f'(x) = \tfrac{1}{2}x^{-1/2}, \qquad f''(x) = -\tfrac{1}{4}x^{-3/2},$$

$$f(1) = 1, \qquad f'(1) = \tfrac{1}{2}, \qquad f''(1) = -\tfrac{1}{4}.$$

Therefore, the desired Taylor polynomial is

$$p_2(x) = 1 + \frac{1/2}{1!}(x - 1) + \frac{-1/4}{2!}(x - 1)^2$$

$$= 1 + \tfrac{1}{2}(x - 1) - \tfrac{1}{8}(x - 1)^2.$$

Since 1.02 is close to 1, $p_2(1.02)$ gives a good approximation to $f(1.02)$, that is, to $\sqrt{1.02}$.

$$p_2(1.02) = 1 + \tfrac{1}{2}(1.02 - 1) - \tfrac{1}{8}(1.02 - 1)^2$$

$$= 1 + \tfrac{1}{2}(.02) - \tfrac{1}{8}(.02)^2$$

$$= 1 + .01 - .00005$$

$$= 1.00995$$

Accuracy of the Approximation   The solution to Example 5 is incomplete in a practical sense, for it offers no information about how close 1.00995 is to the true value of $\sqrt{1.02}$. In general, when we obtain an approximation to some quantity, we also want an indication of the quality of the approximation.

To measure the accuracy of an approximation to a function $f(x)$ by its Taylor polynomial at $x = a$, we define

$$R_n(x) = f(x) - p_n(x).$$

This difference between $f(x)$ and $p_n(x)$ is called the *nth remainder of $f(x)$ at $x = a$*. The following formula is derived in advanced texts:

The Remainder Formula   Suppose that the function $f(x)$ can be differentiated $n + 1$ times on an interval containing the number a. Then, for each x in this interval, there exists a number c between a and x such that

$$R_n(x) = \frac{f^{(n+1)}(c)}{(n + 1)!}(x - a)^{n+1}. \tag{1}$$

Usually the precise value of c is unknown. However, if we can find a number M such that $\left|f^{(n+1)}(c)\right| \leq M$ for all c between a and x, we do not need to know which c appears in (1), because we have

$$|f(x) - p_n(x)| = |R_n(x)| \leq \frac{M}{(n+1)!}\,|x - a|^{n+1}\,.$$

EXAMPLE 6   Determine the accuracy of the estimate in Example 5.

Solution   The second remainder for a function $f(x)$ at $x = 1$ is

$$R_2(x) = \frac{f^{(3)}(c)}{3!}(x - 1)^3,$$

where c is between 1 and x (and where c depends on x). Here $f(x) = \sqrt{x}$, and therefore $f^{(3)}(c) = \frac{3}{8}c^{-5/2}$. We are interested in $x = 1.02$, and so $1 \leq c \leq 1.02$. We observe that since $c^{5/2} \geq 1^{5/2} = 1$, we have $c^{-5/2} \leq 1$. Thus

$$\left|f^{(3)}(c)\right| \leq \tfrac{3}{8} \cdot 1 = \tfrac{3}{8},$$

and

$$|R_2(1.02)| \leq \frac{3/8}{3!}(1.02 - 1)^3$$

$$= \tfrac{3}{8} \cdot \tfrac{1}{6}(.02)^3$$

$$= .0000005.$$

Thus the error in using $p_2(1.02)$ as an approximation of $f(1.02)$ is at most $.0000005$. ∎

INCORPORATING TECHNOLOGY

Taylor Polynomials   Graphing calculators can be used to determine how well a function is approximated by a Taylor polynomial. Figure 4 shows the (heavily shaded) graph of $\mathbf{Y_1} = \sin(x^2)$ and the graph of its sixth Taylor polynomial $\mathbf{Y_2} = x^2 - \dfrac{x^6}{6}$. The two graphs appear identical on the screen for x between -1.1 and 1.1. Figure 5 shows that the distance between the two functions at $x = 1.1$ is about $.02$. As x increases beyond 1.1, the goodness of fit deteriorates. For instance, the two functions are about 5.9 units apart when $x = 2$. ∎

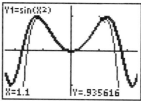

Figure 4. $\sin(x^2)$ and its sixth Taylor polynomial.

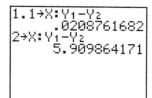

Figure 5.   Two differences between the function and its Taylor polynomial.

Practice Problems 11.1

1. **(a)** Determine the third Taylor polynomial of $f(x) = \cos x$ at $x = 0$.

   (b) Use the result of part (a) to estimate $\cos .12$.

2. Determine all Taylor polynomials of $f(x) = 3x^2 - 17$ at $x = 3$.

EXERCISES 11.1

In Exercises 1–8, determine the third Taylor polynomial of the given function at $x = 0$.

1. $f(x) = \sin x$

2. $f(x) = e^{-x/2}$

3. $f(x) = 5e^{2x}$

4. $f(x) = \cos(\pi - 5x)$

5. $f(x) = \sqrt{4x + 1}$

6. $f(x) = \dfrac{1}{x + 2}$

7. $f(x) = xe^{3x}$

8. $f(x) = \sqrt{1 - x}$

9. Determine the fourth Taylor polynomial of $f(x) = e^x$ at $x = 0$ and use it to estimate $e^{.01}$.

10. Determine the fourth Taylor polynomial of $f(x) = \ln(1 - x)$ at $x = 0$ and use it to estimate $\ln(.9)$.

11. Sketch the graphs of $f(x) = \dfrac{1}{1 - x}$ and its first three Taylor polynomials at $x = 0$.

12. Sketch the graphs of $f(x) = \sin x$ and its first three Taylor polynomials at $x = 0$.

13. Determine the nth Taylor polynomial for $f(x) = e^x$ at $x = 0$.

14. Determine all Taylor polynomials for $f(x) = x^2 + 2x + 1$ at $x = 0$.

15. Use a second Taylor polynomial at $x = 0$ to estimate the area under the curve $y = \ln(1 + x^2)$ from $x = 0$ to $x = \frac{1}{2}$.

16. Use a second Taylor polynomial at $x = 0$ to estimate the area under the curve $y = \sqrt{\cos x}$ from $x = -1$ to $x = 1$. (The exact answer to three decimal places is 1.828.)

17. Determine the third Taylor polynomial of $\dfrac{1}{5 - x}$ at $x = 4$.

18. Determine the fourth Taylor polynomial of $\ln x$ at $x = 1$.

19. Determine the third and fourth Taylor polynomials of $\cos x$ at $x = \pi$.

20. Determine the third and fourth Taylor polynomials of $x^3 + 3x - 1$ at $x = -1$.

21. Use the second Taylor polynomial of $f(x) = \sqrt{x}$ at $x = 9$ to estimate $\sqrt{9.3}$.

22. Use the second Taylor polynomial of $f(x) = \ln x$ at $x = 1$ to estimate $\ln .8$.

23. Determine all Taylor polynomials of $f(x) = x^4 + x + 1$ at $x = 2$.

24. Determine the nth Taylor polynomial of $f(x) = 1/x$ at $x = 1$.

25. If $f(x) = 3 + 4x - \dfrac{5}{2!}x^2 + \dfrac{7}{3!}x^3$, what are $f''(0)$ and $f'''(0)$?

26. If $f(x) = 2 - 6(x - 1) + \dfrac{3}{2!}(x - 1)^2 - \dfrac{5}{3!}(x - 1)^3 + \dfrac{1}{4!}(x - 1)^4$, what are $f''(1)$ and $f'''(1)$?

27. The third remainder for $f(x)$ at $x = 0$ is

$$R_3(x) = \frac{f^{(4)}(c)}{4!}x^4,$$

where c is a number between 0 and x. Let $f(x) = \cos x$, as in Practice Problem 11.1.

   (a) Find a number M such that $|f^{(4)}(c)| \le M$ for all values of c.

   (b) In Practice Problem 11.1, the error in using $p_3(.12)$ as an approximation to $f(.12) = \cos .12$ is given by $R_3(.12)$. Show that this error does not exceed 8.64×10^{-6}.

28. Let $p_4(x)$ be the fourth Taylor polynomial of $f(x) = e^x$ at $x = 0$. Show that the error in using $p_4(.1)$ as an approximation for $e^{.1}$ is at most 2.5×10^{-7}. [*Hint:* Observe that if $x = .1$ and if c is a number between 0 and $.1$ then $|f^{(5)}(c)| \le f^{(5)}(.1) = e^{.1} \le e^1 \le 3$.]

29. Let $p_2(x)$ be the second Taylor polynomial of $f(x) = \sqrt{x}$ at $x = 9$, as in Exercise 21.

   (a) Give the second remainder for $f(x)$ at $x = 9$.

   (b) Show that $|f^{(3)}(c)| \le \frac{1}{648}$ if $c \ge 9$.

   (c) Show that the error in using $p_2(9.3)$ as an approximation for $\sqrt{9.3}$ is at most $\frac{1}{144} \times 10^{-3} < 7 \times 10^{-6}$.

30. Let $p_2(x)$ be the second Taylor polynomial of $f(x) = \ln x$ at $x = 1$, as in Exercise 22.

   (a) Show that $|f^{(3)}(c)| < 4$ if $c \ge .8$.

   (b) Show that the error in using $p_2(.8)$ as an approximation for $\ln .8$ is at most $\frac{16}{3} \times 10^{-3} < .0054$.

Technology Exercises

31. Graph the function $\mathbf{Y_1} = \dfrac{1}{1 - x}$ and its fourth Taylor polynomial in the window $[-1, 1]$ by $[-1, 5]$. Find a number b such that graphs of the two functions appear identical on the screen for x between 0 and b. Calculate the difference between the function and its Taylor polynomial at $x = b$.

32. Repeat Exercise 31 for the function $\mathbf{Y_1} = \dfrac{1}{1-x}$ and its seventh Taylor polynomial.

33. Graph the function $\mathbf{Y_1} = e^x$ and its fourth Taylor polynomial in the window $[0,3]$ by $[-2,20]$. Find a number b such that graphs of the two functions appear identical on the screen for x between 0 and b. Calculate the difference between the function and its Taylor polynomial at $x = b$ and at $x = 3$.

34. Graph the function $\mathbf{Y_1} = \cos x$ and its second Taylor polynomial in the window ZDECIMAL. Find an interval of the form $[-b, b]$ over which the Taylor polynomial is a good fit to the function. What is the greatest difference between the two functions on this interval?

Solutions to Practice Problems 11.1

1. (a)
$$f(x) = \cos x, \qquad f(0) = 1$$
$$f'(x) = -\sin x, \qquad f'(0) = 0$$
$$f''(x) = -\cos x, \qquad f''(0) = -1$$
$$f'''(x) = \sin x, \qquad f'''(0) = 0$$

Therefore,

$$p_3(x) = 1 + \frac{0}{1!}x + \frac{-1}{2!}x^2 + \frac{0}{3!}x^3 = 1 - \frac{1}{2}x^2.$$

[Notice that here the third Taylor polynomial is actually a polynomial of degree 2. The important thing about $p_3(x)$ is not its degree but rather the fact that it agrees with $f(x)$ at $x = 0$ up to its third derivative.]

(b) By part (a), $\cos x \approx 1 - \frac{1}{2}x^2$ when x is near 0. Therefore,

$$\cos .12 \approx 1 - \tfrac{1}{2}(.12)^2 = .9928.$$

(*Note*: To five decimal places, $\cos .12 = .99281$.)

2.
$$f(x) = 3x^2 - 17, \qquad f(3) = 10$$
$$f'(x) = 6x, \qquad f'(3) = 18$$
$$f''(x) = 6, \qquad f''(3) = 6$$
$$f^{(3)}(x) = 0, \qquad f^{(3)}(3) = 0$$

The derivatives $f^{(n)}(x)$ for $n \geq 3$ are all the zero constant function. In particular, $f^{(n)}(3) = 0$ for $n \geq 3$. Therefore,

$$p_1(x) = 10 + 18(x - 3),$$

$$p_2(x) = 10 + 18(x - 3) + \frac{6}{2!}(x - 3)^2,$$

$$p_3(x) = 10 + 18(x - 3) + \frac{6}{2!}(x - 3)^2 + \frac{0}{3!}(x - 3)^3.$$

For $n \geq 3$, we have

$$p_n(x) = p_2(x) = 10 + 18(x - 3) + 3(x - 3)^2.$$

[This is the appropriate form of the Taylor polynomial at $x = 3$. However, it is instructive to multiply out the terms in $p_2(x)$ and collect the like powers of x:

$$p_2(x) = 10 + 18x - 18 \cdot 3 + 3(x^2 - 6x + 9)$$
$$= 10 + 18x - 54 + 3x^2 - 18x + 27 = 3x^2 - 17.$$

That is, $p_2(x)$ is $f(x)$, but written in a different form. This is not too surprising, since $f(x)$ itself is a polynomial that agrees with $f(x)$ and all its derivatives at $x = 3$.]

11.2 The Newton–Raphson Algorithm

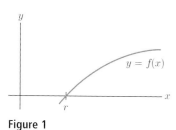

Figure 1

Many applications of mathematics involve the solution of equations. Often we have a function $f(x)$ and must find a value of x, say $x = r$, such that $f(r) = 0$. Such a value of x is called a *zero* of the function or, equivalently, a *root* of the equation $f(x) = 0$. Graphically, a zero of $f(x)$ is a value of x where the graph of $y = f(x)$ crosses the x-axis. (See Fig. 1.) When $f(x)$ is a polynomial, it is sometimes possible to factor $f(x)$ and quickly discover the zeros of $f(x)$. Unfortunately, in most realistic applications there is no simple way to locate zeros. However, there are several methods for finding an approximate value of a zero to any desired degree of accuracy. We shall describe one such method, the Newton–Raphson algorithm.

Suppose that we know that a zero of $f(x)$ is approximately x_0. The idea of the Newton–Raphson algorithm is to obtain an even better approximation of the zero by replacing $f(x)$ by its first Taylor polynomial at x_0, that is, by

$$p(x) = f(x_0) + \frac{f'(x_0)}{1}(x - x_0).$$

Since $p(x)$ closely resembles $f(x)$ near $x = x_0$, the zero of $f(x)$ should be close to the zero of $p(x)$. But solving the equation $p(x) = 0$ for x gives

$$f(x_0) + f'(x_0)(x - x_0) = 0$$
$$x f'(x_0) = f'(x_0)x_0 - f(x_0)$$
$$x = x_0 - \frac{f(x_0)}{f'(x_0)}.$$

That is, if x_0 is an approximation to the zero r, the number

$$x_1 = x_0 - \frac{f(x_0)}{f'(x_0)} \qquad (1)$$

generally provides an improved approximation.

We may visualize the situation geometrically as in Fig. 2. The first Taylor polynomial $p(x)$ at x_0 has as its graph the tangent line to $y = f(x)$ at the point $(x_0, f(x_0))$. The value of x for which $p(x) = 0$, that is, $x = x_1$, corresponds to the point where the tangent line crosses the x-axis.

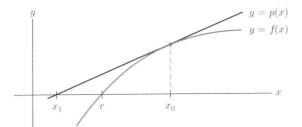

Figure 2. Obtaining x_1 from x_0.

Now let us use x_1 in place of x_0 as an approximation to the zero r. We obtain a new approximation x_2 from x_1 in the same way that we obtained x_1 from x_0:

$$x_2 = x_1 - \frac{f(x_1)}{f'(x_1)}.$$

We may repeat this process over and over. At each stage a new approximation x_{new} is obtained from the old approximation x_{old} by the following formula:

Newton–Raphson Method

$$x_{\text{new}} = x_{\text{old}} - \frac{f(x_{\text{old}})}{f'(x_{\text{old}})}.$$

In this way we obtain a sequence of approximations $x_0, x_1, x_2, \ldots$, which usually approach as close to r as desired. (See Fig. 3.)

EXAMPLE 1   The polynomial $f(x) = x^3 - x - 2$ has a zero between 1 and 2. Let $x_0 = 1$ and find the next three approximations of the zero of $f(x)$ using the Newton–Raphson algorithm.

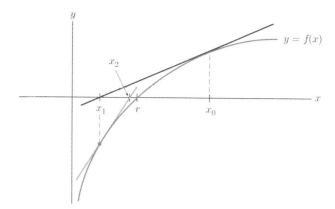

Figure 3. A sequence of approximations to r.

Solution Since $f'(x) = 3x^2 - 1$, formula (1) becomes

$$x_1 = x_0 - \frac{x_0^3 - x_0 - 2}{3x_0^2 - 1}.$$

With $x_0 = 1$, we have

$$x_1 = 1 - \frac{1^3 - 1 - 2}{3(1)^2 - 1} = 1 - \frac{-2}{2} = 2,$$

$$x_2 = 2 - \frac{2^3 - 2 - 2}{3(2)^2 - 1} = 2 - \frac{4}{11} = \frac{18}{11},$$

$$x_3 = \frac{18}{11} - \frac{\left(\frac{18}{11}\right)^3 - \frac{18}{11} - 2}{3\left(\frac{18}{11}\right)^2 - 1} \approx 1.530.$$

The actual value of r to three decimal places is 1.521. ■

EXAMPLE 2   Use four repetitions of the Newton–Raphson algorithm to approximate $\sqrt{2}$.

Solution $\sqrt{2}$ is a zero of the function $f(x) = x^2 - 2$. Since $\sqrt{2}$ clearly lies between 1 and 2, let us take our initial approximation as $x_0 = 1$. ($x_0 = 2$ would do just as well.) Since $f'(x) = 2x$, we have

$$x_1 = x_0 - \frac{x_0^2 - 2}{2x_0} = 1 - \frac{1^2 - 2}{2(1)} = 1 - \left(-\frac{1}{2}\right) = 1.5,$$

$$x_2 = 1.5 - \frac{(1.5)^2 - 2}{2(1.5)} \approx 1.4167,$$

$$x_3 = 1.4167 - \frac{(1.4167)^2 - 2}{2(1.4167)} \approx 1.41422,$$

$$x_4 = 1.41422 - \frac{(1.41422)^2 - 2}{2(1.41422)} \approx 1.41421.$$

This approximation to $\sqrt{2}$ is correct to five decimal places. ■

EXAMPLE 3   Approximate the zeros of the polynomial $x^3 + x + 3$.

Solution   By applying our curve-sketching techniques, we can make a rough sketch of the graph of $y = x^3 + x + 3$. (See Fig. 4.) The graph crosses the x-axis between $x = -2$ and $x = -1$. So the polynomial has one zero lying between -2 and -1. Let us therefore set $x_0 = -1$. Since $f'(x) = 3x^2 + 1$, we have

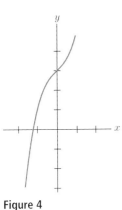

$$x_1 = x_0 - \frac{x_0^3 + x_0 + 3}{3x_0^2 + 1} = -1 - \frac{(-1)^3 + (-1) + 3}{3(-1)^2 + 1} = -1.25,$$

$$x_2 = -1.25 - \frac{(-1.25)^3 + (-1.25) + 3}{3(-1.25)^2 + 1} \approx -1.21429,$$

$$x_3 \approx -1.21341,$$

$$x_4 \approx -1.21341.$$

Figure 4

Therefore, the zero of the given polynomial is approximately -1.21341.   ◾

EXAMPLE 4   Approximate the positive solution of $e^x - 4 = x$.

Solution   The rough sketches of the two graphs in Fig. 5 indicate that the solution lies near 2. Let $f(x) = e^x - 4 - x$. Then the solution of the original equation will be a zero of $f(x)$. We apply the Newton–Raphson algorithm to $f(x)$ with $x_0 = 2$. Since $f'(x) = e^x - 1$,

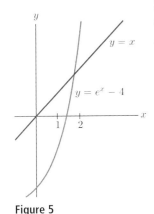

$$x_1 = x_0 - \frac{e^{x_0} - 4 - x_0}{e^{x_0} - 1} = 2 - \frac{e^2 - 4 - 2}{e^2 - 1} \approx 2 - \frac{1.38906}{6.38906} \approx 1.78,$$

$$x_2 = 1.78 - \frac{e^{1.78} - 4 - (1.78)}{e^{1.78} - 1} \approx 1.78 - \frac{.14986}{4.92986} \approx 1.75,$$

$$x_3 = 1.75 - \frac{e^{1.75} - 4 - (1.75)}{e^{1.75} - 1} \approx 1.75 - \frac{.0046}{4.7546} \approx 1.749.$$

Figure 5

Therefore, an approximate solution is $x = 1.749$.   ◾

EXAMPLE 5   **Internal rate of return**   Suppose that an investment of $100 yields the following returns:

   $2 at the end of the first month
   $15 at the end of the second month
   $45 at the end of the third month
   $50 at the end of the fourth (and last) month

The total of these returns is $112. This represents the initial investment of $100, plus earnings of $12 during the 4 months. The *internal rate of return* on this investment is the interest rate (per month) for which the sum of the present values of the returns equals the initial investment, $100. Determine the internal rate of return.

Solution Let i be the *monthly* rate of interest. The present value of an amount A to be received in k months is $A(1 + i)^{-k}$. Therefore, we must solve

$$\begin{bmatrix} \text{amount of initial} \\ \text{investment} \end{bmatrix} = \begin{bmatrix} \text{sum of present} \\ \text{values of returns} \end{bmatrix}$$

$$100 = 2(1 + i)^{-1} + 15(1 + i)^{-2} + 45(1 + i)^{-3} + 50(1 + i)^{-4}.$$

Multiplying both sides of the equation by $(1 + i)^4$ and taking all terms to the left, we obtain

$$100(1 + i)^4 - 2(1 + i)^3 - 15(1 + i)^2 - 45(1 + i) - 50 = 0.$$

Let $x = 1 + i$, and solve the resulting equation by the Newton–Raphson algorithm with $x_0 = 1.1$.

$$100x^4 - 2x^3 - 15x^2 - 45x - 50 = 0$$

$$f(x) = 100x^4 - 2x^3 - 15x^2 - 45x - 50$$

$$f'(x) = 400x^3 - 6x^2 - 30x - 45$$

$$x_1 = x_0 - \frac{100x_0^4 - 2x_0^3 - 15x_0^2 - 45x_0 - 50}{400x_0^3 - 6x_0^2 - 30x_0 - 45}$$

$$= 1.1 - \frac{100(1.1)^4 - 2(1.1)^3 - 15(1.1)^2 - 45(1.1) - 50}{400(1.1)^3 - 6(1.1)^2 - 30(1.1) - 45}$$

$$= 1.1 - \frac{26.098}{447.14} \approx 1.042$$

$$x_2 \approx 1.035$$

$$x_3 \approx 1.035$$

Therefore, an approximate solution is $x = 1.035$. Hence $i = .035$ and the investment had an internal rate of return of 3.5% per month. ◼

In general, if an investment of P dollars produces the returns

R_1 at the end of the first period,
R_2 at the end of the second period,

⋮

R_N at the end of the Nth (and last) period,

then the internal rate of return, i, is obtained by solving* the equation

$$P(1 + i)^N - R_1(1 + i)^{N-1} - R_2(1 + i)^{N-2} - \cdots - R_N = 0$$

for its positive root.

When a loan of P dollars is paid back with N equal periodic payments of R dollars at interest rate i per period, the equation to be solved for i becomes

$$P(1 + i)^N - R(1 + i)^{N-1} - R(1 + i)^{N-2} - \cdots - R = 0.$$

---

*We are assuming that all the returns are nonnegative and add up to at least P. An analysis of the general case can be found in H. Paley, P. Colwell, and R. Cannaday, *Internal Rates of Return*, UMAP Module 640 (Lexington, MA: COMAP, Inc., 1984).

This equation can be simplified to

$$Pi + R\left[(1+i)^{-N} - 1\right] = 0.$$

(See Exercise 41 in Section 11.3.)

EXAMPLE 6

Amortization of a loan A mortgage of $104,880 is repaid in 360 monthly payments of $755. Use two iterations of the Newton–Raphson algorithm to estimate the monthly rate of interest.

Solution Here $P = 104{,}880$, $R = 755$, and $N = 360$. Therefore, we must solve the equation

$$104{,}880i + 755\left[(1+i)^{-360} - 1\right] = 0.$$

Let $f(i) = 104{,}880i + 755\left[(1+i)^{-360} - 1\right]$. Then

$$f'(i) = 104{,}880 - 271{,}800(1+i)^{-361}.$$

Apply the Newton–Raphson algorithm to $f(i)$ with $i_0 = .01$:

$$i_1 = i_0 - \frac{104{,}880i_0 + 755\left[(1+i_0)^{-360} - 1\right]}{104{,}880 - 271{,}800(1+i_0)^{-361}} \approx .00676$$

$$i_2 \approx .00650.$$

Therefore, the monthly interest rate is approximately .65%. ∎

COMMENTS

1. The values of successive approximations in the Newton–Raphson algorithm depend on the extent of round-off used during the calculation.

2. The Newton–Raphson algorithm is an excellent computational tool. However, in some cases it will not work. For instance, if $f'(x_n) = 0$ for some approximation x_n, there is no way to compute the next approximation. Other instances in which the algorithm fails are presented in Exercises 25 and 26.

3. It can be shown that, if $f(x)$, $f'(x)$, and $f''(x)$ are continuous near r [a zero of $f(x)$] and $f'(r) \neq 0$, the Newton–Raphson algorithm will definitely work provided that the initial approximation x_0 is not too far away. ∎

INCORPORATING TECHNOLOGY

The Newton–Raphson Algorithm The TI-83/84 can generate a new approximation for the Newton–Raphson algortihm with each press of the ENTER key. To illustrate, let us use the polynomial $f(x) = x^3 - x - 2$ from Example 1. Begin by pressing Y=, and assign $Y_1 = X^3 - X - 2$. Assign to Y_2 the derivative of Y_1 so that $Y_2 = 3X^2 - 1$. Return to the home screen. Our initial approximation in Example 1 was $x_0 = 1$, so we begin the Newton–Raphson algorithm by assigning the value 1 to the variable X. This is accomplished by pressing $\boxed{1}$ $\boxed{\text{STO}\blacktriangleright}$ $\boxed{\text{X},\text{T},\Theta,n}$ and then $\boxed{\text{ENTER}}$.

Now that we have initialized the algorithm we compute the next approximation by calculating the value of $X - Y_1/Y_2$. As indicated in Fig. 6, after typing in $X - Y_1/Y_2$ we immediately press $\boxed{\text{STO}\blacktriangleright}$ $\boxed{\text{X},\text{T},\Theta,n}$ to assign the value of that calculation to X. Then each time we press the $\boxed{\text{ENTER}}$ key another approximation is displayed. Note that when assigning to Y_2 the derivative of Y_1 we could just as well have set $Y_2 = \text{nDeriv}(Y_1, X, X)$. In this case, the successive approximations will differ slightly from those obtained with Y_2 equal to the exact derivative. ∎

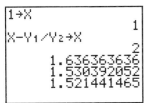
```
1→X
                    1
X-Y₁/Y₂→X
                    2
        1.636363636
        1.530392052
        1.521441465
```

Figure 6. Successive approximations for Example 1.

Practice Problems 11.2

1. Use three repetitions of the Newton–Raphson algorithm to estimate $\sqrt[3]{7}$.

2. Use three repetitions of the Newton–Raphson algorithm to estimate the zeros of $f(x) = 2x^3 + 3x^2 + 6x - 3$.

EXERCISES 11.2

In Exercises 1–8, use three repetitions of the Newton–Raphson algorithm to approximate the following:

1. $\sqrt{5}$ **2.** $\sqrt{7}$ **3.** $\sqrt[3]{6}$ **4.** $\sqrt[3]{11}$

5. The zero of $x^2 - x - 5$ between 2 and 3

6. The zero of $x^2 + 3x - 11$ between -5 and -6

7. The zero of $\sin x + x^2 - 1$ near $x_0 = 0$

8. The zero of $e^x + 10x - 3$ near $x_0 = 0$

9. Sketch the graph of $y = x^3 + 2x + 2$ and use the Newton–Raphson algorithm (three repetitions) to approximate all x-intercepts.

10. Sketch the graph of $y = x^3 + x - 1$ and use the Newton–Raphson algorithm (three repetitions) to approximate all x-intercepts.

11. Use the Newton–Raphson algorithm to find an approximate solution to $e^{-x} = x^2$.

12. Use the Newton–Raphson algorithm to find an approximate solution to $e^{5-x} = 10 - x$.

13. Suppose that an investment of $500 yields returns of $100, $200, and $300 at the end of the first, second, and third months, respectively. Determine the internal rate of return on this investment.

14. An investor buys a bond for $1000. She receives $10 at the end of each month for 2 months and then sells the bond at the end of the second month for $1040. Determine the internal rate of return on this investment.

15. A $663 television set is purchased with a down payment of $100 and a loan of $563 to be repaid in five monthly installments of $116. Determine the monthly rate of interest on the loan.

16. A mortgage of $100,050 is repaid in 240 monthly payments of $900. Determine the monthly rate of interest.

17. A function $f(x)$ has the graph given in Fig. 7. Let x_1 and x_2 be the estimates of a root of $f(x)$ obtained by applying the Newton–Raphson algorithm using an initial approximation of $x_0 = 5$. Draw the appropriate tangent lines and estimate the numerical values of x_1 and x_2.

18. Redo Exercise 17 with $x_0 = 1$.

19. Suppose that the line $y = 4x + 5$ is tangent to the graph of the function $f(x)$ at $x = 3$. If the Newton–Raphson algorithm is used to find a root of $f(x) = 0$ with the initial guess $x_0 = 3$, what is x_1?

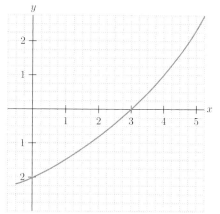

Figure 7

20. Suppose that the graph of the function $f(x)$ has slope -2 at the point $(1, 2)$. If the Newton–Raphson algorithm is used to find a root of $f(x) = 0$ with the initial guess $x_0 = 1$, what is x_1?

21. Figure 8 contains the graph of the function $f(x) = x^2 - 2$. The function has zeros at $x = \sqrt{2}$ and $x = -\sqrt{2}$. When the Newton–Raphson algorithm is applied to find a zero, what values of x_0 lead to the zero $\sqrt{2}$?

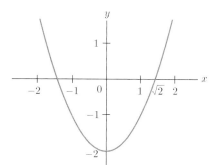

Figure 8. Graph of $f(x) = x^2 - 2$.

22. Figure 9 contains the graph of the function $f(x) = x^3 - 12x$. The function has zeros at $x = -\sqrt{12}$, 0, and $\sqrt{12}$. Which zero of $f(x)$ will be approximated by the Newton–Raphson method starting with $x_0 = 4$? Starting with $x_0 = 1$? Starting with $x_0 = -1.8$?

23. What special occurrence takes place when the Newton–Raphson algorithm is applied to the linear function $f(x) = mx + b$ with $m \neq 0$?

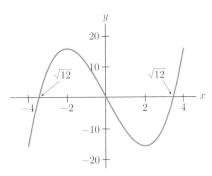

Figure 9. Graph of $f(x) = x^3 - 12x$.

24. What happens when the first approximation, x_0, is actually a zero of $f(x)$?

Exercises 25 and 26 present two examples in which successive repetitions of the Newton–Raphson algorithm do not approach a root.

25. Apply the Newton–Raphson algorithm to the function $f(x) = x^{1/3}$ whose graph is drawn in Fig. 10(a). Use $x_0 = 1$.

26. Apply the Newton–Raphson algorithm to the function whose graph is drawn in Fig. 10(b). Use $x_0 = 1$.

Technology Exercises

27. The functions $f(x) = x^2 - 4$ and $g(x) = (x - 2)^2$ both have a zero at $x = 2$. Apply the Newton–Raphson al-

gorithm to each function with $x_0 = 3$ and determine the value of n for which x_n appears on the screen as exactly 2. Graph the two functions and explain why the sequence for $f(x)$ converges so quickly to 2, whereas the sequence for $g(x)$ converges so slowly.

28. Apply the Newton–Raphson algorithm to the function $f(x) = x^3 - 5x$ with $x_0 = 1$. After observing the behavior, graph the function along with the tangent lines at $x = 1$ and $x = -1$ and explain geometrically what is happening.

29. Draw the graph of $f(x) = x^4 - 2x^2$, $[-2, 2]$ by $[-2, 2]$. The function has zeros at $x = -\sqrt{2}$, $x = 0$, and $x = \sqrt{2}$. By looking at the graph, guess which zero will be approached when applying the Newton–Raphson algorithm to each of the following initial approximations:
(a) $x_0 = 1.1$ **(b)** $x_0 = .95$ **(c)** $x_0 = .9$
Then test your guesses by actually carrying out the computations.

30. Graph the function $f(x) = \dfrac{x^2}{1 + x^2}$, $[-2, 2]$ by $[-.5, 1]$. The function has 0 as a zero. By looking at the graph, guess at a value of x_0 for which x_1 will be exactly 0 when the Newton–Raphson algorithm is invoked. Then test your guess by carrying out the computation.

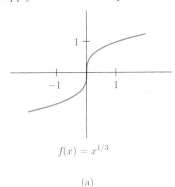

$f(x) = x^{1/3}$

(a)

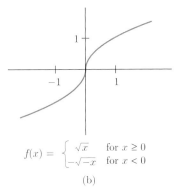

$f(x) = \begin{cases} \sqrt{x} & \text{for } x \geq 0 \\ -\sqrt{-x} & \text{for } x < 0 \end{cases}$

(b)

Figure 10

Solutions to Practice Problems 11.2

1. We wish to approximate a zero of $f(x) = x^3 - 7$. Since $f(1) = -6 < 0$ and $f(2) = 1 > 0$, the graph of $f(x)$ crosses the x-axis somewhere between $x = 1$ and $x = 2$. Take $x_0 = 2$ as the initial approximation to the zero. Since $f'(x) = 3x^2$, we have

$$x_1 = x_0 - \frac{x_0^3 - 7}{3x_0^2} = 2 - \frac{2^3 - 7}{3(2)^2} = \frac{23}{12} \approx 1.9167,$$

$$x_2 = 1.9167 - \frac{(1.9167)^3 - 7}{3(1.9167)^2} \approx 1.91294,$$

$$x_3 = 1.91294 - \frac{(1.91294)^3 - 7}{3(1.91294)^2} \approx 1.91293.$$

(Continued)

2. As a preliminary step, we use the methods of Chapter 2 to sketch the graph of $f(x)$. (See Fig. 11.) We see that $f(x)$ has a zero that occurs for a positive value of x. Since $f(0) = -3$ and $f(1) = 8$, the graph crosses the x-axis between 0 and 1. Let us choose $x_0 = 0$ as our initial approximation to the zero of $f(x)$. Since $f'(x) = 6x^2 + 6x + 6$, we then have

$$x_1 = x_0 - \frac{2x_0^3 + 3x_0^2 + 6x_0 - 3}{6x_0^2 + 6x_0 + 6} = 0 - \frac{-3}{6} = \frac{1}{2},$$

$$x_2 = \frac{1}{2} - \frac{1}{\frac{21}{2}} = \frac{1}{2} - \frac{2}{21} = \frac{17}{42} \approx .40476.$$

Continuing, we find that $x_3 \approx .39916$.

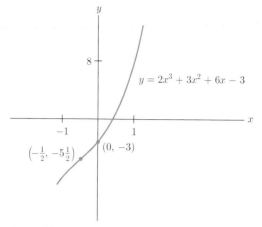

Figure 11

11.3 Infinite Series

An *infinite series* is an infinite addition of numbers

$$a_1 + a_2 + a_3 + a_4 + \cdots .$$

Here are some examples:

$$1 + \tfrac{1}{2} + \tfrac{1}{4} + \tfrac{1}{8} + \tfrac{1}{16} + \cdots , \tag{1}$$

$$1 + 1 + 1 + 1 + \cdots , \tag{2}$$

$$1 - 1 + 1 - 1 + \cdots . \tag{3}$$

Some infinite series can be associated with a "sum." To illustrate how this is done, let us consider the infinite series (1). If we add up the first two, three, four, five, and six terms of the infinite series (1), we obtain

$$1 + \tfrac{1}{2} = 1\tfrac{1}{2},$$

$$1 + \tfrac{1}{2} + \tfrac{1}{4} = 1\tfrac{3}{4},$$

$$1 + \tfrac{1}{2} + \tfrac{1}{4} + \tfrac{1}{8} = 1\tfrac{7}{8},$$

$$1 + \tfrac{1}{2} + \tfrac{1}{4} + \tfrac{1}{8} + \tfrac{1}{16} = 1\tfrac{15}{16},$$

$$1 + \tfrac{1}{2} + \tfrac{1}{4} + \tfrac{1}{8} + \tfrac{1}{16} + \tfrac{1}{32} = 1\tfrac{31}{32}.$$

Each total lies halfway between the preceding total and the number 2. It appears from these calculations that, by increasing the number of terms, we bring the total arbitrarily close to 2. Indeed, this is supported by further calculation. For example,

$$\underbrace{1 + \frac{1}{2} + \frac{1}{4} + \cdots + \frac{1}{2^9}}_{10 \text{ terms}} = 2 - \frac{1}{2^9} \approx 1.998047,$$

$$\underbrace{1 + \frac{1}{2} + \frac{1}{4} + \cdots + \frac{1}{2^{19}}}_{20 \text{ terms}} = 2 - \frac{1}{2^{19}} \approx 1.999998,$$

$$\underbrace{1 + \frac{1}{2} + \frac{1}{4} + \cdots + \frac{1}{2^{n-1}}}_{n \text{ terms}} = 2 - \frac{1}{2^{n-1}}.$$

Therefore, it seems reasonable to assign the infinite series (1) the "sum" 2:

$$1 + \tfrac{1}{2} + \tfrac{1}{4} + \tfrac{1}{8} + \tfrac{1}{16} + \cdots = 2. \tag{4}$$

The sum of the first n terms of an infinite series is called its nth *partial sum* and is denoted S_n. In series (1) we were very fortunate that the partial sums approached a limiting value, 2. This is not always the case. For example, consider the infinite series (2). If we form the first few partial sums, we get

$$S_2 = 1 + 1 \qquad\qquad = 2,$$
$$S_3 = 1 + 1 + 1 \qquad\quad = 3,$$
$$S_4 = 1 + 1 + 1 + 1 = 4.$$

We see that these sums do not approach any limit. Rather, they become larger and larger, eventually exceeding any specified number.

The partial sums need not grow without bound for an infinite series not to have a sum. For example, consider the infinite series (3). Here the sums of initial terms are

$$S_2 = 1 - 1 \qquad\qquad\quad = 0,$$
$$S_3 = 1 - 1 + 1 \qquad\qquad = 1,$$
$$S_4 = 1 - 1 + 1 - 1 \qquad = 0,$$
$$S_5 = 1 - 1 + 1 - 1 + 1 = 1,$$

and so forth. The partial sums alternate between 0 and 1 and do not approach a limit. So the infinite series (3) has no sum.

An infinite series whose partial sums approach a limit is called *convergent*. The limit is then called the *sum* of the infinite series. An infinite series whose partial sums do not approach a limit is called *divergent*. From our preceding discussion, we know that the infinite series (1) is convergent, whereas (2) and (3) are divergent.

It is often an extremely difficult task to determine whether a given infinite series is convergent. And intuition is not always an accurate guide. For example, we might at first suspect that the infinite series

$$1 + \tfrac{1}{2} + \tfrac{1}{3} + \tfrac{1}{4} + \tfrac{1}{5} + \cdots$$

(the *harmonic series*) is convergent. However, it is not. The sums of its initial terms increase without bound, although they do so very slowly. For example, it takes about 12,000 terms before the sum exceeds 10 and about 2.7×10^{43} terms before the sum exceeds 100. Nevertheless, the sum eventually exceeds any prescribed number. (See Exercise 42 and Section 11.4.)

There is an important type of infinite series whose convergence or divergence is easily determined. Let a and r be given nonzero numbers. A series of the form

$$a + ar + ar^2 + ar^3 + ar^4 + \cdots$$

is called a *geometric series with ratio r*. (The "ratio" of consecutive terms is r.)

The Geometric Series   The infinite series

$$a + ar + ar^2 + ar^3 + ar^4 + \cdots$$

converges if and only if $|r| < 1$. When $|r| < 1$, the sum of the series is

$$\frac{a}{1-r}. \tag{5}$$

For example, if $a = 1$ and $r = \frac{1}{2}$, we obtain the infinite series (1). In this case

$$\frac{a}{1-r} = \frac{1}{1-\frac{1}{2}} = \frac{1}{\frac{1}{2}} = 2,$$

in agreement with our previous observation. Also, series (2) and (3) are divergent geometric series, with $r = 1$ and $r = -1$, respectively. A proof of the foregoing result is outlined in Exercise 41.

EXAMPLE 1   Calculate the sums of the following geometric series:

(a) $1 + \dfrac{1}{5} + \dfrac{1}{5^2} + \dfrac{1}{5^3} + \dfrac{1}{5^4} + \cdots$

(b) $\dfrac{2}{3^2} + \dfrac{2}{3^4} + \dfrac{2}{3^6} + \dfrac{2}{3^8} + \dfrac{2}{3^{10}} + \cdots$

(c) $\dfrac{5}{2^2} - \dfrac{5^2}{2^5} + \dfrac{5^3}{2^8} - \dfrac{5^4}{2^{11}} + \dfrac{5^5}{2^{14}} - \cdots$

Solution (a) Here $a = 1$ and $r = \frac{1}{5}$. The sum of the series is

$$\frac{a}{1-r} = \frac{1}{1-\frac{1}{5}} = \frac{1}{\frac{4}{5}} = \frac{5}{4}.$$

(b) We find r by dividing any term by the preceding term. So

$$r = \frac{\frac{2}{3^4}}{\frac{2}{3^2}} = \frac{2}{3^4} \cdot \frac{3^2}{2} = \frac{1}{3^2} = \frac{1}{9}.$$

Since the series is a geometric series, we obtain the same result using any other pair of successive terms. For instance,

$$\frac{\frac{2}{3^8}}{\frac{2}{3^6}} = \frac{2}{3^8} \cdot \frac{3^6}{2} = \frac{1}{3^2} = \frac{1}{9}.$$

The first term of the series is $a = \dfrac{2}{3^2} = \dfrac{2}{9}$, so the sum of the series is

$$\frac{a}{1-r} = a \cdot \frac{1}{1-r} = \frac{2}{9} \cdot \frac{1}{1-\frac{1}{9}} = \frac{2}{9} \cdot \frac{9}{8} = \frac{1}{4}.$$

(c) We may find r as in part (b), or we may observe that the numerator of each fraction in the series (c) is increasing by a factor of 5, while the denominator is increasing by a factor of $2^3 = 8$. So the ratio of successive fractions is $\frac{5}{8}$. However, the terms in the series are alternately positive and negative, so the ratio of successive terms must be negative. Hence $r = -\frac{5}{8}$. Next, $a = \frac{5}{2^2} = \frac{5}{4}$, so the sum of series (c) is

$$a \cdot \frac{1}{1-r} = \frac{5}{4} \cdot \frac{1}{1-\left(-\frac{5}{8}\right)} = \frac{5}{4} \cdot \frac{1}{\frac{13}{8}} = \frac{5}{4} \cdot \frac{8}{13} = \frac{10}{13}.$$ ∎

Sometimes a rational number is expressed as an infinite repeating decimal, such as $.12\overline{12}$. The value of such a "decimal expansion" is in fact the sum of an infinite series.

EXAMPLE 2   What rational number has the decimal expansion $.1212\overline{12}$?

Solution   This number denotes the infinite series

$$.12 + .0012 + .000012 + \cdots = \frac{12}{100} + \frac{12}{100^2} + \frac{12}{100^3} + \cdots,$$

a geometric series with $a = \frac{12}{100}$ and $r = \frac{1}{100}$. The sum of the geometric series is

$$\frac{a}{1-r} = a \cdot \frac{1}{1-r} = \frac{12}{100} \cdot \frac{1}{1-\frac{1}{100}} = \frac{12}{100} \cdot \frac{100}{99} = \frac{12}{99} = \frac{4}{33}.$$

Hence $.1212\overline{12} = \frac{4}{33}$. ∎

EXAMPLE 3   **The multiplier effect in economics**   Suppose that the federal government enacts an income tax cut of \$10 billion. Assume that each person will spend 93% of all resulting extra income and save the rest. Estimate the total effect of the tax cut on economic activity.

Solution   Express all amounts of money in billions of dollars. Of the increase in income created by the tax cut, $(.93)(10)$ billion dollars will be spent. These dollars become extra income to someone and hence 93% will be spent again and 7% saved, so additional spending of $(.93)(.93)(10)$ billion dollars is created. The recipients of those dollars will spend 93% of them, creating again additional spending of

$$(.93)(.93)(.93)(10) = 10(.93)^3$$

billion dollars, and so on. The total amount of new spending created by the tax cut is thus given by the infinite series

$$10(.93) + 10(.93)^2 + 10(.93)^3 + \cdots.$$

This is a geometric series with initial term $10(.93)$ and ratio $.93$. Its sum is

$$\frac{a}{1-r} = \frac{10(.93)}{1-.93} = \frac{9.3}{.07} \approx 132.86.$$

Thus a \$10 billion tax cut creates new spending of about \$132.86 billion. ∎

Example 3 illustrates the *multiplier effect.* The proportion of each extra dollar that a person will spend is called the *marginal propensity to consume,* denoted MPC. In Example 3, MPC = .93. As we observed, the total new spending generated by the tax cut is

$$[\text{total new spending}] = 10 \cdot \frac{.93}{1 - .93} = [\text{tax cut}] \cdot \frac{\text{MPC}}{1 - \text{MPC}}.$$

The tax cut is multiplied by the "multiplier" $\dfrac{\text{MPC}}{1 - \text{MPC}}$ to obtain its true effect.

EXAMPLE 4

Drug therapy Patients with certain heart problems are often treated with digitoxin, a derivative of the digitalis plant. The rate at which a person's body eliminates digitoxin is proportional to the amount of digitoxin present. In 1 day (24 hours) about 10% of any given amount of the drug will be eliminated. Suppose that a maintenance dose of .05 milligram (mg) is given daily to a patient. Estimate the total amount of digitoxin that should be present in the patient after several months of treatment.

Solution For a moment, let us consider what happens to the initial dose of .05 mg, and disregard the subsequent doses. After 1 day, 10% of the .05 mg will have been eliminated and $(.90)(.05)$ mg will remain. By the end of the second day, this smaller amount will be reduced 10% to $(.90)(.90)(.05)$ mg, and so on, until after n days only $(.90)^n(.05)$ mg of the original dose will remain. (See Fig. 1.) To determine the cumulative effect of all the doses of digitoxin, we observe that at the time of the second dose (one day after the first dose), the patient's body will contain the second dose of .05 mg plus $(.90)(.05)$ mg of the first dose. A day later there will be the third dose of .05 mg, plus $(.90)(.05)$ mg of the second dose, plus $(.90)^2(.05)$ of the first dose. At the time of any new dose, the patient's body will contain that dose plus the amounts that remain of earlier doses. Let us tabulate this.

	Total Amount (mg) of Digitoxin
	0 .05
	1 $.05 + (.90)(.05)$
Days after **Initial Dose**	2 $.05 + (.90)(.05) + (.90)^2(.05)$
	$\vdots$
	n $.05 + (.90)(.05) + (.90)^2(.05) + \cdots + (.90)^n(.05)$

We can see that the amounts present at the time of each new dose correspond to the partial sums of the geometric series

$$.05 + (.90)(.05) + (.90)^2(.05) + (.90)^3(.05) + \cdots ,$$

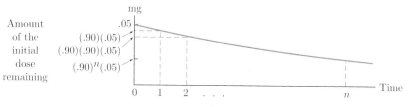

Figure 1. Exponential decrease of the initial dose.

where $a = .05$ and $r = .90$. The sum of this series is

$$\frac{.05}{1-.90} = \frac{.05}{.10} = .5.$$

Since the partial sums of the series approach the sum of .5, we may conclude that a daily maintenance dose of .05 mg will eventually raise the level of digitoxin in the patient to a plateau of .5 mg. Between doses the level will drop 10% down to $(.90)(.5) = .45$ mg. The use of a regular maintenance dose to sustain a certain level of a drug in a patient is an important technique in drug therapy.[*] ∎

Sigma Notation When studying series, it is often convenient to use the Greek capital letter sigma to indicate summation. For example, the sum

$$a_2 + a_3 + \cdots + a_{10}$$

is denoted by

$$\sum_{k=2}^{10} a_k$$

(read "the sum of a sub k from k equals 2 to 10"). The nth partial sum of a series, $a_1 + a_2 + \cdots + a_n$, is written as $\sum_{k=1}^{n} a_k$. In these examples the letter k is called the *index of summation*. Sometimes we require the index of summation to begin with 0 and sometimes with 1, but any integer value may be used for k. Any letter not already in use may be used as the index of summation. For instance, both

$$\sum_{i=0}^{4} a_i \quad \text{and} \quad \sum_{j=0}^{4} a_j$$

indicate the sum $a_0 + a_1 + a_2 + a_3 + a_4$.

Finally, a formal infinite series

$$a_1 + a_2 + a_3 + \cdots$$

is written as

$$\sum_{k=1}^{\infty} a_k \quad \text{or} \quad \sum_{1}^{\infty} a_k.$$

We will also write $\sum_{k=1}^{\infty} a_k$ as the symbol for the numerical value of the series when it is convergent. Using this notation (and writing ar^0 in place of a), the main result about the geometric series may be written as follows:

$$\sum_{k=0}^{\infty} ar^k = \frac{a}{1-r} \qquad \text{if } |r| < 1,$$

$$\sum_{k=0}^{\infty} ar^k \text{ is divergent} \qquad \text{if } |r| \geq 1.$$

EXAMPLE 5 Determine the sums of the following infinite series.

(a) $\displaystyle\sum_{k=0}^{\infty} \left(\frac{2}{3}\right)^k$ (b) $\displaystyle\sum_{j=0}^{\infty} 4^{-j}$ (c) $\displaystyle\sum_{i=3}^{\infty} \frac{2}{7^i}$

[*]See "Principles of Drug Therapy" by John A. Oates and Grant R. Wilkinson, in *Principles of Internal Medicine*, T. R. Harrison, ed., 8th ed. (New York: McGraw-Hill Book Company, 1977), pp. 334–346.

Solution In each case, the first step is to write out the first few terms of the series.

(a) $\displaystyle\sum_{k=0}^{\infty}\left(\frac{2}{3}\right)^{k} = \underset{[k=0]}{1} + \underset{[k=1]}{\frac{2}{3}} + \underset{[k=2]}{\left(\frac{2}{3}\right)^{2}} + \underset{[k=3]}{\left(\frac{2}{3}\right)^{3}} + \cdots$

This is a geometric series with initial term $a = 1$ and ratio $r = \frac{2}{3}$; its sum is

$$\frac{1}{1-\frac{2}{3}} = \frac{1}{\frac{1}{3}} = 3.$$

(b) $\displaystyle\sum_{j=0}^{\infty} 4^{-j} = 4^{0}+4^{-1}+4^{-2}+4^{-3}+\cdots = 1+\frac{1}{4}+\left(\frac{1}{4}\right)^{2}+\left(\frac{1}{4}\right)^{3}+\cdots = \frac{1}{1-\frac{1}{4}} = \frac{4}{3}$

(c) $\displaystyle\sum_{i=3}^{\infty}\frac{2}{7^{i}} = \frac{2}{7^{3}}+\frac{2}{7^{4}}+\frac{2}{7^{5}}+\frac{2}{7^{6}}+\cdots$

This is a geometric series with $a = \dfrac{2}{7^{3}}$ and $r = \dfrac{1}{7}$; its sum is

$$a\cdot\frac{1}{1-r} = \frac{2}{7^{3}}\cdot\frac{1}{1-\frac{1}{7}} = \frac{2}{7^{3}}\cdot\frac{7}{6} = \frac{1}{147}.\qquad\blacksquare$$

INCORPORATING TECHNOLOGY

Finite Sums   Graphing calculators can compute finite sums. The variable **X** can be used as the index of summation. If $f(x)$ is an expression involving x, the sum

$$\sum_{x=m}^{n} f(x)$$

can be computed on TI calculators as

$$\textbf{sum}(\textbf{seq}(\textbf{f}(\textbf{X}), \textbf{X}, \textbf{m}, \textbf{n}, \textbf{1})).$$

For instance,

$$\sum_{x=1}^{99}\frac{1}{x} = 1+\frac{1}{2}+\frac{1}{3}+\cdots+\frac{1}{99}$$

is calculated as **sum(seq(1/X,X,1,99,1))**, and

$$\sum_{x=1}^{10}\frac{2}{3^{2x}} = \frac{2}{3^{2}}+\frac{2}{3^{4}}+\cdots+\frac{2}{3^{20}}$$

```
sum(seq(1/X,X,1,
99,1))
        5.177377518
sum(seq(2/3^(2X)
,X,1,10,1))
         .2499999999
```

Figure 2

```
0→K:1→S
            1
K+1→K:S+(2/3)^K→
S
       1.666666667
       2.111111111
       2.407407407
```

Figure 3

from Example 1(b) is calculated as **sum(seq(2/3^(2X), X, 1, 10, 1))**. (See Fig. 2.) The expressions **sum(** and **seq(** are both accessed by pressing 2nd [LIST]. Then **sum(** is the fifth option under the **MATH** menu, and **seq(** is the fifth option under the **OPS** menu. Figure 2 shows the result of this calculation and also the sum from Example 1(b).

Also, successive partial sums can be generated by repeatedly pressing the ENTER key. In Fig. 3 the variable **S** holds the current partial sum for the series in Example 5(a). $\blacksquare$

Practice Problems 11.3

1. Determine the sum of the geometric series

$$8 - \frac{8}{3} + \frac{8}{9} - \frac{8}{27} + \frac{8}{81} - \cdots .$$

2. Find the value of $\displaystyle\sum_{k=0}^{\infty}(.7)^{-k+1}$

EXERCISES 11.3

Determine the sums of the following geometric series when they are convergent.

1. $1 + \dfrac{1}{6} + \dfrac{1}{6^2} + \dfrac{1}{6^3} + \dfrac{1}{6^4} \cdots$

2. $1 + \dfrac{3}{4} + \left(\dfrac{3}{4}\right)^2 + \left(\dfrac{3}{4}\right)^3 + \left(\dfrac{3}{4}\right)^4 + \cdots$

3. $1 - \dfrac{1}{3^2} + \dfrac{1}{3^4} - \dfrac{1}{3^6} + \dfrac{1}{3^8} - \cdots$

4. $1 + \dfrac{1}{2^3} + \dfrac{1}{2^6} + \dfrac{1}{2^9} + \dfrac{1}{2^{12}} + \cdots$

5. $2 + \dfrac{2}{3} + \dfrac{2}{9} + \dfrac{2}{27} + \dfrac{2}{81} + \cdots$

6. $3 + \dfrac{6}{5} + \dfrac{12}{25} + \dfrac{24}{125} + \dfrac{48}{625} + \cdots$

7. $\dfrac{1}{5} + \dfrac{1}{5^4} + \dfrac{1}{5^7} + \dfrac{1}{5^{10}} + \dfrac{1}{5^{13}} + \cdots$

8. $\dfrac{1}{3^2} - \dfrac{1}{3^3} + \dfrac{1}{3^4} - \dfrac{1}{3^5} + \dfrac{1}{3^6} - \cdots$

9. $3 - \dfrac{3^2}{7} + \dfrac{3^3}{7^2} - \dfrac{3^4}{7^3} + \dfrac{3^5}{7^4} - \cdots$

10. $6 - 1.2 + .24 - .048 + .0096 - \cdots$

11. $\dfrac{2}{5^4} - \dfrac{2^4}{5^5} + \dfrac{2^7}{5^6} - \dfrac{2^{10}}{5^7} + \dfrac{2^{13}}{5^8} - \cdots$

12. $\dfrac{3^2}{2^5} + \dfrac{3^4}{2^8} + \dfrac{3^6}{2^{11}} + \dfrac{3^8}{2^{14}} + \dfrac{3^{10}}{2^{17}} + \cdots$

13. $5 + 4 + 3.2 + 2.56 + 2.048 + \cdots$

14. $\dfrac{5^3}{3} - \dfrac{5^5}{3^4} + \dfrac{5^7}{3^7} - \dfrac{5^9}{3^{10}} + \dfrac{5^{11}}{3^{13}} - \cdots$

Sum an appropriate infinite series to find the rational number whose decimal expansion is given.

15. $.272\overline{72}7$ **16.** $.173\overline{173}$

17. $.22\overline{2}$ **18.** $.151\overline{515}$

19. $4.011\overline{011}$ $(= 4 + .011\overline{011})$

20. $5.44\overline{4}$

21. Show that $.99\overline{9} = 1$.

22. Compute the value of $.1212\overline{1212}$ as a geometric series with $a = .1212$ and $r = .0001$. Compare your answer with the result of Example 2.

23. Compute the total new spending created by a \$10 billion federal income tax cut when the population's marginal propensity to consume is 95%. Compare your result with that of Example 3 and note how a small change in the MPC makes a dramatic change in the total spending generated by the tax cut.

24. Compute the effect of a \$20 billion federal income tax cut when the population's marginal propensity to consume is 98%. What is the "multiplier" in this case?

A perpetuity *is a periodic sequence of payments that continues forever. The* capital value *of the perpetuity is the sum of the present values of all future payments.*

25. Consider a perpetuity that promises to pay \$100 at the beginning of each month. If the interest rate is 12% compounded monthly, the present value of \$100 in k months is $100(1.01)^{-k}$.

   (a) Express the capital value of the perpetuity as an infinite series.

   (b) Find the sum of the infinite series.

26. Consider a perpetuity that promises to pay P dollars at the *end* of each month. (The first payment will be received in 1 month.) If the interest rate per month is r, the present value of P dollars in k months is $P(1+r)^{-k}$. Find a simple formula for the capital value of the perpetuity.

27. A generous corporation not only gives its CEO a \$1,000,000 bonus, but gives her enough money to cover the taxes on the bonus, the taxes on the additional taxes, the taxes on the taxes on the additional taxes, and so on. If she is in the 39.6% tax bracket, how large is her bonus?

28. The *coefficient of restitution* of a ball, a number between 0 and 1, specifies how much energy is conserved when the ball hits a rigid surface. A coefficient of .9, for instance, means a bouncing ball will rise to 90% of its previous height after each bounce. The coefficients of restitution for a tennis ball, basketball, super ball, and softball are .7, .75, .9, and .3, respectively. Find the total distance traveled by a tennis ball dropped from a height of 6 feet.

29. A patient receives 6 milligrams of a certain drug daily. Each day the body eliminates 30% of the amount of the drug present in the system. Estimate the total amount of the drug that should be present after extended treatment immediately after a dose is given.

30. A patient receives 2 milligrams of a certain drug each day. Each day the body eliminates 20% of the amount of drug present in the system. Estimate the total amount of the drug present after extended treatment immediately *before* a dose is given.

31. A patient receives M milligrams of a certain drug each day. Each day the body eliminates 25% of the amount of drug present in the system. Determine the value of the maintenance dose M such that after many days approximately 20 milligrams of the drug is present immediately after a dose is given.

32. A patient receives M milligrams of a certain drug daily. Each day the body eliminates a fraction q of the amount of the drug present in the system. Estimate the total amount of the drug that should be present after extended treatment immediately after a dose is given.

33. The infinite series $a_1 + a_2 + a_3 + \cdots$ has partial sums given by $S_n = 3 - \dfrac{5}{n}$.

  (a) Find $\sum_{k=1}^{10} a_k$.

  (b) Does the infinite series converge? If so, to what value does it converge?

34. The infinite series $a_1 + a_2 + a_3 + \cdots$ has partial sums given by $S_n = n - \dfrac{1}{n}$.

  (a) Find $\sum_{k=1}^{10} a_k$.

  (b) Does the infinite series converge? If so, to what value does it converge?

Determine the sums of the following infinite series:

35. $\displaystyle\sum_{k=0}^{\infty} \left(\frac{5}{6}\right)^k$ **36.** $\displaystyle\sum_{k=0}^{\infty} \frac{7}{10^k}$

37. $\displaystyle\sum_{j=1}^{\infty} 5^{-2j}$ **38.** $\displaystyle\sum_{j=0}^{\infty} \frac{(-1)^j}{3^j}$

39. $\displaystyle\sum_{k=0}^{\infty} (-1)^k \frac{3^{k+1}}{5^k}$ **40.** $\displaystyle\sum_{k=1}^{\infty} \left(\frac{1}{3}\right)^{2k}$

41. Let a and r be given nonzero numbers.

  (a) Show that

$$(1 - r)(a + ar + ar^2 + \cdots + ar^n) = a - ar^{n+1},$$

  and from this conclude that, for $r \neq 1$,

$$a + ar + ar^2 + \cdots + ar^n = \frac{a}{1 - r} - \frac{ar^{n+1}}{1 - r}.$$

  (b) Use the result of part (a) to explain why the geometric series $\sum_0^{\infty} ar^k$ converges to $\dfrac{a}{1 - r}$ when $|r| < 1$.

  (c) Use the result of part (a) to explain why the geometric series diverges for $|r| > 1$.

  (d) Explain why the geometric series diverges for $r = 1$ and $r = -1$.

42. Show that the infinite series

$$1 + \frac{1}{2} + \frac{1}{3} + \frac{1}{4} + \frac{1}{5} + \cdots$$

  diverges. [*Hint:* $\frac{1}{3} + \frac{1}{4} > \frac{1}{2}$; $\frac{1}{5} + \frac{1}{6} + \frac{1}{7} + \frac{1}{8} > \frac{1}{2}$; $\frac{1}{9} + \cdots + \frac{1}{16} > \frac{1}{2}$; etc.]

Technology Exercises

43. What is the exact value of the infinite geometric series whose partial sum appears at the first entry in Fig. 3?

44. What is the exact value of the infinite geometric series whose partial sum appears at the second entry in Fig. 3?

In Exercises 45 and 46, the calculator screen computes a partial sum of an infinite series. Write out the first five terms of the series and determine the exact value of the infinite series.

45.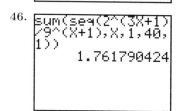

46.
```
sum(seq(2^(3X+1)
/9^(X+1),X,1,40,
1))
            1.761790424
```

47. Verify the formula

$$\sum_{x=1}^{n} x = \frac{n(n + 1)}{2}$$

  for $n = 10$, 50, and 100.

48. The sum of the first n odd numbers is n^2; that is,

$$\sum_{x=1}^{n} (2x - 1) = n^2.$$

  Verify this formula for $n = 5$, 10, and 25.

In Exercises 49 and 50, convince yourself that the equation is correct by summing up the first 999 terms of the infinite series and comparing it with the value on the right.

49. $\displaystyle\sum_{x=1}^{\infty} \frac{1}{x^2} = \frac{\pi^2}{6}$.   **50.** $\displaystyle\sum_{x=1}^{\infty} \frac{(-1)^{x+1}}{x} = \ln 2$.

Solutions to Practice Problems 11.3

1. Answer: 6. To obtain the sum of a geometric series, identify a and r, and (provided that $|r| < 1$) substitute these values into the formula $\dfrac{a}{1-r}$. The initial term a is just the first term of the series: $a = 8$. The ratio r is often obvious by inspection. However, if in doubt, divide any term by the *preceding* term. Here, the second term divided by the first term is $\frac{-8}{3}/8 = -\frac{1}{3}$, so $r = -\frac{1}{3}$. Since $|r| = \frac{1}{3}$, the series is convergent and the sum is

$$\frac{a}{1-r} = \frac{8}{1-\left(-\frac{1}{3}\right)} = \frac{8}{\frac{4}{3}} = 8 \cdot \frac{3}{4} = 6.$$

2. Write out the first few terms of the series and then proceed as in Problem 1.

$$\sum_{k=0}^{\infty}(.7)^{-k+1} = \begin{array}{cc} (.7)^1 & + & (.7)^0 & + & (.7)^{-1} \\ [k=0] & & [k=1] & & [k=2] \end{array}$$

$$\begin{array}{cc} + & (.7)^{-2} & + & (.7)^{-3} \\ & [k=3] & & [k=4] \end{array}$$

$$= .7 + 1 + \frac{1}{.7} + \frac{1}{(.7)^2} + \frac{1}{(.7)^3} + \cdots.$$

Here $a = .7$ and $r = 1/.7 = \frac{10}{7}$. Since $|r| = \frac{10}{7} > 1$, the series is divergent and has no sum. (The formula $\dfrac{a}{1-r}$ yields $\frac{7}{3}$; however, this value is meaningless. The formula applies only to the case in which the series is convergent.)

11.4 Series with Positive Terms

Very often, it is difficult to determine the sum of an infinite series. As a fallback to determining the sum, we can at least check that the series converges and so has a sum (even if we cannot determine its exact value). Calculus includes many tests for telling if an infinite series converges. This section presents two convergence tests for infinite series consisting of positive terms. The tests are derived from geometric models of the series.

Throughout this section, we consider only series for which each term a_k is positive (or zero). Suppose that $\sum_{k=1}^{\infty} ar^k$ is such a series. Consider the corresponding collection of rectangles in Fig. 1. Each rectangle is 1 unit wide, and the height of the kth rectangle is a_k. Hence the area of the kth rectangle is a_k, and the area of the region consisting of the first n rectangles is the nth partial sum $S_n = a_1 + a_2 + \cdots + a_n$. As n increases, the partial sums increase and approach the area of the region consisting of all the rectangles. If this area is finite, the infinite series converges to this area. If this area is infinite, the series is divergent.

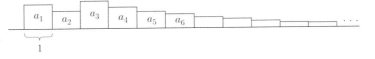

Figure 1. Representation of an infinite series by rectangles.

This geometric "picture" of an infinite series provides a convergence test that relates the convergence of the series to the convergence of an improper integral. For example, consider

$$\sum_{k=1}^{\infty} \frac{1}{k^2} \quad \text{and} \quad \int_{1}^{\infty} \frac{1}{x^2}\, dx.$$

Notice that the series and the integral have a similar form:

$$\sum_{k=1}^{\infty} f(k) \quad \text{and} \quad \int_{1}^{\infty} f(x)\, dx, \tag{1}$$

where $f(x) = 1/x^2$.

The techniques of Section 9.6 show that the integral is convergent. Hence the area under the graph of $y = 1/x^2$ for $x \geq 1$ is finite. Figure 2 shows the graph of $y = 1/x^2$ $(x \geq 1)$ superimposed on a geometric model of the series

$$\sum_{k=1}^{\infty} \frac{1}{k^2} = 1 + \frac{1}{4} + \frac{1}{9} + \frac{1}{16} + \cdots .$$

The area of the first rectangle is 1. The region consisting of all the remaining rectangles has finite area since it is contained in the region under the graph of $y = 1/x^2$ $(x \geq 1)$, which has finite area. Hence the total area of all the rectangles is finite and the series $\sum_{k=1}^{\infty} \frac{1}{k^2}$ is convergent.

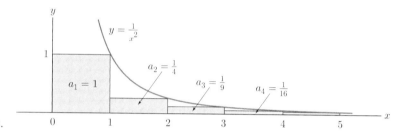

Figure 2.   A convergent series.

As a second example, consider

$$\sum_{k=1}^{\infty} \frac{1}{k} \qquad \text{and} \qquad \int_{1}^{\infty} \frac{1}{x}\, dx.$$

Once again, the series and the integral have the forms in (1), where $f(x) = 1/x$. It is easy to check that the integral is divergent and hence the area under the graph of $y = 1/x$ for $x \geq 1$ is infinite. Figure 3 shows the graph of $y = 1/x$ superimposed on a geometric model of the series

$$\sum_{k=1}^{\infty} \frac{1}{k} = 1 + \frac{1}{2} + \frac{1}{3} + \frac{1}{4} + \cdots .$$

Since the area of the region formed by the rectangles clearly exceeds the infinite area of the region under the graph of $y = 1/x$ $(x \geq 1)$, the series $\sum_{k=1}^{\infty} \frac{1}{k}$ is divergent.

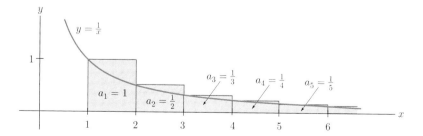

Figure 3.   A divergent series.

The reasoning for these two examples can be used to derive the following important test:

The Integral Test   Let $f(x)$ be continuous, decreasing, and positive for $x \geq 1$. Then the infinite series

$$\sum_{k=1}^{\infty} f(k)$$

is convergent if the improper integral

$$\int_{1}^{\infty} f(x)\,dx$$

is convergent, and the infinite series is divergent if the improper integral is divergent.

EXAMPLE 1   Use the integral test to determine whether the infinite series

$$\sum_{k=1}^{\infty} \frac{1}{e^k}$$

is convergent or divergent.

Solution Here $f(x) = 1/e^x = e^{-x}$. We know from Chapter 4 that $f(x)$ is a positive, decreasing, continuous function. Also,

$$\int_{1}^{\infty} e^{-x}\,dx = \lim_{b \to \infty} \int_{1}^{b} e^{-x}\,dx = \lim_{b \to \infty} -e^{-x}\Big|_{1}^{b}$$

$$= \lim_{b \to \infty} \left(-e^{-b} + e^{-1}\right) = e^{-1} = \frac{1}{e}.$$

Since the improper integral is convergent, so is the infinite series.   ∎

NOTE ▶ The integral test does not provide the exact value of the sum of a convergent infinite series. It only verifies convergence. Other techniques, sometimes quite advanced, must be used to find the sum. (The sum of the series in Example 1 is readily found since the series happens to be a geometric series with ratio $1/e$.)   ∎

Instead of starting our infinite series with $k = 1$, we may start with $k = N$, where N is any positive integer. To test the convergence of such a series, we determine the convergence (or divergence) of the improper integral

$$\int_{N}^{\infty} f(x)\,dx.$$

EXAMPLE 2   Determine whether the series

$$\sum_{k=3}^{\infty} \frac{\ln k}{k}$$

is convergent.

Solution We take $f(x) = (\ln x)/x$. Note that $f(x)$ is continuous and positive for $x \geq 3$. Moreover,

$$f'(x) = \frac{x \cdot \dfrac{1}{x} - \ln x \cdot 1}{x^2} = \frac{1 - \ln x}{x^2}.$$

Since $\ln x > 1$ for $x \geq 3$, we conclude that $f'(x)$ is negative and hence that $f(x)$ is a decreasing function.

To antidifferentiate $(\ln x)/x$, make the substitution $u = \ln x$, $du = (1/x)\,dx$:

$$\int \frac{\ln x}{x}\,dx = \int u\,du = \frac{u^2}{2} + C = \frac{(\ln x)^2}{2} + C.$$

Hence

$$\int_3^\infty \frac{\ln x}{x}\,dx = \lim_{b \to \infty} \int_3^b \frac{\ln x}{x}\,dx = \lim_{b \to \infty} \frac{(\ln x)^2}{2}\Big|_3^b$$

$$= \lim_{b \to \infty} \frac{(\ln b)^2}{2} - \frac{(\ln 3)^2}{2} = \infty.$$

Thus the series $\sum_{k=3}^\infty \frac{\ln k}{k}$ is divergent. ■

When using the integral test, we tested the convergence of an infinite series by relating it to an improper integral. In many situations it is possible to accomplish the same result by comparing the series with another infinite series whose convergence or divergence is already known.

Suppose that $\sum_{k=1}^\infty a_k$ and $\sum_{k=1}^\infty b_k$ have the property that $0 \le a_k \le b_k$ for all k. In Fig. 4 we have superimposed the geometric models for the two series. Each rectangle for the series $\sum_{k=1}^\infty a_k$ lies inside (or coincides with) the corresponding rectangle for the series $\sum_{k=1}^\infty b_k$. Clearly, if the region formed by all the rectangles

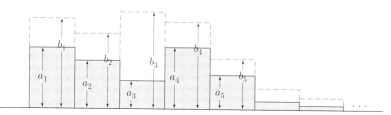

Figure 4. Term-by-term comparison of two series.

for $\sum_{k=1}^\infty b_k$ has finite area, so does the region for $\sum_{k=1}^\infty a_k$. On the other hand, if the region for $\sum_{k=1}^\infty a_k$ has infinite area, so does the region for $\sum_{k=1}^\infty b_k$. These geometric conclusions may be stated in terms of the infinite series as follows:

Comparison Test Suppose that $0 \le a_k \le b_k$ for $k = 1, 2, \ldots$.

$$\text{If } \sum_{k=1}^\infty b_k \text{ converges, so does } \sum_{k=1}^\infty a_k.$$

$$\text{If } \sum_{k=1}^\infty a_k \text{ diverges, so does } \sum_{k=1}^\infty b_k.$$

The comparison test also applies to two series whose terms eventually satisfy $0 \le a_k \le b_k$, say for $k \ge N$, where N is some positive integer. This is so because the convergence or divergence of $\sum_{k=1}^\infty a_k$ and $\sum_{k=1}^\infty b_k$ is not affected by removing some terms from the beginning of the series.

EXAMPLE 3

Determine the convergence or divergence of the series

$$\sum_{k=1}^\infty \frac{3}{1 + 5^k} = \frac{3}{6} + \frac{3}{26} + \frac{3}{126} + \frac{3}{626} + \cdots.$$

Solution Compare the series with the convergent geometric series

$$\sum_{k=1}^{\infty} \frac{3}{5^k} = \frac{3}{5} + \frac{3}{25} + \frac{3}{125} + \frac{3}{625} + \cdots .$$

This series converges since the ratio of successive terms is $r = \frac{1}{5}$. The kth terms of these two series satisfy

$$\frac{3}{1+5^k} < \frac{3}{5^k}$$

because the denominator of the left fraction is greater than the denominator of the right fraction. Since the series $\sum_{k=1}^{\infty} \frac{3}{5^k}$ converges, the comparison test implies that $\sum_{k=1}^{\infty} \frac{3}{1+5^k}$ also converges. ∎

This section has considered convergence tests only for series of positive terms. Here is a version of the comparison test that works even if one of the two series has some negative terms.

Suppose that $\sum_{k=1}^{\infty} b_k$ is a convergent series of positive terms and that $|a_k| \leq b_k$ for $k = 1, 2, 3, \ldots$. Then $\sum_{k=1}^{\infty} a_k$ is convergent.

Practice Problems 11.4

1. **(a)** What is the improper integral associated with the infinite series $\sum_{k=1}^{\infty} \frac{k^2}{(k^3+6)^2}$?

    (b) Is the improper integral found in part (a) convergent or divergent?

    (c) Is the infinite series $\sum_{k=1}^{\infty} \frac{k^2}{(k^3+6)^2}$ convergent or divergent?

2. The two series

    $$\sum_{k=1}^{\infty} \frac{1}{4k} \quad \text{and} \quad \sum_{k=1}^{\infty} \frac{1}{4k+3}$$

    are both divergent. (This is easily established by the integral test.) Which of these series can be used in the comparison test to show that the series $\sum_{k=1}^{\infty} \frac{1}{4k+1}$ is divergent?

EXERCISES 11.4

In Exercises 1–16, use the integral test to determine whether the infinite series is convergent or divergent. (You may assume that the hypotheses of the integral test are satisfied.)

1. $\sum_{k=1}^{\infty} \frac{3}{\sqrt{k}}$

2. $\sum_{k=1}^{\infty} \frac{5}{k^{3/2}}$

3. $\sum_{k=2}^{\infty} \frac{1}{(k-1)^3}$

4. $\sum_{k=0}^{\infty} \frac{7}{k+100}$

5. $\sum_{k=1}^{\infty} \frac{2}{5k-1}$

6. $\sum_{k=2}^{\infty} \frac{1}{k\sqrt{\ln k}}$

7. $\sum_{k=2}^{\infty} \frac{k}{(k^2+1)^{3/2}}$

8. $\sum_{k=1}^{\infty} \frac{1}{(2k+1)^3}$

9. $\sum_{k=2}^{\infty} \frac{1}{k(\ln k)^2}$

10. $\sum_{k=1}^{\infty} \frac{1}{(3k)^2}$

11. $\sum_{k=1}^{\infty} e^{3-k}$

12. $\sum_{k=1}^{\infty} \frac{1}{e^{2k+1}}$

13. $\sum_{k=1}^{\infty} ke^{-k^2}$

14. $\sum_{k=1}^{\infty} k^{-3/4}$

15. $\sum_{k=1}^{\infty} \frac{2k+1}{k^2+k+2}$

16. $\sum_{k=2}^{\infty} \frac{k+1}{(k^2+2k+1)^2}$

17. It can be shown that

$$\int_0^\infty \frac{3}{9 + x^2}\, dx$$

is convergent. Use this fact to show that an appropriate infinite series converges. Give the series and show that the hypotheses of the integral test are satisfied.

18. Use the integral test to determine if $\sum_{k=1}^\infty \frac{e^{1/k}}{k^2}$ is convergent. Show that the hypotheses of the integral test are satisfied.

19. It can be shown that $\lim_{b\to\infty} be^{-b} = 0$. Use this fact and the integral test to show that $\sum_{k=1}^\infty \frac{k}{e^k}$ is convergent.

20. Is the series $\sum_{k=1}^\infty \frac{3^k}{4^k}$ convergent? What is the easiest way to answer this question? Can you tell if

$$\int_1^\infty \frac{3^x}{4^x}\, dx$$

is convergent?

In Exercises 21–26, use the comparison test to determine whether the infinite series is convergent or divergent.

21. $\sum_{k=2}^\infty \frac{1}{k^2 + 5}$ $\left[\text{Compare with } \sum_{k=2}^\infty \frac{1}{k^2}.\right]$

22. $\sum_{k=2}^\infty \frac{1}{\sqrt{k^2 - 1}}$ $\left[\text{Compare with } \sum_{k=2}^\infty \frac{1}{k}.\right]$

23. $\sum_{k=1}^\infty \frac{1}{2^k + k}$ $\left[\text{Compare with } \sum_{k=1}^\infty \frac{1}{2^k} \text{ or } \sum_{k=1}^\infty \frac{1}{k}.\right]$

24. $\sum_{k=1}^\infty \frac{1}{k3^k}$ $\left[\text{Compare with } \sum_{k=1}^\infty \frac{1}{k} \text{ or } \sum_{k=1}^\infty \frac{1}{3^k}.\right]$

25. $\sum_{k=1}^\infty \frac{1}{5^k} \cos^2\left(\frac{k\pi}{4}\right)$ $\left[\text{Compare with } \sum_{k=1}^\infty \cos^2\left(\frac{k\pi}{4}\right)\right.$ or $\left.\sum_{k=1}^\infty \frac{1}{5^k}.\right]$

26. $\sum_{k=0}^\infty \frac{1}{\left(\frac{3}{4}\right)^k + \left(\frac{5}{4}\right)^k}$ $\left[\text{Compare with } \sum_{k=0}^\infty \left(\frac{3}{4}\right)^{-k}\right.$ or $\left.\sum_{k=0}^\infty \left(\frac{5}{4}\right)^{-k}.\right]$

27. Can the comparison test be used with $\sum_{k=2}^\infty \frac{1}{k \ln k}$ and $\sum_{k=2}^\infty \frac{1}{k}$ to deduce anything about the first series?

28. Can the comparison test be used with $\sum_{k=2}^\infty \frac{1}{k^2 \ln k}$ and $\sum_{k=2}^\infty \frac{1}{k^2}$ to deduce anything about the first series?

29. The following property is true for any two series (with possibly some negative terms): Let $\sum_{k=1}^\infty a_k$ and $\sum_{k=1}^\infty b_k$ be convergent series whose sums are S and T, respectively. Then $\sum_{k=1}^\infty (a_k + b_k)$ is a convergent series whose sum is $S + T$. Make a geometric picture to illustrate why this property is true when the terms a_k and b_k are all positive.

30. Let $\sum_{k=1}^\infty a_k$ be a convergent series with sum S, and let c be a constant. Then $\sum_{k=1}^\infty ca_k$ is a convergent series whose sum is $c \cdot S$. Make a geometric picture to illustrate why this is true when $c = 2$ and the terms a_k are all positive.

31. Use Exercise 29 to show that the series $\sum_{k=0}^\infty \frac{8^k + 9^k}{10^k}$ is convergent and determine its sum.

32. Use Exercise 30 to show that the series $\sum_{k=1}^\infty \frac{3}{k^2}$ is convergent. Then use the comparison test to show that the series $\sum_{k=1}^\infty \frac{e^{1/k}}{k^2}$ is convergent.

Solutions to Practice Problems 11.4

1. (a) $\int_1^\infty \dfrac{x^2}{(x^3+6)^2}\,dx$. In general, to find the function $f(x)$, replace each occurrence of k by x; then replace the summation sign by an integral sign and adjoin dx.

(b) A substitution must first be made to antidifferentiate the function. Let $u = x^3 + 6$. Then $du = 3x^2\,dx$ and

$$\int \frac{x^2}{(x^3+6)^2}\,dx = \frac{1}{3}\int \frac{3x^2}{(x^3+6)^2}\,dx$$

$$= \frac{1}{3}\int \frac{1}{u^2}\,du$$

$$= -\frac{1}{3}u^{-1} + C$$

$$= -\frac{1}{3}\cdot\frac{1}{x^3+6} + C.$$

Hence

$$\int_1^\infty \frac{x^2}{(x^3+6)^2}\,dx = \lim_{b\to\infty}\left[-\frac{1}{3}\cdot\frac{1}{x^3+6}\right]\Big|_1^b$$

$$= \lim_{b\to\infty}\left[-\frac{1}{3}\cdot\frac{1}{b^3+6} + \frac{1}{3}\cdot\frac{1}{7}\right]$$

$$= \frac{1}{21}.$$

Therefore, the improper integral is convergent.

(c) Convergent, since the infinite series is convergent if and only if the associated improper integral is convergent.

2. To show that a series is divergent, we need to show that its terms are *greater* than the corresponding terms of some divergent series. Since

$$\frac{1}{4k+3} < \frac{1}{4k+1},$$

the comparison should be made with

$$\sum_{k=1}^\infty \frac{1}{4k+3}.$$

(*Note:* If instead we had been trying to establish the *convergence* of an infinite series, we would try to show that its terms are *less* than the corresponding terms of a convergent series.)

11.5 Taylor Series

Consider the infinite series $1 + x + x^2 + x^3 + x^4 + \cdots$. This series is of a different type from those discussed in the preceding two sections. Its terms are not numbers but rather are powers of x. However, for some specific values of x, the series is convergent. In fact, for any value of x between -1 and 1, the series is a convergent geometric series with ratio x and sum $\dfrac{1}{1-x}$. We write

$$\frac{1}{1-x} = 1 + x + x^2 + x^3 + x^4 + \cdots, \qquad |x| < 1. \tag{1}$$

Looking at (1) from a different point of view, we see that the function $f(x) = \dfrac{1}{1-x}$ is represented as a series involving the powers of x. This representation is not valid throughout the entire domain of the function $\dfrac{1}{1-x}$, but just for values of x with $-1 < x < 1$.

In many important cases, a function $f(x)$ may be represented by a series of the form

$$f(x) = a_0 + a_1 x + a_2 x^2 + a_3 x^3 + \cdots, \tag{2}$$

where $a_0, a_1, a_2, \ldots$ are suitable constants and where x ranges over values that make the series converge to $f(x)$. The series is called a *power series* (because it involves powers of x). It may be shown that when a function $f(x)$ has a representation by a power series as in (2), the coefficients $a_0, a_1, a_2, \ldots$ are uniquely determined by $f(x)$ and its derivatives at $x = 0$. In fact, $a_0 = f(0)$, and $a_k = f^{(k)}(0)/k!$ for $k = 1, 2, \ldots$, so

$$f(x) = f(0) + \frac{f'(0)}{1!}x + \frac{f''(0)}{2!}x^2 + \cdots + \frac{f^{(k)}(0)}{k!}x^k + \cdots . \qquad (3)$$

The series in (3) is often called the *Taylor series of $f(x)$ at $x = 0$* because the partial sums of the series are the Taylor polynomials of $f(x)$ at $x = 0$. The entire equation (3) is called the *Taylor series expansion of $f(x)$ at $x = 0$*.

EXAMPLE 1

Find the Taylor series expansion of

$$\frac{1}{1-x} \quad \text{at } x = 0.$$

Solution We already know how to represent $\dfrac{1}{1-x}$ as a power series for $|x| < 1$. However, let us use the formula for the Taylor series to see if we get the same result.

$$f(x) = \frac{1}{1-x} = (1-x)^{-1}, \qquad f(0) = 1,$$

$$f'(x) = (1-x)^{-2}, \qquad f'(0) = 1,$$

$$f''(x) = 2(1-x)^{-3}, \qquad f''(0) = 2,$$

$$f'''(0) = 3 \cdot 2(1-x)^{-4}, \qquad f'''(0) = 3 \cdot 2,$$

$$f^{(4)}(x) = 4 \cdot 3 \cdot 2(1-x)^{-5}, \qquad f^{(4)}(0) = 4 \cdot 3 \cdot 2,$$

$$\vdots \qquad\qquad\qquad \vdots$$

Therefore,

$$\frac{1}{1-x} = 1 + \frac{1}{1!}x + \frac{2}{2!}x^2 + \frac{3 \cdot 2}{3!}x^3 + \frac{4 \cdot 3 \cdot 2}{4!}x^4 + \cdots$$

$$= 1 + x + x^2 + x^3 + x^4 + \cdots .$$

We have verified that the Taylor series for $\dfrac{1}{1-x}$ is the familiar geometric power series. The Taylor series expansion is valid for $|x| < 1$. ∎

EXAMPLE 2

Find the Taylor series at $x = 0$ for $f(x) = e^x$.

Solution

$$f(x) = e^x, \quad f'(x) = e^x, \quad f''(x) = e^x, \quad f'''(x) = e^x, \ldots$$
$$f(0) = 1, \quad f'(0) = 1, \quad f''(0) = 1, \quad f'''(0) = 1, \ldots .$$

Therefore,

$$e^x = 1 + x + \frac{1}{2!}x^2 + \frac{1}{3!}x^3 + \frac{1}{4!}x^4 + \cdots .$$

It can be shown that this Taylor series expansion of e^x is valid for all x. (*Note:* A Taylor polynomial of e^x gives only an approximation of e^x, but the infinite Taylor series actually *equals* e^x for all x, in the sense that for any given x the sum of the series is the same as the value of e^x.) ∎

Operations on Taylor Series It is often helpful to think of a Taylor series as a polynomial of infinite degree. Many operations on polynomials are also legitimate for Taylor series, provided that we restrict attention to values of x within an appropriate interval. For example, if we have a Taylor series expansion of $f(x)$, we may differentiate the series term by term to obtain the Taylor series expansion of $f'(x)$. An analogous result holds for antiderivatives. Other permissible operations that produce Taylor series include multiplying a Taylor series expansion by a constant or a power of x, replacing x by a power of x or by a constant times a power of x, and adding or subtracting two Taylor series expansions. The use of such operations often makes it possible to find the Taylor series of a function without directly using the formal definition of a Taylor series. (The process of computing high-order derivatives can become quite laborious when the product or quotient rule is involved.) Once a power series expansion of a function $f(x)$ is found, that series *must* be the Taylor series of the function, since the coefficients of the series are uniquely determined by $f(x)$ and its derivatives at $x = 0$.

EXAMPLE 3

Use the Taylor series at $x = 0$ for

$$\frac{1}{1-x}$$

to find the Taylor series at $x = 0$ for the following functions:

(a) $\dfrac{1}{(1-x)^2}$ (b) $\dfrac{1}{(1-x)^3}$ (c) $\ln(1-x)$

Solution We begin with the series expansion

$$\frac{1}{1-x} = 1 + x + x^2 + x^3 + x^4 + x^5 + \cdots, \quad |x| < 1.$$

(a) When we differentiate both sides of this equation, we obtain

$$\frac{1}{(1-x)^2} = 1 + 2x + 3x^2 + 4x^3 + 5x^4 + \cdots, \quad |x| < 1.$$

(b) Differentiating the series in part (a), we find that

$$\frac{2}{(1-x)^3} = 2 + 3 \cdot 2x + 4 \cdot 3x^2 + 5 \cdot 4x^3 + \cdots, \quad |x| < 1.$$

We may multiply a convergent series by a constant. Multiplying by $\frac{1}{2}$, we have

$$\frac{1}{(1-x)^3} = 1 + 3x + 6x^2 + 10x^3 + \cdots + \frac{(n+2)(n+1)}{2}x^n + \cdots$$

for $|x| < 1$.

(c) For $|x| < 1$, we have

$$\int \frac{1}{1-x}\, dx = \int (1 + x + x^2 + x^3 + \cdots)\, dx,$$

$$-\ln(1-x) + C = x + \tfrac{1}{2}x^2 + \tfrac{1}{3}x^3 + \tfrac{1}{4}x^4 + \cdots,$$

where C is the constant of integration. If we set $x = 0$ in both sides, we obtain

$$0 + C = 0,$$

so $C = 0$. Thus

$$\ln(1-x) = -x - \tfrac{1}{2}x^2 - \tfrac{1}{3}x^3 - \tfrac{1}{4}x^4 - \cdots, \quad |x| < 1. \quad \blacksquare$$

EXAMPLE 4   Use the result of Example 3(c) to compute $\ln 1.1$.

Solution Take $x = -.1$ in the Taylor series expansion of $\ln(1-x)$. Then

$$\ln(1-(-.1)) = -(-.1) - \tfrac{1}{2}(-.1)^2 - \tfrac{1}{3}(-.1)^3 - \tfrac{1}{4}(-.1)^4 - \cdots$$

$$\ln 1.1 = .1 - \frac{.01}{2} + \frac{.001}{3} - \frac{.0001}{4} + \frac{.00001}{5} - \cdots .$$

This infinite series may be used to compute $\ln 1.1$ to any degree of accuracy required. For instance, the fifth partial sum gives $\ln 1.1 \approx .09531$, which is correct to five decimal places. ◼

EXAMPLE 5   Use the Taylor series at $x = 0$ for e^x to find the Taylor series at $x = 0$ for

(a) $x(e^x - 1)$ (b) e^{x^2}

Solution (a) If we subtract 1 from the Taylor series for e^x, we obtain a series that converges to $e^x - 1$:

$$e^x - 1 = \left(1 + x + \frac{1}{2!}x^2 + \frac{1}{3!}x^3 + \frac{1}{4!}x^4 + \cdots\right) - 1$$

$$= x + \frac{1}{2!}x^2 + \frac{1}{3!}x^3 + \frac{1}{4!}x^4 + \cdots .$$

Now we multiply this series by x, term by term:

$$x(e^x - 1) = x^2 + \frac{1}{2!}x^3 + \frac{1}{3!}x^4 + \frac{1}{4!}x^5 + \cdots .$$

(b) To obtain the Taylor series for e^{x^2}, we replace every occurrence of x by x^2 in the Taylor series for e^x,

$$e^{x^2} = 1 + (x^2) + \frac{1}{2!}(x^2)^2 + \frac{1}{3!}(x^2)^3 + \frac{1}{4!}(x^2)^4 + \cdots$$

$$= 1 + x^2 + \frac{1}{2!}x^4 + \frac{1}{3!}x^6 + \frac{1}{4!}x^8 + \cdots .$$ ◼

EXAMPLE 6   Find the Taylor series at $x = 0$ for

(a) $\dfrac{1}{1 + x^3}$ (b) $\dfrac{x^2}{1 + x^3}$

Solution (a) In the Taylor series at $x = 0$ for $\dfrac{1}{1-x}$, we replace x by $-x^3$, to obtain

$$\frac{1}{1-(-x^3)} = 1 + (-x^3) + (-x^3)^2 + (-x^3)^3 + (-x^3)^4 + \cdots$$

$$\frac{1}{1+x^3} = 1 - x^3 + x^6 - x^9 + x^{12} - \cdots .$$

(b) If we multiply the series in part (a) by x^2, we obtain

$$\frac{x^2}{1+x^3} = x^2 - x^5 + x^8 - x^{11} + x^{14} - \cdots .$$ ◼

Definite Integrals   The standard normal curve of statistics has the equation

$$y = \frac{1}{\sqrt{2\pi}}\, e^{-x^2/2}.$$

Areas under the curve cannot be found by direct integration since there is no simple formula for an antiderivative of $e^{-x^2/2}$. However, Taylor series can be used to calculate these areas with a high degree of accuracy.

EXAMPLE 7   Find the area under the standard normal curve from $x = 0$ to $x = .8$; that is, calculate

$$\frac{1}{\sqrt{2\pi}} \int_0^{.8} e^{-x^2/2}\, dx.$$

Solution   A Taylor expansion for e^x was obtained in Example 2.

$$e^x = 1 + x + \frac{1}{2!}x^2 + \frac{1}{3!}x^3 + \frac{1}{4!}x^4 + \cdots .$$

Replace each occurrence of x by $-x^2/2$. Then

$$e^{-x^2/2} = 1 + \left(-\frac{x^2}{2}\right) + \frac{1}{2!}\left(-\frac{x^2}{2}\right)^2 + \frac{1}{3!}\left(-\frac{x^2}{2}\right)^3 + \frac{1}{4!}\left(-\frac{x^2}{2}\right)^4 + \cdots ,$$

$$e^{-x^2/2} = 1 - \frac{1}{2\cdot 1!}x^2 + \frac{1}{2^2\cdot 2!}x^4 - \frac{1}{2^3\cdot 3!}x^6 + \frac{1}{2^4\cdot 4!}x^8 - \cdots .$$

Integrating, we obtain

$$\frac{1}{\sqrt{2\pi}} \int_0^{.8} e^{-x^2/2}\, dx$$

$$= \frac{1}{\sqrt{2\pi}}\left(x - \frac{1}{3\cdot 2\cdot 1!}x^3 + \frac{1}{5\cdot 2^2\cdot 2!}x^5 - \frac{1}{7\cdot 2^3\cdot 3!}x^7 + \frac{1}{9\cdot 2^4\cdot 4!}x^9 - \cdots \right)\Bigg|_0^{.8}$$

$$= \frac{1}{\sqrt{2\pi}}\left[.8 - \frac{1}{6}(.8)^3 + \frac{1}{40}(.8)^5 - \frac{1}{336}(.8)^7 + \frac{1}{3456}(.8)^9 - \cdots \right].$$

The infinite series on the right converges to the value of the definite integral. Summing up the five terms displayed gives the approximation .28815, which is accurate to four places. This approximation can be made arbitrarily accurate by summing additional terms. ■

Convergence of Power Series   When we differentiate, integrate, or perform algebraic operations on Taylor series, we are using the fact that Taylor series are *functions*. In fact, any power series in x is a function of x, whether or not its coefficients are obtained from the derivatives of some function. The domain of a **power series function** is the set of all x for which the series converges. The function value at a specific x in its domain is the number to which the series converges.

For instance, the geometric series $\sum_{k=0}^{\infty} x^k$ defines a function whose domain is the set of all x for which $|x| < 1$. The familiar Taylor series expansion

$$\frac{1}{1-x} = \sum_{k=0}^{\infty} x^k$$

simply states that the functions $\dfrac{1}{1-x}$ and $\sum_{k=0}^{\infty} x^k$ have the same value for each x such that $|x| < 1$.

Given any power series $\sum_{k=0}^{\infty} a_k x^k$, one of three possibilities must occur:

(i) There is a positive constant R such that the series converges for $|x| < R$ and diverges for $|x| > R$.

(ii) The series converges for all x.

(iii) The series converges only for $x = 0$.

In case (i) we call R the *radius of convergence* of the series. The series converges for all x in the interval $-R < x < R$ and may or may not converge at one or both of the endpoints of this interval. In case (ii), we say that the radius of convergence is ∞, and in case (iii) we say that the radius of convergence is 0.

When a power series with a positive radius of convergence is differentiated term by term, the new series will have the same radius of convergence. An analogous result holds for antiderivatives. Other operations, such as replacing x by a constant times a power of x, may affect the radius of convergence.

Suppose that we begin with a function that has derivatives of all orders, and we write down its formal Taylor series at $x = 0$. Can we conclude that the Taylor series and the function have the same values for every x within the radius of convergence of the series? For all the functions that we consider, the answer is yes. However, it is possible for the two values to differ. In this case we say that the function does not admit a power series expansion. To show that a function admits a power series expansion, it is necessary to show that the partial sums of the Taylor series converge to the function. The nth partial sum of the series is the nth Taylor polynomial p_n. Recall from Section 11.1 that we considered the nth remainder of $f(x)$,

$$R_n(x) = f(x) - p_n(x).$$

For a fixed x, the Taylor series converges to $f(x)$ if and only if $R_n(x) \to 0$ as $n \to \infty$. Exercises 45 and 46 illustrate how convergence can be verified by using the remainder formula from Section 11.1.

Taylor Series at $x = a$ To simplify the discussion in this section, we have restricted our attention to series that involve powers of x, rather than powers of $x - a$. However, Taylor series, just like Taylor polynomials, can be formed as sums of powers of $x - a$. The Taylor expansion of $f(x)$ at $x = a$ is

$$f(x) = f(a) + \frac{f'(a)}{1!}(x - a) + \frac{f''(a)}{2!}(x - a)^2 + \frac{f'''(a)}{3!}(x - a)^3 + \cdots$$

$$+ \frac{f^{(n)}(a)}{n!}(x - a)^n + \cdots .$$

Practice Problems 11.5

1. Find the Taylor series expansion of $\sin x$ at $x = 0$.

2. Find the Taylor series expansion of $\cos x$ at $x = 0$.

3. Find the Taylor series expansion of $x^3 \cos 7x$ at $x = 0$.

4. If $f(x) = x^3 \cos 7x$, find $f^{(5)}(0)$. [*Hint:* How are the coefficients in the Taylor series of $f(x)$ related to $f(x)$ and its derivatives at $x = 0$?]

EXERCISES 11.5

In Exercises 1–4, find the Taylor series at $x = 0$ of the given function by computing three or four derivatives and using the definition of the Taylor series.

1. $\dfrac{1}{2x + 3}$

2. $\ln(1 - 3x)$

3. $\sqrt{1 + x}$

4. $(1 + x)^3$

In Exercises 5–20, find the Taylor series at $x = 0$ of the given function. Use suitable operations (differentiation, substitution, etc.) on the Taylor series at $x = 0$ of $\dfrac{1}{1-x}$, e^x, or $\cos x$. These series are derived in Examples 1 and 2 and Practice Problem 2.

5. $\dfrac{1}{1-3x}$ **6.** $\dfrac{1}{1+x}$

7. $\dfrac{1}{1+x^2}$ **8.** $\dfrac{x}{1+x^2}$

9. $\dfrac{1}{(1+x)^2}$ **10.** $\dfrac{x}{(1-x)^3}$

11. $5e^{x/3}$ **12.** $x^3 e^{x^2}$

13. $1 - e^{-x}$ **14.** $3(e^{-2x} - 2)$

15. $\ln(1+x)$ **16.** $\ln(1+x^2)$

17. $\cos 3x$ **18.** $\cos x^2$

19. $\sin 3x$ **20.** $x \sin x^2$

21. Find the Taylor series of xe^{x^2} at $x = 0$.

22. Show that $\ln\left(\dfrac{1+x}{1-x}\right) = 2x + \frac{2}{3}x^3 + \frac{2}{5}x^5 + \frac{2}{7}x^7 + \cdots$, $|x| < 1$. [*Hint:* Use Exercise 15 and Example 3.] This series converges much more quickly than the series for $\ln(1-x)$ in Example 3, particularly for x close to zero. The series gives a formula for $\ln y$, where y is any number and $x = \dfrac{y-1}{y+1}$.

23. The *hyperbolic cosine* of x, denoted by $\cosh x$, is defined by
$$\cosh x = \tfrac{1}{2}(e^x + e^{-x}).$$
This function occurs often in physics and probability theory. The graph of $y = \cosh x$ is called a *catenary*.

(a) Use differentiation and the definition of a Taylor series to compute the first four nonzero terms in the Taylor series of $\cosh x$ at $x = 0$.

(b) Use the known Taylor series for e^x to obtain the Taylor series for $\cosh x$ at $x = 0$.

24. The *hyperbolic sine* of x is defined by
$$\sinh x = \tfrac{1}{2}(e^x - e^{-x}).$$
Repeat parts (a) and (b) of Exercise 23 for $\sinh x$.

25. Given the Taylor series expansion
$$\frac{1}{\sqrt{1+x}} = 1 - \frac{1}{2}x + \frac{1 \cdot 3}{2 \cdot 4}x^2 - \frac{1 \cdot 3 \cdot 5}{2 \cdot 4 \cdot 6}x^3 +$$
$$\frac{1 \cdot 3 \cdot 5 \cdot 7}{2 \cdot 4 \cdot 6 \cdot 8}x^4 - \cdots,$$
find the first four terms in the Taylor series of $\dfrac{1}{\sqrt{1-x}}$ at $x = 0$.

26. Find the first four terms in the Taylor series of $\dfrac{1}{\sqrt{1-x^2}}$ at $x = 0$. (See Exercise 25.)

27. Use Exercise 25 and the fact that
$$\int \frac{1}{\sqrt{1+x^2}}\, dx = \ln(x + \sqrt{1+x^2}) + C$$
to find the Taylor series of $\ln(x + \sqrt{1+x^2})$ at $x = 0$.

28. Use the Taylor series expansion for $\dfrac{x}{(1-x)^2}$ to find the function whose Taylor series is $1 + 4x + 9x^2 + 16x^3 + 25x^4 + \cdots$.

29. Use the Taylor series for e^x to show that $\dfrac{d}{dx}e^x = e^x$.

30. Use the Taylor series for $\cos x$ (see Practice Problem 2) to show that $\cos(-x) = \cos x$.

31. The Taylor series at $x = 0$ for
$$f(x) = \ln\left(\frac{1+x}{1-x}\right)$$
is given in Exercise 22. Find $f^{(5)}(0)$.

32. The Taylor series at $x = 0$ for $f(x) = \sec x$ is $1 + \frac{1}{2}x^2 + \frac{5}{24}x^4 + \frac{61}{720}x^6 + \cdots$. Find $f^{(4)}(0)$.

33. The Taylor series at $x = 0$ for $f(x) = \tan x$ is $x + \frac{1}{3}x^3 + \frac{2}{15}x^5 + \frac{17}{315}x^7 + \cdots$. Find $f^{(4)}(0)$.

34. The Taylor series at $x = 0$ for $\dfrac{1+x^2}{1-x}$ is $1 + x + 2x^2 + 2x^3 + 2x^4 + \cdots$. Find $f^{(4)}(0)$, where $f(x) = \dfrac{1+x^4}{1-x^2}$.

In Exercises 35–37, find the Taylor series expansion at $x = 0$ of the given antiderivative.

35. $\displaystyle\int e^{-x^2}\, dx$ **36.** $\displaystyle\int xe^{x^3}\, dx$ **37.** $\displaystyle\int \frac{1}{1+x^3}\, dx$

In Exercises 38–40, find an infinite series that converges to the value of the given definite integral.

38. $\displaystyle\int_0^1 \sin x^2\, dx$ **39.** $\displaystyle\int_0^1 e^{-x^2}\, dx$ **40.** $\displaystyle\int_0^1 xe^{x^3}\, dx$

41. (a) Use the Taylor series for e^x at $x = 0$ to show that $e^x > x^2/2$ for $x > 0$.

(b) Deduce that $e^{-x} < 2/x^2$ for $x > 0$.

(c) Show that xe^{-x} approaches 0 as $x \to \infty$.

42. Let k be a positive constant.

(a) Show that $e^{kx} > \dfrac{k^2 x^2}{2}$, for $x > 0$.

(b) Deduce that $e^{-kx} < \dfrac{2}{k^2 x^2}$, for $x > 0$.

(c) Show that xe^{-kx} approaches 0 as $x \to \infty$.

43. Show that $e^x > x^3/6$ for $x > 0$, and from this deduce that $x^2 e^{-x}$ approaches 0 as $x \to \infty$.

44. If k is a positive constant, show that $x^2 e^{-kx}$ approaches 0 as $x \to \infty$.

Exercises 45 and 46 rely on the fact that

$$\lim_{n \to \infty} \frac{|x|^{n+1}}{(n+1)!} = 0.$$

The proof of this fact is omitted.

45. Let $R_n(x)$ be the nth remainder of $f(x) = \cos x$ at $x = 0$. See Section 11.1. Show that, for any fixed value of x, $|R_n(x)| \le |x|^{n+1}/(n+1)!$, and hence conclude

that $|R_n(x)| \to 0$ as $n \to \infty$. This shows that the Taylor series for $\cos x$ converges to $\cos x$ for every value of x.

46. Let $R_n(x)$ be the nth remainder of $f(x) = e^x$ at $x = 0$. See Section 11.1. Show that, for any fixed value of x, $|R_n(x)| \le e^{|x|} \cdot |x|^{n+1}/(n+1)!$, and hence conclude that $|R_n(x)| \to 0$ as $n \to \infty$. This shows that the Taylor series for e^x converges to e^x for every value of x.

Solutions to Practice Problems 11.5

1. Use the definition of the Taylor series as an extended Taylor polynomial.

$$f(x) = \sin x, \qquad f'(x) = \cos x,$$
$$f(0) = 0, \qquad f'(0) = 1,$$

$$f''(x) = -\sin x, \quad f'''(x) = -\cos x,$$
$$f''(0) = 0 \qquad f'''(0) = -1,$$

$$f^{(4)}(x) = \sin x, \qquad f^{(5)}(x) = \cos x,$$
$$f^{(4)}(0) = 0, \qquad f^{(5)}(0) = 1.$$

Therefore,

$$\sin x = 0 + 1 \cdot x + \frac{0}{2!}x^2 + \frac{-1}{3!}x^3 + \frac{0}{4!}x^4 + \frac{1}{5!}x^5 + \cdots$$

$$= x - \frac{1}{3!}x^3 + \frac{1}{5!}x^5 - \cdots.$$

2. Differentiate the Taylor series in Problem 1.

$$\frac{d}{dx}\sin x = \frac{d}{dx}\left(x - \frac{1}{3!}x^3 + \frac{1}{5!}x^5 - \cdots\right),$$

$$\cos x = 1 - \frac{1}{2!}x^2 + \frac{1}{4!}x^4 - \cdots.$$

$\left[\text{Note: We use the fact that } \dfrac{3}{3!} = \dfrac{3}{1\cdot2\cdot3} = \dfrac{1}{1\cdot2} = \dfrac{1}{2!} \text{ and } \dfrac{5}{5!} = \dfrac{1}{4!}.\right]$

3. Replace x by $7x$ in the Taylor series for $\cos x$ and then multiply by x^3.

$$\cos x = 1 - \frac{1}{2!}x^2 + \frac{1}{4!}x^4 - \cdots$$

$$\cos 7x = 1 - \frac{1}{2!}(7x)^2 + \frac{1}{4!}(7x)^4 - \cdots$$

$$= 1 - \frac{7^2}{2!}x^2 + \frac{7^4}{4!}x^4 - \cdots$$

$$x^3 \cos 7x = x^3\left(1 - \frac{7^2}{2!}x^2 + \frac{7^4}{4!}x^4 - \cdots\right)$$

$$= x^3 - \frac{7^2}{2!}x^5 + \frac{7^4}{4!}x^7 - \cdots.$$

4. The coefficient of x^5 in the Taylor series of $f(x)$ is $\dfrac{f^{(5)}(0)}{5!}$. By Problem 3, this coefficient is $-\dfrac{7^2}{2!}$. Therefore,

$$\frac{f^{(5)}(0)}{5!} = -\frac{7^2}{2!}$$

$$f^{(5)}(0) = -\frac{7^2}{2!}\cdot 5! = -\frac{49}{2}\cdot 120$$

$$= -(49)(60) = -2940.$$

REVIEW OF FUNDAMENTAL CONCEPTS

1. Define the nth Taylor polynomial of $f(x)$ at $x = a$.

2. In what way is the nth Taylor polynomial of $f(x)$ at $x = a$ like $f(x)$ at $x = a$?

3. State the remainder formula for the nth Taylor polynomial of $f(x)$ at $x = a$.

4. Explain how the Newton–Raphson algorithm is used to approximate a zero of a function.

5. What is the nth partial sum of an infinite series?

6. What is a convergent infinite series? Divergent?

7. What is meant by the sum of a convergent infinite series?

8. What is a geometric series and when does it converge?

9. What is the sum of a convergent geometric series?

10. Define the Taylor series of $f(x)$ at $x = 0$.

11. Discuss the three possibilities for the radius of convergence of a Taylor series.

SUPPLEMENTARY EXERCISES

1. Find the second Taylor polynomial of $x(x+1)^{3/2}$ at $x = 0$.

2. Find the fourth Taylor polynomial of $(2x+1)^{3/2}$ at $x = 0$.

3. Find the fifth Taylor polynomial of $x^3 - 7x^2 + 8$ at $x = 0$.

4. Find the nth Taylor polynomial of $\dfrac{2}{2-x}$ at $x = 0$.

5. Find the third Taylor polynomial of x^2 at $x = 3$.

6. Find the third Taylor polynomial of e^x at $x = 2$.

7. Use a second Taylor polynomial at $t = 0$ to estimate the area under the graph of $y = -\ln(\cos 2t)$ between $t = 0$ and $t = \frac{1}{2}$.

8. Use a second Taylor polynomial at $x = 0$ to estimate the value of $\tan(.1)$.

9. (a) Find the second Taylor polynomial of $\sqrt{x}$ at $x = 9$.

    (b) Use part (a) to estimate $\sqrt{8.7}$ to six decimal places.

    (c) Use the Newton–Raphson algorithm with $n = 2$ and $x_0 = 3$ to approximate the solution of the equation $x^2 - 8.7 = 0$. Express your answer to six decimal places.

10. (a) Use the third Taylor polynomial of $\ln(1-x)$ at $x = 0$ to approximate $\ln 1.3$ to four decimal places.

    (b) Find an approximate solution of the equation $e^x = 1.3$ using the Newton–Raphson algorithm with $n = 2$ and $x_0 = 0$. Express your answer to four decimal places.

11. Use the Newton–Raphson algorithm with $n = 2$ to approximate the zero of $x^2 - 3x - 2$ near $x_0 = 4$.

12. Use the Newton–Raphson algorithm with $n = 2$ to approximate the solution of the equation $e^{2x} = 1 + e^{-x}$.

In Exercises 13–20, find the sum of the given infinite series if it is convergent.

13. $1 - \dfrac{3}{4} + \dfrac{9}{16} - \dfrac{27}{64} + \dfrac{81}{256} - \cdots$

14. $\dfrac{5^2}{6} + \dfrac{5^3}{6^2} + \dfrac{5^4}{6^3} + \dfrac{5^5}{6^4} + \dfrac{5^6}{6^5} + \cdots$

15. $\dfrac{1}{8} + \dfrac{1}{8^2} + \dfrac{1}{8^3} + \dfrac{1}{8^4} + \dfrac{1}{8^5} + \cdots$

16. $\dfrac{2^2}{7} - \dfrac{2^5}{7^2} + \dfrac{2^8}{7^3} - \dfrac{2^{11}}{7^4} + \dfrac{2^{14}}{7^5} - \cdots$

17. $\dfrac{1}{m+1} + \dfrac{m}{(m+1)^2} + \dfrac{m^2}{(m+1)^3} + \dfrac{m^3}{(m+1)^4} + \cdots,$

    where m is a positive number

18. $\dfrac{1}{m} - \dfrac{1}{m^2} + \dfrac{1}{m^3} - \dfrac{1}{m^4} + \dfrac{1}{m^5} - \cdots,$ where m is a positive number

19. $1 + 2 + \dfrac{2^2}{2!} + \dfrac{2^3}{3!} + \dfrac{2^4}{4!} + \cdots$

20. $1 + \dfrac{1}{3} + \dfrac{1}{2!}\left(\dfrac{1}{3}\right)^2 + \dfrac{1}{3!}\left(\dfrac{1}{3}\right)^3 + \dfrac{1}{4!}\left(\dfrac{1}{3}\right)^4 + \cdots$

21. Use properties of convergent series to find $\displaystyle\sum_{k=0}^{\infty} \dfrac{1 + 2^k}{3^k}$.

22. Find $\displaystyle\sum_{k=0}^{\infty} \dfrac{3^k + 5^k}{7^k}$.

In Exercises 23–26, determine if the given series is convergent.

23. $\displaystyle\sum_{k=1}^{\infty} \dfrac{1}{k^3}$

24. $\displaystyle\sum_{k=1}^{\infty} \dfrac{1}{3^k}$

25. $\displaystyle\sum_{k=1}^{\infty} \dfrac{\ln k}{k}$

26. $\displaystyle\sum_{k=0}^{\infty} \dfrac{k^3}{(k^4 + 1)^2}$

27. For what values of p is $\displaystyle\sum_{k=1}^{\infty} \dfrac{1}{k^p}$ convergent?

28. For what values of p is $\displaystyle\sum_{k=1}^{\infty} \dfrac{1}{p^k}$ convergent?

In Exercises 29–32, find the Taylor series at $x = 0$ of the given function. Use suitable operations on the Taylor series at $x = 0$ of $\dfrac{1}{1-x}$ and e^x.

29. $\dfrac{1}{1 + x^3}$

30. $\ln(1 + x^3)$

31. $\dfrac{1}{(1 - 3x)^2}$

32. $\dfrac{e^x - 1}{x}$

33. (a) Find the Taylor series of $\cos 2x$ at $x = 0$, either by direct calculation or by using the known series for $\cos x$.

    (b) Use the trigonometric identity

$$\sin^2 x = \tfrac{1}{2}(1 - \cos 2x)$$

    to find the Taylor series of $\sin^2 x$ at $x = 0$.

34. (a) Find the Taylor series of $\cos 3x$ at $x = 0$.

    (b) Use the trigonometric identity

$$\cos^3 x = \tfrac{1}{4}(\cos 3x + 3\cos x)$$

    to find the fourth Taylor polynomial of $\cos^3 x$ at $x = 0$.

35. Use the decomposition

$$\dfrac{1 + x}{1 - x} = \dfrac{1}{1 - x} + \dfrac{x}{1 - x}$$

to find the Taylor series of $\dfrac{1 + x}{1 - x}$ at $x = 0$.

36. Find an infinite series that converges to

$$\int_0^{1/2} \frac{e^x - 1}{x}\, dx.$$

[*Hint*: Use Exercise 32.]

37. It can be shown that the sixth Taylor polynomial of $f(x) = \sin x^2$ at $x = 0$ is $x^2 - \frac{1}{6}x^6$. Use this fact in parts (a), (b), and (c).

(a) What is the fifth Taylor polynomial of $f(x)$ at $x = 0$?

(b) What is $f'''(0)$?

(c) Estimate the area under the graph of $y = \sin x^2$ between $x = 0$ and $x = 1$. Use four decimal places, and compare your answer with the values given in Example 4 of Section 11.1.

38. Let $f(x) = \ln|\sec x + \tan x|$. It can be shown that $f'(0) = 1$, $f''(0) = 0$, $f'''(0) = 1$, and $f^{(4)}(0) = 0$. What is the fourth Taylor polynomial of $f(x)$ at $x = 0$?

39. Let $f(x) = 1 + x^2 + x^4 + x^6 + \cdots$.

(a) Find the Taylor series expansion of $f'(x)$ at $x = 0$.

(b) Find the simple formula for $f'(x)$ not involving a series. [*Hint*: First find a simple formula for $f(x)$.]

40. Let $f(x) = x - 2x^3 + 4x^5 - 8x^7 + 16x^9 - \cdots$.

(a) Find the Taylor series expansion of $\int f(x)\, dx$ at $x = 0$.

(b) Find a simple formula for $\int f(x)\, dx$ not involving a series. [*Hint*: First find a simple formula for $f(x)$.]

41. Fractional Reserve Banking Suppose that the Federal Reserve (the Fed) buys $100 million of government debt obligations from private owners. This creates $100 million of new money and sets off a chain reaction because of the "fractional reserve" banking system. When the $100 million is deposited into private bank accounts, the banks keep only 15% in reserve and may loan out the remaining 85%, creating more new money: $(.85)(100)$ million dollars. The companies who borrow this money turn around and spend it, and the recipients deposit the money in their bank accounts. Assuming that all the $(.85)(100)$ million is redeposited, the banks may again loan out 85% of this amount, creating $(.85)^2(100)$ million additional dollars. This process may be repeated indefinitely. Compute the total amount of new money that can be created theoretically by this process, beyond the original $100 million. (In practice, only about an additional $300 million is created, usually within a few weeks of the action of the Fed.)

42. Suppose that the Federal Reserve creates $100 million of new money, as in Exercise 41, and the banks lend 85% of all new money they receive. However, suppose that out of each loan, only 80% is redeposited into the banking system. Thus, whereas the first set of loans totals $(.85)(100)$ million dollars, the second set is only 85% of $(.80)(.85)(100)$, or $(.80)(.85)^2(100)$ million, and the next set is 85% of $(.80)^2(.85)^2(100)$, or $(.80)^2(.85)^3(100)$ million dollars, and so on. Compute the total theoretical amount that may be loaned in this situation.

Suppose that when you die the proceeds of a life insurance policy will be deposited into a trust fund that will earn 8% interest, compounded continuously. According to the terms of your will, the trust fund must pay to your descendants and their heirs c_1 dollars (total) at the end of the first year, c_2 dollars at the end of the second year, c_3 dollars at the end of the third year, and so on, forever. The amount that must be in the trust fund initially to make the kth payment is $c_k e^{-.08k}$, the present value of the amount to be paid in k years. So the life insurance policy should pay a total of $\sum_{k=1}^{\infty} c_k e^{-.08k}$ dollars into the trust fund to provide for all the payments.

43. How large must the insurance policy be if $c_k = 10{,}000$ for all k? (Find the sum of the series.)

44. How large must the insurance policy be if $c_k = 10{,}000(.9)^k$ for all k?

45. Suppose that $c_k = 10{,}000(1.08)^k$ for all k. Find the sum of the series above if the series converges.

PROBABILITY AND CALCULUS

In this chapter we shall survey a few applications of calculus to the theory of probability. Since we do not intend this chapter to be a self-contained course in probability, we shall select only a few salient ideas to present a taste of probability theory and provide a starting point for further study.

12.1 Discrete Random Variables

We will motivate the concepts of mean, variance, standard deviation, and random variable by analyzing examination grades.

Suppose that the grades on an exam taken by 10 people are 50, 60, 60, 70, 70, 90, 100, 100, 100, 100. This information is displayed in a frequency table in Fig. 1.

One of the first things we do when looking over the results of an exam is to compute the *mean* or *average* of the grades. We do this by totaling the grades and dividing by the number of people. This is the same as multiplying each distinct grade by the frequency with which it occurs, adding up those products, and dividing by the sum of the frequencies:

$$[\text{mean}] = \frac{50 \cdot 1 + 60 \cdot 2 + 70 \cdot 2 + 90 \cdot 1 + 100 \cdot 4}{10} = \frac{800}{10} = 80.$$

Grade	50	60	70	90	100
Frequency	1	2	2	1	4

Figure 1

[Grade] − [Mean]	−30	−20	−10	10	20
Frequency	1	2	2	1	4

Figure 2

To get an idea of how spread out the grades are, we can compute the difference between each grade and the average grade. We have tabulated these differences in Fig. 2. For example, if a person received a 50, then [grade] − [mean] is $50 - 80 = -30$. As a measure of the spread of the grades, statisticians compute the average of the squares of these differences and call it the *variance* of the grade distribution. We have

$$[\text{variance}] = \frac{(-30)^2 \cdot 1 + (-20)^2 \cdot 2 + (-10)^2 \cdot 2 + (10)^2 \cdot 1 + (20)^2 \cdot 4}{10}$$

$$= \frac{900 + 800 + 200 + 100 + 1600}{10} = \frac{3600}{10} = 360.$$

The square root of the variance is called the *standard deviation* of the grade distribution. In this case, we have

$$[\text{standard deviation}] = \sqrt{360} \approx 18.97.$$

There is another way of looking at the grade distribution and its mean and variance. This new point of view is useful because it can be generalized to other situations. We begin by converting the frequency table to a relative frequency table. (See Fig. 3.) Below each grade we list the fraction of the class receiving that grade. The grade of 50 occurred $\frac{1}{10}$ of the time, the grade of 60 occurred $\frac{2}{10}$ of the time, and so on. Note that the relative frequencies add up to 1, because they represent the various fractions of the class grouped by test scores.

Grade	50	60	70	90	100
Relative frequency	$\frac{1}{10}$	$\frac{2}{10}$	$\frac{2}{10}$	$\frac{1}{10}$	$\frac{4}{10}$

Figure 3

It is sometimes helpful to display the data in the relative frequency table by constructing a *relative frequency histogram*. (See Fig. 4.) Over each grade we place a rectangle whose height equals the relative frequency of that grade.

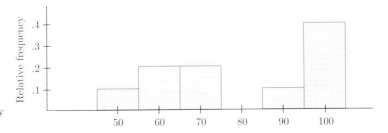

Figure 4. A relative frequency histogram.

An alternative way to compute the mean grade is

$$[\text{mean}] = \frac{50\cdot 1 + 60\cdot 2 + 70\cdot 2 + 90\cdot 1 + 100\cdot 4}{10}$$

$$= 50\cdot\frac{1}{10} + 60\cdot\frac{2}{10} + 70\cdot\frac{2}{10} + 90\cdot\frac{1}{10} + 100\cdot\frac{4}{10}$$

$$= 5 + 12 + 14 + 9 + 40 = 80.$$

Looking at the second line of this computation, we see that the mean is a sum of the various grades times their relative frequencies. We say that the mean is the *weighted sum* of the grades. (Grades are weighted by their relative frequencies.)

In a similar manner we see that the variance is also a weighted sum.

$$[\text{variance}] = \big[(50-80)^2\cdot 1 + (60-80)^2\cdot 2 + (70-80)^2\cdot 2$$

$$+ (90-80)^2\cdot 1 + (100-80)^2\cdot 4\big]\frac{1}{10}$$

$$= (50-80)^2\cdot\frac{1}{10} + (60-80)^2\cdot\frac{2}{10} + (70-80)^2\cdot\frac{2}{10}$$

$$+ (90-80)^2\cdot\frac{1}{10} + (100-80)^2\cdot\frac{4}{10}$$

$$= 90 + 80 + 20 + 10 + 160 = 360.$$

The relative frequency table shown in Fig. 3 is also called a *probability table*. The reason for this terminology is as follows. Suppose that we perform an *experiment* that consists of picking an exam paper at random from among the 10 papers. If the experiment is repeated many times, we expect the grade of 50 to occur about one-tenth of the time, the grade of 60 about two-tenths of the time, and so on. We say that the *probability* of the grade of 50 being chosen is $\frac{1}{10}$, the probability of the grade of 60 being chosen is $\frac{2}{10}$, and so on. In other words, the probability associated with a given grade measures the likelihood that an exam having that grade is chosen.

In this section we consider various experiments described by probability tables similar to the one in Fig. 3. The results of these experiments will be numbers (such as the preceding exam scores) called the *outcomes* of the experiment. We will also be given the probability of each outcome, indicating the relative frequency with which the given outcome is expected to occur if the experiment is repeated very often. If the outcomes of an experiment are $a_1, a_2, \ldots, a_n$, with respective probabilities $p_1, p_2, \ldots, p_n$, we describe the experiment by a probability table. (See Fig. 5.) Since the probabilities indicate relative frequencies, we see that

$$0 \le p_i \le 1$$

and

$$p_1 + p_2 + \cdots + p_n = 1.$$

Outcome	a_1	a_2	a_3	$\cdots$	a_n
Probability	p_1	p_2	p_3	$\cdots$	p_n

Figure 5

The last equation indicates that the outcomes $a_1, \ldots, a_n$ comprise all possible results of the experiment. We will usually list the outcomes of our experiments in ascending order, so $a_1 < a_2 < \cdots < a_n$.

We may display the data of a probability table in a histogram that has a rectangle of height p_i over the outcome a_i. (See Fig. 6.)

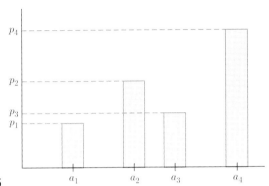

Figure 6

Let us define the *expected value* (or *mean*) of the probability table of Fig. 5 to be the weighted sum of the outcomes $a_1, \ldots, a_n$, each outcome weighted by the probability of its occurrence. That is,

$$[\text{expected value}] = a_1 p_1 + a_2 p_2 + \cdots + a_n p_n.$$

Similarly, let us define the *variance* of the probability table to be the weighted sum of the squares of the differences between each outcome and the expected value. That is, if m denotes the expected value, then

$$[\text{variance}] = (a_1 - m)^2 p_1 + (a_2 - m)^2 p_2 + \cdots + (a_n - m)^2 p_n.$$

To keep from writing the "outcome" so many times, we shall abbreviate by X the outcome of our experiment. That is, X is a variable that takes on the values $a_1, a_2, \ldots, a_n$ with respective probabilities $p_1, p_2, \ldots, p_n$. We will assume that our experiment is performed many times, being repeated in an unbiased (or random) way. Then X is a variable whose value depends on chance, and for this reason we say that X is a *random variable*. Instead of speaking of the expected value (mean) and the variance of a probability table, let us speak of the *expected value* and the *variance of the random variable* X that is associated with the probability table. We shall denote the expected value of X by $\mathrm{E}(X)$ and the variance of X by $\mathrm{Var}(X)$. The *standard deviation* of X is defined to be $\sqrt{\mathrm{Var}(X)}$.

EXAMPLE 1

One possible bet in roulette is to wager \$1 on red. The two possible outcomes are: lose \$1 and win \$1. These outcomes and their probabilities are given in Fig. 7. (*Note*: A roulette wheel in Las Vegas has 18 red numbers, 18 black numbers, and two green numbers.) Compute the expected value and the variance of the amount won.

Solution Let X be the random variable "amount won." Then

$$E(X) = -1 \cdot \frac{20}{38} + 1 \cdot \frac{18}{38} = -\frac{2}{38} \approx -.0526,$$

$$Var(X) = \left[-1 - \left(-\frac{2}{38}\right)\right]^2 \cdot \frac{20}{38} + \left[1 - \left(-\frac{2}{38}\right)\right]^2 \cdot \frac{18}{38}$$

$$= \left(-\frac{36}{38}\right)^2 \cdot \frac{20}{38} + \left(\frac{40}{38}\right)^2 \cdot \frac{18}{38} \approx .997.$$

Amount won	-1	1
Probability	$\frac{20}{38}$	$\frac{18}{38}$

Figure 7. Las Vegas roulette.

The expected value of the amount won is approximately $-5\frac{1}{4}$ cents. In other words, sometimes we will win \$1 and sometimes we will lose \$1, but in the long run we can expect to lose an average of about $5\frac{1}{4}$ cents for each time we bet. ■

EXAMPLE 2

An experiment consists of selecting a number at random from the set of integers $\{1, 2, 3\}$. The probabilities are given by the table in Fig. 8. Let X designate the outcome. Find the expected value and the variance of X.

Number	1	2	3
Probability	$\frac{1}{3}$	$\frac{1}{3}$	$\frac{1}{3}$

Figure 8

Solution

$$E(X) = 1 \cdot \frac{1}{3} + 2 \cdot \frac{1}{3} + 3 \cdot \frac{1}{3} = 2,$$

$$Var(X) = (1-2)^2 \cdot \frac{1}{3} + (2-2)^2 \cdot \frac{1}{3} + (3-2)^2 \cdot \frac{1}{3}$$

$$= (-1)^2 \cdot \frac{1}{3} + 0 + (1)^2 \cdot \frac{1}{3} = \frac{2}{3}.$$

EXAMPLE 3

A cement company plans to bid on a contract for constructing the foundations of new homes in a housing development. The company is considering two bids: a high bid that will produce \$75,000 profit (if the bid is accepted) and a low bid that will produce \$40,000 profit. From past experience the company estimates that the high bid has a 30% chance of acceptance and the low bid a 50% chance. Which bid should the company make?

Solution The standard method of decision is to choose the bid that has the higher expected value. Let X be the amount the company makes if it submits the high bid, and let Y be the amount it makes if it submits the low bid. Then the company must analyze the situation using the probability table shown in Table 1. The expected values are

$$E(X) = (75{,}000)(.30) + 0(.70) = 22{,}500,$$

$$E(Y) = (40{,}000)(.50) + 0(.50) = 20{,}000.$$

If the cement company has many opportunities to bid on similar contracts, a high bid each time will be accepted sufficiently often to produce an average profit of \$22,500 per bid. A consistently low bid will produce an average profit of \$20,000 per bid. Thus the company should submit the high bid. ■

TABLE 1   Bids on a Cement Contract

| | High Bid | | | Low Bid | |
	Accepted	Rejected		Accepted	Rejected
Value of X	75,000	0	Value of Y	40,000	0
Probability	.30	.70	Probability	.50	.50

When a probability table contains a large number of possible outcomes of an experiment, the associated histogram for the random variable X becomes a valuable aid for visualizing the data in the table. Look at Fig. 9, for example. Since the rectangles that make up the histogram all have the same width, their areas are in the same ratios as their heights. By an appropriate change of scale on the y-axis, we may assume that the *area* (instead of the height) of each rectangle gives the associated probability of X. Such a histogram is sometimes referred to as a *probability density histogram.*

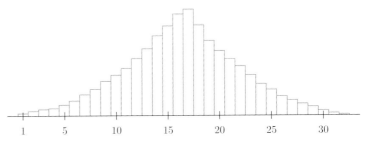

Figure 9.   Probabilities displayed as areas.

A histogram that displays probabilities as areas is useful when we wish to visualize the probability that X has a value between two specified numbers. For example, in Fig. 9 suppose that the probabilities associated with $X = 5, X = 6, \ldots, X = 10$ are $p_5, p_6, \ldots, p_{10}$, respectively. Then the probability that X lies between 5 and 10 inclusive is $p_5 + p_6 + \cdots + p_{10}$. In terms of areas, this probability is just the total area of those rectangles over the values $5, 6, \ldots, 10$. (See Fig. 10.) We will consider analogous situations in the next section.

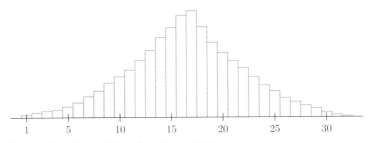

Figure 10.   Probability that $5 \leq x \leq 10$.

Practice Problems 12.1

1. Compute the expected value and the variance of the random variable X with Table 2 as its probability table.

TABLE 2

Value of X	-1	0	1	2
Probability	$\frac{1}{8}$	$\frac{1}{8}$	$\frac{3}{8}$	$\frac{3}{8}$

2. The production department at a radio factory sends CB radios to the inspection department in lots of 100. There an inspector examines three radios at random from each lot. If at least one of the three radios is defective and needs adjustment, the entire lot is sent back to the production department. Records of the inspection department show that the number X of

defective radios in a sample of three radios has Table 3 as its probability table.

TABLE 3 Quality Control Data

Defectives	0	1	2	3
Probability	.7265	.2477	.0251	.0007

(a) What percentage of the lots does the inspection department reject?

(b) Find the mean number of defective radios in the samples of three radios.

(c) Based on the evidence in part (b), estimate the average number of defective radios in each lot of 100 radios.

EXERCISES 12.1

1. Table 4 is the probability table for a random variable X. Find E(X), Var(X), and the standard deviation of X.

TABLE 4

Outcome	0	1
Probability	$\frac{1}{5}$	$\frac{4}{5}$

2. Find E(X), Var(X), and the standard deviation of X, where X is the random variable whose probability table is given in Table 5.

TABLE 5

Outcome	1	2	3
Probability	$\frac{4}{9}$	$\frac{4}{9}$	$\frac{1}{9}$

3. Compute the variances of the three random variables whose probability tables are given in Table 6. Relate the sizes of the variances to the spread of the values of the random variable.

TABLE 6

	Outcome	Probability
(a)	4	.5
	6	.5
(b)	3	.5
	7	.5
(c)	1	.5
	9	.5

4. Compute the variances of the two random variables whose probability tables are given in Table 7. Relate

the sizes of the variances to the spread of the values of the random variables.

TABLE 7

	Outcome	Probability
(a)	2	.1
	4	.4
	6	.4
	8	.1
(b)	2	.3
	4	.2
	6	.2
	8	.3

5. The number of accidents per week at a busy intersection was recorded for a year. There were 11 weeks with no accidents, 26 weeks with one accident, 13 weeks with two accidents, and 2 weeks with three accidents. A week is to be selected at random and the number of accidents noted. Let X be the outcome. Then X is a random variable taking on the values 0, 1, 2, and 3.

(a) Write out a probability table for X.

(b) Compute E(X). (c) Interpret E(X).

6. The number of phone calls coming into a telephone switchboard during each minute was recorded during an entire hour. During 30 of the 1-minute intervals there were no calls, during 20 intervals there was one call, and during 10 intervals there were two calls. A 1-minute interval is to be selected at random and the number of calls noted. Let X be the outcome. Then X is a random variable taking on the values 0, 1, and 2.

(a) Write out a probability table for X.

(b) Compute $E(X)$. **(c)** Interpret $E(X)$.

7. Consider a circle with radius 1.

(a) What percentage of the points lies within $\frac{1}{2}$ unit of the center?

(b) Let c be a constant with $0 < c < 1$. What percentage of the points lies within c units of the center?

8. Consider a circle with circumference 1. An arrow (or spinner) is attached at the center so that, when flicked, it spins freely. Upon stopping, it points to a particular point on the circumference of the circle. Determine the likelihood that the point is

(a) On the top half of the circumference.

(b) On the top quarter of the circumference.

(c) On the top one-hundredth of the circumference.

(d) Exactly at the top of the circumference.

9. A citrus grower anticipates a profit of $100,000 this year if the nightly temperatures remain mild. Unfortunately, the weather forecast indicates a 25% chance that the temperatures will drop below freezing during the next week. Such freezing weather will destroy 40% of the crop and reduce the profit to $60,000. However, the grower can protect the citrus fruit against the possible freezing (using smudge pots, electric fans, and so on) at a cost of $5000. Should the grower spend the $5000 and thereby reduce the profit to $95,000? [*Hint*: Compute $E(X)$, where X is the profit the grower will get if he does nothing to protect the fruit.]

10. Suppose that the weather forecast in Exercise 9 indicates a 10% chance that cold weather will reduce the citrus grower's profit from $100,000 to $85,000 and a 10% chance that cold weather will reduce the profit to $75,000. Should the grower spend $5000 to protect the citrus fruit against the possible bad weather?

Solutions to Practice Problems 12.1

1. $E(X) = (-1)\cdot\frac{1}{8} + 0\cdot\frac{1}{8} + 1\cdot\frac{3}{8} + 2\cdot\frac{3}{8} = 1,$

$\text{Var}(X) = (-1-1)^2\cdot\frac{1}{8} + (0-1)^2\cdot\frac{1}{8}$

$\qquad + (1-1)^2\cdot\frac{3}{8} + (2-1)^2\cdot\frac{3}{8}$

$\qquad = 4\cdot\frac{1}{8} + 1\cdot\frac{1}{8} + 0 + 1\cdot\frac{3}{8} = 1.$

2. (a) In three cases a lot will be rejected: $X = 1$, 2, or 3. Adding the corresponding probabilities, we find that the probability of rejecting a lot is $.2477 + .0251 + .0007 = .2735$, or 27.35%. (An alternative method of solution uses the fact that the sum of the probabilities for *all* possible cases must be 1. From the table we see that the probability of accepting a lot is .7265, so the proba-

bility of rejecting a lot is $1 - .7265 = .2735$.)

(b) $E(X) = 0(.7265) + 1(.2477)$

$\qquad + 2(.0251) + 3(.0007)$

$\qquad = .3000.$

(c) In part (b) we found that an average of .3 radio in every sample of three radios is defective. Thus about 10% of the radios in the sample are defective. Since the samples are chosen at random, we may assume that about 10% of *all* the radios are defective. Thus we estimate that on the average 10 out of each lot of 100 radios will be defective.

12.2 Continuous Random Variables

Consider a cell population that is growing vigorously. When a cell is T days old it divides and forms two new daughter cells. If the population is sufficiently large, it will contain cells of many different ages between 0 and T. It turns out that the proportion of cells of various ages remains constant. That is, if a and b are any two numbers between 0 and T, with $a < b$, the proportion of cells whose ages lie between a and b is essentially constant from one moment to the next, even though individual cells are aging and new cells are being formed all the time. In fact, biologists have found that under the ideal circumstances described, the proportion of cells whose ages are between a and b is given by the area under the graph of the function $f(x) = 2ke^{-kx}$ from $x = a$ to $x = b$, where $k = (\ln 2)/T$.[*] (See Fig. 1.)

---

[*]See J. R. Cook and T. W. James, "Age Distribution of Cells in Logarithmically Growing Cell Populations," in *Synchrony in Cell Division and Growth*, Erik Zeuthen, ed. (New York: John Wiley & Sons, 1964), pp. 485–495.

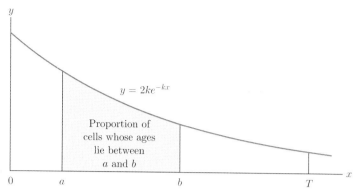

Figure 1. Age distribution in a cell population.

Now consider an experiment in which we select a cell at random from the population and observe its age, X. Then the probability that X lies between a and b is given by the area under the graph of $f(x) = 2ke^{-kx}$ from a to b. (See Fig. 1.) Let us denote this probability by $\Pr(a \leq X \leq b)$. Using the fact that the area under the graph of $f(x)$ is given by a definite integral, we have

$$\Pr(a \leq X \leq b) = \int_a^b f(x)\,dx = \int_a^b 2ke^{-kx}\,dx. \tag{1}$$

Since X can assume any one of the (infinitely many) numbers in the continuous interval from 0 to T, we say that X is a *continuous random variable*. The function $f(x)$ that determines the probability in (1) for each a and b is called the (*probability*) *density function* of X (or of the experiment whose outcome is X).

More generally, consider an experiment whose outcome may be any value between A and B. The outcome of the experiment, denoted X, is called a *continuous random variable*. For the cell population described previously, $A = 0$ and $B = T$. Another typical experiment might consist of choosing a number X at random between $A = 5$ and $B = 6$. Or we could observe the duration X of a random telephone call passing through a given telephone switchboard. If we have no way of knowing how long a call might last, X might be any nonnegative number. In this case it is convenient to say that X lies between 0 and ∞ and to take $A = 0$ and $B = \infty$. On the other hand, if the possible values of X for some experiment include rather large negative numbers, we sometimes takes $A = -\infty$.

Given an experiment whose outcome is a continuous random variable X, the probability $\Pr(a \leq X \leq b)$ is a measure of the likelihood that an outcome of the experiment will lie between a and b. If the experiment is repeated many times, the proportion of times X has a value between a and b should be close to $\Pr(a \leq X \leq b)$. In experiments of practical interest involving a continuous random variable X, it is usually possible to find a function $f(x)$ such that

$$\Pr(a \leq X \leq b) = \int_a^b f(x)\,dx \tag{2}$$

for all a and b in the range of possible values of X. Such a function $f(x)$ is called a *probability density function* and satisfies the following properties:

(I) $f(x) \geq 0$ for $A \leq x \leq B$.

(II) $\displaystyle\int_A^B f(x) = 1.$

Indeed, Property I means that, for x between A and B, the graph of $f(x)$ must lie on or above the x-axis. Property II simply says that there is probability 1 that X has a value between A and B. (Of course, if $B = \infty$ and/or $A = -\infty$, the integral in Property II is an improper integral.) Properties I and II characterize probability density functions, in the sense that any function $f(x)$ satisfying I and II is the probability density function for some continuous random variable X. Moreover, $\Pr(a \le X \le b)$ can then be calculated using equation (2).

Unlike a probability table for a discrete random variable, a density function $f(x)$ does *not* give the probability that X has a certain value. Instead, $f(x)$ can be used to find the probability that X is *near* a specific value in the following sense. If x_0 is a number between A and B and if Δx is the width of a small interval centered at x_0, the probability that X is between $x_0 - \frac{1}{2}\Delta x$ and $x_0 + \frac{1}{2}\Delta x$ is approximately $f(x_0)\Delta x$, that is, the area of the rectangle shown in Fig. 2.

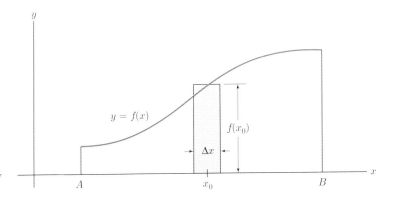

Figure 2. Area of rectangle gives approximate probability that X is near x_0.

EXAMPLE 1

Consider the cell population described earlier. Let $f(x) = 2ke^{-kx}$, where $k = (\ln 2)/T$. Show that $f(x)$ is indeed a probability density function on $0 \le x \le T$.

Solution Clearly, $f(x) \ge 0$, since $\ln 2$ is positive and the exponential function is never negative. Thus Property I is satisfied. For Property II we check that

$$\int_0^T f(x)\,dx = \int_0^T 2ke^{-kx}\,dx = -2e^{-kx}\Big|_0^T = -2e^{-kT} + 2e^0$$

$$= -2e^{-[(\ln 2)/T]T} + 2 = -2e^{-\ln 2} + 2$$

$$= -2e^{\ln(1/2)} + 2 = -2\left(\frac{1}{2}\right) + 2 = 1.$$ ■

EXAMPLE 2

Let $f(x) = kx^2$.

(a) Find the value of k that makes $f(x)$ a probability density function on $0 \le x \le 4$.

(b) Let X be a continuous random variable whose density function is $f(x)$. Compute $\Pr(1 \le X \le 2)$.

Solution (a) We must have $k \ge 0$ so that Property I is satisfied. For Property II, we calculate

$$\int_0^4 f(x)\,dx = \int_0^4 kx^2\,dx = \frac{1}{3}kx^3\Big|_0^4 = \frac{1}{3}k(4)^3 - 0 = \frac{64}{3}k.$$

To satisfy Property II we must have $\frac{64}{3}k = 1$, or $k = \frac{3}{64}$. Thus $f(x) = \frac{3}{64}x^2$.

(b) $\Pr(1 \le X \le 2) = \displaystyle\int_1^2 f(x)\,dx = \int_1^2 \frac{3}{64}x^2\,dx = \frac{1}{64}x^3\Big|_1^2 = \frac{8}{64} - \frac{1}{64} = \frac{7}{64}.$

The area corresponding to this probability is shown in Fig. 3.   ■

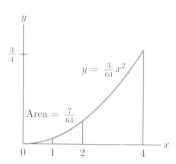

Figure 3

The density function in the next example is a special case of what statisticians sometimes call a **beta probability density**.

EXAMPLE 3   The parent corporation for a franchised chain of fast-food restaurants claims that the proportion of their new restaurants that make a profit during their first year of operation has the probability density function

$$f(x) = 12x(1-x)^2, \qquad 0 \le x \le 1.$$

(a) What is the probability that less than 40% of the restaurants opened this year will make a profit during their first year of operation?

(b) What is the probability that more than 50% of the restaurants will make a profit during their first year of operation?

Solution   Let X be the proportion of new restaurants opened this year that make a profit during their first year of operation. Then the possible values of X range between 0 and 1.

(a) The probability that X is less than .4 equals the probability that X is between 0 and .4. We note that $f(x) = 12x(1 - 2x + x^2) = 12x - 24x^2 + 12x^3$ and therefore,

$$\Pr(0 \le X \le .4) = \int_0^{.4} f(x)\,dx = \int_0^{.4} (12x - 24x^2 + 12x^3)\,dx$$

$$= (6x^2 - 8x^3 + 3x^4)\Big|_0^{.4} = .5248.$$

(b) The probability that X is greater than .5 equals the probability that X is between .5 and 1. Thus

$$\Pr(.5 \le X \le 1) = \int_{.5}^1 (12x - 24x^2 + 12x^3)\,dx$$

$$= (6x^2 - 8x^3 + 3x^4)\Big|_{.5}^1 = .3125.$$ ■

Each probability density function is closely related to another important function called a cumulative distribution function. To describe this relationship, let us consider an experiment whose outcome is a continuous random variable X, with values between A and B, and let $f(x)$ be the associated density function. For each number x between A and B, let $F(x)$ be the probability that X is less than or equal to the number x. Sometimes we write $F(x) = \Pr(X \leq x)$; however, since X is never less than A, we may also write

$$F(x) = \Pr(A \leq X \leq x). \tag{3}$$

Graphically, $F(x)$ is the area under the graph of the probability density function $f(x)$ from A to x. (See Fig. 4.) The function $F(x)$ is called the *cumulative distri-*

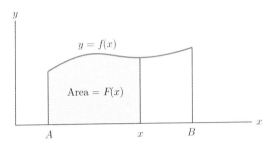

Figure 4. The cumulative distribution function $F(x)$.

bution function of the random variable X (or of the experiment whose outcome is X). Note that $F(x)$ also has the properties

$$F(A) = \Pr(A \leq X \leq A) = 0, \tag{4}$$
$$F(B) = \Pr(A \leq X \leq B) = 1. \tag{5}$$

Since $F(x)$ is an area function that gives the area under the graph of $f(x)$ from A to x, we know from Section 6.3 that $F(x)$ is an antiderivative of $f(x)$. That is,

$$F'(x) = f(x), \qquad A \leq x \leq B. \tag{6}$$

It follows that we may use $F(x)$ to compute probabilities, since

$$\Pr(a \leq X \leq b) = \int_a^b f(x)\,dx = F(b) - F(a), \tag{7}$$

for any a and b between A and B.

The relation (6) between $F(x)$ and $f(x)$ makes it possible to find one of these functions when the other is known, as we see in the following two examples.

EXAMPLE 4   Let X be the age of a cell selected at random from the cell population described earlier. The probability density function for X is $f(x) = 2ke^{-kx}$, where $k = (\ln 2)/T$. (See Fig. 5.) Find the cumulative distribution function $F(x)$ for X.

Solution   Since $F(x)$ is an antiderivative of $f(x) = 2ke^{-kx}$, we have $F(x) = -2e^{-kx} + C$ for some constant C. Now $F(x)$ is defined for $0 \leq x \leq T$. Thus (4) implies that $F(0) = 0$. Setting $F(0) = -2e^0 + C = 0$, we find that $C = 2$, so

$$F(x) = -2e^{-kx} + 2.$$

(See Fig. 6.)

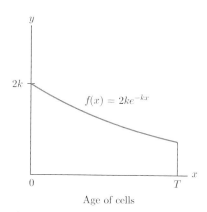

Figure 5. Probability density function.

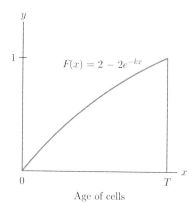

Figure 6. Cumulative distribution function.

EXAMPLE 5

Let X be the random variable associated with the experiment that consists of selecting a point at random from a circle of radius 1 and observing its distance from the center. Find the probability density function $f(x)$ and cumulative distribution function $F(x)$ of X.

Solution The distance of a point from the center of the unit circle is a number between 0 and 1. Suppose that $0 \leq x \leq 1$. Let us first compute the cumulative distribution function $F(x) = \Pr(0 \leq X \leq x)$. That is, let us find the probability that a point selected at random lies within x units of the center of the circle, in other words, lies inside the circle of radius x. See the shaded region in Fig. 7(b). Since the area of this shaded region is πx^2 and the area of the entire unit circle is $\pi \cdot 1^2 = \pi$, the proportion of points inside the shaded region is $\pi x^2 / \pi = x^2$. Thus the probability is x^2 that a point selected at random will be in this shaded region. Hence

$$F(x) = x^2.$$

Differentiating, we find that the probability density function for X is

$$f(x) = F'(x) = 2x.$$ ∎

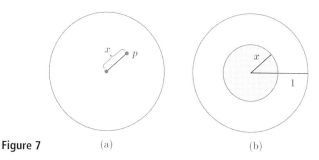

Figure 7   (a)   (b)

Our final example involves a continuous random variable X whose possible values lie between $A = 1$ and $B = \infty$; that is, X is any number greater than or equal to 1.

EXAMPLE 6

Let $f(x) = 3x^{-4}$, $x \geq 1$.

(a) Show that $f(x)$ is the probability density function of some random variable X.

(b) Find the cumulative distribution function $F(x)$ of X.

(c) Compute $\Pr(X \le 4)$, $\Pr(4 \le X \le 5)$, and $\Pr(4 \le X)$.

Solution **(a)** It is clear that $f(x) \ge 0$ for $x \ge 1$. Thus Property I holds. To check for Property II, we must compute

$$\int_1^{\infty} 3x^{-4}\, dx.$$

But

$$\int_1^b 3x^{-4}\, dx = -x^{-3}\Big|_1^b = -b^{-3} + 1 \to 1$$

as $b \to \infty$. Thus

$$\int_1^{\infty} 3x^{-4}\, dx = 1,$$

and Property II holds.

(b) Since $F(x)$ is an antiderivative of $f(x) = 3x^{-4}$, we have

$$F(x) = \int 3x^{-4}\, dx = -x^{-3} + C.$$

Since X has values greater than or equal to 1, we must have $F(1) = 0$. Setting $F(1) = -1 + C = 0$, we find that $C = 1$, so

$$F(x) = 1 - x^{-3}.$$

(c) $\Pr(X \le 4) = F(4) = 1 - 4^{-3} = 1 - \frac{1}{64} = \frac{63}{64}.$

Since we know $F(x)$, we may use it to compute $\Pr(4 \le X \le 5)$, as follows:

$$\Pr(4 \le X \le 5) = F(5) - F(4) = (1 - 5^{-3}) - (1 - 4^{-3})$$

$$= \frac{1}{4^3} - \frac{1}{5^3} \approx .0076.$$

We may compute $\Pr(4 \le X)$ directly by evaluating the improper integral

$$\int_4^{\infty} 3x^{-4}\, dx.$$

However, there is a simpler method. We know that

$$\int_1^4 3x^{-4}\, dx + \int_4^{\infty} 3x^{-4}\, dx = \int_1^{\infty} 3x^{-4}\, dx = 1. \tag{8}$$

In terms of probabilities, (8) may be written as

$$\Pr(X \le 4) + \Pr(4 \le X) = 1.$$

Hence

$$\Pr(4 \le X) = 1 - \Pr(X \le 4) = 1 - \frac{63}{64} = \frac{1}{64}. \qquad \blacksquare$$

Practice Problems 12.2

1. In a certain farming region and in a certain year, the number of bushels of wheat produced per acre is a random variable X with a density function

$$f(x) = \frac{x - 30}{50}, \qquad 30 \le x \le 40.$$

(a) What is the probability that an acre selected at random produced less than 35 bushels of wheat?

(b) If the farming region had 20,000 acres of wheat, how many acres produced less than 35 bushels of wheat per acre?

2. The density function for a continuous random variable X on the interval $1 \le x \le 2$ is $f(x) = 8/(3x^3)$. Find the corresponding cumulative distribution function for X.

EXERCISES 12.2

Verify that each of the following functions is a probability density function.

1. $f(x) = \frac{1}{18}x, \ 0 \le x \le 6$

2. $f(x) = 2(x-1), \ 1 \le x \le 2$

3. $f(x) = \frac{1}{4}, \ 1 \le x \le 5$

4. $f(x) = \frac{8}{9}x, \ 0 \le x \le \frac{3}{2}$

5. $f(x) = 5x^4, \ 0 \le x \le 1$

6. $f(x) = \frac{3}{2}x - \frac{3}{4}x^2, \ 0 \le x \le 2$

In Exercises 7–12, find the value of k that makes the given function a probability density function on the specified interval.

7. $f(x) = kx, \ 1 \le x \le 3$

8. $f(x) = kx^2, \ 0 \le x \le 2$

9. $f(x) = k, \ 5 \le x \le 20$

10. $f(x) = k/\sqrt{x}, \ 1 \le x \le 4$

11. $f(x) = kx^2(1-x), \ 0 \le x \le 1$

12. $f(x) = k(3x - x^2), \ 0 \le x \le 3$

13. The density function of a continuous random variable X is $f(x) = \frac{1}{8}x, \ 0 \le x \le 4$. Sketch the graph of $f(x)$ and shade in the areas corresponding to (a) $\Pr(X \le 1)$; (b) $\Pr(2 \le X \le 2.5)$; (c) $\Pr(3.5 \le X)$.

14. The density function of a continuous random variable X is $f(x) = 3x^2, \ 0 \le x \le 1$. Sketch the graph of $f(x)$ and shade in the areas corresponding to (a) $\Pr(X \le .3)$; (b) $\Pr(.5 \le X \le .7)$; (c) $\Pr(.8 \le X)$.

15. Find $\Pr(1 \le X \le 2)$ when X is a random variable whose density function is given in Exercise 1.

16. Find $\Pr(1.5 \le X \le 1.7)$ when X is a random variable whose density function is given in Exercise 2.

17. Find $\Pr(X \le 3)$ when X is a random variable whose density function is given in Exercise 3.

18. Find $\Pr(1 \le X)$ when X is a random variable whose density function is given in Exercise 4.

19. Suppose that the lifetime X (in hours) of a certain type of flashlight battery is a random variable on the interval $30 \le x \le 50$ with density function $f(x) = \frac{1}{20}, \ 30 \le x \le 50$. Find the probability that a battery selected at random will last at least 35 hours.

20. At a certain supermarket the amount of wait time at the express lane is a random variable with density function $f(x) = 11/[10(x+1)^2], \ 0 \le x \le 10$. (See Fig. 8.) Find the probability of having to wait less than 4 minutes at the express lane.

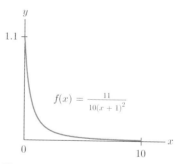

Figure 8. A density function.

21. The cumulative distribution function for a random variable X on the interval $1 \le x \le 5$ is $F(x) = \frac{1}{2}\sqrt{x-1}$. (See Fig. 9.) Find the corresponding density function.

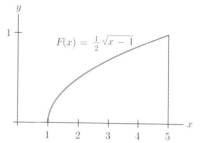

Figure 9. A cumulative distribution function.

22. The cumulative distribution function for a random variable X on the interval $1 \le x \le 2$ is $F(x) = \frac{4}{3} - 4/(3x^2)$. Find the corresponding density function.

23. Compute the cumulative distribution function corresponding to the density function $f(x) = \frac{1}{5}, \ 2 \le x \le 7$.

24. Compute the cumulative distribution function corresponding to the density function $f(x) = \frac{1}{2}(3-x), \ 1 \le x \le 3$.

25. The time (in minutes) required to complete a certain subassembly is a random variable X with density function $f(x) = \frac{1}{21}x^2, \ 1 \le x \le 4$.
   (a) Use $f(x)$ to compute $\Pr(2 \le X \le 3)$.
   (b) Find the corresponding cumulative distribution function $F(x)$.
   (c) Use $F(x)$ to compute $\Pr(2 \le X \le 3)$.

26. The density function for a continuous random variable X on the interval $1 \le x \le 4$ is $f(x) = \frac{4}{9}x - \frac{1}{9}x^2$.
   (a) Use $f(x)$ to compute $\Pr(3 \le X \le 4)$.
   (b) Find the corresponding cumulative distribution function $F(x)$.
   (c) Use $F(x)$ to compute $\Pr(3 \le X \le 4)$.

An experiment consists of selecting a point at random from the square in Fig. 10(a). Let X be the maximum of the coordinates of the point.

27. Show that the cumulative distribution function of X is $F(x) = x^2/4$, $0 \le x \le 2$.

28. Find the corresponding density function of X.

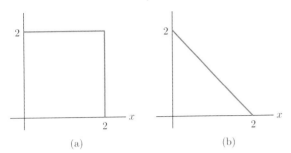

(a)   (b)

Figure 10

An experiment consists of selecting a point at random from the triangle in Fig. 10(b). Let X be the sum of the coordinates of the point.

29. Show that the cumulative distribution function of X is $F(x) = x^2/4$, $0 \le x \le 2$.

30. Find the corresponding density function of X.

In a certain cell population, cells divide every 10 days, and the age of a cell selected at random is a random variable X with the density function $f(x) = 2ke^{-kx}$, $0 \le x \le 10$, $k = (\ln 2)/10$.

31. Find the probability that a cell is at most 5 days old.

32. Upon examination of a slide, 10% of the cells are found to be undergoing mitosis (a change in the cell leading to division). Compute the length of time required for mitosis; that is, find the number M such that

$$\int_{10-M}^{10} 2ke^{-kx}\, dx = .10.$$

33. A random variable X has a density function $f(x) = \frac{1}{3}$, $0 \le x \le 3$. Find b such that $\Pr(0 \le X \le b) = .6$.

34. A random variable X has a density function $f(x) = \frac{2}{3}x$ on $1 \le x \le 2$. Find a such that $\Pr(a \le X) = \frac{1}{3}$.

35. A random variable X has a cumulative distribution function $F(x) = \frac{1}{4}x^2$ on $0 \le x \le 2$. Find b such that $\Pr(X \le b) = .09$.

36. A random variable X has a cumulative distribution function $F(x) = (x-1)^2$ on $1 \le x \le 2$. Find b such that $\Pr(X \le b) = \frac{1}{4}$.

37. Let X be a continuous random variable with values between $A = 1$ and $B = \infty$, and with the density function $f(x) = 4x^{-5}$.

(a) Verify that $f(x)$ is a probability density function for $x \ge 1$.

(b) Find the corresponding cumulative distribution function $F(x)$.

(c) Use $F(x)$ to compute $\Pr(1 \le X \le 2)$ and $\Pr(2 \le X)$.

38. Let X be a continuous random variable with the density function $f(x) = 2(x+1)^{-3}$, $x \ge 0$.

(a) Verify that $f(x)$ is a probability density function for $x \ge 0$.

(b) Find the cumulative distribution function for X.

(c) Compute $\Pr(1 \le X \le 2)$ and $\Pr(3 \le X)$.

Solutions to Practice Problems 12.2

1. (a) $\Pr(X \le 35) = \displaystyle\int_{30}^{35} \frac{x-30}{50}\, dx = \left. \frac{(x-30)^2}{100} \right|_{30}^{35}$

$$= \frac{5^2}{100} - 0 = .25.$$

(b) Using part (a), we see that 25% of the 20,000 acres, or 5000 acres, produced less that 35 bushels of wheat per acre.

2. The cumulative distribution function $F(x)$ is an antiderivative of $f(x) = 8/(3x^3) = \frac{8}{3}x^{-3}$. Thus $F(x) = -\frac{4}{3}x^{-2} + C$ for some constant C. Since X varies over the interval $1 \le x \le 2$, we must have $F(1) = 0$; that is, $-\frac{4}{3}(1)^{-2} + C = 0$. Thus $C = \frac{4}{3}$, and

$$F(x) = \frac{4}{3} - \frac{4}{3}x^{-2}.$$

12.3 Expected Value and Variance

When studying the cell population described in Section 12.2, we might reasonably ask for the average age of the cells. In general, given an experiment described by a random variable X and a probability density function $f(x)$, it is often important to know the average outcome of the experiment and the degree to which the experimental outcomes are spread out around the average. To provide this information in Section 12.1, we introduced the concepts of expected value and variance of a discrete random variable. Let us now examine the analogous definition for a continuous random variable.

DEFINITION Let X be a continuous random variable whose possible values lie between A and B, and let $f(x)$ be the probability density function for X. Then the *expected value* (or *mean*) of X is the number $E(X)$ defined by

$$E(X) = \int_A^B x f(x)\, dx. \tag{1}$$

The *variance* of X is the number $\text{Var}(X)$ defined by

$$\text{Var}(X) = \int_A^B [x - E(X)]^2 f(x)\, dx. \tag{2}$$

The expected value of X has the same interpretation as in the discrete case: if the experiment whose outcome is X is performed many times, the average of all the outcomes will approximately equal $E(X)$. As in the case of a discrete random variable, the variance of X is a quantitative measure of the likely spread of the values of X about the mean $E(X)$ when the experiment is performed many times.

To explain why definition (1) of $E(X)$ is analogous to the definition in Section 12.1, let us approximate the integral in (1) by a Riemann sum of the form

$$x_1 f(x_1)\Delta x + x_2 f(x_2)\Delta x + \cdots + x_n f(x_n)\Delta x. \tag{3}$$

Here $x_1, \ldots, x_n$ are the midpoints of subintervals of the interval from A to B, each subinterval of width $\Delta x = (B - A)/n$. (See Fig. 1.) Now recall from Section 12.2 that, for $i = 1, \ldots, n$, the quantity $f(x_i)\Delta x$ is approximately the probability that X is close to x_i, that is, the probability that X lies in the subinterval centered at x_i. If we write $\Pr(X \approx x_i)$ for this probability, then (3) is nearly the same as

$$x_1 \cdot \Pr(X \approx x_1) + x_2 \cdot \Pr(X \approx x_2) + \cdots + x_n \cdot \Pr(X \approx x_n). \tag{4}$$

As the number of subintervals increases, the sum becomes closer and closer to the integral in equation (1) defining $E(X)$. Furthermore, each approximating sum in (4) resembles the sum in the definition of the expected value of a discrete random variable, where we compute the weighted sum over all possible outcomes, with each outcome weighted by the probability of its occurrence.

Figure 1

A similar analysis will show that definition (2) of variance is analogous to the definition for the discrete case.

EXAMPLE 1

Let us consider the experiment of selecting a number at random from among the numbers between 0 and B. Let X denote the associated random variable. Determine the cumulative distribution function of X, the density function of X, and the mean and variance of X.

Solution

$$F(x) = \frac{[\text{length of the interval from 0 to } x]}{[\text{length of the interval from 0 to } B]} = \frac{x}{B}.$$

Since $f(x) = F'(x)$, we see that $f(x) = 1/B$. Thus we have

$$\mathrm{E}(X) = \int_0^B x \cdot \frac{1}{B}\, dx = \frac{1}{B}\int_0^B x\, dx = \frac{1}{B}\cdot\frac{B^2}{2} = \frac{B}{2},$$

$$\mathrm{Var}(X) = \int_0^B \left(x - \frac{B}{2}\right)^2 \cdot \frac{1}{B}\, dx = \frac{1}{B}\int_0^B \left(x - \frac{B}{2}\right)^2 dx$$

$$= \frac{1}{B}\cdot\frac{1}{3}\left(x - \frac{B}{2}\right)^3\Bigg|_0^B = \frac{1}{3B}\left[\left(\frac{B}{2}\right)^3 - \left(-\frac{B}{2}\right)^3\right] = \frac{B^2}{12}.$$

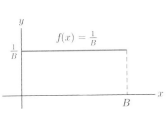

Figure 2. A uniform probability density function.

The graph of the density function $f(x)$ is shown in Fig. 2. Since the density function has a flat graph, the random variable X is called the *uniform random variable* on the interval from 0 to B. ◼

EXAMPLE 2

Let X be the age of a cell chosen at random from the population described in Section 12.2, where the density function for X was given as

$$f(x) = 2ke^{-kx}, \qquad 0 \le x \le T,$$

and $k = (\ln 2)/T$. Find the average age, $\mathrm{E}(X)$, of the cell population.

Solution By definition,

$$\mathrm{E}(X) = \int_0^T x \cdot 2ke^{-kx}\, dx.$$

To calculate this integral, we need integration by parts, with $f(x) = 2x$, $g(x) = ke^{-kx}$, $f'(x) = 2$, and $G(x) = -e^{-kx}$. We have

$$\int_0^T 2xke^{-kx}\, dx = -2xe^{-kx}\Big|_0^T - \int_0^T -2e^{-kx}\, dx$$

$$= -2Te^{-kT} - \left(\frac{2}{k}e^{-kx}\right)\Big|_0^T$$

$$= -2Te^{-kT} - \frac{2}{k}e^{-kT} + \frac{2}{k}.$$

This formula for $\mathrm{E}(X)$ may be simplified by noting that $e^{-kT} = e^{-\ln 2} = \frac{1}{2}$. Thus

$$\mathrm{E}(X) = -2T\left(\frac{1}{2}\right) - \frac{2}{k}\left(\frac{1}{2}\right) + \frac{2}{k} = \frac{1}{k} - T$$

$$= \frac{T}{\ln 2} - T = \left(\frac{1}{\ln 2} - 1\right)T$$

$$\approx .4427T.$$ ◼

EXAMPLE 3

Consider the experiment of selecting a point at random in a circle of radius 1, and let X be the distance from this point to the center. Compute the expected value and variance of the random variable X.

Solution We showed in Example 5 of Section 12.2 that the density function for X is given by $f(x) = 2x$, $0 \le x \le 1$. Therefore, we see that

$$\mathrm{E}(X) = \int_0^1 x \cdot 2x\, dx = \int_0^1 2x^2\, dx = \frac{2x^3}{3}\Big|_0^1 = \frac{2}{3}$$

and

$$\text{Var}(X) = \int_0^1 \left(x - \frac{2}{3}\right)^2 \cdot 2x\, dx \qquad \left[\text{since } \text{E}(X) = \frac{2}{3}\right]$$

$$= \int_0^1 \left(x^2 - \frac{4}{3}x + \frac{4}{9}\right) \cdot 2x\, dx$$

$$= \int_0^1 \left(2x^3 - \frac{8}{3}x^2 + \frac{8}{9}x\right) dx$$

$$= \left(\frac{1}{2}x^4 - \frac{8}{9}x^3 + \frac{4}{9}x^2\right)\Big|_0^1$$

$$= \frac{1}{2} - \frac{8}{9} + \frac{4}{9} = \frac{1}{18}.$$

From our first calculation, we see that if a large number of points is chosen randomly from a circle of radius 1 their average distance to the center should be about $\frac{2}{3}$. ■

The following alternative formula for the variance of a random variable is usually easier to use than the actual definition of $\text{Var}(X)$.

Let X be a continuous random variable whose values lie between A and B, and let $f(x)$ be the density function for X. Then

$$\text{Var}(X) = \int_A^B x^2 f(x)\, dx - \text{E}(X)^2. \qquad (5)$$

To prove (5), we let $m = \text{E}(X) = \int_A^B x f(x)\, dx$. Then

$$\text{Var}(X) = \int_A^B (x - m)^2 f(x)\, dx = \int_A^B (x^2 - 2xm + m^2) f(x)\, dx$$

$$= \int_A^B x^2 f(x)\, dx - 2m \int_A^B x f(x)\, dx + m^2 \int_A^B f(x)\, dx$$

$$= \int_A^B x^2 f(x)\, dx - 2m \cdot m + m^2 \cdot 1 \qquad \text{(by Property II)}$$

$$= \int_A^B x^2 f(x)\, dx - m^2.$$

EXAMPLE 4

A college library has found that, in any given month during a school year, the proportion of students who make some use of the library is a random variable X with the cumulative distribution function

$$F(x) = 4x^3 - 3x^4, \qquad 0 \le x \le 1.$$

(a) Compute $\text{E}(X)$ and give an interpretation of this quantity.

(b) Compute $\text{Var}(X)$.

Solution (a) To compute $\text{E}(X)$ we first find the probability density function $f(x)$. From Section 12.2 we know that

$$f(x) = F'(x) = 12x^2 - 12x^3.$$

Hence

$$E(X) = \int_0^1 x f(x)\, dx = \int_0^1 (12x^3 - 12x^4)\, dx$$

$$= \left(3x^4 - \frac{12}{5}x^5\right)\Big|_0^1 = 3 - \frac{12}{5} = \frac{3}{5}.$$

The meaning of $E(X)$ in this example is that over a period of many months (during school years) the average proportion of students each month who make some use of the library should be close to $\frac{3}{5}$.

(b) We first compute

$$\int_0^1 x^2 f(x)\, dx = \int_0^1 (12x^4 - 12x^5)\, dx = \left(\frac{12}{5}x^5 - 2x^6\right)\Big|_0^1$$

$$= \frac{12}{5} - 2 = \frac{2}{5}.$$

Then, from the alternative formula (5) for the variance, we find that

$$\text{Var}(X) = \frac{2}{5} - E(X)^2 = \frac{2}{5} - \left(\frac{3}{5}\right)^2 = \frac{1}{25}. \qquad \blacksquare$$

Practice Problems 12.3

1. Find the expected value and variance of the random variable X whose density function is $f(x) = 1/(2\sqrt{x})$, $1 \le x \le 4$.

2. An insurance company finds that the proportion X of their salespeople who sell more than \$25,000 worth of insurance in a given week is a random variable with

the beta probability density function

$$f(x) = 60x^3(1-x)^2, \qquad 0 \le x \le 1.$$

(a) Compute $E(X)$ and give an interpretation of this quantity.

(b) Compute $\text{Var}(X)$.

EXERCISES 12.3

Find the expected value and variance for each random variable whose probability density function is given. When computing the variance, use formula (5).

1. $f(x) = \frac{1}{18}x$, $0 \le x \le 6$
2. $f(x) = 2(x-1)$, $1 \le x \le 2$
3. $f(x) = \frac{1}{4}$, $1 \le x \le 5$
4. $f(x) = \frac{8}{9}x$, $0 \le x \le \frac{3}{2}$
5. $f(x) = 5x^4$, $0 \le x \le 1$
6. $f(x) = \frac{3}{2}x - \frac{3}{4}x^2$, $0 \le x \le 2$
7. $f(x) = 12x(1-x)^2$, $0 \le x \le 1$
8. $f(x) = \dfrac{3\sqrt{x}}{16}$, $0 \le x \le 4$

9. A newspaper publisher estimates that the proportion X of space devoted to advertising on a given day is a random variable with the beta probability density $f(x) = 30x^2(1-x)^2$, $0 \le x \le 1$.

(a) Find the cumulative distribution function for X.

(b) Find the probability that less than 25% of the newspaper's space on a given day contains advertising.

(c) Find $E(X)$ and give an interpretation of this quantity.

(d) Compute $\text{Var}(X)$.

10. Let X be the proportion of new restaurants in a given year that make a profit during their first year of operation, and suppose that the density function for X is $f(x) = 20x^3(1-x)$, $0 \le x \le 1$.

(a) Find $E(X)$ and give an interpretation of this quantity.

(b) Compute $\text{Var}(X)$.

11. The useful life (in hundreds of hours) of a certain machine component is a random variable X with the cumulative distribution function $F(x) = \frac{1}{9}x^2$, $0 \le x \le 3$.
    (a) Find $E(X)$ and give an interpretation of this quantity.
    (b) Compute $\text{Var}(X)$.

12. The time (in minutes) required to complete an assembly on a production line is a random variable X with the cumulative distribution function $F(x) = \frac{1}{125}x^3$, $0 \le x \le 5$.
    (a) Find $E(X)$ and give an interpretation of this quantity.
    (b) Compute $\text{Var}(X)$.

13. The amount of time (in minutes) that a person spends reading the editorial page of the newspaper is a random variable with the density function $f(x) = \frac{1}{72}x$, $0 \le x \le 12$. Find the average time spent reading the editorial page.

14. At a certain bus stop the time between buses is a random variable X with the density function $f(x) = 6x(10 - x)/1000$, $0 \le x \le 10$. Find the average time between buses.

15. When preparing a bid on a large construction project, a contractor analyzes how long each phase of the construction will take. Suppose that the contractor estimates that the time required for the electrical work will be X hundred worker-hours, where X is a random variable with density function $f(x) = x(6-x)/18$, $3 \le x \le 6$. (See Fig. 3.)
    (a) Find the cumulative distribution function $F(x)$.
    (b) What is the likelihood that the electrical work will take less than 500 worker-hours?
    (c) Find the mean time to complete the electrical work.
    (d) Find $\text{Var}(X)$.

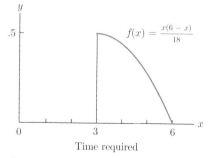

Figure 3. Density function for construction bid.

16. The amount of milk (in thousands of gallons) that a dairy sells each week is a random variable X with the density function $f(x) = 4(x-1)^3$, $1 \le x \le 2$. (See Fig. 4.)

    (a) What is the likelihood that the dairy will sell more than 1500 gallons?
    (b) What is the average amount of milk that the dairy sells each week?

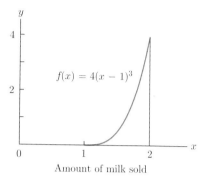

Figure 4. Density function for sales of milk.

17. Let X be a continuous random variable with values between $A = 1$ and $B = \infty$, and with the density function $f(x) = 4x^{-5}$. Compute $E(X)$ and $\text{Var}(X)$.

18. Let X be a continuous random variable with density function $f(x) = 3x^{-4}$, $x \ge 1$. Compute $E(X)$ and $\text{Var}(X)$.

If X is a random variable with density function $f(x)$ on $A \le x \le B$, the median *of X is that number M such that*

$$\int_A^M f(x)\, dx = \frac{1}{2}.$$

In other words, $\Pr(X \le M) = \frac{1}{2}$.

19. Find the median of the random variable whose density function is $f(x) = \frac{1}{18}x$, $0 \le x \le 6$.

20. Find the median of the random variable whose density function is $f(x) = 2(x-1)$, $1 \le x \le 2$.

21. The machine component described in Exercise 11 has a 50% chance of lasting at least how long?

22. In Exercise 12, find the length of time T such that half of the assemblies are completed in T minutes or less.

23. In Exercise 20 of Section 12.2, find the length of time T such that about half of the time you wait only T minutes or less in the express lane at the supermarket.

24. Find the number M such that half of the time the dairy in Exercise 16 sells M thousand gallons of milk or less.

25. Show that $E(X) = B - \int_A^B F(x)\, dx$, where $F(x)$ is the cumulative distribution function for X on $A \le x \le B$.

26. Use the formula in Exercise 25 to compute $E(X)$ for the random variable X in Exercise 12.

Solutions to Practice Problems 12.3

1. $E(X) = \int_1^4 x \cdot \frac{1}{2\sqrt{x}}\,dx = \int_1^4 \frac{1}{2}x^{1/2}\,dx = \frac{1}{3}x^{3/2}\Big|_1^4$

$= \frac{1}{3}(4)^{3/2} - \frac{1}{3} = \frac{8}{3} - \frac{1}{3} = \frac{7}{3}.$

To find $\text{Var}(X)$, we first compute

$\int_1^4 x^2 \cdot \frac{1}{2\sqrt{x}}\,dx = \int_1^4 \frac{1}{2}x^{3/2}\,dx = \frac{1}{5}x^{5/2}\Big|_1^4$

$= \frac{1}{5}(4)^{5/2} - \frac{1}{5} = \frac{32}{5} - \frac{1}{5} = \frac{31}{5}.$

Then, from formula (5),

$\text{Var}(X) = \frac{31}{5} - \left(\frac{7}{3}\right)^2 = \frac{34}{45}.$

2. (a) First note that $f(x) = 60x^3(1-x)^2 = 60x^3(1 - 2x + x^2) = 60x^3 - 120x^4 + 60x^5.$ Then

$E(X) = \int_0^1 x f(x)\,dx$

$= \int_0^1 (60x^4 - 120x^5 + 60x^6)\,dx$

$= \left(12x^5 - 20x^6 + \frac{60}{7}x^7\right)\Big|_0^1$

$= 12 - 20 + \frac{60}{7} = \frac{4}{7}.$

Thus, in an average week, about four-sevenths of the salespeople sell more than \$25,000 worth of insurance. More precisely, over a period of many weeks, we expect an average of four-sevenths of the salespeople each week to sell more than \$25,000 worth of insurance.

(b) $\int_0^1 x^2 f(x)\,dx = \int_0^1 (60x^5 - 120x^6 + 60x^7)\,dx$

$= \left(10x^6 - \frac{120}{7}x^7 + \frac{60}{8}x^8\right)\Big|_0^1$

$= 10 - \frac{120}{7} + \frac{60}{8} = \frac{5}{14}.$

Hence

$\text{Var}(X) = \frac{5}{14} - \left(\frac{4}{7}\right)^2 = \frac{3}{98}.$

12.4 Exponential and Normal Random Variables

This section is devoted to the two most important types of probability density functions, the exponential and normal density functions. These functions are associated with random variables that arise in a wide variety of applications. We will describe some typical examples.

Exponential Density Functions Let k be a positive constant. Then the function

$$f(x) = ke^{-kx}, \qquad x \geq 0,$$

is called an *exponential density function*. (See Fig. 1.) This function is indeed a probability density function. First, $f(x)$ is clearly greater than or equal to 0. Second,

$$\int_0^b ke^{-kx}\,dx = -e^{-kx}\Big|_0^b = 1 - e^{-kb} \to 1 \quad \text{as} \quad b \to \infty,$$

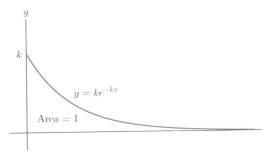

Figure 1. Exponential density function.

so

$$\int_0^\infty k e^{-kx}\, dx = 1.$$

A random variable X with an exponential density function is called an *exponential random variable*, and the values of X are said to be *exponentially distributed*. Exponential random variables are used in reliability calculations to represent the lifetime (or time to failure) of electronic components such as computer chips. They are used to describe the length of time between two successive random events, such as the interarrival times between successive telephone calls at a switchboard. Also, exponential random variables can arise in the study of service times, such as the length of time a person spends in a doctor's office or at a gas station.

Let us compute the expected value of an exponential random variable X:

$$\mathrm{E}(X) = \int_0^\infty x f(x)\, dx = \int_0^\infty x k e^{-kx}\, dx.$$

We may approximate this improper integral by a definite integral and use integration by parts to find that

$$\int_0^b x k e^{-kx}\, dx = -x e^{-kx}\Big|_0^b - \int_0^b -e^{-kx}\, dx$$

$$= (-b e^{-kb} + 0) - \frac{1}{k} e^{-kx}\Big|_0^b$$

$$= -b e^{-kb} - \frac{1}{k} e^{-kb} + \frac{1}{k}. \qquad (1)$$

As $b \to \infty$, this quantity approaches $1/k$, because the numbers $-b e^{-kb}$ and $-(1/k)e^{-kb}$ both approach 0. (See Section 11.5, Exercise 42.) Thus

$$\mathrm{E}(X) = \int_0^\infty x k e^{-kx}\, dx = \frac{1}{k}.$$

Let us now compute the variance of X. From the alternative formula for $\mathrm{Var}(X)$ given in Section 12.3, we have

$$\mathrm{Var}(X) = \int_0^\infty x^2 f(x)\, dx - \mathrm{E}(X)^2$$

$$= \int_0^\infty x^2 k e^{-kx}\, dx - \frac{1}{k^2}. \qquad (2)$$

Using integration by parts, we obtain

$$\int_0^b x^2 k e^{-kx}\, dx = x^2(-e^{-kx})\Big|_0^b - \int_0^b 2x(-e^{-kx})\, dx$$

$$= (-b^2 e^{-kb} + 0) + 2\int_0^b x e^{-kx}\, dx$$

$$= -b^2 e^{-kb} + \frac{2}{k}\int_0^b x k e^{-kx}\, dx. \qquad (3)$$

Now let $b \to \infty$. We know from our calculation (1) of $\mathrm{E}(X)$ that the integral in the second term of (3) approaches $1/k$; also, it can be shown that $-b^2 e^{-kb}$ approaches 0 (see Section 11.5, Exercise 44). Therefore,

$$\int_0^\infty x^2 k e^{-kx}\, dx = \frac{2}{k} \cdot \frac{1}{k} = \frac{2}{k^2}.$$

And by equation (2) we have

$$\text{Var}(X) = \frac{2}{k^2} - \frac{1}{k^2} = \frac{1}{k^2}.$$

Let us summarize our results:

Let X be a random variable with an exponential density function $f(x) = ke^{-kx}$ ($x \geq 0$). Then

$$E(X) = \frac{1}{k} \quad \text{and} \quad \text{Var}(X) = \frac{1}{k^2}.$$

EXAMPLE 1   Suppose that the number of days of continuous use provided by a certain brand of light bulb is an exponential random variable X with expected value 100 days.

(a) Find the density function of X.

(b) Find the probability that a randomly chosen bulb will last between 80 and 90 days.

(c) Find the probability that a randomly chosen bulb will last for more than 40 days.

Solution (a) Since X is an exponential random variable, its density function must be of the form $f(x) = ke^{-kx}$ for some $k > 0$. Since the expected value of such a density function is $1/k$ and is equal to 100 in this case, we see that

$$\frac{1}{k} = 100,$$

$$k = \frac{1}{100} = .01.$$

Thus $f(x) = .01e^{-.01x}$.

(b) $\Pr(80 \leq X \leq 90) = \int_{80}^{90} .01e^{-.01x}\, dx = -e^{-.01x}\Big|_{80}^{90} = -e^{-.9} + e^{-.8} \approx .04276.$

(c) $\Pr(X \geq 40) = \int_{40}^{\infty} .01e^{-.01x}\, dx = 1 - \int_{0}^{40} .01e^{-.01x}\, dx$

[since $\int_{0}^{\infty} f(x)\, dx = 1$], so

$$\Pr(X \geq 40) = 1 + (e^{-.01x})\Big|_{0}^{40} = 1 + (e^{-.4} - 1) = e^{-.4} \approx .67032. \quad \blacksquare$$

EXAMPLE 2   During a certain part of the day, the interarrival time between successive phone calls at a central telephone exchange is an exponential random variable X with expected value $\frac{1}{3}$ second.

(a) Find the density function of X.

(b) Find the probability that between $\frac{1}{3}$ and $\frac{2}{3}$ second elapses between consecutive phone calls.

(c) Find the probability that the time between successive phone calls is more than 2 seconds.

Solution (a) Since X is an exponential random variable, its density function is $f(x) = ke^{-kx}$ for some $k > 0$. Since the expected value of X is $1/k = \frac{1}{3}$, we have $k = 3$ and $f(x) = 3e^{-3x}$.

(b) $\Pr\left(\frac{1}{3} \leq X \leq \frac{2}{3}\right) = \int_{1/3}^{2/3} 3e^{-3x}\, dx = -e^{-3x}\Big|_{1/3}^{2/3} = -e^{-2} + e^{-1} \approx .23254.$

(c) $\Pr(X \geq 2) = \int_{2}^{\infty} 3e^{-3x}\, dx = 1 - \int_{0}^{2} 3e^{-3x}\, dx = 1 + (e^{-3x})\Big|_{0}^{2} = e^{-6} \approx .00248.$

In other words, about .25% of the time, the waiting time between consecutive calls is at least 2 seconds.   ∎

Normal Density Functions   Let μ and σ be given numbers, with $\sigma > 0$. Then the function

$$f(x) = \frac{1}{\sigma\sqrt{2\pi}}\, e^{-(1/2)[(x-\mu)/\sigma]^2} \tag{4}$$

is called a *normal density function*. A random variable X whose density function has this form is called a *normal random variable*, and the values of X are said to be *normally distributed*. Many random variables in applications are approximately normal. For example, errors that occur in physical measurements and various manufacturing processes, as well as many human physical and mental characteristics, are all conveniently modeled by normal random variables.

The graph of the density function in definition (4) is called a *normal curve* (Fig. 2). A normal curve is symmetric about the line $x = \mu$ and has inflection points at $\mu - \sigma$ and $\mu + \sigma$. Figure 3 shows three normal curves corresponding to different values of σ. The parameters μ and σ determine the shape of the curve. The value of μ determines the point where the curve reaches its maximum height, and the value of σ determines how sharp a peak the curve has.

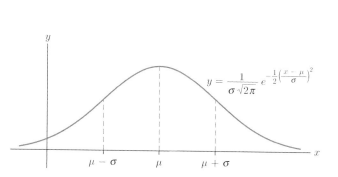

Figure 2. A normal density function.

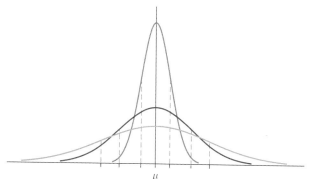

Figure 3. Several normal curves.

It can be shown that the constant $1/(\sigma\sqrt{2\pi})$ in definition (4) of a normal density function $f(x)$ is needed to make the area under the normal curve equal to 1, that is, to make $f(x)$ a probability density function. The theoretical values of a normal random variable X include all positive and negative numbers, but the normal curve approaches the horizontal axis so rapidly beyond the inflection points that the probabilities associated with intervals on the x-axis far to the left or right of $x = \mu$ are negligible.

Using techniques outside the scope of this book, we can verify the following basic facts about a normal random variable.

Let X be a random variable with the normal density function

$$f(x) = \frac{1}{\sigma\sqrt{2\pi}} e^{-(1/2)[(x-\mu)/\sigma]^2}.$$

Then the expected value (mean), variance, and standard deviation of X are given by

$$E(X) = \mu, \quad \mathrm{Var}(X) = \sigma^2, \quad \text{and} \quad \sqrt{\mathrm{Var}(X)} = \sigma.$$

A normal random variable with expected value $\mu = 0$ and standard deviation $\sigma = 1$ is called a *standard normal random variable* and is often denoted by the letter Z. Using these values for μ and σ in (4) and writing z in place of the variable x, we see that the density function for Z is

$$f(z) = \frac{1}{\sqrt{2\pi}} e^{-(1/2)z^2}.$$

The graph of this function is called the *standard normal curve*. (See Fig. 4.)

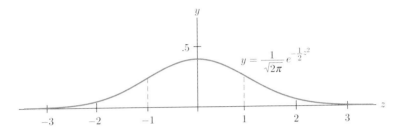

Figure 4. The standard normal curve.

Probabilities involving a standard normal random variable Z may be written in the form

$$\Pr(a \le Z \le b) = \int_a^b \frac{1}{\sqrt{2\pi}} e^{-(1/2)z^2}\, dz.$$

Such an integral cannot be evaluated directly, because the density function for Z cannot be antidifferentiated in terms of elementary functions. However, tables of such probabilities have been compiled using numerical approximations to the definite integrals. For $z \ge 0$, let $A(z) = \Pr(0 \le Z \le z)$ and $A(-z) = \Pr(-z \le Z \le 0)$. That is, let $A(z)$ and $A(-z)$ be the areas of the regions shown in Fig. 5. From the symmetry of the standard normal curve, it is clear that $A(-z) = A(z)$. Values of $A(z)$ for $z \ge 0$ are listed in Table 1 of the Appendix.

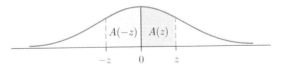

Figure 5. Areas under the standard normal curve.

EXAMPLE 3   Let Z be a standard normal random variable. Use Table 1 to compute the following probabilities:

(a) $\Pr(0 \le Z \le 1.84)$ (b) $\Pr(-1.65 \le Z \le 0)$

(c) $\Pr(.7 \le Z)$ (d) $\Pr(.5 \le Z \le 2)$ (e) $\Pr(-.75 \le Z \le 1.46)$

Solution (a) $\Pr(0 \le Z \le 1.84) = A(1.84)$. In Table 1 we move down the column under z until we reach 1.8; then we move right in the same row to the column with the heading .04. There we find that $A(1.84) = .4671$.

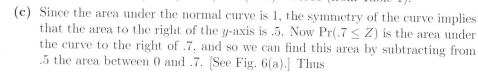

(b) $\Pr(-1.65 \leq Z \leq 0) = A(-1.65) = A(1.65) = .4505$ (from Table 1).

(c) Since the area under the normal curve is 1, the symmetry of the curve implies that the area to the right of the y-axis is .5. Now $\Pr(.7 \leq Z)$ is the area under the curve to the right of .7, and so we can find this area by subtracting from .5 the area between 0 and .7. [See Fig. 6(a).] Thus

$$\Pr(.7 \leq Z) = .5 - \Pr(0 \leq Z \leq .7)$$
$$= .5 - A(.7) = .5 - .2580 \quad \text{(from Table 1)}$$
$$= .2420.$$

(d) The area under the standard normal curve from .5 to 2 equals the area from 0 to 2 minus the area from 0 to .5. [See Fig. 6(b).] Thus we have

$$\Pr(.5 \leq Z \leq 2) = A(2) - A(.5)$$
$$= .4772 - .1915 = .2857.$$

(e) The area under the standard normal curve from $-.75$ to 1.46 equals the area from $-.75$ to 0 plus the area from 0 to 1.46. [See Fig. 6(c).] Thus

$$\Pr(-.75 \leq Z \leq 1.46) = A(-.75) + A(1.46)$$
$$= A(.75) + A(1.46)$$
$$= .2734 + .4279 = .7013. \qquad \blacksquare$$

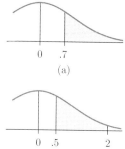
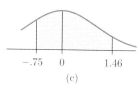

Figure 6

When X is an *arbitrary* normal random variable, with mean μ and standard deviation σ, we may compute a probability such as $\Pr(a \leq X \leq b)$ by making the change of variable $z = (x - \mu)/\sigma$. This converts the integral for $\Pr(a \leq X \leq b)$ into an integral involving the standard normal density function. The following example illustrates this procedure.

EXAMPLE 4   A metal flange on a truck must be between 92.1 and 94 millimeters long to fit properly. The lengths of the flanges supplied to the truck manufacturer are normally distributed with mean $\mu = 93$ millimeters and standard deviation $\sigma = .4$ millimeter.

(a) What percentage of the flanges have an acceptable length?

(b) What percentage of the flanges are too long?

Solution   Let X be the length of a metal flange selected at random from the supply of flanges.

(a) We have

$$\Pr(92.1 \leq X \leq 94) = \int_{92.1}^{94} \frac{1}{(.4)\sqrt{2\pi}} e^{-(1/2)[(x-93)/.4]^2} \, dx.$$

Using the substitution $z = (x - 93)/.4$, $dz = (1/.4) \, dx$, we note that if $x = 92.1$ then $z = (92.1 - 93)/.4 = -.9/.4 = -2.25$, and if $x = 94$, then $z = (94 - 93)/.4 = 1/.4 = 2.5$. Hence

$$\Pr(92.1 \leq X \leq 94) = \int_{-2.25}^{2.5} \frac{1}{\sqrt{2\pi}} e^{-(1/2)z^2} \, dz.$$

The value of this integral is the area under the standard normal curve from -2.25 to 2.5, which equals the area from -2.25 to 0 plus the area from 0 to 2.5. Thus

$$\Pr(92.1 \leq X \leq 94) = A(-2.25) + A(2.5)$$
$$= A(2.25) + A(2.5)$$
$$= .4878 + .4938 = .9816.$$

From this probability we conclude that about 98% of the flanges will have an acceptable length.

(b)
$$\Pr(94 \le X) = \int_{94}^{\infty} \frac{1}{(.4)\sqrt{2\pi}}\, e^{-(1/2)[(x-93)/.4]^2}\, dx$$

This integral is approximated by an integral from $x = 94$ to $x = b$, where b is large. If we substitute $z = (x - 93)/.4$, we find that

$$\int_{94}^{b} \frac{1}{(.4)\sqrt{2\pi}}\, e^{-(1/2)[(x-93)/.4]^2}\, dx = \int_{2.5}^{(b-93)/.4} \frac{1}{\sqrt{2\pi}}\, e^{-(1/2)z^2}\, dz. \qquad (5)$$

Now when $b \to \infty$ the quantity $(b-93)/.4$ also becomes arbitrarily large. Since the left integral in (5) approaches $\Pr(94 \le X)$, we conclude that

$$\Pr(94 \le X) = \int_{2.5}^{\infty} \frac{1}{\sqrt{2\pi}}\, e^{-(1/2)z^2}\, dz.$$

To calculate this integral, we use the method of Example 3(c). The area under the standard normal curve to the right of 2.5 equals the area to the right of 0 minus the area from 0 to 2.5. That is,

$$\Pr(94 \le X) = .5 - A(2.5)$$
$$= .5 - .4938 = .0062.$$

Approximately .6% of the flanges exceed the maximum acceptable length. ■

INCORPORATING TECHNOLOGY

The TI-83 graphing calculator can easily calculate normal probabilities with the **normalcdf** function from the DISTR menu. The area under the normal curve with mean μ and standard deviation σ from $x = a$ to $x = b$ is given by **normalcdf(a,b,μ,σ)**. The normal probabilities from Example 4 are calculated in Fig. 7. (*Note*: E99, which equals 10^{99}, is generated by pressing **1** [2nd] [EE] **99** and is used in place of infinity. Minus infinity is represented by −E99.) ■

```
normalcdf(92.1,9
4,93,.4)
        .9815658867
normalcdf(94,E99
,93,.4)
        .0062096799
```

Figure 7. Probabilities from Example 4.

Practice Problems 12.4

1. The emergency flasher on an automobile is warranted for the first 12,000 miles that the car is driven. During that period a defective flasher will be replaced free. If the time before failure of the emergency flasher (measured in thousands of miles) is an exponential random variable X with mean 50 (thousand miles), what percentage of the flashers will have to be replaced during the warranty period?

2. The lead time between ordering furniture from a certain company and receiving delivery is a normal random variable with $\mu = 18$ weeks and $\sigma = 5$ weeks. Find the likelihood that a customer will have to wait more than 16 weeks.

EXERCISES 12.4

Find (by inspection) the expected values and variances of the exponential random variables with the density functions given in Exercises 1–4.

1. $3e^{-3x}$

2. $\frac{1}{4}e^{-x/4}$

3. $.2e^{-.2x}$

4. $1.5e^{-1.5x}$

In a large factory there is an average of two accidents per day, and the time between accidents has an exponential density function with expected value of $\frac{1}{2}$ day.

5. Find the probability that the time between two accidents will be more than $\frac{1}{2}$ day and less than 1 day.

6. Find the probability that the time between accidents will be less than 8 hours ($\frac{1}{3}$ day).

The amount of time required to serve a customer at a bank has an exponential density function with mean 3 minutes.

7. Find the probability that a customer is served in less than 2 minutes.

8. Find the probability that serving a customer will require more than 5 minutes.

During a certain part of the day, the time between arrivals of automobiles at the tollgate on a turnpike is an exponential random variable with expected value 20 seconds.

9. Find the probability that the time between successive arrivals is more than 60 seconds.

10. Find the probability that the time between successive arrivals is greater than 10 seconds and less than 30 seconds.

Upon studying the vacancies occurring in the U.S. Supreme Court, it has been determined that the time elapsed between successive resignations is an exponential random variable with expected value 2 years.[*]

11. A new president takes office at the same time that a justice retires. Find the probability that the next vacancy on the court will take place during the president's 4-year term.

12. Find the probability that the composition of the U.S. Supreme Court will remain unchanged for a period of 5 years or more.

13. Suppose that the average life span of an electronic component is 72 months and that the life spans are exponentially distributed.

    (a) Find the probability that a component lasts for more than 24 months.

    (b) The *reliability function* $r(t)$ gives the probability that a component will last for more than t months. Compute $r(t)$ in this case.

14. Consider a group of patients that have been treated for an acute disease such as cancer, and let X be the

number of years a person lives after receiving the treatment (the survival time). Under suitable conditions, the density function for X will be $f(x) = ke^{-kx}$ for some constant k.

    (a) The *survival function* $S(x)$ is the probability that a person chosen at random from the group of patients survives until at least time x. Explain why $S(x) = 1 - F(x)$, where $F(x)$ is the cumulative distribution function for X, and compute $S(x)$.

    (b) Suppose that the probability is .90 that a patient will survive at least 5 years [$S(5) = .90$]. Find the constant k in the exponential density function $f(x)$.

Find the expected values and the standard deviations (by inspection) of the normal random variables with the density functions given in Exercises 15–18.

15. $\dfrac{1}{\sqrt{2\pi}}e^{-(1/2)(x-4)^2}$

16. $\dfrac{1}{\sqrt{2\pi}}e^{-(1/2)(x+5)^2}$

17. $\dfrac{1}{3\sqrt{2\pi}}e^{-(1/18)x^2}$

18. $\dfrac{1}{5\sqrt{2\pi}}e^{-(1/2)[(x-3)/5]^2}$

19. Show that the function $f(x) = e^{-x^2/2}$ has a relative maximum at $x = 0$.

20. Show that the function $f(x) = e^{-(1/2)[(x-\mu)/\sigma]^2}$ has a relative maximum at $x = \mu$.

21. Show that the function $f(x) = e^{-x^2/2}$ has inflection points at $x = \pm 1$.

22. Show that the function $f(x) = e^{-(1/2)[(x-\mu)/\sigma]^2}$ has inflection points at $x = \mu \pm \sigma$.

23. Let Z be a standard normal random variable. Calculate:

    (a) $\Pr(-1.3 \le Z \le 0)$ **(b)** $\Pr(.25 \le Z)$

    (c) $\Pr(-1 \le Z \le 2.5)$ **(d)** $\Pr(Z \le 2)$

24. Calculate the area under the standard normal curve for values of z

    (a) between .5 and 1.5,

    (b) between $-.75$ and .75,

    (c) to the left of $-.3$,

    (d) to the right of -1.

25. The gestation period (length of pregnancy) of a certain species is approximately normally distributed with a mean of 6 months and standard deviation of $\frac{1}{2}$ month.

    (a) Find the percentage of births that occur after a gestation period of between 6 and 7 months.

    (b) Find the percentage of births that occur after a gestation period of between 5 and 6 months.

---

[*]See W. A. Wallis, "The Poisson Distribution and the Supreme Court," *Journal of the American Statistical Association*, 31 (1936), 376–380.

26. Suppose that the life span of a certain automobile tire is normally distributed, with $\mu = 25{,}000$ miles and $\sigma = 2000$ miles.

    (a) Find the probability that a tire will last between 28,000 and 30,000 miles.

    (b) Find the probability that a tire will last more than 29,000 miles.

27. If the amount of milk in a gallon container is a normal random variable, with $\mu = 128.2$ ounces and $\sigma = .2$ ounce, find the probability that a random container of milk contains less than 128 ounces.

28. The amount of weight required to break a certain brand of twine has a normal density function, with $\mu = 43$ kilograms and $\sigma = 1.5$ kilograms. Find the probability that the breaking weight of a piece of the twine is less than 40 kilograms.

29. A student with an eight o'clock class at the University of Maryland commutes to school by car. She has discovered that along each of two possible routes her traveling time to school (including the time to get to class) is approximately a normal random variable. If she uses the Capital Beltway for most of her trip, $\mu = 25$ minutes and $\sigma = 5$ minutes. If she drives a longer route over local city streets, $\mu = 28$ minutes and $\sigma = 3$ minutes. Which route should the student take if she leaves home at 7:30 A.M.? (Assume that the best route is one that minimizes the probability of being late to class.)

30. Which route should the student in Exercise 29 take if she leaves home at 7:26 A.M.?

31. A certain type of bolt must fit through a 20-millimeter test hole or else it is discarded. If the diameters of the bolts are normally distributed, with $\mu = 18.2$ millimeters and $\sigma = .8$ millimeters, what percentage of the bolts will be discarded?

32. The Math SAT scores of a recent freshman class at a university were normally distributed, with $\mu = 535$ and $\sigma = 100$.

    (a) What percentage of the scores were between 500 and 600?

    (b) Find the minimum score needed to be in the top 10% of the class.

33. Let X be the time to failure (in years) of a transistor, and suppose that the transistor has been operating properly for a years. Then it can be shown that the probability that the transistor will fail within the next b years is

$$\frac{\Pr(a \le X \le a+b)}{\Pr(a \le X)}. \qquad (6)$$

Compute this probability for the case when X is an exponential random variable with density function $f(x) = ke^{-kx}$, and show that this probability equals $\Pr(0 \le X \le b)$. This means that the probability given

by (6) does not depend on how long the transistor has already been operating. Exponential random variables are therefore said to be *memoryless*.

34. Recall that the *median* of an exponential density function is that number M such that $\Pr(X \le M) = \frac{1}{2}$. Show that $M = (\ln 2)/k$. (We see that the median is less than the mean.)

35. If the lifetime (in weeks) of a certain brand of light bulb has an exponential density function and 80% of all light bulbs fail within the first 100 weeks, find the average lifetime of a light bulb.

Technology Exercises

36. The computations of the expected value and variance of an exponential random variable relied on the fact that, for any positive number k, be^{-kb} and $b^2 e^{-kb}$ approach 0 as b gets large. That is,

$$\lim_{x \to \infty} \frac{x}{e^{kx}} = 0 \quad \text{and} \quad \lim_{x \to \infty} \frac{x^2}{e^{kx}} = 0.$$

The validity of these limits for the case $k = 1$ is shown in Figs. 8 and 9. Convince yourself that these limits hold for all positive values of k by generating graphs for $k = .1$, $k = .5$, and $k = 2$.

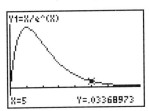

Figure 8. Graph of $Y_1 = \dfrac{x}{e^x}$.

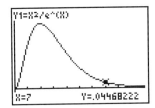

Figure 9. Graph of $Y_1 = \dfrac{x^2}{e^x}$.

37. Use the integral routine to convince yourself that $\int_{-\infty}^{\infty} x^2 f(x)\,dx = 1$, where $f(x)$ is the standard normal density function. [*Note:* Since $f(x)$ approaches zero so rapidly as x gets large in magnitude, the value of the improper integral is nearly the same as the definite integral of $x^2 f(x)$ from $x = -8$ to $x = 8$.] Conclude that the standard deviation of the standard normal random variable is 1.

Solutions to Practice Problems 12.4

1. The density function for X is $f(x) = ke^{-kx}$, where $1/k = 50$ (thousand miles) and $k = 1/50 = .02$. Then

$$\Pr(X \le 12) = \int_0^{12} .02e^{-.02x}\, dx = -e^{-.02x}\Big|_0^{12}$$

$$= 1 - e^{-.24} \approx .21337.$$

About 21% of the flashers will have to be replaced during the warranty period.

2. Let X be the time between ordering and receiving the furniture. Since $\mu = 18$ and $\sigma = 5$, we have

$$\Pr(16 \le X) = \int_{16}^{\infty} \frac{1}{5\sqrt{2\pi}} e^{-(1/2)[(x-18)/5]^2}\, dx.$$

If we substitute $z = (x-18)/5$, then $dz = \frac{1}{5}\, dx$, and $z = -.4$ when $x = 16$.

$$\Pr(16 \le X) = \int_{-.4}^{\infty} \frac{1}{\sqrt{2\pi}} e^{-(1/2)z^2}\, dz.$$

[A similar substitution was made in Example 4(b).] The preceding integral gives the area under the standard normal curve to the right of $-.4$. Since the area between $-.4$ and 0 is $A(-.4) = A(.4)$, and the area to the right of 0 is $.5$, we have

$$\Pr(16 \le X) = A(.4) + .5 = .1554 + .5 = .6554.$$

12.5 Poisson and Geometric Random Variables

Probability theory is widely applied in business, biology and the social sciences to situations that involve counting. The probability models in this section involve a random variable X whose values are the discrete numbers $0, 1, 2, \ldots$. Usually there is no specific upper limit to the value of X, even though extremely large values of X are highly unlikely. Here are typical examples of such experiments. In each case, X represents the outcome of the experiment.

1. At an insurance company, count the number of fire insurance claims submitted in any one month (selected at random).

2. In a microbiological study of a pond, count the number of protozoa in a drop-size random sample of water.

3. In a factory, count the number of times per month that a certain type of machine breaks down.

Suppose X denotes a random variable for an experiment whose outcome is one of the values $0, 1, 2, \ldots$, and for each possible value n, let p_n be the associated probability of occurrence. That is,

$$p_0 = \Pr(X = 0),$$
$$p_1 = \Pr(X = 1),$$
$$\vdots$$
$$p_n = \Pr(X = n)$$
$$\vdots$$

Notice that, since $p_0, p_1, p_2, \ldots$ are probabilities, each lies between 0 and 1. Also, the sum of these probabilities must be 1. (One of the outcomes $0, 1, 2, \ldots$ always occurs.) That is,

$$p_0 + p_1 + p_2 + \cdots + p_n + \cdots = 1.$$

Unlike the situation in Section 12.1, this sum is an infinite series such as those studied in Sections 11.3 and 11.5.

In analogy with the case of experiments having a finite number of possible outcomes, we may define the *expected value* (or average value) of the random variable

X (or of the experiment whose outcome is X) to be the number $E(X)$ given by the following formula:

$$E(X) = 0 \cdot p_0 + 1 \cdot p_1 + 2 \cdot p_2 + 3 \cdot p_3 + \cdots$$

(provided that the infinite series converges). That is, the expected value $E(X)$ is formed by adding the products of the possible outcomes by their respective probabilities of occurrence.

In a similar fashion, letting m denote $E(X)$, we define the *variance* of X by

$$\mathrm{Var}(x) = (0 - m)^2 \cdot p_0 + (1 - m)^2 \cdot p_1 + (2 - m)^2 \cdot p_2 + (3 - m)^2 \cdot p_3 + \cdots .$$

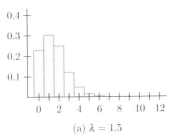

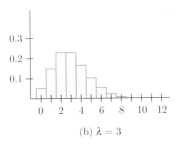

(a) $\lambda = 1.5$

Poisson Random Variables In many experiments, the probabilities p_n involve a parameter λ (depending on the particular experiment), and they have the following special form:

$$p_0 = e^{-\lambda},$$

$$p_1 = \frac{\lambda}{1} e^{-\lambda},$$

$$p_2 = \frac{\lambda^2}{2 \cdot 1} e^{-\lambda},$$

$$p_3 = \frac{\lambda^3}{3 \cdot 2 \cdot 1} e^{-\lambda},$$

$$\vdots$$

$$p_n = \frac{\lambda^n}{n!} e^{-\lambda}. \tag{1}$$

(b) $\lambda = 3$

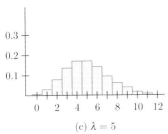

(c) $\lambda = 5$

Figure 1

The constant $e^{-\lambda}$ in each probability is necessary to make the sum of all the probabilities equal to 1. A random variable X whose probabilities are given by formula (1) is called a *Poisson random variable*, and the probabilities for X are said to form a *Poisson distribution* with parameter λ. The histograms in Fig. 1 show Poisson distributions for $\lambda = 1.5$, 3, and 5.

EXAMPLE 1

The annual number of deaths in a certain town due to a particular disease has a Poisson distribution with parameter $\lambda = 3$. Verify that the associated probabilities sum to 1.

Solution The first few probabilities are (to four decimal places)

$$p_0 = e^{-3} \approx .0498,$$

$$p_1 = \frac{3}{1} e^{-3} = 3 \cdot p_0 \approx .1494,$$

$$p_2 = \frac{3^2}{2 \cdot 1} e^{-3} = \frac{3 \cdot 3}{2 \cdot 1} e^{-3} = \frac{3}{2} p_1 \approx .2240,$$

$$p_3 = \frac{3^3}{3 \cdot 2 \cdot 1} e^{-3} = \frac{3 \cdot 3 \cdot 3}{3 \cdot 2 \cdot 1} e^{-3} = \frac{3}{3} p_2 \approx .2240,$$

$$p_4 = \frac{3^4}{4 \cdot 3 \cdot 2 \cdot 1} e^{-3} = \frac{3 \cdot \boxed{3 \cdot 3 \cdot 3}}{4 \cdot \boxed{3 \cdot 2 \cdot 1}} e^{-3} = \frac{3}{4} p_3 \approx .1680,$$

$$p_5 = \frac{3^5}{5 \cdot 4 \cdot 3 \cdot 2 \cdot 1} e^{-3} = \frac{3 \cdot \boxed{3 \cdot 3 \cdot 3 \cdot 3}}{5 \cdot \boxed{4 \cdot 3 \cdot 2 \cdot 1}} e^{-3} = \frac{3}{5} p_4 \approx .1008.$$

Notice how each probability p_n for $n \geq 1$ is computed from the preceding probability p_{n-1}. In general, $p_n = (\lambda/n)p_{n-1}$.

To sum the probabilities for all n, use the exact values, not the decimal approximations:

$$e^{-3} + \frac{3}{1}e^{-3} + \frac{3^2}{2 \cdot 1}e^{-3} + \frac{3^3}{3 \cdot 2 \cdot 1}e^{-3} + \frac{3^4}{4 \cdot 3 \cdot 2 \cdot 1}e^{-3} + \cdots$$

$$= e^{-3}\left(1 + 3 + \frac{1}{2!}3^2 + \frac{1}{3!}3^3 + \frac{1}{4!}3^4 + \cdots\right).$$

From Section 11.5, you should recognize that the series inside the parentheses is the power series for e^x evaluated at $x = 3$. The preceding sum is $e^{-3} \cdot e^3$, which equals 1.   ■

The following facts about Poisson random variables provide an interpretation for the parameter λ.

Let X be a random variable whose probabilities are Poisson distributed with parameter λ; that is,

$$p_0 = e^{-\lambda},$$

$$p_n = \frac{\lambda^n}{n!}e^{-\lambda} \qquad (n = 1, 2, \dots).$$

Then the expected value and variance of X are given by

$$E(X) = \lambda, \qquad \text{Var}(X) = \lambda.$$

We shall verify only the statement about $E(X)$. The argument uses the Taylor series for e^λ. We have

$$E(X) = 0 \cdot p_0 + 1 \cdot p_1 + 2 \cdot p_2 + 3 \cdot p_3 + 4 \cdot p_4 + \cdots$$

$$= 0 \cdot e^{-\lambda} + 1 \cdot \frac{\lambda}{1}e^{-\lambda} + 2 \cdot \frac{\lambda^2}{1 \cdot 2}e^{-\lambda}$$

$$+ 3 \cdot \frac{\lambda^3}{1 \cdot 2 \cdot 3}e^{-\lambda} + 4 \cdot \frac{\lambda^4}{1 \cdot 2 \cdot 3 \cdot 4}e^{-\lambda} + \cdots$$

$$= \lambda e^{-\lambda} + \frac{\lambda^2}{1}e^{-\lambda} + \frac{\lambda^3}{1 \cdot 2}e^{-\lambda} + \frac{\lambda^4}{1 \cdot 2 \cdot 3}e^{-\lambda} + \cdots$$

$$= \lambda e^{-\lambda}\left(1 + \frac{\lambda}{1} + \frac{\lambda^2}{1 \cdot 2} + \frac{\lambda^3}{1 \cdot 2 \cdot 3} + \cdots\right)$$

$$= \lambda e^{-\lambda} \cdot e^\lambda$$

$$= \lambda.$$

The next two examples illustrate some applications of Poisson random variables.

EXAMPLE 2   Suppose that we observe the number X of calls received by a telephone switchboard during a 1-minute interval. Experience suggests that X is Poisson distributed with $\lambda = 5$.

(a) Determine the probability that zero, one, or two calls arrive during a particular minute.

(b) Determine the probability that three or more calls arrive during a particular minute.

(c) Determine the average number of calls received per minute.

Solution (a) The probability that zero, one, or two calls arrive during a given minute is $p_0 + p_1 + p_2$. Moreover,

$$p_0 = e^{-\lambda} = e^{-5} \approx .00674,$$

$$p_1 = \frac{\lambda}{1}e^{-\lambda} = 5e^{-5} \approx .03369,$$

$$p_2 = \frac{\lambda^2}{1 \cdot 2}e^{-\lambda} = \frac{5}{2}p_1 \approx .0842.$$

Thus $p_0 + p_1 + p_2 \approx .12465$. That is, during approximately 12% of the minutes, either zero, one, or two calls are received.

(b) The probability of receiving three or more calls is the same as the probability of *not* receiving zero, one, or two calls and so is equal to

$$1 - (p_0 + p_1 + p_2) = 1 - .12465 = .87535.$$

(c) The average number of calls received per minute is equal to λ. That is, on average the switchboard receives five calls per minute.   ∎

EXAMPLE 3   Drop-size water samples are drawn from a New England pond. The numbers of protozoa in many different samples are counted and the average number is found to be about 8.3. What is the probability that a sample chosen at random contains at most four protozoa?

Solution Under the assumption that the protozoa are thoroughly spread throughout the pond, without clumping, the number of protozoa per drop is a Poisson random variable, call it X. From the experimental data, we assume that $E(X) = 8.3$. Since $\lambda = E(X)$, the probabilities for X are given by

$$p_n = \frac{8.3^n}{n!}e^{-8.3}.$$

The probability of "at most four" is $\Pr(X \le 4)$. Using a calculator to generate the probabilities, we find that

$$\Pr(X \le 4) = p_0 + p_1 + p_2 + p_3 + p_4$$
$$\approx .00025 + .00206 + .00856 + .02368 + .04914$$
$$= .08369.$$

The probability of at most four protozoa is about 8.4%.   ∎

Geometric Random Variables   The following two experiments give rise to discrete random variables whose values are $0, 1, \ldots,$ but whose distributions are not Poisson.

- Toss a coin until a head appears and count the number of tails that precede it.

- As part of a quality-control procedure, test the items coming off an assembly line. Count the number of acceptable items before the first defective item is found.

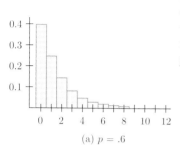

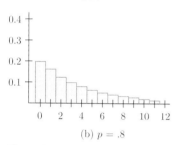

(a) $p = .6$

(b) $p = .8$

Figure 2

Each of these experiments involves a trial having two results (tail, head) or (acceptable, defective). In general, the two results are named *success* and *failure*, and the trial is repeated until a failure occurs. The outcome of the experiment is the number X of successes $(0, 1, 2, \ldots)$ that precede the first failure. If for some number p between 0 and 1 the probabilities for X have the form

$$
\begin{aligned}
p_0 &= 1 - p, \\
p_1 &= p(1 - p), \\
p_2 &= p^2(1 - p), \\
&\vdots \\
p_n &= p^n(1 - p), \\
&\vdots
\end{aligned}
\tag{2}
$$

then X is called a *geometric random variable*, and the probabilities for X are said to form a *geometric distribution* with parameter p. In this case, each trial of the experiment has the same probability p of success. (The probability of failure is $1 - p$.) Also, the outcome of each trial is independent of the other trials. The histograms in Fig. 2 display geometric distributions for $p = .6$ and .8.

The term "geometric" is associated with formula (2) because the probabilities form a geometric series, with initial term $a = 1 - p$ and ratio $r = p$. The sum of the series is

$$
p_0 + p_1 + p_2 + \cdots = \frac{a}{1 - r} = \frac{1 - p}{1 - p} = 1.
$$

This is just what you would expect: The probabilities add up to 1.

EXAMPLE 4

An assembly line produces a small mechanical toy and about 2% of the toys are defective. A quality-control person selects a toy at random, inspects it, and repeats this process until a defective toy is found. The probability of success (passing the test) is .98 for each inspection (trial).

(a) Find the probability that exactly three toys pass the test before a defective toy is found.

(b) Find the probability that at most three toys pass the test before a defective toy is found.

(c) What is the probability that at least four toys will pass the test before the first defective toy is found?

Solution   Let X be the number of acceptable toys found before the first defective toy. A reasonable assumption is that the random variable X has a geometric distribution with parameter $p = .98$.

(a) The probability that $X = 3$ is $p_3 = (.98)^3(1 - .98) \approx .0188$.

(b) $\Pr(X \le 3) = p_0 + p_1 + p_2 + p_3$

$$= .02 + (.98)(.02) + (.98)^2(.02) + (.98)^3(.02)$$

$$\approx .02 + .0196 + .0192 + .0188 = .0776.$$

(c) $\Pr(X \ge 4) = 1 - \Pr(X \le 3) \approx 1 - .0776 = .9224.$ ∎

The following properties of a geometric distribution can be established with facts about power series.

Let X be a geometric random variable with parameter p, that is,

$$p_n = p^n(1 - p) \qquad (n = 0, 1, \dots).$$

Then the expected value and variance of X are given by

$$\mathrm{E}(X) = \frac{p}{1 - p}, \qquad \mathrm{Var}(X) = \frac{p}{(1 - p)^2}.$$

EXAMPLE 5   For the situation described in Example 4, what is the average number of toys that pass inspection before the first defective toy is found?

Solution   Since $p = .98$, $\mathrm{E}(X) = .98/(1 - .98) = 49$. If many inspections are made, then we can expect on average that 49 toys will pass inspection before a defective toy is found. ∎

INCORPORATING TECHNOLOGY

Poisson Probabilities   The TI-83 graphing calculator has two functions that calculate Poisson probabilities. The value of **poissonpdf(λ,n)** is $p_n = \dfrac{\lambda^n}{n!}e^{-\lambda}$, and the value of **poissoncdf(λ,n)** is $p_0 + p_1 + p_2 + \cdots + p_n$. (These two functions are invoked from the DISTR menu.) In Fig. 3 the functions are used to calculate two probabilities from Example 2(a). With other graphing calculators, you can find the sum of successive Poisson probabilities with **sum(seq**, as shown in the last computation of Fig. 3. In Fig. 4 **sum(seq** is used to compute the geometric probabilities from parts (b) and (c) of Example 4. ∎

Figure 3. Two probabilities from Example 2.

Figure 4. Two probabilities from Example 4.

Practice Problems 12.5

1. A Public Health Officer is tracking down the source of a bacterial infection in a certain city. She analyzes the reported incidence of the infection in each city block and finds an average of three cases per block. A certain block is found to have seven cases. What is the probability that a randomly chosen block has at least seven cases, assuming that the number of cases per block is Poisson distributed?

EXERCISES 12.5

1. Suppose that a random variable X has a Poisson distribution with $\lambda = 3$, as in Example 1. Compute the probabilities p_6, p_7, p_8.

2. Let X be a Poisson random variable with parameter $\lambda = 5$. Compute the probabilities $p_0, \ldots, p_6$ to four decimal places.

3. Repeat Exercise 2 with $\lambda = .75$ and make a histogram.

4. Repeat Exercise 2 with $\lambda = 2.5$ and make a histogram.

5. The monthly number of fire insurance claims filed with the Firebug Insurance Company is Poisson distributed with $\lambda = 10$.

   (a) What is the probability that in a given month no claims are filed?

   (b) What is the probability that in a given month no more than two claims are filed? (The number of claims is either zero, one, or two.)

   (c) What is the probability that in a given month at least three claims are filed?

6. On a typical weekend evening at a local hospital, the number of persons waiting for treatment in the emergency room is Poisson distributed with $\lambda = 6.5$.

   (a) What is the likelihood that either no one or only one person is waiting for treatment?

   (b) What is the likelihood that no more than four persons are waiting?

   (c) What is the likelihood that at least five persons are waiting?

7. The number of typographical errors per page of a certain newspaper has a Poisson distribution, and there is an average of 1.5 errors per page.

   (a) What is the probability that a randomly selected page is error free?

   (b) What is the probability that a page has either two or three errors?

   (c) What is the probability that a page has at least four errors?

8. During a certain part of the day, an average of five automobiles arrives every minute at the tollgate on a turnpike. Let X be the number of automobiles that arrives in any 1-minute interval selected at random. Let Y be the interarrival time between any two successive arrivals. (The average interarrival time is $\frac{1}{5}$ minute.) Assume that X is a Poisson random variable and that Y is an exponential random variable.

   (a) Find the probability that at least five cars arrive during a given 1-minute interval.

   (b) Find the probability that the time between any two successive cars is less than $\frac{1}{5}$ minute.

9. A bakery makes gourmet cookies. For a batch of 4800 oatmeal and raisin cookies, how many raisins should be used so that the probability of a cookie having no raisins is .01? [*Note*: A reasonable assumption is that the number of raisins in a random cookie has a Poisson distribution.]

10. If X is a geometric random variable with parameter $p = .9$, compute the probabilities $p_0, \ldots, p_5$ and make a histogram.

11. Repeat Exercise 10 with $p = .6$.

12. The quality-control department at a sewing machine factory has determined that 1 out of 40 machines does not pass inspection. Let X be the number of machines on an assembly line that passes inspection before a machine is found that fails inspection.

   (a) Write the formula for $\Pr(X = n)$.

   (b) What is the probability that of five machines coming off the assembly line the first four pass inspection and the fifth does not?

13. In a certain town, there are two competing taxicab companies, Red Cab and Blue Cab. The taxis mix with downtown traffic in a random manner. There are three times as many Red taxis as there are Blue taxis. Suppose that you stand on a downtown street corner and count the number X of Red taxis that appear before the first Blue taxi appears.

   (a) Determine the formula for $\Pr(X = n)$.

   (b) What is the likelihood of observing at least three Red taxis before the first Blue taxi?

   (c) What is the average number of consecutive Red taxis prior to the appearance of a Blue taxi?

14. At a certain junior high school, two-thirds of the students have at least one tooth cavity. A dental survey is made of the students. What is the probability that the first student to have a cavity is the third student examined?

15. Let X be a geometric random variable with parameter $p < 1$. Find a formula for $\Pr(X < n)$, for $n > 0$. [*Note*: The partial sum of a geometric series with ratio r is given by

$$1 + r + \cdots + r^{n-1} = \frac{1 - r^n}{1 - r}.]$$

16. Whenever a document is fed into a high-speed copy machine, there is a .5% chance that a paper jam will stop the machine.

   (a) What is the expected number of documents that can be copied before a paper jam occurs?

   (b) Determine the probability that at least 100 documents can be copied before a paper jam occurs. [*Hint*: See Exercise 15.]

17. Suppose that a large number of persons become infected by a particular strain of staphylococcus that is present in food served by a fast-food restaurant and that the germ usually produces a certain symptom in 5% of the persons infected. What is the probability that when customers are examined the first person to have the symptom is the fifth customer examined?

18. Suppose that you toss a fair coin until a head appears and count the number X of consecutive tails that precede it.

   (a) Determine the probability that exactly n consecutive tails occur.

   (b) Determine the average number of consecutive tails that occur.

   (c) Write down the infinite series that gives the variance for the number of consecutive tails. Use Exercise 28 in Section 11.5 to show that the variance equals 2.

Exercises 19 and 20 illustrate a technique from statistics (called the method of maximum likelihood*) that estimates a parameter for a probability distribution.*

19. In a production process a box of fuses is examined and found to contain two defective fuses. Suppose that the probability of having two defective fuses in a box selected at random is $(\lambda^2/2)e^{-\lambda}$ for some λ. Take first and second derivatives to determine the value of λ for which the probability has its maximum value.

20. A person shooting at a target has five successive hits and then a miss. If x is the probability of success on each shot, the probability of having five successive hits followed by a miss is $x^5(1-x)$. Take first and second derivatives to determine the value of x for which the probability has its maximum value.

21. Let X be a geometric random variable with parameter p. Derive the formula for $E(X)$ by using the power series formula (see Example 3 in Section 11.5):

$$1 + 2x + 3x^2 + \cdots = \frac{1}{(1-x)^2} \quad \text{for } |x| < 1$$

22. Let X be a Poisson random variable with parameter λ. Use Exercise 23 in Section 11.5 to show that the probability that X is an even integer (including 0) is $e^{-\lambda}\cosh\lambda$.

Technology Exercises

23. The number of times a printing press breaks down each month is Poisson distributed with $\lambda = 4$. What is the probability that the printing press breaks down between 2 and 8 times during a particular month?

24. The number of people arriving during a 5-minute interval at a supermarket checkout counter is Poisson distributed with $\lambda = 8$.

   (a) What is the probability that exactly eight people arrive during a particular 5-minute period?

   (b) What is the probability that at most eight people arrive during a particular 5-minute period?

25. The number of babies born each day in a certain hospital is Poisson distributed with $\lambda = 6.9$.

   (a) During a particular day, are seven babies more likely to be born than six babies?

   (b) What is the probability that at most 15 babies will be born during a particular day?

26. The number of accidents occurring each month at a certain intersection is Poisson distributed with $\lambda = 4.8$.

   (a) During a particular month, are five accidents more likely to occur than four accidents?

   (b) What is the probability that more than eight accidents will occur during a particular month?

Solutions to Practice Problems 12.5

1. The number of cases per block is Poisson distributed with $\lambda = 3$. So the probability of having at least seven cases in a given block is

$$p_7 + p_8 + p_9 + \ldots$$
$$= 1 - (p_0 + p_1 + p_2 + p_3 + p_4 + p_5 + p_6).$$

However,

$$p_n = \frac{3^n}{1 \cdot 2 \cdots n}e^{-3}$$

so

$$p_0 = .04979, \quad p_1 = .14936, \quad p_2 = .22404$$
$$p_3 = .22404, \quad p_4 = .16803, \quad p_5 = .10082,$$
$$p_6 = .05041.$$

Therefore, the probability of at least seven cases in a given block is $1 - (.04979 + .14936 + .22404 + .22404 + .16803 + .10082 + .05041) = .03351$. (See Figure 5.)

```
1-poissoncdf(3,6
)
          .0335085353
1-sum(seq((3^X/X
!)e^(-3),X,0,6,1
))
          .0335085353
```

Figure 5

REVIEW OF FUNDAMENTAL CONCEPTS

1. What is a probability table?

2. What is a discrete random variable?

3. Make a small probability table for a discrete random variable X and use it to define $E(X)$, $Var(X)$, and the standard deviation of X.

4. Explain how to create a probability density histogram.

5. What is the difference between a discrete random variable and a continuous random variable?

6. What are the two properties of a probability density function?

7. How is a probability density function used to calculate probabilities?

8. What is a cumulative distribution function and how is it related to the corresponding probability density function?

9. How is the expected value of a continuous random variable computed?

10. Give two ways to compute the variance of a continuous random variable.

11. What is an exponential density function? Give an example.

12. What is the expected value of an exponential random variable?

13. What is the density function for a normal random variable with mean μ and standard deviation σ?

14. What is a standard normal random variable? Write the density function.

15. How is an integral involving a normal density function converted to an integral involving a standard normal density function?

16. What is $\Pr(X = n)$ for a Poisson random variable with parameter λ? What is $E(X)$ in this case?

17. What is $\Pr(X = n)$ for a geometric random variable with parameter p (the probability of success)? What is $E(X)$ in this case?

SUPPLEMENTARY EXERCISES

1. Let X be a continuous random variable on $0 \le x \le 2$, with the density function $f(x) = \frac{3}{8}x^2$.
   (a) Calculate $\Pr(X \le 1)$ and $\Pr(1 \le X \le 1.5)$.
   (b) Find $E(X)$ and $Var(X)$.

2. Let X be a continuous random variable on $3 \le x \le 4$, with the density function $f(x) = 2(x - 3)$.
   (a) Calculate $\Pr(3.2 \le X)$ and $\Pr(3 \le X)$.
   (b) Find $E(X)$ and $Var(X)$.

3. For any number A, verify that $f(x) = e^{A-x}$, $x \ge A$, is a density function. Compute the associated cumulative distribution for X.

4. For any positive constants k and A, verify that the function $f(x) = kA^k/x^{k+1}$, $x \ge A$, is a density function. The associated cumulative distribution function $F(x)$ is called a *Pareto distribution*. Compute $F(x)$.

5. For any positive integer n, the function $f_n(x) = c_n x^{(n-2)/2} e^{-x/2}$, $x \ge 0$, where c_n is an appropriate constant, is called the *chi-square density function* with n degrees of freedom. Find c_2 and c_4 such that $f_2(x)$ and $f_4(x)$ are probability density functions.

6. For any positive number k, verify that $f(x) = 1/(2k^3)x^2 e^{-x/k}$, $x \ge 0$, is a density function.

7. A medical laboratory tests many blood samples for a certain disease that occurs in about 5% of the samples. The lab collects samples from 10 persons and mixes together some blood from each sample. If a test on the mixture is positive, an additional 10 tests must be run, one on each individual sample. But if the test on the

mixture is negative, no other tests are needed. It can be shown that the test of the mixture will be negative with probability $(.95)^{10} = .599$, because each of the 10 samples has a 95% chance of being free of the disease. If X is the total number of tests required, X has the probability table shown in Table 1.
   (a) Find $E(X)$.
   (b) If the laboratory uses the procedure described on 200 blood samples (that is, 20 batches of 10 samples), about how many tests can it expect to run?

TABLE 1 Blood Test Probabilities for Batches of 10 Samples

	Test of Mixture	
	Negative	*Positive*
Total tests	1	11
Probability	.599	.401

8. If the laboratory in Exercise 7 uses batches of 5 instead of 10 samples, the probability of a negative test on the mixture of 5 samples is $(.95)^5 = .774$. Thus Table 2 gives the probabilities for the number X of tests required.
   (a) Find $E(X)$.
   (b) If the laboratory uses this procedure on 200 blood samples (that is, 40 batches of 5 samples), about how many tests can it expect to run?

TABLE 2 Blood Test Probabilities for Batches of 5 Samples

Test of Mixture		
	Negative	*Positive*
Total tests	1	6
Probability	.774	.226

9. A certain gas station sells X thousand gallons of gas each week. Suppose that the cumulative distribution function for X is $F(x) = 1 - \frac{1}{4}(2 - x)^2$, $0 \leq x \leq 2$.

(a) If the tank contains 1.6 thousand gallons at the beginning of the week, find the probability that the gas station will have enough gas for its customers throughout the week.

(b) How much gas must be in the tank at the beginning of the week to have a probability of .99 that there will be enough gasoline for the week?

(c) Compute the density function for X.

10. A service contract on a computer costs $100 per year. The contract covers all necessary maintenance and repairs on the computer. Suppose that the actual cost to the manufacturer for providing this service is a random variable X (measured in hundreds of dollars) whose probability density function is $f(x) = (x - 5)^4/625$, $0 \leq x \leq 5$. Compute $E(X)$ and determine how much money the manufacturer expects to make on each service contract on average.

11. A random variable X has a uniform density function $f(x) = \frac{1}{5}$ on $20 \leq x \leq 25$.

(a) Find $E(X)$ and $Var(X)$.

(b) Find b such that $Pr(X \leq b) = .3$.

12. A random variable X has a cumulative distribution function $F(x) = (x^2 - 9)/16$ on $3 \leq x \leq 5$.

(a) Find the density function for X.

(b) Find a such that $Pr(a \leq X) = \frac{1}{4}$.

13. The annual incomes of the households in a certain community range between 5 and 25 thousand dollars. Let X represent the annual income (in thousands of dollars) of a household chosen at random in this community, and suppose that the probability density function for X is $f(x) = kx$, $5 \leq x \leq 25$.

(a) Find the value of k that makes $f(x)$ a density function.

(b) Find the fraction of households whose income exceeds $20,000.

(c) Find the mean annual income of the households in the community.

14. The density function $f(x)$ for the lifetime of a certain battery is shown in Fig. 1. Each battery lasts between 3 and 10 hours.

(a) Sketch the graph of the corresponding cumulative distribution function $F(x)$.

(b) What is the meaning of the number $F(7) - F(5)$?

(c) Formulate the number in part (b) in terms of $f(x)$.

Figure 1

15. A point is selected at random from the rectangle of Fig. 2; call its coordinates (θ, y). Find the probability that $y \leq \sin \theta$.

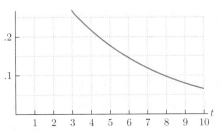

Figure 2

16. **Buffon Needle Problem** A needle of length 1 unit is dropped on a floor that is ruled with parallel lines, 1 unit apart. [See Fig. 3.] Let P be the lowest point of the needle, y the distance of P from the ruled line above it, and θ the angle the needle makes with a line parallel to the ruled lines. Show that the needle touches a ruled line if and only if $y \leq \sin \theta$. Conclude that the probability of the needle touching a ruled line is the probability found in Exercise 15.

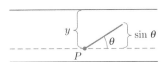

Figure 3

17. The lifetime of a certain TV picture tube is an exponential random variable with an expected value of 5 years. The tube manufacturer sells the tube for $100, but will give a complete refund if the tube burns out within 3 years. Then the revenue that the manufacturer receives on each tube is a discrete random variable Y, with values 100 and 0. Determine the expected revenue per tube.

18. The condenser motor in an air conditioner costs $300 to replace, but a home air conditioning service will guarantee to replace it free when it burns out if you will pay

an annual insurance premium of $25. The life span of the motor is an exponential random variable with an expected life of 10 years. Should you take out the insurance for the first year? [*Hint:* Consider the random variable Y such that $Y = 300$ if the motor burns out during the year and $Y = 0$ otherwise. Compare $E(Y)$ with the cost of 1 year's insurance.]

19. An exponential random variable X has been used to model the relief times (in minutes) of arthritic patients who have taken an analgesic for their pain. Suppose that the density function for X is $f(x) = ke^{-kx}$ and that a certain analgesic provides relief within 4 minutes for 75% of a large group of patients. Then we may estimate that $\Pr(X \leq 4) = .75$. Use this estimate to find an approximate value for k. [*Hint:* First show that $\Pr(X \leq 4) = 1 - e^{-4k}$.]

20. A piece of new equipment has a useful life of X thousand hours, where X is a random variable with the density function $f(x) = .01xe^{-x/10}$, $x \geq 0$. A manufacturer expects the machine to generate $5000 of additional income for every thousand hours of use, but the machine costs $60,000. Should the manufacturer purchase the new equipment? [*Hint:* Compute the expected value of the additional earnings generated by the machine.]

21. Extensive records are kept of the life spans (in months) of a certain product, and a relative frequency histogram is constructed from the data, using areas to represent relative frequencies (as in Fig. 4 in Section 12.1). It turns out that the upper boundary of the relative frequency histogram is approximated closely by the graph of the function

$$f(x) = \frac{1}{8\sqrt{2\pi}} e^{-(1/2)[(x-50)/8]^2}.$$

Determine the probability that the life span of such a product is between 30 and 50 months.

22. A certain machine part has a nominal length of 80 millimeters, with a tolerance of $\pm.05$ millimeter. Suppose that the actual length of the parts supplied is a normal random variable with mean 79.99 millimeters and standard deviation .02 millimeter. How many parts in a lot of 1000 should you expect to lie outside the tolerance limits?

23. The men hired by a certain city police department must be at least 69 inches tall. If the heights of adult men in the city are normally distributed, with $\mu = 70$ inches and $\sigma = 2$ inches, what percentage of the men are tall enough to be eligible for recruitment by the police department?

24. Suppose that the police force in Exercise 23 maintains the same height requirements for women as men and that the heights of women in the city are normally distributed, with $\mu = 65$ inches and $\sigma = 1.6$ inches. What percentage of the women are eligible for recruitment?

25. Let Z be a standard normal random variable. Find the number a such that $\Pr(a \leq Z) = .40$.

26. Scores on a school's entrance exam are normally distributed, with $\mu = 500$ and $\sigma = 100$. If the school wishes to admit only the students in the top 40%, what should be the cutoff grade?

27. It is useful in some applications to know that about 68% of the area under the standard normal curve lies between -1 and 1.
    (a) Verify this statement.
    (b) Let X be a normal random variable with expected value μ and variance σ^2. Compute
    $$\Pr(\mu - \sigma \leq X \leq \mu + \sigma).$$

28. (a) Show that about 95% of the area under the standard normal curve lies between -2 and 2.
    (b) Let X be a normal random variable with expected value μ and variance σ^2. Compute
    $$\Pr(\mu - 2\sigma \leq X \leq \mu + 2\sigma).$$

29. The Chebyshev inequality says that for any random variable X with expected value μ and standard deviation σ,
    $$\Pr(\mu - n\sigma \leq X \leq \mu + n\sigma) \geq 1 - \frac{1}{n^2}.$$
    (a) Take $n = 2$. Apply the Chebyshev inequality to an exponential random variable.
    (b) By integrating, find the exact value of the probability in part (a).

30. Do the same as in Exercise 29 with a normal random variable.

A small volume of blood is selected and examined under a microscope, and the number of white blood cells is counted. Suppose that for healthy people the number of white blood cells in such a specimen is Poisson distributed with $\lambda = 4$.

31. What is the probability that a specimen from a healthy person has exactly four white blood cells?

32. What is the probability that a specimen from a healthy person has eight or more white blood cells?

33. What is the average number of white blood cells per specimen from a healthy person?

A pair of dice is rolled until a 7 or 11 appears, and the number of rolls preceding the final roll is observed. The probability of rolling 7 or 11 is $\frac{2}{9}$.

34. Determine the formula for p_n, the probability of exactly n consecutive rolls preceding the final roll.

35. Determine the average number of consecutive rolls preceding the final roll.

36. What is the probability that at least three consecutive rolls precede the final roll?

APPENDIX

Areas under the Standard Normal Curve

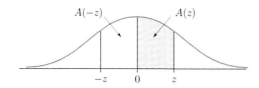

TABLE 1   Areas under the Standard Normal Curve

z	.00	.01	.02	.03	.04	.05	.06	.07	.08	.09
0.0	.0000	.0040	.0080	.0120	.0160	.0199	.0239	.0279	.0319	.0359
0.1	.0398	.0438	.0478	.0517	.0557	.0596	.0636	.0675	.0714	.0754
0.2	.0793	.0832	.0871	.0910	.0948	.0987	.1026	.1064	.1103	.1141
0.3	.1179	.1217	.1255	.1293	.1331	.1368	.1406	.1443	.1480	.1517
0.4	.1554	.1591	.1628	.1664	.1700	.1736	.1772	.1808	.1844	.1879
0.5	.1915	.1950	.1985	.2019	.2054	.2088	.2123	.2157	.2190	.2224
0.6	.2258	.2291	.2324	.2357	.2389	.2422	.2454	.2486	.2518	.2549
0.7	.2580	.2612	.2642	.2673	.2704	.2734	.2764	.2794	.2823	.2852
0.8	.2881	.2910	.2939	.2967	.2996	.3023	.3051	.3078	.3106	.3133
0.9	.3159	.3186	.3212	.3238	.3264	.3289	.3315	.3340	.3365	.3389
1.0	.3413	.3438	.3461	.3485	.3508	.3531	.3554	.3577	.3599	.3621
1.1	.3643	.3665	.3686	.3708	.3729	.3749	.3770	.3790	.3810	.3820
1.2	.3849	.3869	.3888	.3907	.3925	.3944	.3962	.3980	.3997	.4015
1.3	.4032	.4049	.4066	.4082	.4099	.4115	.4131	.4147	.4162	.4177
1.4	.4192	.4207	.4222	.4236	.4251	.4265	.4279	.4292	.4306	.4319
1.5	.4332	.4345	.4357	.4370	.4382	.4394	.4406	.4418	.4429	.4441
1.6	.4452	.4463	.4474	.4484	.4495	.4505	.4515	.4525	.4535	.4545
1.7	.4554	.4564	.4573	.4582	.4591	.4599	.4608	.4616	.4625	.4633
1.8	.4641	.4649	.4656	.4664	.4671	.4678	.4686	.4693	.4699	.4706
1.9	.4713	.4719	.4726	.4732	.4738	.4744	.4750	.4756	.4761	.4767
2.0	.4772	.4778	.4783	.4788	.4793	.4798	.4803	.4808	.4812	.4817
2.1	.4821	.4826	.4830	.4834	.4838	.4842	.4846	.4850	.4854	.4857
2.2	.4861	.4864	.4868	.4871	.4875	.4878	.4881	.4884	.4887	.4890
2.3	.4893	.4896	.4898	.4901	.4904	.4906	.4909	.4911	.4913	.4916
2.4	.4918	.4920	.4922	.4925	.4927	.4929	.4931	.4932	.4934	.4936
2.5	.4938	.4940	.4941	.4943	.4945	.4946	.4948	.4949	.4951	.4952
2.6	.4953	.4955	.4956	.4957	.4959	.4960	.4961	.4962	.4963	.4964
2.7	.4965	.4966	.4967	.4968	.4969	.4970	.4971	.4972	.4973	.4974
2.8	.4974	.4975	.4976	.4977	.4977	.4978	.4979	.4979	.4980	.4981
2.9	.4981	.4982	.4982	.4983	.4984	.4984	.4985	.4985	.4986	.4986
3.0	.4987	.4987	.4987	.4988	.4988	.4989	.4989	.4989	.4990	.4990
3.1	.4990	.4991	.4991	.4991	.4992	.4992	.4992	.4992	.4993	.4993
3.2	.4993	.4993	.4994	.4994	.4994	.4994	.4994	.4995	.4995	.4995
3.3	.4995	.4995	.4995	.4996	.4996	.4996	.4996	.4996	.4996	.4997
3.4	.4997	.4997	.4997	.4997	.4997	.4997	.4997	.4997	.4997	.4998
3.5	.4998	.4998	.4998	.4998	.4998	.4998	.4998	.4998	.4998	.4998

ANSWERS

CHAPTER 0

Exercises 0.1, page 12

1.
−1 0   4

3.
−2 0 $\sqrt{2}$

5.
0   3

7. $[2, 3)$ **9.** $[-1, 0)$

11. $(-\infty, 3)$ **13.** $0, 10, 0, 70$ **15.** $0, 0, -\frac{9}{8}, a^3 + a^2 - a - 1$ **17.** $\frac{1}{3}, 3, \dfrac{a+1}{a+2}$ **19.** $a^2 - 1, a^2 + 2a$

21. (a) 1990 sales   (b) 60   **23.** $x \neq 1, 2$ **25.** $x < 3$ **27.** Function   **29.** Not a function   **31.** Not a function   **33.** 1   **35.** 3   **37.** Positive   **39.** Positive   **41.** $-1, 5, 9$ **43.** .03   **45.** .04   **47.** No

49. Yes   **51.** $(a+1)^3$ **53.** 1, 3, 4   **55.** $\pi, 3, 12$ **57.** $f(x) = \begin{cases} .06x & \text{for } 50 \leq x \leq 300 \\ .02x + 12 & \text{for } 300 < x \leq 600 \\ .015x + 15 & \text{for } 600 < x \end{cases}$

59.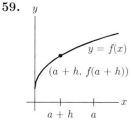

61. You need parentheses $Y_1 = X\hat{\ }(3/4)$

63.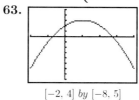
$[-2, 4]$ by $[-8, 5]$

65.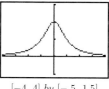
$[-4, 4]$ by $[-.5, 1.5]$

Exercises 0.2, page 20

1.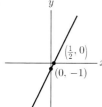

3.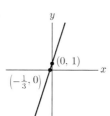

5.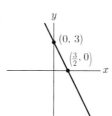

7. $\left(-\frac{1}{3}, 0\right), (0, 3)$ **9.** y-intercept $(0, 5)$

11. $(12, 0), (0, 3)$ **13.** (a) $K = \frac{1}{250}, V = \frac{1}{50}$ (b) $\left(-\dfrac{1}{K}, 0\right), \left(0, \dfrac{1}{V}\right)$ **15.** (a) $58

(b) $f(x) = .20x + 18$ **17.** $300x + 1500$, $x = $ number of days   **19.** The cost for another 5% is $25 million. The cost for the final 5% is 21 times as much.   **21.** $a = 3, b = -4, c = 0$ **23.** $a = -2, b = 3, c = 1$

25. $a = -1, b = 0, c = 1$ **27.**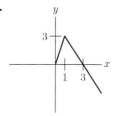

29.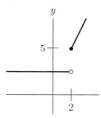

31.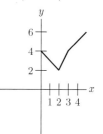

33. 1   **35.** 10^{-2} **37.** 2.5   **39.** $-3985, 3008$ **41.** $-4.60569, 231.499$

Exercises 0.3, page 25

1. $x^2 + 9x + 1$ **3.** $9x^3 + 9x$ **5.** $\dfrac{t^2 + 1}{9t}$ **7.** $\dfrac{3x + 1}{x^2 - x - 6}$ **9.** $\dfrac{4x}{x^2 - 12x + 32}$ **11.** $\dfrac{2x^2 + 5x + 50}{x^2 - 100}$

13. $\dfrac{2x^2 - 2x + 10}{x^2 + 3x - 10}$ **15.** $\dfrac{-x^2 + 5x}{x^2 + 3x - 10}$ **17.** $\dfrac{x^2 + 5x}{-x^2 + 7x - 10}$ **19.** $\dfrac{-x^2 + 3x + 4}{x^2 + 5x - 6}$ **21.** $\dfrac{-x^2 - 3x}{x^2 + 15x + 50}$

23. $\dfrac{5u - 1}{5u + 1}, u \neq 0$ **25.** $\left(\dfrac{x}{1 - x}\right)^6$ **27.** $\left(\dfrac{x}{1 - x}\right)^3 - 5\left(\dfrac{x}{1 - x}\right)^2 + 1$ **29.** $\dfrac{t^3 - 5t^2 + 1}{-t^3 + 5t^2}$ **31.** $2xh + h^2$

33. $4 - 2t - h$ **35.** (a) $C(A(t)) = 3000 + 1600t - 40t^2$ (b) $6040   **37.** $h(x) = x + \dfrac{1}{8}; h(x)$ converts from British sizes to U.S. sizes.   **39.** The graph of $f(x) + c$ is the graph of $f(x)$ shifted up (if $c > 0$) or down (if $c < 0$) by $|c|$ units.   **41.**   **43.** $f(f(x)) = x, x \neq 1$

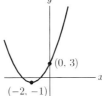

Exercises 0.4, page 32

1. $2, \frac{3}{2}$ **3.** $\frac{3}{2}$ **5.** No zeros   **7.** $1, -\frac{1}{5}$ **9.** $5, 4$ **11.** $2 + \dfrac{\sqrt{6}}{3}, 2 - \dfrac{\sqrt{6}}{3}$ **13.** $(x + 5)(x + 3)$

15. $(x - 4)(x + 4)$ **17.** $3(x + 2)^2$ **19.** $-2(x - 3)(x + 5)$ **21.** $x(3 - x)$ **23.** $-2x(x - \sqrt{3})(x + \sqrt{3})$

25. $(-1, 1), (5, 19)$ **27.** $(-1, 9), (4, 4)$ **29.** $(0, 0), (2, -2)$ **31.** $(0, 5), (2 - \sqrt{3}, 25 - 23\sqrt{3}/2)$,

$(2 + \sqrt{3}, 25 + 23\sqrt{3}/2)$ **33.** $-7, 3$ **35.** $-2, 3$ **37.** -7 **39.** 16,667 and 78,571 subscribers   **41.** $-1, 2$

43. ≈ 4.56 **45.** $\approx (-.41, -1.83), (2.41, 3.83)$ **47.** $\approx (2.14, -25.73), (4.10, -21.80)$

49. $[-5, 22]$ by $[-1400, 100]$ **51.** $[-20, 4]$ by $[-500, 2500]$

Exercises 0.5, page 39

1. 27   **3.** 1   **5.** .0001   **7.** -16 **9.** 4   **11.** .01   **13.** $\frac{1}{6}$ **15.** 100   **17.** 16   **19.** 125   **21.** 1

23. 4   **25.** $\frac{1}{2}$ **27.** 1000   **29.** 10   **31.** 6   **33.** 16   **35.** 18   **37.** $\frac{4}{9}$ **39.** 7   **41.** $x^6 y^6$ **43.** $x^3 y^3$

45. $\dfrac{1}{x^{1/2}}$ **47.** $\dfrac{x^{12}}{y^6}$ **49.** $x^{12} y^{20}$ **51.** $x^2 y^6$ **53.** $16x^4$ **55.** x^2 **57.** $\dfrac{1}{x^7}$ **59.** x **61.** $\dfrac{27x^6}{8y^3}$

63. $2\sqrt{x}$ **65.** $\dfrac{1}{8x^6}$ **67.** $\dfrac{1}{32x^2}$ **69.** $9x^3$ **71.** $x - 1$ **73.** $1 + 6x^{1/2}$ **75.** $a^{1/2} \cdot b^{1/2} = (ab)^{1/2}$ (Law 5)

77. 16   **79.** $\frac{1}{4}$ **81.** 8   **83.** $\frac{1}{32}$ **85.** $709.26   **87.** $127,857.61   **89.** $164.70   **91.** $1592.75

93. $3268.00   **95.** $\frac{500}{256}(256 + 256r + 96r^2 + 16r^3 + r^4) = A$ **97.** $\frac{1}{20}(2x)^2 = \frac{1}{20}(4x^2) = 4(\frac{1}{20}x^2)$

99. .0008103   **101.** .00000823

Exercises 0.6, page 47

1.   **3.**   **5.**   **7.** $P = 8x; 3x^2 = 25$

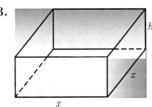

9. $A = \pi r^2; 2\pi r = 15$

11. $V = x^2 h; x^2 + 4xh = 65$

13. $\pi r^2 h = 100; C = 11\pi r^2 + 14\pi rh$ **15.** $2x + 3h = 5000; A = xh$ **17.** $C = 36x + 20h$

19. 75 cm^2 **21.** (a) 38   (b) $40   **23.** (a) 200   (b) 275   (c) 25   **25.** (a) $P(x) = 12x - 800$

(b) $640   (c) $3150   **27.** 270 cents   **29.** A 100-in.^{3} cylinder of radius 3 in. costs $1.62 to construct.

31. $1.08   **33.** $R(30) = 1800$; $C(30) = 1200$ **35.** 40   **37.** $C(1000) = 4000$ **39.** Find the y-coordinate of the point on the graph whose x-coordinate is 400.   **41.** The greatest profit, \$52,500, occurs when 2500 units of goods are produced.   **43.** Find the x-coordinate of the point on the graph whose y-coordinate is 30,000.   **45.** Find $h(3)$. Find the y-coordinate of the point on the graph whose t coordinate is 3.   **47.** Find the maximum value of $h(t)$. Find the y-coordinate of the highest point of the graph.   **49.** Solve $h(t) = 100$. Find the t-coordinates of the points whose y-coordinate is 100.   **51. (a)**

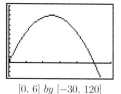

$[0, 6]$ by $[-30, 120]$

(b) 96 feet   **53. (a)**
(c) 1 and 4 seconds
(d) 5 seconds
(e) 2.5 seconds; 100 feet

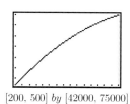

$[200, 500]$ by $[42000, 75000]$
(b) 350 bicycles per year   **(c)** \$68,000   **(d)** \$5000   **(e)** No, revenue would only increase by \$4000.

Chapter 0: Supplementary Exercises, page 51

1. $2, 27\frac{1}{3}, -2, -2\frac{1}{8}, \frac{5\sqrt{2}}{2}$ **3.** $a^2 - 4a + 2$ **5.** $x \neq 0, -3$ **7.** All x **9.** Yes   **11.** $5x(x-1)(x+4)$

13. $(-1)(x-6)(x+3)$ **15.** $-\frac{2}{5}, 1$ **17.** $\left(\dfrac{5+3\sqrt{5}}{10}, \dfrac{3\sqrt{5}}{5}\right), \left(\dfrac{5-3\sqrt{5}}{10}, -\dfrac{3\sqrt{5}}{5}\right)$ **19.** $x^2 + x - 1$

21. $x^{5/2} - 2x^{3/2}$ **23.** $x^{3/2} - 2x^{1/2}$ **25.** $\dfrac{x^2 - x + 1}{x^2 - 1}$ **27.** $-\dfrac{3x^2 + 1}{3x^2 + 4x + 1}$ **29.** $\dfrac{-3x^2 + 9x - 10}{3x^2 - 5x - 8}$

31. $\dfrac{1}{x^4} - \dfrac{2}{x^2} + 4$ **33.** $(\sqrt{x} - 1)^2$ **35.** $\dfrac{1}{(\sqrt{x}-1)^2} - \dfrac{2}{\sqrt{x}-1} + 4$ **37.** $27, 32, 4$ **39.** $301 + 10t + .04t^2$

41. $x^2 + 2x + 1$ **43.** x

CHAPTER 1

Exercises 1.1, page 63

1. $m = -7, b = 3$ **3.** $m = \frac{1}{2}, b = \frac{3}{2}$ **5.** $m = \frac{1}{7}, b = -5$ **7.** $y - 1 = -(x - 7)$ **9.** $y - 1 = \frac{1}{2}(x - 2)$

11. $y - 5 = \frac{63}{10}(x - \frac{5}{7})$ **13.** $y = 0$ **15.** $y = 9$ **17.** $-\dfrac{x}{\pi} + y = 1$ or $y = \dfrac{x}{\pi} + 1$ **19.** $y = -2x - 4$

21. $y = x - 2$ **23.** $y = 3x - 6$ **25.** $y = x - 2$ **27.** Start at $(1,0)$. To get back to the line, move one unit to the right and then one unit up.   **29.** Start at $(1, -1)$. To get back to the line, move

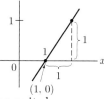

(1, 0)

three units to the right and then one unit down.   **31. (a)** C   **(b)** B

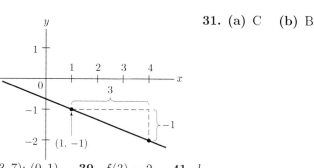

(c) D   (d) A   **33.** 1   **35.** $-\frac{3}{4}$ **37.** $(2, 5); (3, 7); (0, 1)$ **39.** $f(3) = 2$ **41.** l_1

43.

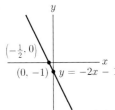

45. $a = 2$, $f(2) = 2$ **47. (a)** $C(10) = 1220$ dollars   **(b)** Marginal cost is 12

dollars per item.   **(c)** $C(11) - C(10)$ = marginal cost = \$12   **49.** $P(x) = .06x + 4.89$ dollars, where $P(x)$ is the price of one gallon x months since January 1st. Price of one gallon on April 1st is $P(3) = \$5.07$. Price of 15 gallons is \$76.05. Price of one gallon on September 1st is $P(8) = \$5.37$. Price of 15 gallons is \$80.55.
51. $C(x) = .03x + 5$ **53.** $G(x) = -\frac{5000}{3}x + \frac{25,000}{3}$, $G(4.35) \approx 1083.3$ gallons   **55. (a)** $C(x) = 7x + 1500$.
(b) Marginal cost is \$7 per rod.   **(c)** \$7   **57.** If the monopolist wants to sell one more unit of goods, then the price per unit must be lowered by 2 ¢. No one is willing to pay \$7 or more for a unit of goods.   **59.** Let $A(x)$ be the amount in ml of the drug in the blood after x minutes, then $A(x) = 6x + 1.5$.
65. (a) $y = .38x + 39.5$ **(b)**   **(c)** Every year, .38% more of the world becomes urban.

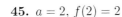

$[0, 30]$ by $[30, 60]$

(d) 43.3%   **(e)** 2007   **(f)** 1.9%

Exercises 1.2, page 70

1. $-\frac{4}{3}$ **3.** 1   **5.** Small positive slope   **7.** Zero slope   **9.** Zero slope   **11.** Approximately \$22. The price was rising on both days.   **13.** \$104.50; $m \approx \dfrac{107 - 104.50}{2} = 1.25$ dollars/day   **15.** The slope of the tangent line is approximately 1/2. Thus the federal debt rose at the rate of .5 trillion dollars per year in 1990.

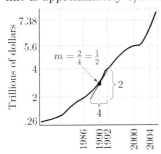

17. (a) The debt per capita was approximately \$1000 in 1950, \$15,000 in 1990, \$21,000 in 2000, and \$24,000 in 2004.

(b) The slope of the tangent line is 0. Thus, in 2000, the debt per capita held steady (at about \$21,000)

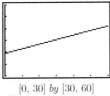

19. -1; $y - .16 = -1(x + .5)$ **21.** $\frac{2}{3}$; $y - \frac{1}{9} = \frac{2}{3}(x - \frac{1}{3})$

23. $y - 6.25 = 5(x - 2.5)$ **25.** $(\frac{7}{4}, \frac{49}{16})$ **27.** $(-\frac{1}{3}, \frac{1}{9})$ **29.** 12   **31.** $\frac{3}{4}$ **33.** $a = 1$, $f(1) = 1$, slope is 2
35. $\left(\dfrac{1}{\sqrt{2}}, \dfrac{1}{2\sqrt{2}}\right), \left(-\dfrac{1}{\sqrt{2}}, -\dfrac{1}{2\sqrt{2}}\right)$ **37. (a)** 3, 9   **(b)** increase   **39.** -3 **41.** Approximately .35.

Exercises 1.3, page 80

1. 3 **3.** $\frac{3}{4}$ **5.** $7x^6$ **7.** $\frac{2}{3}x^{-1/3} = \dfrac{2}{3\sqrt[3]{x}}$ **9.** $f(x) = x^{-5/2}$; $f'(x) = -\frac{5}{2}x^{-7/2}$ **11.** $\frac{1}{3}x^{-2/3}$

13. $f(x) = x^2$; $f'(x) = 2x$ **15.** 0 **17.** $\frac{3}{4}$ **19.** $-\frac{9}{4}$ **21.** 1 **23.** 2 **25.** 32 **27.** $f(-5) = -125$, $f'(-5) = 75$ **29.** $f(8) = 2$, $f'(8) = \frac{1}{12}$ **31.** $f(-2) = -\frac{1}{32}$, $f'(-2) = -\frac{5}{64}$ **33.** $y - 8 = 12(x + 2)$ **35.** $y = 3x + 1$ **37.** $y - \frac{1}{3} = \frac{3}{2}(x - \frac{1}{9})$ **39.** $y - 1 = -\frac{1}{2}(x - 1)$ **41.** $f(x) = x^4$, $f'(x) = 4x^3$, $f(1) = 1$, $f'(1) = 4$, then (6) (with $a = 1$) becomes $y - 1 = 4(x - 1)$, which is the given equation of the tangent line. **43.** $P = (\frac{1}{16}, \frac{1}{4})$, $b = \frac{1}{8}$. **45. (a)** $(16, 4)$ **(b)** **47.** No, such a point would have to

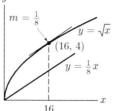

have an x-coordinate satisfying $3x^2 = -1$, which has no real solutions. **49.** $8x^7$ **51.** $\frac{3}{4}x^{-1/4}$ **53.** 0 **55.** $\frac{1}{5}x^{-4/5}$ **57.** $4, \frac{1}{3}$ **59.** $a = 4$, $b = 1$ **61.** 1, 1.5; 2 **63.** $y - 5 = \frac{1}{2}(x - 4)$ **65.** $4x + 2h$ **67.** $-2x + 2 - h$ **69.** $3x^2 + 3xh + h^2$ **71.** $f'(x) = -2x$ **73.** $f'(x) = 14x + 1$ **75.** $f'(x) = 3x^2$ **77. (a)** and **(b) (c)** Parallel lines have equal slopes: Slope of the graph of $y = f(x)$ at the point $(x, f(x))$ is equal to the slope of the graph of $y = f(x) + 3$ at the point $(x, f(x) + 3)$, which implies the given equation **79.** .69315 **81.** .70711 **83.** .11111 **85.**

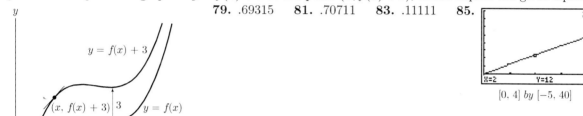

$[0, 4]$ by $[-5, 40]$

87. $y = \dfrac{x}{6} + \dfrac{3}{2}$ **89.** $y = -16x + 12$ **91.** 2 **93.** 4

Exercises 1.4, page 91

1. No limit **3.** 1 **5.** No limit **7.** -5 **9.** 5 **11.** No limit **13.** 288 **15.** 0 **17.** 3 **19.** -4 **21.** -8 **23.** $\frac{6}{7}$ **25.** No limit **27. (a)** 0 **(b)** $-\frac{3}{2}$ **(c)** $-\frac{1}{4}$ **(d)** -1 **29.** 6 **31.** 3

33. Step 1: $\dfrac{f(x+h) - f(x)}{h} = \dfrac{(x+h)^2 + 1 - (x^2 + 1)}{h}$ Step 2: $\dfrac{f(x+h) - f(x)}{h} = 2x + h$ Step 3: $f'(x) = 2x$.

35. Step 1: $\dfrac{f(x+h) - f(x)}{h} = \dfrac{(x+h)^3 - 1 - (x^3 - 1)}{h}$ Step 2: $\dfrac{f(x+h) - f(x)}{h} = 3x^2 + 3xh + h^2$

Step 3: $f'(x) = 3x^2$. **37.** Steps 1, 2: $\dfrac{f(3+h) - f(3)}{h} = 3$. Step 3: $f'(x) = \lim\limits_{h \to 0} 3 = 3$.

39. Steps 1, 2: $\dfrac{f(x+h) - f(x)}{h} = 1 + \dfrac{-1}{x(x+h)}$. Step 3: $f'(x) = \lim\limits_{h \to 0} 1 + \dfrac{-1}{x(x+h)} = 1 - \dfrac{1}{x^2}$.

41. Steps 1, 2: $\dfrac{f(x+h) - f(x)}{h} = \dfrac{1}{(x+1)(x+h+1)}$.

Step 3: $f'(x) = \lim\limits_{h \to 0} \dfrac{1}{(x+1)(x+h+1)} = \dfrac{1}{(x+1)^2}$.

43. Steps 1, 2: $\dfrac{f(x+h) - f(x)}{h} = \dfrac{-2x - h}{((x+h)^2 + 1)(x^2 + 1)}$.

Step 3: $f'(x) = \lim\limits_{h \to 0} \dfrac{-2x - h}{((x+h)^2 + 1)(x^2 + 1)} = \dfrac{-2x}{(x^2 + 1)^2}$.

45. Steps 1, 2: $\dfrac{f(x+h) - f(x)}{h} = \dfrac{1}{\sqrt{x+h+2} + \sqrt{x+2}}$.

Step 3: $f'(x) = \lim\limits_{h \to 0} \dfrac{1}{\sqrt{x+h+2} + \sqrt{x+2}} = \dfrac{1}{2\sqrt{x+2}}$.

47. Steps 1, 2: $\dfrac{f(x+h) - f(x)}{h} = \dfrac{-1}{\sqrt{x}\sqrt{x+h}(\sqrt{x} + \sqrt{x+h})}$.

Step 3: $f'(x) = \lim\limits_{h \to 0} \dfrac{-1}{\sqrt{x}\sqrt{x+h}(\sqrt{x} + \sqrt{x+h})} = \dfrac{-1}{2x\sqrt{x}} = \dfrac{-1}{2x^{3/2}}$. **49.** $f(x) = x^2; a = 1$

51. $f(x) = \dfrac{1}{x}; a = 10$ **53.** $f(x) = \sqrt{x}; a = 9$ **55.** Take $f(x) = x^2$, then the given limit is $f'(2) = 4$.

57. Take $f(x) = \sqrt{x}$, then the given limit is $f'(2) = \dfrac{1}{2\sqrt{2}}$.   **59.** Take $f(x) = x^{1/3}$, then the given limit is

$f'(8) = \frac{1}{12}$.   **61.** 0   **63.** 0   **65.** 0   **67.** $\frac{3}{4}$ **69.** 0   **71.** 0   **73.** 0   **75.** .5

Exercises 1.5, page 98

1. No   **3.** Yes   **5.** No   **7.** No   **9.** Yes   **11.** No   **13.** Continuous, differentiable   **15.** Continuous, not differentiable   **17.** Continuous, not differentiable   **19.** Not continuous, not differentiable   **21.** $f(5) = 3$

23. Not possible   **25.** $f(0) = 12$ **27. (a)** $T(x) = \begin{cases} .15x & \text{for } 0 < x \le 27{,}050 \\ .275x - 3381.25 & \text{for } 27{,}050 < x \le 65{,}550 \\ .305x - 5347.75 & \text{for } 65{,}550 < x \le 136{,}750 \end{cases}$

(c) $T(65{,}550) - T(27{,}050) = 10{,}587.5$ dollars

(b)

Taxable income in dollars

29. (a) $R(x) = \begin{cases} .07x + 2.5 & \text{for } 0 \le x \le 100 \\ .04x + 5.5 & \text{for } 100 < x \end{cases}$ **(b)** $P(x) = \begin{cases} .04x + 2.5 & \text{for } 0 \le x \le 100 \\ .01x + 5.5 & \text{for } 100 < x \end{cases}$ **31. (a)** 3

thousand dollars per hour   **(b)** 3 thousand dollars per hour, between 8 A.M and 10 A.M   **33.** $a = 1$

Exercises 1.6, page 106

1. $3x^2 + 2x$ **3.** $2(\frac{1}{2})x^{-1/2}$ or $\dfrac{1}{\sqrt{x}}$ **5.** $\dfrac{1}{2} - 2(-1)x^{-2}$ or $\dfrac{1}{2} + \dfrac{2}{x^2}$ **7.** $4x^3 + 3x^2 + 1$ **9.** $3(2x+4)^2(2)$ or

$6(2x+4)^2$ **11.** $7(x^3 + x^2 + 1)^6(3x^2 + 2x)$ **13.** $-\dfrac{8}{x^3}$ **15.** $3(\frac{1}{3})(2x^2 + 1)^{-\frac{2}{3}}(4x)$ or $4x(2x^2 + 1)^{-\frac{2}{3}}$

17. $2 + 3(x+2)^2$ **19.** $\frac{1}{5}(-5)x^{-6}$ or $-\dfrac{1}{x^6}$ **21.** $(-1)(x^3 + 1)^{-2}(3x^2)$ or $-\dfrac{3x^2}{(x^3 + 1)^2}$ **23.** $1 - (x+1)^{-2}$

25. $\dfrac{45x^2 + 5}{2\sqrt{3x^3 + x}}$ **27.** 3   **29.** $\frac{1}{2}(1 + x + x^2)^{-\frac{1}{2}}(1 + 2x)$ **31.** $10(1 - 5x)^{-2}$

33. $-45(1 + x + \sqrt{x})^{-2}(1 + \frac{1}{2}x^{-\frac{1}{2}})$ **35.** $1 + \frac{1}{2}(x+1)^{-\frac{1}{2}}$ **37.** $\dfrac{3}{2}\left(\dfrac{\sqrt{x}}{2} + 1\right)^{1/2}\left(\dfrac{1}{4}x^{-1/2}\right)$ or

$\dfrac{3}{8\sqrt{x}}\left(\dfrac{\sqrt{x}}{2} + 1\right)^{1/2}$ **39.** 4   **41.** 15   **43.** $f'(4) = 48, y = 48x - 191$

45. (a) $y' = 2(3x^2 + x - 2) \cdot (6x + 1) = 36x^3 + 18x^2 - 22x - 4$ **(b)** $y = 9x^4 + 6x^3 - 11x^2 - 4x + 4$, $y' = 36x^3 + 18x^2 - 22x - 4$ **47.** 4.8; 1.8   **49.** 14; 11   **51.** 10; $\frac{15}{4}$ **53.** $(5, \frac{161}{3})$; $(3, 49)$ **55.** $f(4) = 5$, $f'(4) = \frac{1}{2}$ **57. (a)** $S(1) = 120.560$, $S'(1) = 1.5$.   **(b)** $S(3) = 80$, $S'(3) = -6$.
59. (a) $S(10) = \frac{372}{121} \approx 3.074$ thousand dollars, $S'(10) = -\frac{18}{11^3} \approx -.014$ thousand dollars per day.
(b) $S(11) \approx S(10) + S'(10) \approx 3.061$ thousand dollars. $S(11) = \frac{49}{16} = 3.0625$ thousand dollars.
61. (a) $A(8) = 12$, $A'(8) = .5$.   **(b)** $A(9) \approx A(8) + A'(8) = 12.5$. If the company spends $9000, it should expect to sell 12,500 computers.   **63. (a)** $D(4) \approx 5.583$ trillion dollars, $D'(4) = .082$ or 82 billion dollars per year.

Exercises 1.7, page 114

1. $10t(t^2 + 1)^4$ **3.** $8t + \frac{11}{2}t^{-\frac{1}{2}}$ **5.** $5T^4 - 16T^3 + 6T - 1$ **7.** $6P - \frac{1}{2}$ **9.** $2a^2t + b^2$ **11.** $y' = 1, y'' = 0$
13. $y' = \frac{1}{2}x^{-1/2}, y'' = -\frac{1}{4}x^{-3/2}$ **15.** $y' = \frac{1}{2}(x+1)^{-\frac{1}{2}}, y'' = -\frac{1}{4}(x+1)^{-\frac{3}{2}}$ **17.** $f'(r) = 2\pi r, f''(r) = 2\pi$
19. $f'(P) = 15(3P+1)^4, f''(P) = 180(3P+1)^3$ **21.** 36   **23.** 0   **25.** 34   **27.** $f'(1) = -\frac{1}{9}, f''(1) = \frac{2}{27}$
29. 0   **31.** 20   **33. (a)** $f'''(x) = 60x^2 - 24x$ **(b)** $f'''(x) = \dfrac{15}{2\sqrt{x}}$ **35. (a)** $2Tx + 3P$ **(b)** $3x$
(c) $x^2 + 2T$ **37.** When 50 bicycles are manufactured, the cost is $5000. For every additional bicycle manufactured, there is an additional cost of $45.   **39. (a)** 2.60 dollars per unit   **(b)** 100 or 200 more units
41. (a) $R(12) = 22, R'(12) = .075$ **(b)** $P(x) = R(x) - C(x)$ so $P'(x) = R'(x) - C'(x)$. When 1200 chips are produced, the marginal profit is $.75 - 1.5 = -.75$ dollars per chip.   **43.**

$[-4, 4]$ by $[-2, 2]$

Exercises 1.8, page 122

1. (a) 12; 10; 8.4   **(b)** 8   **3. (a)** 14   **(b)** 13   **5. (a)** $-\frac{7}{4}$ **(b)** $\frac{5}{6}$ **(c)** January 1, 1980   **7. (a)** 28 km/hour   **(b)** 96 km   **(c)** $\frac{1}{2}$hr   **9.** 63 units/hour   **11. (a)** $v(3) = -12$ ft/sec and $v(6) = 24$ ft/sec.
(b) When $t > 5$ or when $0 \le t < 2$.   **(c)** 131 ft.   **13. (a)** 160 ft/sec   **(b)** 96 ft/sec   **(c)** -32 ft/sec^2
(d) 10 sec   **(e)** -160 ft/sec   **15.** A–b; B–d; C–f; D–e; E–a; F–c; G–g   **17. (a)** 15 ft/sec   **(b)** No; positive velocity indicates the object is moving away from the reference point   **(c)** 5 ft/sec   **19. (a)** 5010
(b) 5005   **(c)** 4990   **(d)** 4980   **(e)** 4997.5   **21.** Four minutes after it has been poured, the coffee is 120°. At that time, its temperature is decreasing by 5°/min; 119.5°   **23.** When the price of a car is $10,000, 200,000 cars are sold. At that price, the number of cars sold decreases by 3 for each dollar increase in price.
25. When the price is set at $1200, 60,000 computers are sold. For every $100 increase in price, the sales decrease by 2000 computers. 59,000 computers.   **27.** The profit from manufacturing and selling 100 luxury cars is $90,000. Each additional car made and sold creates an additional profit of $1200; $88,800
29. (a) $C'(5) = 74$ thousand dollars per unit   **(b)** $C(5.25) \approx C(5) + C'(5)(.25) = 256.5$ thousand dollars
(c) $x = 4$ **(d)** $C'(4) = 62, R'(4) = 29$. If the production is increased by one unit, cost will rise by $62,000 and revenue will increase by $29,000. The company should not increase production beyond the break-even point.
31. (a) $500 billion   **(b)** $50 billion/yr   **(c)** 1994   **(d)** 1994

33. (a)

$y = f(t)$

$y = f'(t)$

$[.5, 6]$ by $[-3, 3]$

(b) .85 sec   **(c)** 5 days   **(d)** $-.05$ sec/day   **(e)** 3 days

Chapter 1: Supplementary Exercises, page 127

1.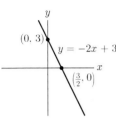
$y = -2x + 3$
$(0, 3)$
$(\frac{3}{2}, 0)$

3.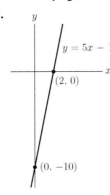
$y = 5x - 10$
$(2, 0)$
$(0, -10)$

5.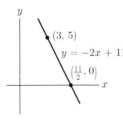
$(3, 5)$
$y = -2x + 11$
$(\frac{11}{2}, 0)$

7.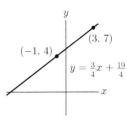
$(3, 7)$
$(-1, 4)$
$y = \frac{3}{4}x + \frac{19}{4}$

9.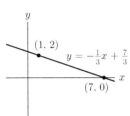
$(1, 2)$
$y = -\frac{1}{3}x + \frac{7}{3}$
$(7, 0)$

11.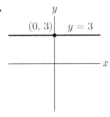
$(0, 3)$ $y = 3$

13.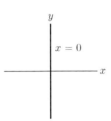
$x = 0$

15. $7x^6 + 3x^2$ **17.** $\dfrac{3}{\sqrt{x}}$

19. $-\dfrac{3}{x^2}$ **21.** $48x(3x^2 - 1)^7$ **23.** $-\dfrac{5}{(5x - 1)^2}$ **25.** $\dfrac{x}{\sqrt{x^2 + 1}}$ **27.** $-\dfrac{1}{4x^{5/4}}$ **29.** 0

31. $10[x^5 - (x - 1)^5]^9[5x^4 - 5(x - 1)^4]$ **33.** $\dfrac{3}{2}t^{-1/2} + \dfrac{3}{2}t^{-3/2}$ **35.** $\dfrac{2(9t^2 - 1)}{(t - 3t^3)^2}$ **37.** $\dfrac{9}{4}x^{1/2} - 4x^{-1/3}$

39. 28 **41.** $14; 3$ **43.** $\frac{15}{2}$ **45.** 33 **47.** $4x^3 - 4x$ **49.** $-\frac{3}{2}(1 - 3P)^{-1/2}$ **51.** 29 **53.** $300(5x + 1)^2$

55. -2 **57.** $3x^{-1/2}$ **59.** Slope -4; tangent $y = -4x + 6$ **61.** 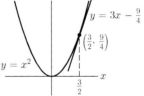   **63.** $y = 2$

$y = 3x - \frac{9}{4}$
$(\frac{3}{2}, \frac{9}{4})$
$y = x^2$
$\frac{3}{2}$

65. $f(2) = 3, f'(2) = -1$ **67.** 96 ft/s   **69.** 11 ft   **71.** $\frac{5}{3}$ ft/s   **73.** (a) \$16.10   (b) \$16   **75.** $\frac{3}{4}$in.
77. 4 **79.** Does not exist   **81.** $-\frac{1}{50}$ **83.** The slope of a secant line at $(3, 9)$

CHAPTER 2

Exercises 2.1, page 138

1. (a), (e), (f)   **3.** (b), (c), (d)   **5.** Increasing for $x < \frac{1}{2}$, relative maximum point at $x = \frac{1}{2}$, maximum value $= 1$, decreasing for $x > \frac{1}{2}$, concave down, y-intercept $(0, 0)$, x- intercepts $(0, 0)$ and $(1, 0)$.   **7.** Decreasing for $x < 0$, relative minimum point at $x = 0$, relative minimum value $= 2$, increasing for $0 < x < 2$, relative maximum point at $x = 2$, relative maximum value $= 4$, decreasing for $x > 2$, concave up for $x < 1$, concave down for $x > 1$, inflection point at $(1, 3)$, y-intercept $(0, 2)$, x-intercept $(3.6, 0)$ **9.** Decreasing for $x < 2$, relative minimum at $x = 2$, minimum value $=3$, increasing for $x > 2$, concave up for all x, no inflection point, defined for $x > 0$, the line $y = x$ is an asymptote, the y-axis is an asymptote   **11.** Decreasing for $1 \leq x < 3.2$, relative minimum point at $x = 3.2$, increasing for $x > 3.2$, maximum value $= 6$ (at $x = 1$), minimum value $= .9$ (at $x = 3.2$), inflection point at $x = 4$, concave up for $1 \leq x < 4$, concave down for $x > 4$, the line $y = 4$ is an asymptote.   **13.** Slope decreases for all x.   **15.** Slope decreases for $x < 1$, increases for $x > 1$. Minimum slope occurs at $x = 1$.

17. (a) C, F (b) A, B, F (c) C **19.** 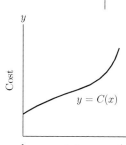   **21.**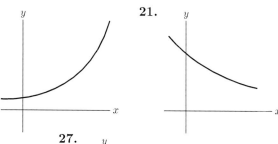

23. 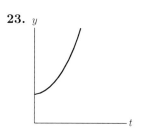   **25.** 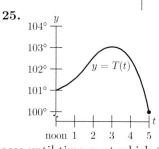   **27.**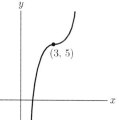

29. Oxygen content decreases until time a, at which time it reaches a minimum. After a, oxygen content steadily increases. The rate of increase increases until b, and then decreases. Time b is the time when oxygen content is increasing fastest.   **31.** 1960   **33.** The parachutist's speed levels off to 15 ft/sec

35. 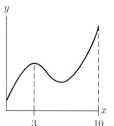   **37.** 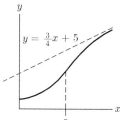   **39.** (a) Yes (b) Yes   **41.** Relatively low

43. $x = 2$ **45.** $\frac{1}{6}$ unit apart

Exercises 2.2, page 147

1. (e)   **3.** (a), (b), (d), (e)   **5.** (d)   **7.** 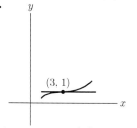   **9.**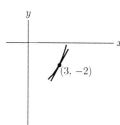

11. 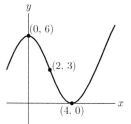   **13.** 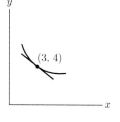   **15.** 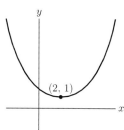   **17.**

19.

	f	f'	f''
A	POS	POS	NEG
B	0	NEG	0
C	NEG	0	POS

21. $t = 1$ **23.** (a) decreasing   (b) The function $f(x)$ is increasing for $1 \le x < 2$ because the values of $f'(x)$ are positive. The function $f(x)$ is decreasing for $2 < x \le 3$ because the values of $f'(x)$ are negative. Therefore, $f(x)$ has a relative maximum at $x = 2$. Coordinates: $(2, 9)$ **(c)** The function $f(x)$ is decreasing for $9 \le x < 10$ because the values of $f'(x)$ are negative. The function $f(x)$ is increasing for $10 < x \le 11$ because the values of $f'(x)$ are positive. Therefore, $f(x)$ has a relative minimum at $x = 10$.   **(d)** concave down   **(e)** at $x = 6$; coordinates: $(6, 5)$ **(f)** $x = 15$ **25.** The slope is positive because $f'(6) = 2$, a positive number.   **27.** The slope is 0 because $f'(3) = 0$. Also, $f'(x)$ is positive for x slightly less than 3, and $f'(x)$ is negative for x slightly greater than 3. Hence $f(x)$ changes from increasing to decreasing at $x = 3$.   **29.** $f'(x)$ is increasing at $x = 0$, so the graph of $f(x)$ is concave up.   **31.** At $x = 1$, $f'(x)$ changes from increasing to decreasing, so the concavity of the graph of $f(x)$ changes from concave up to concave down.   **33.** $y - 3 = 2(x - 6)$ **35.** 3.25   **37. (a)** $\frac{1}{6}$ in.   **(b)** (ii), because the water level is falling.   **39.** II   **41.** I   **43. (a)** 2 million   **(b)** 30,000 farms per year   **(c)** 1940   **(d)** 1945 and 1978   **(e)** 1960   **45.** rel. max: $x \approx -2.34$; rel. min: $x \approx 2.34$; inflection point: $x = 0, x \approx \pm 1.41$

Exercises 2.3, page 159

1. $f'(x) = 3(x+3)(x-3)$; relative maximum point $(-3, 54)$; relative minimum point $(3, -54)$.

Critical Values		−3		3	
	$x < -3$		$-3 < x < 3$		$3 < x$
$3(x+3)$	−	0	+		+
$x - 3$	−		−	0	+
$f'(x)$	+	0	−	0	+
$f(x)$	Increasing on $(-\infty, -3)$	54	Decreasing on $(-3, 3)$	−54	Increasing on $(3, \infty)$

Local maximum $(-3, 54)$ Local minimum $(3, -54)$

3. $f'(x) = -3(x-1)(x-3)$; relative maximum point $(3, 1)$; relative minimum point $(1, -3)$.

Critical Values		1		3	
	$x < 1$		$1 < x < 3$		$3 < x$
$-3(x-1)$	+	0	−		−
$x - 3$	−		−	0	+
$f'(x)$	−	0	+	0	−
$f(x)$	Decreasing on $(-\infty, 1)$	−3	Increasing on $(1, 3)$	1	Decreasing on $(3, \infty)$

Local minimum $(1, -3)$ Local maximum $(3, 1)$

5. $f'(x) = x(x-2)$; relative maximum point $(0, 1)$; relative minimum point $(2, -1/3)$.

Critical Values		0		2	
	$x < 0$		$0 < x < 2$		$2 < x$
x	−	0	+		+
$x - 2$	−		−	0	+
$f'(x)$	+	0	−	0	+
$f(x)$	Increasing on $(-\infty, 0)$	1	Decreasing on $(0, 2)$	−1/3	Increasing on $(2, \infty)$

Local maximum $(0, 1)$ Local minimum $(2, -1/3)$

7. $f'(x) = -3x(x+8)$; relative maximum point $(0, -2)$; relative minimum point $(-8, -258)$.

Critical Values	$x < -8$	-8	$-8 < x < 0$	0	$0 < x$
$x + 8$	$-$	0	$+$		$+$
$-3x$	$+$		$+$	0	$-$
$f'(x)$	$-$	0	$+$	0	$-$
$f(x)$	Decreasing on $(-\infty, -8)$	-258	Increasing on $(-8, 0)$	-2	Decreasing on $(0, \infty)$

Local minimum $(-8, -258)$ Local maximum $(0, -2)$

9.
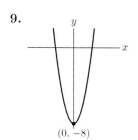
$(0, -8)$

11.
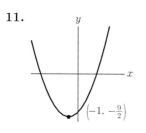
$\left(-1, -\frac{9}{2}\right)$

13.
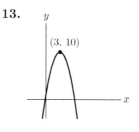
$(3, 10)$

15.
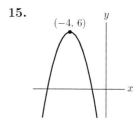
$(-4, 6)$

17.
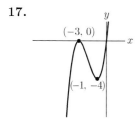
$(-3, 0)$
$(-1, -4)$

19.
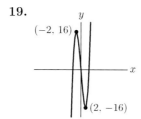
$(-2, 16)$
$(2, -16)$

21.
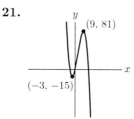
$(9, 81)$
$(-3, -15)$

23.
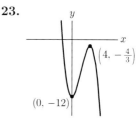
$\left(4, -\frac{4}{3}\right)$
$(0, -12)$

25.
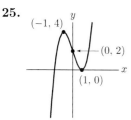
$(-1, 4)$
$(0, 2)$
$(1, 0)$

27.
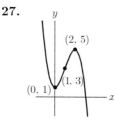
$(2, 5)$
$(1, 3)$
$(0, 1)$

29.
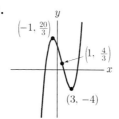
$\left(-1, \frac{20}{3}\right)$
$\left(1, \frac{4}{3}\right)$
$(3, -4)$

31.
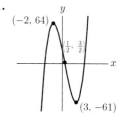
$(-2, 64)$
$\left(\frac{1}{2}, \frac{3}{2}\right)$
$(3, -61)$

33. No, $f''(x) = 2a \neq 0$ **35.** $(4, 3)$ min   **37.** $(1, 5)$ max   **39.** $(-.1, -3.05)$ min   **41.** $f'(x) = g'(x)$
43. (a) f has a relative minimum **(b)** f has an inflection point   **45. (a)** $A(x) = -893.103x + 460.759$ (billion dollars).   **(b)** Revenue is $x\%$ of assets or $R(x) = \frac{xA(x)}{100} = \frac{x}{100}(-893.103x + 460.759)$. $R(.3) \approx .578,484$ billion dollars or 578.484 million dollars; $R(.1) \approx .371, 449$ billion dollars or 371.449 million dollars.   **(c)** Maximum revenue when $R'(x) = 0$ or $x \approx .258$. Maximum revenue $R(.258) \approx .594,273$ or 594.273 million dollars.
47. $f'(x)$ is always nonnegative.   **49.** They both have a minimum point. The parabola does not have a vertical asymptote.

Exercises 2.4, page 165

1. $\left(\dfrac{3 \pm \sqrt{5}}{2}, 0\right)$ **3.** $(-2, 0)$, $\left(-\frac{1}{2}, 0\right)$ **5.** $\left(\frac{1}{2}, 0\right)$ **7.** The derivative $x^2 - 4x + 5$ has no zeros. No relative extreme points.

9.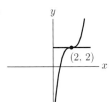

(2, 2)

11.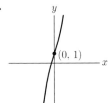

(0, 1)

13.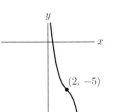

(2, −5)

15.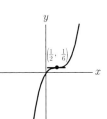

$\left(\frac{1}{2}, \frac{1}{6}\right)$

17.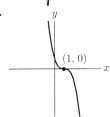

(1, 0)

19.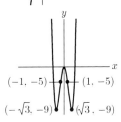

(−1, −5) (1, −5)

$(-\sqrt{3}, -9)$ $(\sqrt{3}, -9)$

21.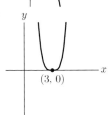

(3, 0)

23.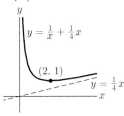

$y = \frac{1}{x} + \frac{1}{4}x$

(2, 1)

$y = \frac{1}{4}x$

25.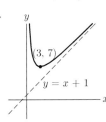

(3, 7)

$y = x + 1$

27.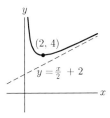

(2, 4)

$y = \frac{x}{2} + 2$

29.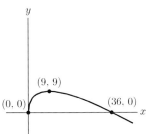

(9, 9)

(0, 0)   (36, 0)

31. $g(x) = f'(x)$

33. $f(2) = 0$ implies $4a + 2b + c = 0$. Local maximum at $(0, 1)$ implies $f'(0) = 0$ and $f(0) = 1$. $a = -1/4$, $b = 0$, $c = 1$, $f(x) = -1/4x^2 + 1$.   **35.** If $f'(a) = 0$ and f' is increasing at $x = a$, then $f'(x) < 0$ for $x < a$ and $f'(x) > 0$ for $x > a$. By the first derivative test (case (b)), f has a local minimum at $x = a$.

37. (a)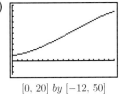

$[0, 20]$ by $[-12, 50]$

(b) 15.0 g   **(c)** after 12.0 days   **(d)** 1.6 g/day
(e) after 6.0 days and after 17.6 days   **(f)** after 11.8 days

Exercises 2.5, page 172

1. 20   **3.** $t = 4$, $f(4) = 8$ **5.** $x = 1, y = 1$, maximum $= 1$ **7.** $x = 3, y = 3$, minimum $= 18$
9. $x = 6, y = 6$, minimum $= 12$ **11. (a)** Objective: $A = xy$, constraint: $8x + 4y = 320$
(b) $A = -2x^2 + 80x$ **(c)** $x = 20$ ft, $y = 40$ ft   **13. (a)**   **(b)** $h + 4x$ **(c)** Objective:

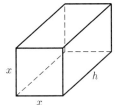

$V = x^2h$; constraint: $h + 4x = 84$ **(d)** $V = -4x^3 + 84x^2$ **(e)** $x = 14$ in., $h = 28$ in   **15.** Let x be the length of the fence and y the other dimension. Objective: $C = 15x + 20y$; constraint: $xy = 75$; $x = 10$ ft, $y = 7.5$ ft   **17.** Let x be the length of each edge of the base and h the height. Objective: $A = 2x^2 + 4xh$; constraint: $x^2h = 8000$; 20 cm by 20 cm by 20 cm   **19.** Let x be the length of the fence parallel to the river and y the length of each section perpendicular to the river. Objective: $A = xy$; constraint: $6x + 15y = 1500$; $x = 125$ ft, $y = 50$ ft   **21.** Objective: $P = xy$; constraint: $x + y = 100$; $x = 50, y = 50$

23. Objective: $A = \dfrac{\pi x^2}{2} + 2xh$; constraint: $(2 + \pi)x + 2h = 14$; $x = \dfrac{14}{4 + \pi}$ ft

25. $w = 20$ ft, $x = 10$ ft

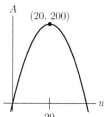

A
$(20, 200)$
w
20

27. (a) $C(x) = 6x + 10\sqrt{(20 - x)^2 + 24^2}$;

$C'(x) = 6 - \dfrac{10(20 - x)}{\sqrt{(20 - x)^2 + 24^2}}$; $C'(x) = 0$ $(0 \leq x \leq 20)$ implies $x = 2$. Use the first derivative test to conclude

that the minimum cost is $C(2) = 312$ dollars.   **29.** $\left(\frac{3}{2}, \sqrt{\frac{3}{2}}\right)$ **31.** $x = 2$, $y = 1$

Exercises 2.6, page 181

1. (a) 90   **(b)** 180   **(c)** 6   **(d)** 1080 pounds   **3. (a)** $C = 16r + 2x$ **(b)** Constraint $rx = 800$
(c) $x = 80$, $r = 10$, minimum inventory cost $= \$320$ **5.** Let x be the number of cases per order and r the
number of orders per year. Objective: $C = 80r + 5x$; constraint: $rx = 10,000$ **(a)** \$4100   **(b)** 400 cases
7. Let r be the number of production runs and x the number of microscopes manufactured per run. Objective:
$C = 2500r + 25x$; constraint: $rx = 1600$; 4 runs   **11.** Objective: $A = (100 + x)w$; constraint: $2x + 2w = 300$;
$x = 25$ ft, $w = 125$ ft   **13.** Objective: $F = 2x + 3w$; constraint: $xw = 54$; $x = 9$ m, $w = 6$ m
15. (a) $A(x) = 100x + 1000$.   **(b)** $R(x) = A(x) \cdot (\text{Price}) = (100x + 1000)(18 - x)$ $(0 \leq x \leq 18)$. The graph of
$R(x)$ is a parabola looking downward, with a maximum at $x = 4$.   **(c)** $A(x)$ does not change,
$R(x) = (100x + 1000)(9 - x)$ $(0 \leq x \leq 9)$. Maximum value when $x = 0$.   **17.** Let x be the length of each edge
of the base and h the height. Objective: $C = 6x^2 + 10xh$; constraint: $x^2h = 150$; 5 ft by 5 ft by 6 ft   **19.** Let x
be the length of each edge of the end and h the length. Objective: $V = x^2h$; constraint: $2x + h = 120$; 40 cm by
40 cm by 40 cm   **21.** Objective: $V = w^2x$; constraint: $2x + w = 16$; $\frac{8}{3}$ in.   **23.** After 20 days
25. $2\sqrt{3}$ by 6   **27.** 10 in. by 10 in. by 4 in.   **29.** ≈ 3.77 cm

Exercises 2.7, page 190

1. \$1   **3.** 32   **5.** 5   **7.** $x = 20$ units, $p = \$133.33$ **9.** 2 million tons, \$156 per ton   **11. (a)** \$2.00
(b) \$2.30   **13.** Let x be the number of prints and p the price per print. Demand equation: $p = 650 - 5x$;
revenue: $R(x) = (650 - 5x)x$; 65 prints   **15.** Let x be the number of tables and p the profit per table.
$p = 16 - .5x$; profit from the cafe: $R = (16 - .5x)x$; 16 tables   **17. (a)** $x = 15 \cdot 10^5$, $p = \$45$.   **(b)** No. Profit
is maximized when price is increased to \$50.   **19.** 5%   **21. (a)** \$75,000   **(b)** \$3200 per unit   **(c)** 15 units
(d) 32.5 units   **(e)** 35 units

Chapter 2: Supplementary Exercises, page 194

1. (a) increasing: $-3 < x < 1, x > 5$; decreasing: $x < -3, 1 < x < 5$ **(b)** concave up: $x < -1, x > 3$; concave
down: $-1 < x < 3$ **3.**   **5.**   **7.** d, e   **9.** c, d   **11.** e   **13.** Graph

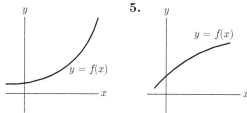

y
$y = f(x)$

y
$y = f(x)$

x
x

goes through $(1, 2)$, increasing at $x = 1$.   **15.** Increasing and concave up at $x = 3$.   **17.** $(10, 2)$ is a relative
minimum point.   **19.** Graph goes through $(5, -1)$, decreasing at $x = 5$.   **21. (a)** after 2 hours   **(b)** .8

(c) after 3 hours   **(d)** $-.02$ units per hour   **23.**

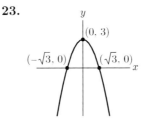

25.

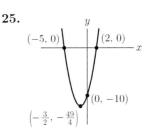

27.

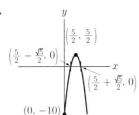

29.

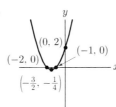

31.

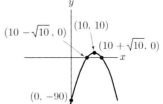

33.

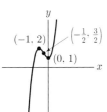

35.

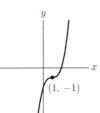

37.

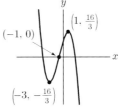

39.

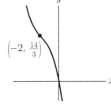

41.

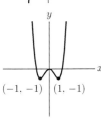

43.

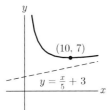

44.

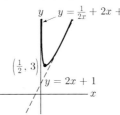

45. $f'(x) = 3x(x^2 + 2)^{1/2}$, $f'(0) = 0$ **47.** $f''(x) = -2x(1 + x^2)^{-2}$, $f''(x)$ is positive for $x < 0$ and negative for $x > 0$.   **49.** A–c, B–e, C–f, D–b, E–a, F–d   **51. (a)** The number of people living between $10 + h$ and 10 mi from the center of the city.   **(b)** If so, $f(x)$ would be decreasing at $x = 10$ **53.** The endpoint maximum value of 2 occurs at $x = 0$.   **55.** Let x be the width and h the height. Objective: $A = 4x + 2xh + 8h$; constraint: $4xh = 200$; 4 ft by 10 ft by 5 ft   **57.** $\frac{15}{2}$ in.   **59.** Let r be the number of production runs and x the number of books manufactured per run. Objective: $C = 1000r + (.25)x$; constraint: $rx = 400,000$; $x = 40,000$
61. $x = 3500$ **63.** Let x be the number of people and c the cost. Objective: $R = xc$; constraint: $c = 1040 - 20x$; 25 people.

CHAPTER 3

Exercises 3.1, page 205

1. $(x + 1) \cdot (3x^2 + 5) + (x^3 + 5x + 2) \cdot 1$, or $4x^3 + 3x^2 + 10x + 7$
3. $(2x^4 - x + 1) \cdot (-5x^4) + (-x^5 + 1) \cdot (8x^3 - 1)$, or $-18x^8 + 6x^5 - 5x^4 + 8x^3 - 1$
5. $x(4)(x^2 + 1)^3(2x) + (x^2 + 1)^4(1)$ or $(x^2 + 1)^3(9x^2 + 1)$ **7.** $(x^2 + 3) \cdot 10(x^2 - 3)^9(2x) + (x^2 - 3)^{10} \cdot 2x$, or $2x(x^2 - 3)^9(11x^2 + 27)$ **9.** $(5x + 1) \cdot 2x + (x^2 - 1) \cdot 5 + \frac{2}{3}$, or $15x^2 + 2x - \frac{13}{3}$ **11.** $\dfrac{(x + 1) \cdot 1 - (x - 1) \cdot 1}{(x + 1)^2}$, or $\dfrac{2}{(x + 1)^2}$ **13.** $\dfrac{(x^2 + 1) \cdot 2x - (x^2 - 1) \cdot 2x}{(x^2 + 1)^2}$ or $\dfrac{4x}{(x^2 + 1)^2}$ **15.** $\dfrac{(2x + 1)^2 - 2(2x + 1)(2)(x + 3)}{(2x + 1)^4}$ or $\dfrac{-2x - 11}{(2x + 1)^3}$ **17.** $\dfrac{-4x}{(x^2 + 1)^2}$ **19.** $\dfrac{(3 - x^2) \cdot (6x + 5) - (3x^2 + 5x + 1) \cdot (-2x)}{(3 - x^2)^2}$, or $\dfrac{5(x + 1)(x + 3)}{(3 - x^2)^2}$
21. $2[(3x^2 + 2x + 2)(x - 2)][(3x^2 + 2x + 2) \cdot 1 + (x - 2) \cdot (6x + 2)]$, or $2(3x^2 + 2x + 2)(x - 2)(9x^2 - 8x - 2)$

23. $\dfrac{-1}{2\sqrt{x}(\sqrt{x}+1)^2}$ **25.** $\dfrac{3x^4-4x^2-3}{x^2}$ **27.** $\sqrt{x+2}\,2\,(2x+1)(2)+(2x+1)^2\dfrac{1}{2\sqrt{x+2}}$ or $\dfrac{(2x+1)(10x+17)}{2\sqrt{x+2}}$

29. $y-16=88(x-3)$ **31.** $2,7$ **33.** $0,\pm2,\perp\frac{5}{4}$ **35.** $(\frac{1}{2},\frac{3}{2}),\,(-\frac{1}{2},\frac{9}{2})$ **37.** $\dfrac{dy}{dx}=8x(x^2+1)^3,$

$\dfrac{d^2y}{dx^2}=8(x^2+1)^2(7x^2+1)$ **39.** $\dfrac{dy}{dx}=\dfrac{x}{2\sqrt{x+1}}+\sqrt{x+1}$ or $\dfrac{dy}{dx}=\dfrac{3x+2}{2\sqrt{x+1}},\,\dfrac{d^2y}{dx^2}=\dfrac{3x+4}{4(x+1)^{3/2}}$

41. $x\cdot f'(x)+f(x)$ **43.** $\dfrac{(x^2+1)\cdot f'(x)-2x\cdot f(x)}{(x^2+1)^2}$ **45.** $2\times3\times1$ **47.** $150;\,AC(150)=35=C'(150)$

49. AR is maximized where $0=\dfrac{d}{dx}(AR)=\dfrac{x\cdot R'(x)-R(x)\cdot1}{x^2}$. This happens when the production level x satisfies $xR'(x)-R(x)=0$, and hence $R'(x)=R(x)/x=AR$.   **51.** 38 in.^{2}/s   **53.** $150{,}853{,}600$ gal/yr

55. $(2,10)$ **59.** $\dfrac{1-2x\cdot f(x)}{(1+x^2)^2}$ **61.** $\frac{1}{8}$ **63.** (b) $f'(x)\cdot g'(x)=-\dfrac{1}{x^2}(3x^2)=-3;\,[f(x)g(x)]'=2x$

65. $f(x)g(x)h'(x)+f(x)g'(x)h(x)+f'(x)g(x)h(x)$ **67.** $\dfrac{h(t)w'(t)-2w(t)h'(t)}{[h(t)]^3}$ **69.** (a)

$[0,\,6]\ by\ [-5,\,20]$

(b) 10.8 mm^2 (c) 2.61 units of light
(d) $-.55$ mm^2/unit of light

Exercises 3.2, page 212

1. $\dfrac{x^3}{x^3+1}$ **3.** $\sqrt{x}(x+1)$ **5.** $f(x)=x^5,\,g(x)=x^3+8x-2$ **7.** $f(x)=\sqrt{x},\,g(x)=4-x^2$ **9.** $f(x)=\dfrac{1}{x},$
$g(x)=x^3-5x^2+1$ **11.** $30x(x^2+5)^{14}$ **13.** $6x^2\cdot3(x-1)^2(1)+(x-1)^3\cdot12x$, or $6x(x-1)^2(5x-2)$
15. $2(x^3-1)\cdot4(3x^2+1)^3(6x)+(3x^2+1)^4\cdot2(3x^2)$, or $6x(3x^2+1)^3(11x^3+x-8)$
17. $\dfrac{d}{dx}[4^3(1-x)^{-3}]=192(1-x)^{-4}$ **19.** $3\left(\dfrac{4x-1}{3x+1}\right)^2\cdot\dfrac{(3x+1)\cdot4-(4x-1)\cdot3}{(3x+1)^2}$, or $\dfrac{21(4x-1)^2}{(3x+1)^4}$
21. $2xf'(x^2)$ **23.** $f'(-x)$ **25.** $\dfrac{2x^2f'(x^2)-f(x^2)}{x^2}$ **27.**   **29.** $30(6x-1)^4$

31. $-(1-x^2)^{-2}\cdot(-2x)$, or $2x(1-x^2)^{-2}$ **33.** $[4(x^2-4)^3-2(x^2-4)]\cdot(2x)$, or $8x(x^2-4)^3-4x(x^2-4)$
35. $2[(x^2+5)^3+1]3(x^2+5)^2\cdot(2x)$, or $12x[(x^2+5)^3+1](x^2+5)^2$ **37.** $6(4x+1)^{1/2}$
39. $\dfrac{dy}{dx}=\left(\dfrac{1}{2}-\dfrac{2}{u^2}\right)(1-2x)$ or $\dfrac{dy}{dx}=\left(\dfrac{1}{2}-\dfrac{2}{(x-x^2)^2}\right)(1-2x)$ **41.** $\dfrac{dy}{dt}=(2x-3)(2t)$ when $t=0,\,x=3,$
$\dfrac{dy}{dt}=0$ **43.** $\dfrac{dy}{dt}=\dfrac{-2}{(x-1)^2}\cdot\dfrac{t}{2}$ when $t=3,\,x=\dfrac{9}{4},\,\dfrac{dy}{dt}=-\dfrac{48}{25}$ **45.** $y=62x-300$ **47.** $1;\,2;\,3$
49. (a) $\dfrac{dV}{dt}=\dfrac{dV}{dx}\cdot\dfrac{dx}{dt}$ (b) 2 **51.** (a) $\dfrac{dy}{dt},\dfrac{dP}{dy},\dfrac{dP}{dt}$ (b) $\dfrac{dP}{dt}=\dfrac{dP}{dy}\cdot\dfrac{dy}{dt}$ **53.** (a) $\dfrac{200(100-x^2)}{(100+x^2)^2}$
(b) $\dfrac{400[100-(4+2t)^2]}{[100+(4+2t)^2]^2}$ (c) Falling at the rate of \$480 per week   **55.** (a) $.4+.0002x$ (b) increasing at the rate of 25 thousand persons per year   (c) rising at the rate of 14 ppm per year   **57.** x^3+1 **59.** 24
61. (a) $t=1.5,\,x=40,\,W\approx77.209$ million dollars; $t=3.5,\,x=30,\,W\approx76.364$ million dollars
(b) $\dfrac{dx}{dt}\Big|_{t=1.5}=20$; the price of one share is \$40 and is rising at the rate of \$20 per month. $\dfrac{dx}{dt}\Big|_{t=3.5}=0$; the

price of one share is steady at \$30 a share.   **63. (a)** $t = 2.5$, $x = 40$, $\dfrac{dx}{dt}\Big|_{t=2.5} = -20$; the price of one share is

\$40 and is falling at the rate of \$20 per month. $t = 4$, $x = 30$, $\dfrac{dx}{dt}\Big|_{t=4} = 0$; the price of one share is steady at \$30

a share.   **(b)** $\dfrac{dW}{dt}\Big|_{t=2.5} = \dfrac{dW}{dx}\Big|_{x=40}\dfrac{dx}{dt}\Big|_{t=2.5} = \dfrac{120}{1849}\cdot(-20) \approx -1.3$; the total value of the company is falling at

the rate of 1.3 million dollars per month. $\dfrac{dW}{dt} = \dfrac{dW}{dx}\dfrac{dx}{dt} = 0$; when $x = 30$, the total value of the company was

steady at $W \approx 76.364$ million dollars.   **65.** The derivative of the composite function $f(g(x))$ is the derivative
of the outer function evaluated at the inner function and then multiplied by the derivative of the inner function.

Exercises 3.3, page 222

1. $\dfrac{x}{y}$ **3.** $\dfrac{1+6x}{5y^4}$ **5.** $\dfrac{2x^3 - x}{2y^3 - y}$ **7.** $\dfrac{1 - 6x^2}{1 - 6y^2}$ **9.** $-\dfrac{y}{x}$ **11.** $-\dfrac{y+2}{5x}$ **13.** $\dfrac{8 - 3xy^2}{2x^2y}$ **15.** $\dfrac{x^2(y^3 - 1)}{y^2(1 - x^3)}$

17. $-\dfrac{y^2 + 2xy}{x^2 + 2xy}$ **19.** $\dfrac{1}{2}$ **21.** $-\dfrac{8}{3}$ **23.** $-\dfrac{2}{15}$ **25.** $y - \dfrac{1}{2} = -\dfrac{1}{16}(x - 4)$, $y + \dfrac{1}{2} = \dfrac{1}{16}(x - 4)$

27. (a) $\dfrac{2x - x^3 - xy^2}{2y + y^3 + x^2y}$ **(b)** 0 **29. (a)** $\dfrac{-y}{2x}$ **(b)** $\dfrac{-27}{16}$ **31.** $-\dfrac{x^3}{y^3}\dfrac{dx}{dt}$ **33.** $\dfrac{2x - y}{x}\dfrac{dx}{dt}$

35. $\dfrac{2x + 2y}{3y^2 - 2x}\dfrac{dx}{dt}$ **37.** $-\dfrac{15}{8}$ units per second   **39.** Rising at 3 thousand units per week   **41.** Increasing at

\$20 thousand per month   **43.** Decreasing at $\dfrac{1}{14}$ L per second   **45. (a)** $x^2 + y^2 = 100$ **(b)** $\dfrac{dy}{dt} = -4$, so the

top of the ladder is falling at the rate of 4 ft/sec.   **47.** Decreasing at $\dfrac{22}{\sqrt{5}}$ ft/sec (or 9.84 ft/sec)

Chapter 3: Supplementary Exercises, page 225

1. $(4x - 1)\cdot 4(3x + 1)^3(3) + (3x + 1)^4\cdot 4$, or $4(3x + 1)^3(15x - 2)$ **3.** $x\cdot 3(x^5 - 1)^2\cdot 5x^4 + (x^5 - 1)^3\cdot 1$, or
$(x^5 - 1)^2(16x^5 - 1)$ **5.** $5(x^{1/2} - 1)^4\cdot 2(x^{1/2} - 2)(\frac{1}{2}x^{-1/2}) + (x^{1/2} - 2)^2\cdot 20(x^{1/2} - 1)^3(\frac{1}{2}x^{-1/2})$, or
$5x^{-1/2}(x^{1/2} - 1)^3(x^{1/2} - 2)(3x^{1/2} - 5)$ **7.** $3(x^2 - 1)^3\cdot 5(x^2 + 1)^4(2x) + (x^2 + 1)^5\cdot 9(x^2 - 1)^2(2x)$, or
$12x(x^2 - 1)^2(x^2 + 1)^4(4x^2 - 1)$ **9.** $\dfrac{(x - 2)\cdot(2x - 6) - (x^2 - 6x)\cdot 1}{(x - 2)^2}$, or $\dfrac{x^2 - 4x + 12}{(x - 2)^2}$

11. $2\left(\dfrac{3 - x^2}{x^3}\right)\cdot\dfrac{x^3\cdot(-2x) - (3 - x^2)\cdot 3x^2}{x^6}$, or $\dfrac{2(3 - x^2)(x^2 - 9)}{x^7}$ **13.** $-\dfrac{1}{3}, 3, \dfrac{31}{27}$ **15.** $y + 32 = 176(x + 1)$

17. $x = 44$ m, $y = 22$ m   **19.** $\dfrac{dC}{dt} = \dfrac{dC}{dx}\cdot\dfrac{dx}{dt} = 40\cdot 3 = 120$. Costs are rising \$120 per day.   **21.** $0; -\dfrac{7}{2}$

23. $\dfrac{3}{2}; -\dfrac{7}{8}$ **25.** $1; -\dfrac{3}{2}$ **27.** $\dfrac{3x^2}{x^6 + 1}$ **29.** $\dfrac{2x}{(x^2 + 1)^2 + 1}$ **31.** $\dfrac{1}{2}\sqrt{1 - x}$ **33.** $\dfrac{3x^2}{2(x^3 + 1)}$

35. $-\dfrac{25}{x(25 + x^2)}$ **37.** $\dfrac{x^{1/2}}{(1 + x^2)^{1/2}}\cdot\dfrac{1}{2}(x^{-1/2})$, or $\dfrac{1}{2\sqrt{1 + x^2}}$ **39. (a)** $\dfrac{dR}{dA}, \dfrac{dA}{dt}, \dfrac{dR}{dx}$, and $\dfrac{dx}{dA}$

(b) $\dfrac{dR}{dt} = \dfrac{dR}{dx}\dfrac{dx}{dA}\dfrac{dA}{dt}$ **41. (a)** $-y^{1/3}/x^{1/3}$ **(b)** 1 **43.** -3 **45.** $\dfrac{3}{5}$ **47. (a)** $\dfrac{dy}{dx} = \dfrac{15x^2}{2y}$ **(b)** $\dfrac{20}{3}$

thousand dollars per thousand unit increase in production   **(c)** $\dfrac{dy}{dt} = \dfrac{15x^2}{2y}\dfrac{dx}{dt}$ **(d)** 2 thousand dollars per

week   **49.** Increasing at the rate of 2.5 units per unit time   **51.** 1.89 m^2/year

CHAPTER 4

Exercises 4.1, page 233

1. $2^{2x}, 3^{(1/2)x}, 3^{-2x}$ **3.** $2^{2x}, 3^{3x}, 2^{-3x}$ **5.** $2^{-4x}, 2^{9x}, 3^{-2x}$ **7.** $2^x, 3^x, 3^x$ **9.** $3^{2x}, 2^{6x}, 3^{-x}$ **11.** $2^{(1/2)x}$,
$3^{(4/3)x}$ **13.** $2^{-2x}, 3^x$ **15.** $\dfrac{1}{9}$ **17.** 1 **19.** 2 **21.** -1 **23.** $\dfrac{1}{5}$ **25.** $\dfrac{5}{2}$ **27.** -1 **29.** 4 **31.** 1

33. 1 or 2   **35.** 1 or 2   **37.** 2^h **39.** $2^h - 1$ **41.** $3^x + 1$ **43.**

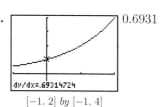

dy/dx=.69314724

$[-1, 2]$ by $[-1, 4]$

0.6931   **45.** 2.7

Exercises 4.2, page 237

1. 1.16, 1.11, 1.10   **3. (a)** $2m$ **(b)** $m/4$ where $m \approx .693$ **5. (a)** e **(b)** $1/e$ **7.** 1.005, 1.001, 1.000
9. $10e^{10x}$ **11. (a)** $4e^{4x}$ **(b)** ke^{kx} **13.** e^{2x}, e^{-x} **15.** e^{-6x}, e^{2x} **17.** e^{6x}, e^{2x} **19.** $x = 4$
21. $x = 4, -2$ **23.** 1 or -1 **25.** $3e^x - 7$ **27.** $xe^x + e^x = (x+1)e^x$
29. $8e^x(2)(1+2e^x)(2e^x) + 8e^x(1+2e^x)^2$ or $8e^x(6e^x+1)(1+2e^x)$ **31.** $\dfrac{e^x(x+1)-e^x}{(x+1)^2}$ or $\dfrac{xe^x}{(x+1)^2}$
33. $\dfrac{e^x(e^x+1)-e^x(e^x-1)}{(e^x+1)^2}$ or $\dfrac{2e^x}{(e^x+1)^2}$ **35.** $\dfrac{e^x}{\sqrt{2e^x+1}}$ **37.** $y' = e^x(1+x)^2$, $y' = 0$ when $x = -1$. The
point is $(-1, 2/e)$.   **39.** 1   **41.** $y - \frac{1}{3} = \frac{1}{9}x$ **43.** $f'(x) = e^x(x^2+4x+3)$, $f''(x) = e^x(x^2+6x+7)$
45. (a) 800 g/cm^2 **(b)** 14 km   **(c)** -50 g/cm^2 per km   **(d)** 2 km   **47.** $y = x + 1$
49.   **51.** $\dfrac{d}{dx}(10^x)\Big|_{x=0} \approx 2.3026$; $\dfrac{d}{dx}(10^x) = m10^x$ where $m = \dfrac{d}{dx}(10^x)\Big|_{x=0}$

$[-1, 3]$ by $[-3, 20]$

Exercises 4.3, page 242

1. $8e^{2x}$ **3.** $4 - 2e^{-2x}$ **5.** $e^{t^2}(2t^2+2t+1)$ **7.** $3(e^x+e^{-x})^2(e^x-e^{-x})$ **9.** $\frac{1}{8}e^{\frac{t}{4}+1}$ **11.** $-\frac{3}{t^2}e^{\frac{3}{t}}$
13. $e^{x^2-5x+4}(2x-5)$ **15.** $\dfrac{1-x+e^{2x}}{e^x}$ **17.** $2e^{2t} - 4e^{-4t}$ **19.** $2(t+1)e^{2t} + 2(t+1)^2e^{2t} = 2(t+1)(t+2)e^{2t}$
21. $e^xe^{e^x}$ **23.** $\dfrac{(15+4x)e^{4x}}{(4+x)^2}$ **25.** $(-x^{-2}+2x^{-1}+6)e^{2x}$ **27.** Max at $x = -2/3$ **29.** Min at $x = 5/4$
31. Max at $x = 9/10$ **33.** \$54,366 per year   **35. (a)** 45 m/sec   **(b)** 10 m/sec^2 **(c)** 4 sec   **(d)** 4 sec
37. 2 in./week   **39.** $.02e^{-2e^{-.01x}}e^{-.01x}$ **41.** $y = Ce^{-4x}$ **43.** $y = e^{-.5x}$ **47.** 1   **49. (a)** Volume seems
to stabilize near 6 ml   **(b)** 3.2 ml   **(c)** 7.7 wk   **(d)** .97 ml/wk   **(e)** 3.7 wk   **(f)** 1.13 ml/wk

Exercises 4.4, page 247

1. $\frac{1}{2}$ **3.** $\ln 5$ **5.** $\frac{1}{e}$ **7.** 3   **9.** e **11.** 0   **13.** x^2 **15.** $\frac{1}{49}$ **17.** $2x$ **19.** $\frac{1}{2}\ln 5$ **21.** $4 - e^{1/2}$
23. $\pm e^{9/2}$ **25.** $-\dfrac{\ln .5}{.00012}$ **27.** $\frac{5}{3}$ **29.** $\frac{e}{3}$ **31.** $3\ln \frac{9}{2}$ **33.** $\frac{1}{2}e^{8/5}$ **35.** $\frac{1}{2}\ln 4$ **37.** $-\ln \frac{3}{2}$
39. $x = \ln 5$, $y = 5(1 - \ln 5) \approx -3.047$ **41. (a)** $y' = -e^{-x}$, $y' = -2$ when $x = -\ln 2 = \ln(\frac{1}{2})$. The point is
$(\ln(\frac{1}{2}), 2)$.   **(b)**   **43.** $(-\ln 3, 3 - 3\ln 3)$, minimum   **45.** Max at $t = 2\ln 51$

$y = e^{-x}$

Slope $= -2$

2

$-\ln 2 \approx -.69$ 0

y

x

47. $\ln 2$ **49.** The graph of $y = e^{\ln x}$ is the same as the graph of $y = x$ for $x > 0$.

51. 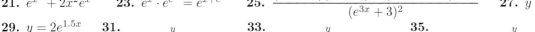 $\frac{1}{5}e^2 \approx 1.4778$

$[-1, 3] \; by \; [-3, 3]$

Exercises 4.5, page 251

1. $\dfrac{1}{x}$ **3.** $\dfrac{1}{x+3}$ **5.** $\dfrac{e^x - e^{-x}}{e^x + e^{-x}}$ **7.** $\left(\dfrac{1}{x} + 1\right)e^{\ln x + x}$ **9.** $\dfrac{1}{x}(\ln x + \ln 2x)$ **11.** $\dfrac{2\ln x}{x} + \dfrac{2}{x}$ or $\dfrac{2}{x}(\ln x + 1)$

13. $\dfrac{1}{x}$ **15.** $2x(1 + \ln(x^2 + 1))$ **17.** $\dfrac{2}{x^2 - 1}$ **19.** $\dfrac{5e^{5x}}{e^{5x} + 1}$ **21.** $3 + 2\ln t$ **23. (a)** $t > 1$.   **(b)** $t > e$.

25. $y = 1$ **27.** $\left(e^2, \dfrac{2}{e}\right)$ **29.** $y' = x(1 + 2\ln x)$, $y'' = 3 + 2\ln x$, $y' = 0$ when $x = e^{-1/2}$, $y''(e^{-1/2}) > 0$,

relative minimum at $x = e^{-1/2}$, $y = -e^{-1}/2$.   **31.** $1 + 3\ln 10$ **33.** $R'(x) = \dfrac{45(\ln x - 1)}{(\ln x)^2}$; $R'(20) \approx 10$

35. $\frac{1}{7}$ **37.**

$[-5, 5] \; by \; [-2, 2]$

Exercises 4.6, page 255

1. $\ln 5x$ **3.** $\ln 3$ **5.** $\ln 2$ **7.** x^2 **9.** $\ln \dfrac{x^5 z^3}{y^{1/2}}$ **11.** $3\ln x$ **13.** $3\ln 3$ **15. (a)** $2\ln 2 = 2(.69) = 1.38$

(b) $\ln 2 + \ln 3 = 1.79$ **(c)** $3\ln 3 + \ln 2 = 3.99$ **17. (a)** $-\ln 2 - \ln 3 = -1.79$ **(b)** $\ln 2 - 2\ln 3 = -1.51$

(c) $-\frac{1}{2}\ln 2 = -.345$ **19.** d   **21.** d   **23.** 3   **25.** $\sqrt{e}$ **27.** e or e^{-1} **29.** 1 or e^4 **31.** $\dfrac{1 + 2e}{e - 1}$

33. $\dfrac{1}{x+5} + \dfrac{2}{2x - 1} - \dfrac{1}{4 - x}$ **35.** $\dfrac{2}{1 + x} + \dfrac{3}{2 + x} + \dfrac{4}{3 + x}$ **37.** $\dfrac{1}{2x} + x$ **39.** $\dfrac{4}{x + 1} - 1$

41. $\ln(3x + 1)\dfrac{5}{5x + 1} + \ln(5x + 1)\dfrac{3}{3x + 1}$ **43.** $(x + 1)^4(4x - 1)^2 \left(\dfrac{4}{x + 1} + \dfrac{8}{4x - 1}\right)$

45. $\dfrac{(x + 1)(2x + 1)(3x + 1)}{\sqrt{4x + 1}} \left(\dfrac{1}{x + 1} + \dfrac{2}{2x + 1} + \dfrac{3}{3x + 1} - \dfrac{2}{4x + 1}\right)$ **47.** $2^x \ln 2$ **49.** $x^x[1 + \ln x]$

51. $y = cx^k$ **53.** $h = 3$, $k = \ln 2$

Chapter 4: Supplementary Exercises, page 257

1. 81   **3.** $\frac{1}{25}$ **5.** 4   **7.** 9   **9.** e^{3x^2} **11.** e^{2x} **13.** $e^{11x} + 7e^x$ **15.** $x = 4$ **17.** $x = -5$ **19.** $70e^{7x}$

21. $e^{x^2} + 2x^2 e^{x^2}$ **23.** $e^x \cdot e^{e^x} = e^{x + e^x}$ **25.** $\dfrac{(e^{3x} + 3)(2x - 1) - (x^2 - x + 5)3e^{3x}}{(e^{3x} + 3)^2}$ **27.** $y = Ce^{-x}$

29. $y = 2e^{1.5x}$ **31.**   **33.**   **35.**

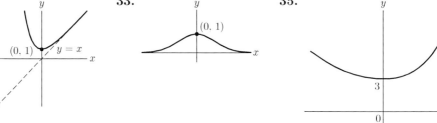

37. $y = \frac{1}{4}x + \frac{1}{2}$ **39.** $\sqrt{5}$ **41.** $\frac{2}{3}$ **43.** 1   **45.** e, $\dfrac{1}{e}$ **47.** $\frac{1}{2}\ln 5$ **49.** $e^{5/2}$ **51.** $\dfrac{6x^5 + 12x^3}{x^6 + 3x^4 + 1}$

53. $\dfrac{5}{5x-7}$ **55.** $\dfrac{2\ln x}{x}$ **57.** $\dfrac{1}{x}+1-\dfrac{1}{2(1+x)}$ **59.** $\ln x$ **61.** $\dfrac{1}{x\ln x}$ **63.** $\dfrac{e^x}{x}+e^x\ln x$

65. $\dfrac{x}{x^2+1}-\dfrac{1}{2x+3}$ **67.** $2x-\dfrac{1}{x}$ **69.** $\ln 2$ **71.** $\dfrac{1}{x-1}$ **73.** $-\tfrac{1}{2}x^{-\frac{1}{2}}$ or $\dfrac{-1}{2\sqrt{x}}$

75. $\sqrt[5]{\dfrac{x^5+1}{x^5+5x+1}}\left[\dfrac{x^4}{x^5+1}-\dfrac{x^4+1}{x^5+5x+1}\right]$ **77.** $x^{\sqrt{x}-\frac{1}{2}}[1+\tfrac{1}{2}\ln x]$

79. $(x^2+5)^6(x^3+7)^8(x^4+9)^{10}\left[\dfrac{12x}{x^2+5}+\dfrac{24x^2}{x^3+7}+\dfrac{40x^3}{x^4+9}\right]$ **81.** $10^x\ln 10$ **83.** $\dfrac{1}{2}\sqrt{\dfrac{xe^x}{x^3+3}}\left[\dfrac{1}{x}+1-\dfrac{3x^2}{x^3+3}\right]$

85. $e^{x+1}(x^2+1)x\left[1+\dfrac{2x}{x^2+1}+\dfrac{1}{x}\right]$ or $e^{x+1}(x^3+3x^2+x+1)$ **87.**

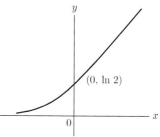

(0, ln 2)

89.

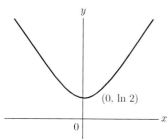

(0, ln 2)

91.

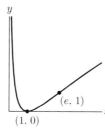

(e, 1)
(1, 0)

93.

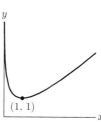

(1, 1)

95. $\dfrac{e^x}{3+e^x}$ **97.** 1

CHAPTER 5

Exercises 5.1, page 266

1. (a) $P(t)=3e^{.02t}$ **(b)** 3 million   **(c)** .02   **(d)** 3.52 million   **(e)** 80,000 people per year   **(f)** 3.5 million   **3. (a)** 5000   **(b)** $P'(t)=.2P(t)$ **(c)** 3.5 h   **(d)** 6.9 h   **5.** .017   **7.** 22 yr   **9.** 27 million cells **11.** 34.0 million   **13. (a)** $P(t)=8e^{-.021t}$ **(b)** 8 g   **(c)** .021   **(d)** 6.5 g   **(e)** .021 g/yr   **(f)** 5 g **(g)** 4 g; 2 g; 1 g   **15. (a)** $f'(t)=-.6f(t)$ **(b)** 14.9 mg   **(c)** 1.2 h   **17.** 30.1 yr   **19.** 176 days **21.** $f(t)=8e^{-.014t}$ **23. (a)** 8 g   **(b)** 3.5 h   **(c)** .6 g/h   **(d)** 8 h   **25.** 13,412 years   **27.** 58.3% **29.** 10,900 years ago   **31.** a–D, b–G, c–E, d–B, e–H, f–F, g–A, h–C   **33. (a)** $y-10=-5t$ or $y=-5t+10$ **(b)** $P(t)=10e^{-.5t}$ **(c)** $T=2.$

Exercises 5.2, page 273

1. (a) $5000   **(b)** 4%   **(c)** $7459.12   **(d)** $A'(t)=.04A(t)$ **(e)** $298.36 per year   **(f)** $7000 **3. (a)** $A(t)=4000e^{.035t}$ **(b)** $A'(t)=.035A(t)$ **(c)** $4290.03   **(d)** 6.4 yr   **(e)** $175 per year   **5.** $378 per year   **7.** 15.3 yr   **9.** 29.3%   **11.** 17.3 years   **13.** 7.3%   **15.** 2002   **17.** 2006   **19.** $786.63 **21.** $7985.16   **23.** 15.7 yr   **25.** a–B, b–D, c–G, d–A, e–F, f–E, g–H, h–C   **27. (a)** $200   **(b)** $8 per year **(c)** 4%   **(d)** 30 yr   **(e)** 30 yr   **(f)** $A'(t)$ is a constant multiple of $A(t)$ since $A'(t)=rA(t)$. **29.**

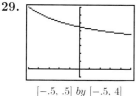

$[-.5, .5]$ by $[-.5, 4]$

31. .06

Exercises 5.3, page 282

1. 20%, 4%   **3.** 30%, 30%   **5.** 60%, 300%   **7.** -25%, -10% **9.** 12.5%   **11.** 5.8 yr   **13.** $p/(140-p)$, elastic   **15.** $2p^2/(116-p^2)$, inelastic   **17.** $p-2$, elastic   **19. (a)** inelastic   **(b)** raised   **21. (a)** elastic **(b)** increase   **23. (a)** 2   **(b)** yes   **29. (a)** $p<2$ **(b)** $p<2$

Exercises 5.4, page 291

1. (a) $f'(x) = 10e^{-2x} > 0$, $f(x)$ increasing; $f''(x) = -20e^{-2x} < 0$, $f(x)$ concave down   **(b)** As x becomes large, $e^{-2x} = \dfrac{1}{e^{2x}}$ approaches 0.   **(c)**

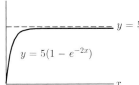

3. $y' = 2e^{-x} = 2 - (2 - 2e^{-x}) = 2 - y$

5. $y' = 30e^{-10x} = 30 - (30 - 30e^{-10x}) = 30 - 10y = 10(3-y)$, $f(0) = 3(1-1) = 0$ **7.** 4.8 h   **11. (a)** 2500 **(b)** 500 people/day   **(c)** day 12   **(d)** day 6 and day 14   **(e)** at time 10 days **(f)** $f'(t) = .00004f(t)(10,000 - f(t))$ **(g)** 1000 people per day   **13. (a)**

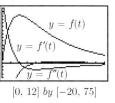

$[0, 12]$ by $[-20, 75]$

(b) 30 units   **(c)** 25 units per hour   **(d)** 9 hr   **(e)** 65.3 units after 2 hr   **(f)** 4 hr

Chapter 5: Supplementary Exercises, page 293

1. $29.92e^{-.2x}$ **3.** \$5488.12   **5.** .058   **7. (a)** $17e^{.018t}$ **(b)** 20.4 million   **(c)** 2011   **9. (a)** \$36,693 **(b)** The alternative investment is superior by \$3859.   **11.** .02; 60,000 people per year; 5 million people **13.** a–F, b–D, c–A, d–G, e–H, f–C, g–B, h–E   **15.** 6%   **17.** 400%   **19.** 3%, decrease   **21.** increase **23.** $100(1 - e^{-.083t})$ **25. (a)** $400°$ **(b)** decreasing at a rate of $100°/\text{sec}$ **(c)** 17 sec   **(d)** 2 sec

CHAPTER 6

Exercises 6.1, page 304

1. $\frac{1}{2}x^2 + C$ **3.** $\frac{1}{3}e^{3x} + C$ **5.** $3x + C$ **7.** $x^4 + C$ **9.** $7x + C$ **11.** $\dfrac{x^2}{2c} + C$ **13.** $2\ln|x| + \dfrac{x^2}{4} + C$ **15.** $\frac{2}{5}x^{5/2} + C$ **17.** $\frac{1}{2}x^2 - \frac{2}{3}x^3 + \frac{1}{3}\ln|x| + C$ **19.** $-\frac{3}{2}e^{-2x} + C$ **21.** $ex + C$ **23.** $-e^{2x} - 2x + C$ **25.** $-\frac{5}{2}$ **27.** $\frac{1}{2}$ **29.** $-\frac{1}{5}$ **31.** -1 **33.** $\frac{1}{15}$ **35.** 3   **37.** $\frac{2}{5}t^{5/2} + C$ **39.** C **41.** $-\frac{5}{2}e^{-.2x} + \frac{5}{2}$ **43.** $\dfrac{x^2}{2} + 3$ **45.** $\frac{2}{3}x^{3/2} + x - \frac{28}{3}$ **47.** $2\ln|x| + 2$ **49.** Testing all three functions reveals that (b) is the only one that works.   **51.**

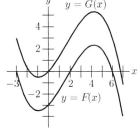

53. $\frac{1}{4}$ **55. (a)** $-16t^2 + 96t + 256$ **(b)** 8 sec   **(c)** 400 ft

57. $P(t) = 60t + t^2 - \frac{1}{12}t^3$ **59.** $20 - 25e^{-.4t}$ °C   **61.** $-95 + 1.3x + .03x^2 - .0006x^3$ **63.** $5875(e^{.016t} - 1)$

65. $C(x) = 25x^2 + 1000x + 10{,}000$ **67.** $F(x) = \frac{1}{2}e^{2x} - e^{-x} + \frac{1}{6}x^3$

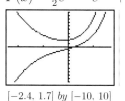

$[-2.4,\ 1.7]\ by\ [-10,\ 10]$

Exercises 6.2, page 313

1. .5; .25, .75, 1.25, 1.75   **3.** .6; 1.3, 1.9, 2.5, 3.1, 3.7   **5.** 8.625   **7.** 15.12   **9.** .077278   **11.** 40   **13.** 15
15. 5.625; 4.5   **17.** 1.61321; error = .04241   **19.** 1.08 L   **21.** 2800 ft   **23.** Increase in the population (in millions) from 1910 to 1950; rate of cigarette consumption t years after 1985; 20 to 50   **25.** Tons of soil eroded during a 5-day period   **29.** 9.5965   **31.** 1.7641   **33.** .8427

Exercises 6.3, page 323

1. $\displaystyle\int_{1/2}^{2} \frac{1}{x}\,dx$ **3.** $\displaystyle\int_{1}^{3}(1-x)(x-3)\,dx$ **5.**   **7.** 0   **9.** 5   **11.** 1   **13.** $\frac{4}{3}(1-e^{-3})$

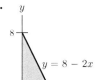

15. $e - e^{-1}$ **17.** $\frac{4}{9}$ **19.** $\ln 2$ **21.** $4\ln 5$ **23.** $\frac{13}{4} - 2\sqrt{e}$ **25.** $3\frac{3}{4}$ **27.** $\frac{1}{5}$ **29.** 10   **31.** $2(e^{1/2}-1)$
33. $6\frac{3}{5}$ **35.** Positive   **37.** 95.4 trillion   **39. (a)** 30 ft   **(b)**   **41. (a)** \$1185.75

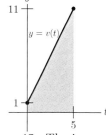

(b) The area under the marginal cost curve from $x = 2$ to $x = 8$.   **43.** The increase in profits resulting from increasing the production level from 44 to 48 units   **45. (a)** $368/15 \approx 24.5$ **(b)** The amount the temperature falls during the first 2 h   **47.** 2088 million m^3 **49.** 10   **51.** $\ln \frac{3}{2}$ **53.** $\frac{80}{3}$

Exercises 6.4, page 331

1. $\displaystyle\int_{1}^{2} f(x)\,dx + \int_{3}^{4} -f(x)\,dx$ **3.**   **5.** $\frac{64}{3}$ **7.** $\frac{52}{3}$ **9.** $e^2 - e - \frac{1}{2}$ **11.** $\frac{1}{6}$ **13.** $\frac{32}{3}$

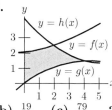

15. $\frac{1}{2}$ **17.** $\frac{1}{24}$ **19. (a)** $\frac{9}{2}$ **(b)** $\frac{19}{3}$ **(c)** $\frac{79}{6}$ **21.** $\frac{3}{2}$ **23.** $2 + 12\ln \frac{3}{2}$
25. $\displaystyle\int_{0}^{20}(76.2e^{.03t} - 50 + 6.03e^{.09t})\,dt$ **27.** No; 20; the additional profit from using the original plan
29. (a) The distance between the two cars after 1 h   **(b)** after 2 h   **31.** 1.4032   **33.** 1.4293

Exercises 6.5, page 340

1. 3　**3.** $50(1 - e^{-2})$　**5.** $\frac{3}{4}\ln 3$　**7.** $55°$　**9.** ≈ 82 g　**11.** \$20　**13.** \$404.72　**15.** \$200　**17.** \$25
19. Intersection $(100, 10)$, consumers' surplus $= \$100$, producers' surplus $= \$250$　**21.** \$3236.68　**23.** \$75,426
25. 13.35 y　**27. (b)** $1000e^{-.04t_1}\Delta t + 1000e^{-.04t_2}\Delta t + \cdots + 1000e^{-.04t_n}\Delta t$　**(c)** $f(t) = 1000e^{-.04t}; 0 \le t \le 5$

(d) $\displaystyle\int_0^5 1000e^{-.04t}\,dt$　**(e)** \$4531.73　**29.** $\frac{32}{3}\pi$　**31.** $\frac{31\pi}{5}$　**33.** 8π　**35.** $\frac{\pi}{2}(1 - e^{-2})$　**37.** $n = 4$, $b = 10$,

$f(x) = x^3$　**39.** $n = 3$, $b = 7$, $f(x) = x + e^x$　**41.** The sum is approximated by $\displaystyle\int_0^3 (3 - x)^2\,dx = 9$.

43. (a) $\dfrac{1000}{3r}(e^{3r} - 1)$　**(b)** 4.5%　**45. (a)** $\dfrac{1000}{r}(e^{6r} - 1)$　**(b)** 5%

Chapter 6: Supplementary Exercises, page 343

1. $9x + C$　**3.** $\frac{2}{3}(x + 1)^{3/2} + C$　**5.** $2(\frac{1}{4}x^4 + x^3 - x) + C$　**7.** $-2e^{-x/2} + C$　**9.** $\frac{3}{5}x^5 - x^4 + C$
11. $-\frac{2}{3}(4 - x)^{3/2} + C$　**13.** $\frac{8}{3}$　**15.** $\frac{14}{3}\sqrt{2}$　**17.** $\frac{15}{16}$　**19.** $\frac{3}{4}$　**21.** $\frac{1}{3}\ln 4$　**23.** $\frac{1}{2}$　**25.** $\frac{80}{81}$　**27.** $\frac{5}{32}$
29. $\frac{1}{3}$　**31.** $\frac{1}{2}$　**33.** $\frac{28}{3}$　**35.** $\frac{e}{2} - 1$　**37.** 8　**39.** $\frac{1}{3}(x - 5)^3 - 7$　**41. (a)** $2t^2 + C$　**(b)** Ce^{4t}
(c) $\frac{1}{4}e^{4t} + C$　**43.** $.02x^2 + 150x + 500$ dollars　**45.** The total quantity of drug (in cubic centimeters) injected
during the first 4 min　**47.** 25　**49.** .68571; .69315　**51.** \$433.33　**53.** 15　**55.** .26; 1.96
57. (a) $f(t) = Q - \dfrac{Q}{A}t$　**(b)** $\dfrac{Q}{2}$　**59. (a)** The area under the curve $y = \dfrac{1}{1 + t^2}$ from $t = 0$ to $t = 3$

(b) $\dfrac{1}{1 + x^2}$　**63.** $\frac{15}{4}$　**65.** True　**67.** $65{,}000$ km^3　**69.** $f(x) = x^3 - x^2 + x$

CHAPTER 7

Exercises 7.1, page 352

1. $f(5, 0) = 25$, $f(5, -2) = 51$, $f(a, b) = a^2 - 3ab - b^2$　**3.** $g(2, 3, 4) = -2$, $g(7, 46, 44) = \frac{7}{2}$
7. $C(x, y, z) = 6xy + 10xz + 10yz$　**9.** $f(8, 1) = 40$, $f(1, 27) = 180$, $f(8, 27) = 360$　**11.** $\approx \$50$. \$50 invested
at 5% continuously compounded interest will yield \$100 in 13.8 years　**13. (a)** \$1875　**(b)** \$2250; yes
15.　　　　　　**17.**　　　　　**19.** $f(x, y) = y - 3x$　**21.** They correspond to the points

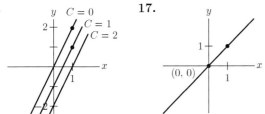

having the same altitude above sea level.　**23.** d　**25.** c

Exercises 7.2, page 361

1. $5y$, $5x$　**3.** $4xe^y$, $2x^2 e^y$　**5.** $\dfrac{1}{y} - \dfrac{y}{x^2}$; $\dfrac{-x}{y^2} + \dfrac{1}{x}$　**7.** $4(2x - y + 5)$, $-2(2x - y + 5)$　**9.** $(2xe^{3x} + 3x^2 e^{3x})\ln y$,

$x^2 e^{3x}/y$　**11.** $\dfrac{2y}{(x + y)^2}$, $-\dfrac{2x}{(x + y)^2}$　**13.** $\dfrac{3}{2}\sqrt{\dfrac{K}{L}}$　**15.** $\dfrac{2xy}{z}$, $\dfrac{x^2}{z}$, $-\dfrac{1 + x^2 y}{z^2}$　**17.** ze^{yz}, $xz^2 e^{yz}$, $x(yz + 1)e^{yz}$

19. 1, 3　**21.** -12　**23.** $\dfrac{\partial f}{\partial x} = 3x^2 y + 2y^2$, $\dfrac{\partial^2 f}{\partial x^2} = 6xy$, $\dfrac{\partial f}{\partial y} = x^3 + 4xy$, $\dfrac{\partial^2 f}{\partial y^2} = 4x$, $\dfrac{\partial^2 f}{\partial y \partial x} = \dfrac{\partial^2 f}{\partial x \partial y} = 3x^2 + 4y$
25. (a) Marginal productivity of labor $= 480$; of capital $= 40$　**(b)** $480h$　**(c)** Production decreases by 240
units.　**27.** If the price of a bus ride increases and the price of a train ticket remains constant, fewer people will
ride the bus. An increase in train-ticket prices coupled with constant bus fare should cause more people to ride
the bus.　**29.** If the average price of DVDs increases and the average price of a DVD player remains constant,
people will purchase fewer DVDs. An increase in average DVD player prices coupled with constant DVD prices
should cause a decline in the number of DVD players purchased.　**31.** $\dfrac{\partial V}{\partial P}(20, 300) = -.06$, $\dfrac{\partial V}{\partial T}(20, 300) = .004$

33. $\dfrac{\partial f}{\partial r} > 0$, $\dfrac{\partial f}{\partial m} > 0$, $\dfrac{\partial f}{\partial p} < 0$　**35.** $\dfrac{\partial^2 f}{\partial x^2} = -\dfrac{45}{4}x^{-5/4}y^{1/4}$. Marginal productivity of labor is decreasing.

Exercises 7.3, page 369

1. $(-2, 1)$ **3.** $(26, 11)$ **5.** $(1, -3), (-1, -3)$ **7.** $(\sqrt{5}, 1), (\sqrt{5}, -1), (-\sqrt{5}, 1), (-\sqrt{5}, -1)$ **9.** $\left(\frac{1}{3}, \frac{4}{3}\right)$
11. Relative minimum; neither relative maximum nor relative minimum   **13.** Relative maximum; neither relative maximum nor relative minimum; relative maximum   **15.** Neither relative maximum nor relative minimum   **17.** $(0, 0)$ min   **19.** $(-1, -4)$ max   **21.** $(0, -1)$ min   **23.** $(-1, 2)$ max; $(1, 2)$ neither max nor min   **25.** $\left(\frac{1}{4}, 2\right)$ min; $\left(\frac{1}{4}, -2\right)$ neither max nor min   **27.** $\left(\frac{1}{2}, \frac{1}{6}, \frac{1}{2}\right)$ **29.** 14 in. × 14 in. × 28 in.
31. $x = 120$, $y = 80$

Exercises 7.4, page 377

1. 58 at $x = 6$, $y = 2$, $\lambda = 12$ **3.** 13 at $x = 8$, $y = -3$, $\lambda = 13$ **5.** $x = \frac{1}{2}$, $y = 2$ **7.** 5, 5   **9.** Base 10 in.,
height 5 in.   **11.** $F(x, y, \lambda) = 4xy + \lambda(1 - x^2 - y^2)$; $\dfrac{\sqrt{2}}{2} \times \dfrac{\sqrt{2}}{2}$
13. $F(x, y, \lambda) = 3x + 4y + \lambda(18,000 - 9x^2 - 4y^2)$; $x = 20$, $y = 60$
15. (a) $F(x, y, \lambda) = 96x + 162y + \lambda(3456 - 64x^{3/4}y^{1/4})$; $x = 81$, $y = 16$ (b) $\lambda = 3$ **17.** $x = 12$, $y = 2$, $z = 4$
19. $x = 2$, $y = 3$, $z = 1$ **21.** $F(x, y, z, \lambda) = 3xy + 2xz + 2yz + \lambda(12 - xyz)$; $x = 2$, $y = 2$, $z = 3$
23. $F(x, y, z, \lambda) = xy + 2xz + 2yz + \lambda(32 - xyz)$; $x = y = 4$, $z = 2$

Exercises 7.5, page 384

1. $E = 6.7$ **3.** $E = (2A + B - 6)^2 + (5A + B - 10)^2 + (9A + B - 15)^2$ **5.** $y = 4.5x - 3$ **7.** $y = -2x + 11.5$
9. $y = -1.4x + 8.5$ **11.** (a) $y = .2073x + 2.7$ (b) \$4773   (c) 2006   **13.** (a) $y = .497x + 11.2$
(b) 22.6 percent   (c) 2002   **15.** (a) $y = -4.24x + 22.01$ (b) $y = 8.442$ degrees Celsius

Exercises 7.6, page 390

1. $e^2 - 2e + 1$ **3.** $2 - e^{-2} - e^2$ **5.** $309\frac{3}{8}$ **7.** $\frac{5}{3}$ **9.** $\frac{38}{3}$ **11.** $e^{-5} + e^{-2} - e^{-3} - e^{-4}$ **13.** $9\frac{1}{3}$

Chapter 7: Supplementary Exercises, page 391

1. $2, \frac{5}{6}, 0$ **3.** ≈ 19.94. Ten dollars increases to 20 dollars in 11.5 y.   **5.** $6x + y, x + 10y$ **7.** $\dfrac{1}{y}e^{x/y}$,
$-\dfrac{x}{y^2}e^{x/y}$ **9.** $3x^2, -z^2, -2yz$ **11.** 6, 1   **13.** $20x^3 - 12xy, 6y^2, -6x^2, -6x^2$ **15.** $-201, 5.5$. At the level
$p = 25$, $t = 10,000$, an increase in price of \$1 will result in a loss in sales of approximately 201 calculators, and
an increase in advertising of \$1 will result in the sale of approximately 5.5 additional calculators.   **17.** $(3, 2)$
19. $(0, 1), (-2, 1)$ **21.** Min at $(2, 3)$ **23.** Min at $(1, 4)$; neither max nor min at $(-1, 4)$ **25.** 20; $x = 3$,
$y = -1$ **27.** $x = \frac{1}{2}$, $y = \frac{3}{2}$, $z = 2$ **29.** $F(x, y, \lambda) = xy + \lambda(40 - 2x - y)$; $x = 10$, $y = 20$ **31.** $y = \frac{5}{2}x - \frac{5}{3}$
33. $y = -2x + 1$ **35.** 5160   **37.** 40

CHAPTER 8

Exercises 8.1, page 396

1. $\dfrac{\pi}{6}, \dfrac{2\pi}{3}, \dfrac{7\pi}{4}$ **3.** $\dfrac{5\pi}{2}, -\dfrac{7\pi}{6}, -\dfrac{\pi}{2}$ **5.** 4π **7.** $\dfrac{7\pi}{2}$ **9.** -3π **11.** $\dfrac{2\pi}{3}$
13.

15.

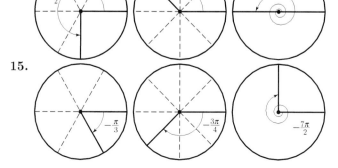

17.

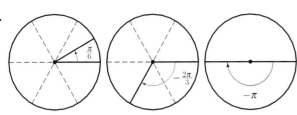

Exercises 8.2, page 401

1. $\sin t = \dfrac{1}{2}$, $\cos t = \dfrac{\sqrt{3}}{2}$ **3.** $\sin t = \dfrac{2}{\sqrt{13}}$, $\cos t = \dfrac{3}{\sqrt{13}}$ **5.** $\sin t = \frac{12}{13}$, $\cos t = \frac{5}{13}$ **7.** $\sin t = \dfrac{1}{\sqrt{5}}$,

$\cos t = -\dfrac{2}{\sqrt{5}}$ **9.** $\sin t = \dfrac{\sqrt{2}}{2}$, $\cos t = -\dfrac{\sqrt{2}}{2}$ **11.** $\sin t = -.8$, $\cos t = -.6$ **13.** .4   **15.** 3.6   **17.** 10.9

19. $b = 1.3$, $c = 2.7$ **21.** $\dfrac{\pi}{6}$ **23.** $\dfrac{3\pi}{4}$ **25.** $\dfrac{5\pi}{8}$ **27.** $\dfrac{\pi}{4}$ **29.** $\dfrac{\pi}{3}$ **31.** $-\dfrac{\pi}{6}$ **33.** $\dfrac{\pi}{4}$ **35.** Here $\cos t$
decreases from 1 to -1.   **37.** 0, 0, 1, -1 **39.** .2, .98, .98, $-.2$ **41. (a)**   **(b)** $46°$

[0, 365] by [−10, 75]

(c) $45°$ coldest, $73°$ warmest   **(d)** January 26   **(e)** July 27   **(f)** October 27 and April 27

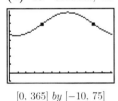

[0, 365] by [−10, 75]

Exercises 8.3, page 410

1. $4\cos 4t$ **3.** $4\cos t$ **5.** $-6\sin 3t$ **7.** $1 - \pi\sin \pi t$ **9.** $-\cos(\pi - t)$ **11.** $-3\cos^2 t \sin t$

13. $\dfrac{\cos\sqrt{x-1}}{2\sqrt{x-1}}$ **15.** $\dfrac{\cos(x-1)}{2\sqrt{\sin(x-1)}}$ **17.** $-8\sin t(1+\cos t)^7$ **19.** $-6x^2\cos x^3 \sin x^3$ **21.** $e^x(\sin x + \cos x)$

23. $2\cos(2x)\cos(3x) - 3\sin(2x)\sin(3x)$ **25.** $\cos^{-2} t$ **27.** $-\dfrac{\sin t}{\cos t}$ **29.** $\dfrac{\cos(\ln t)}{t}$ **31.** -3 **33.** $y = 2$

35. $\frac{1}{2}\sin 2x + C$ **37.** $-\dfrac{7}{2}\sin\dfrac{x}{7} + C$ **39.** $\sin x + \cos x + C$ **41.** $\cos x + \sin 3x + C$

43. $-\frac{1}{4}\cos(4x+1) + C$ **45.** $-\frac{7}{3}\cos(3x-2) + C$ **47.** **(a))** $\max = 120$ at 0, $\dfrac{\pi}{3}$; $\min = 80$ at $\dfrac{\pi}{6}$, $\dfrac{\pi}{2}$
(b) 57   **49.** 0   **51. (a)** $69°$ **(b)** increasing $1.6°/\text{wk}$ **(c)** weeks 6 and 44   **(d)** weeks 28 and 48
(e) week 25, week 51   **(f)** week 12, week 38

Exercises 8.4, page 414

1. $\sec t = \dfrac{\text{hypotenuse}}{\text{adjacent}}$ **3.** $\tan t = \frac{5}{12}$, $\sec t = \frac{13}{12}$ **5.** $\tan t = -\frac{1}{2}$, $\sec t = -\dfrac{\sqrt{5}}{2}$ **7.** $\tan t = -1$, $\sec t = -\sqrt{2}$
9. $\tan t = \frac{4}{3}$, $\sec t = -\frac{5}{3}$ **11.** $75\tan(.7) \approx 63$ ft   **13.** $\tan t \sec t$ **15.** $-\csc^2 t$ **17.** $4\sec^2(4t)$
19. $-3\sec^2(\pi - x)$ **21.** $4(2x+1)\sec^2(x^2+x+3)$ **23.** $\dfrac{\sec^2\sqrt{x}}{2\sqrt{x}}$ **25.** $\tan x + x\sec^2 x$ **27.** $2\tan x \sec^2 x$

29. $6[1 + \tan(2t)]^2 \sec^2(2t)$ **31.** $\sec t$ **33. (a)** $y - 1 = 2(x - \frac{\pi}{4})$ **(b)**

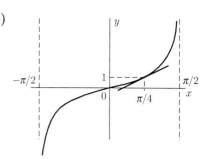

35. $\frac{1}{3}\tan 3x + C$ **37.** 2   **39.** $\tan x + C$

Chapter 8: Supplementary Exercises, page 416

1. $\dfrac{3\pi}{2}$ **3.** $-\dfrac{3\pi}{4}$ **5.**

   7. $\frac{4}{5}, \frac{3}{5}, \frac{4}{3}$ **9.** $-.8, -.6, \frac{4}{3}$ **11.** $\pm\dfrac{2\sqrt{6}}{5}$

13. $\dfrac{\pi}{4}, \dfrac{5\pi}{4}, \dfrac{3\pi}{4}, -\dfrac{7\pi}{4}$ **15.** Negative   **17.** 16.3 ft   **19.** $3\cos t$ **21.** $(\cos\sqrt{t}) \cdot \frac{1}{2}t^{-1/2}$

23. $x^3\cos x + 3x^2\sin x$ **25.** $-\dfrac{2\sin(3x)\sin(2x) + 3\cos(2x)\cos(3x)}{\sin^2(3x)}$ **27.** $-12\cos^2(4x)\sin(4x)$

29. $[\sec^2(x^4 + x^2)](4x^3 + 2x)$ **31.** $\cos(\tan x)\sec^2 x$ **33.** $\sin x\sec^2 x + \sin x$ **35.** $\cot x$

37. $4e^{3x}\sin^3 x\cos x + 3e^{3x}\sin^4 x$ **39.** $\dfrac{\tan(3t)\cos t - 3\sin t\sec^2(3t)}{\tan^2(3t)}$ **41.** $e^{\tan t}\sec^2 t$ **43.** $2(\cos^2 t - \sin^2 t)$

45. $\dfrac{\partial f}{\partial s} = \cos s\cos(2t)$, $\dfrac{\partial f}{\partial t} = -2\sin s\sin(2t)$ **47.** $\dfrac{\partial f}{\partial s} = t^2\cos(st)$, $\dfrac{\partial f}{\partial t} = \sin(st) + st\cos(st)$

49. $y - 1 = 2\left(t - \dfrac{\pi}{4}\right)$ **51.**

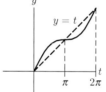

   53. 4   **55.** $\dfrac{\pi^2}{2} - 2$ **57. (a)** $V'(t) = 8\pi\cos\left(160\pi t - \dfrac{\pi}{2}\right)$

(b) 8π L/min   **(c)** 16 L/min   **59.** $\cos(\pi - x) + C$ **61.** 0   **63.** $\dfrac{\pi^2}{2}$ **65.** $2\tan\dfrac{x}{2} + C$ **67.** $\sqrt{2} - 1$

69. $\sqrt{2}$ **71.** 1   **73.** $1000 + \dfrac{400}{3\pi}$ **75.** $\tan x - x + C$ **77.** $\tan x + C$ **79.** $1 - \dfrac{\pi}{4}$

CHAPTER 9

Exercises 9.1, page 425

1. $\frac{1}{6}(x^2 + 4)^6 + C$ **3.** $2\sqrt{x^2 + x + 3} + C$ **5.** $e^{(x^3-1)} + C$ **7.** $-\frac{1}{3}(4 - x^2)^{3/2} + C$ **9.** $(2x + 1)^{1/2} + C$

11. $\frac{1}{2}e^{x^2} + C$ **13.** $\frac{1}{2}(\ln 2x)^2 + C$ **15.** $\frac{1}{5}\ln|x^5 + 1| + C$ **17.** $-(2 - 12x + 2x^2)^{-1} + C$

19. $\frac{1}{4}(\ln x)^2 + C = (\ln\sqrt{x})^2 + C$ **21.** $\frac{1}{3}\ln|x^3 - 3x^2 + 1| + C$ **23.** $-4e^{-x^2} + C$ **25.** $\frac{1}{2}\ln|\ln x^2| + C$

27. $-\frac{1}{10}(x^2 - 6x)^5 + C$ **29.** $\frac{1}{6}(1 + e^x)^6 + C$ **31.** $\frac{1}{2}\ln(1 + 2e^x) + C$ **33.** $\ln|1 - e^{-x}| + C$

35. $-\ln(e^{-x} + 1) + C$ **37.** $f(x) = (x^2 + 9)^{1/2} + 3$ **39.** $2e^{\sqrt{x+5}} + C$ **41.** $\frac{1}{2}\tan x^2 + C$ **43.** $\frac{1}{2}(\sin x)^2 + C$

45. $2\sin\sqrt{x} + C$ **47.** $-\frac{1}{4}\cos^4 x + C$ **49.** $-\frac{2}{3}\sqrt{2 - \sin 3x} + C$ **51.** $\ln|\sin x - \cos x| + C$

53. $\frac{1}{2}(x^2 + 5)^2 + C = \frac{1}{2}x^4 + 5x^2 + \frac{25}{2} + C; \frac{1}{2}x^4 + 5x^2 + C_1$

Exercises 9.2, page 430

1. $\frac{1}{5}xe^{5x} - \frac{1}{25}e^{5x} + C$ **3.** $\frac{x}{5}(x+7)^5 - \frac{1}{30}(x+7)^6 + C$ **5.** $-xe^{-x} - e^{-x} + C$
7. $2x(x+1)^{1/2} - \frac{4}{3}(x+1)^{3/2} + C$ **9.** $(1-3x)(\frac{1}{2}e^{2x}) + \frac{3}{4}e^{2x} + C$ **11.** $-2xe^{-3x} - \frac{2}{3}e^{-3x} + C$
13. $\frac{2}{3}x(x+1)^{3/2} - \frac{4}{15}(x+1)^{5/2} + C$ **15.** $\frac{1}{3}x^{3/2}\ln x - \frac{2}{9}x^{3/2} + C$ **17.** $x\sin x + \cos x + C$
19. $\frac{x^2}{2}\ln 5x - \frac{1}{4}x^2 + C$ **21.** $4x\ln x - 4x + C$ **23.** $-e^{-x}(x^2 + 2x + 2) + C$
25. $\frac{1}{5}x(x+5)^5 - \frac{1}{30}(x+5)^6 + C$ **27.** $\frac{1}{10}(x^2+5)^5 + C$ **29.** $3(3x+1)e^{x/3} - 27e^{x/3} + C$
31. $\frac{1}{2}\tan(x^2+1) + C$ **33.** $\frac{1}{2}xe^{2x} - \frac{1}{4}e^{2x} + \frac{1}{3}x^3 + C$ **35.** $\frac{1}{2}e^{x^2} - x^2 + C$ **37.** $2x\sqrt{x+9} - \frac{4}{3}(x+9)^{3/2} + 38$

Exercises 9.3, page 434

1. $\frac{1}{15}$ **3.** 312 **5.** $\frac{8}{3}$ **7.** $\frac{64}{3}$ **9.** 0 **11.** $\frac{1}{2}\ln(\frac{4}{3})$ **13.** $\frac{1}{3}(e^{27} - e)$ **15.** $\frac{1}{2}$ **17.** 0 **19.** $\frac{1}{\pi}$ **21.** $\frac{\pi}{2}$
23. $\frac{9\pi}{2}$ **25.** $\frac{16}{3}$

Exercises 9.4, page 442

1. $\Delta x = .4$; $3, 3.4, 3.8, 4.2, 4.6, 5$ **3.** $\Delta x = .5$; $-.75, -.25, .25, .75$ **5.**

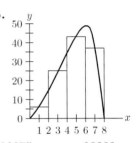

7. $(n=2)$ 40, $(n=4)$ 41, exact: $41\frac{1}{3}$ **9.** .63107, exact: .63212   **11.** .09375, exact: .08333   **13.** 1.03740, exact: .8   **15.** $M = 72$, $T = 90$, $S = 78$, exact: 78   **17.** $M = 44.96248$, $T = 72.19005$, $S = 54.03834$, exact: 53.59815   **19.** $M = 573.41797$, $T = 612.10806$, $S = 586.31466$, exact: 586.26358   **21.** 3.24124   **23.** 1.61347
25. 25,750 ft^2 **27.** 2150 ft   **29.** (a) $f''(x) = x^2 + 6$ (b) $A = 10$ (c) .0333

(d) $-.0244$, satisfies the bound in (c)   **(e)** quartered   **35.** $f(x) = \dfrac{1}{25 - x^2}$, $a = 3$, $b = 5$, $n = 10$
37. Midpoint rule: 2.361749156; trapezoidal rule: 2.474422799; Simpson's rule: 2.399307037; Exact value: 2.397895273; Error using midpoint rule: $-.036146117$; Error using trapezoidal rule: .076527526; Error using Simpson's rule: .001411764   **39.** Midpoint rule: .9989755866; trapezoidal rule: 1.00205197; Simpson's rule: 1.000001048; Exact value: 1; Error using midpoint rule: $-.0010244134$; Error using trapezoidal rule: .00205197; Error using Simpson's rule: .000001048   **41.** bound on the error is .0008333

Exercises 9.5, page 449

1. $147,656   3. $35,797   5. $182,937   7. (a) $\int_0^2 (30+5t)e^{-.10t}\,dt$ (b) $63.1 million

9. (a) $240\pi \int_0^5 te^{-.65t}\,dt$ (b) 1,490,623   11. $\approx 1,400,000$;

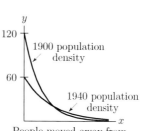

13. (a) $80\pi te^{-.5t}\Delta t$ thousand people   (b) $P'(t)$ (c) the number of people who live between 5 mi and 5 + Δt mi from the city center   (d) $P'(t) = 80\pi te^{-.5t}$ (e) $P(b) - P(a) = \int_a^b P'(t)\,dt = \int_a^b 80\pi te^{-.5t}\,dt$

Exercises 9.6, page 454

1. 0   3. No limit   5. $\frac{1}{4}$ 7. 2   9. 0   11. 5   13. $\frac{1}{2}$ 15. 2   17. 1   19. Area under the graph from 1 to b is $\frac{5}{14}(14b+18)^{1/5} - \frac{5}{7}$. This has no limit as $b \to \infty$.   21. $\frac{1}{2}$ 23. $\frac{1}{6}$ 25. Divergent   27. $\frac{2}{3}$

29. 1   31. $2e$ 33. Divergent   35. $\frac{1}{2}$ 37. 2   39. $\frac{1}{4}$ 41. 2   43. $\frac{1}{6}$ 45. $\dfrac{K}{r}$ 49. $\dfrac{K}{r}$

Chapter 9: Supplementary Exercises, page 456

1. $-\frac{1}{6}\cos(3x^2) + C$ 3. $-\frac{1}{36}(1-3x^2)^6 + C$ 5. $\frac{1}{3}[\ln x]^3 + C$ 7. $-\frac{1}{3}(4-x^2)^{3/2} + C$ 9. $-\frac{1}{3}e^{-x^3} + C$

11. $\frac{1}{3}x^2\sin(3x) - \frac{2}{27}\sin(3x) + \frac{2}{9}x\cos(3x) + C$ 13. $2(x\ln x - x) + C$ 15. $\frac{2}{3}x(3x-1)^{1/2} - \frac{4}{27}(3x-1)^{3/2} + C$

17. $\frac{1}{4}\left[\dfrac{x}{(1-x)^4}\right] - \frac{1}{12}\left[\dfrac{1}{(1-x)^3}\right] + C$ 19. $f(x) = x,\ g(x) = e^{2x}$ 21. $u = \sqrt{x+1}$ 23. $u = x^4 - x^2 + 4$

25. $f(x) = (3x-1)^2,\ g(x) = e^{-x}$; then integrate by parts again.   27. $f(x) = 500 - 4x,\ g(x) = e^{-x/2}$

29. $f(x) = \ln(x+2),\ g(x) = \sqrt{x+2}$ 31. $u = x^2 + 6x$ 33. $u = x^2 - 9$ 35. $u = x^3 - 6x$ 37. $\frac{3}{8}$

39. $1 - e^{-2}$ 41. $\frac{3}{4}e^{-2} - \frac{5}{4}e^{-4}$ 43. $M = 3.93782,\ T = 4.13839,\ S = 4.00468$

45. $M = 12.84089,\ T = 13.20137,\ S = 12.96105$ 47. $\frac{1}{3}e^6$ 49. Divergent   51. $2^{7/4}$ 53. $2e^{-1}$

55. $137,668   57. (a) $M(t_1)\Delta t + \cdots + M(t_n)\Delta t \approx \int_0^2 M(t)\,dt$

(b) $M(t_1)e^{-.1t_1}\Delta t + \cdots + M(t_n)e^{-.1t_n}\Delta t \approx \int_0^2 M(t)e^{-.1t}\,dt$

CHAPTER 10

Exercises 10.1, page 465

5. Order = 2   7. Yes   9. $y = 5$ 11. $f(0) = 4,\ f'(0) = 5$ 13. 20 feet per second per second
15. (a) Decreasing at $2500 per year   (b) $y' = .05(y - 200{,}000)$ (c) The rate of change of the savings account balance is proportional to the difference between the balance at the end of t years and $200,000.
17. The number of people who have heard the news broadcast after t hours is increasing at a rate that is proportional to the difference between that number and 200,000. At the beginning of the broadcast there are 10 people tuned in.   19. $y' = k(C - y),\ k > 0$ 21. $y' = k(P_b - y),\ y(0) = P_0$, where k is a positive constant.
25. No, it will come very close to 5000 but will not attain or exceed this value.   27. $y = 0$ and $y = 1$
29. All solution curves with $y(0) > 1$ will decrease and tend to 1. A typical solution curve is shown in Fig. 7.

31. (a)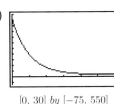

$[0, 30]$ by $[-75, 550]$

(b) $.2(10 - f(5)) = -36.78794412$, using nDeriv $f'(5) = -36.78794436$

Exercises 10.2, page 473

1. $y = \sqrt[3]{15t - \frac{3}{2}t^2 + C}$ **3.** $y = \ln|e^t + C|$ **5.** $y = (-\frac{2}{3}t^{3/2} + C)^{-1}$ or $y = 0$ **7.** $y = (e^{t^3} + C)^{1/3}$

9. $y = (\sqrt{t} + C)^2$ or $y = 0$ **11.** $y = \dfrac{-1}{t^3 + C}$ or $y = 0$ **13.** $y = \ln(\frac{1}{2}e^{t^2} + C)$ **15.** $y = \pm\sqrt{(\ln t)^2 + C}$

17. $y = \dfrac{1}{t - t\ln t + C} + 3$ or $y = 3$ **19.** $y = \frac{1}{2}\ln(2t^2 - 2t + e^6)$ **21.** $y = \sqrt[3]{3t\sin t + 3\cos t + 5}$

23. $y = \sqrt[3]{\cos t + 1}$ **25.** $y = -\sqrt{2t + 2\ln t + 7}$ **27.** $y = \frac{2}{5} + \frac{3}{5}e^{(5/2)t^2}$ **29.** $y = (3x^{1/2}\ln x - 6x^{1/2} + 14)^{2/3}$

31. $y = A(p + 3)^{-1/2}$, $A > 0$ **33.** $y' = k(1 - y)$, where $y = p(t)$, $y(0) = 0$; $y = 1 - e^{-kt}$ **35.** $\dfrac{dV}{dt} = kV^{2/3}$,

where $k < 0$; $V = (3 - \frac{1}{8}t)^3$, $V = 0$ when $t = 24$ weeks.   **37.** $y = be^{Ce^{-at}}$, C any number   **39. (a)** The
population will decrease and approach 5000.   **(b)** The population will increase and approach 5000.
The solution curve represents the number of fish in the
pond, if we start with an initial population of 1000 fish.

(c)

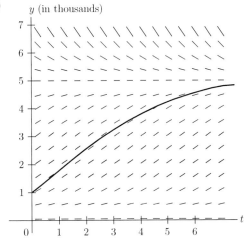

y (in thousands)

Exercises 10.3, page 479

1. e^{-2t} **3.** $e^{-\frac{1}{2t^2}}$ **5.** $\dfrac{1}{10 + t}$ **7.** $y = 1 + Ce^{-t}$ **9.** $y = 2 + Ce^{t^2}$ **11.** $y = 35 + Ce^{-.5t}$

13. $y = \dfrac{C}{10 + t}$ **15.** $y = \dfrac{C - t}{1 + t}$ **17.** $y = 1 + Ce^{-\frac{1}{12}t^2}$ **19.** $y = 2 - \frac{1}{2}e^t + Ce^{-t}$ **21.** $y = \frac{1}{2} + \frac{1}{2}e^{-2t}$

23. $y = 10 + 10t$ **25.** $y = \frac{1}{3}e^{2t} - \frac{4}{3}e^{-t}$ **27.** $y = 1 - e^{-\sin 2t}$ **29. (a)** $y'(0) = -40$, $y(t)$ is decreasing at

$t = 0$.   **(b)** $y = \dfrac{50 + 10t + 5t^2}{1 + t}$

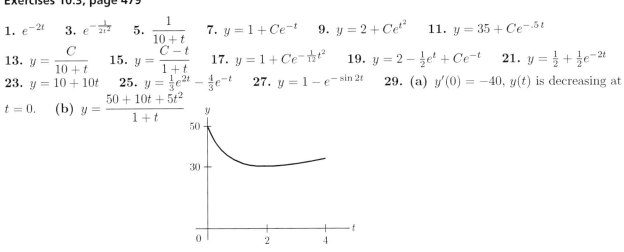

Exercises 10.4, page 485

1. (a) 4200 dollars per year   (b) 40,000 dollars   (c) $t = \frac{1}{.06}\ln(\frac{80}{41}) \approx 11.1$ years   3. (a) $y' = .05y + 3600$
(b) $f(t) = -72,000 + 72,000e^{.05t}$, $f(25) = 179,305$ dollars.   5. At retirement, Kelly has \$41,239 in her
savings account, and John has \$31,139 in his savings account.   7. Approximately \$14,214 per year.
9. (a) $y' = .0676y - A$, $y(0) = 197,640$ (b) $A = 15,385$ dollars per year, or 1282.1 dollars per month
(c) \$263,914   11. (a) $py' + (p+1)y = 0$ (b) $f(p) = 100\,\frac{e^{-p+1}}{p}$ 13. $f(t) = 10 + 340e^{-.1t}$
15. (a) $T = 70$ (b) $k = .5$ (c) $f(t) = 70 + 28e^{-.5t}$ (d) Approximately one hour and 15 minutes
17. $y' = .45y + e^{.03t} + 2$ 19. (a) $k = \frac{2}{7} \approx .286$ (b) $\frac{220}{7} \approx 31.43$ grams per liter per hour. Replacing the
dialysate with a fresh solution after 4 hours triples the rate at which waste products are filtered from the body.
21. (a) $y' - .04y = -500\,t - 2000$, $y(0) = 100,000$ (b) $f(t) = 362,500 - 262,500e^{.04t} + 12,500t$
(c)   The account is depleted in approximately 22.4 years.

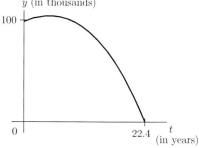

23. (a) 6 years   (b) $y' - .04y = 3000 - 500t$, $y(0) = 10,000$ 25. (a) $y' + .35y = t$
(b) $f(t) = \frac{1}{(.35)^2}(.35t - 1 + e^{-.35t})$, $f(8) \approx 15.2$ milligrams

Exercises 10.5, page 494

1. 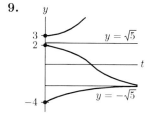   3. 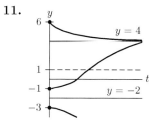   5. 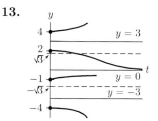   7.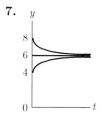

9. 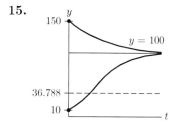   11. 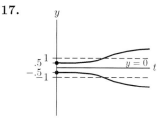   13.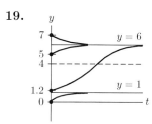

15.   17.   19.

21.

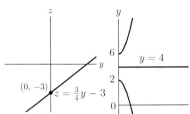

23.

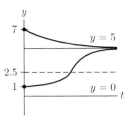

25.

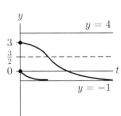

27.

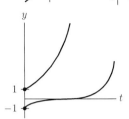

29.

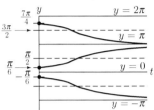

31.

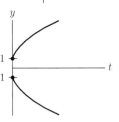

33.

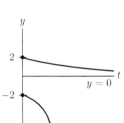

35.

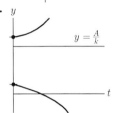

37.

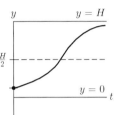

39.

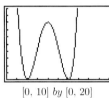

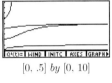

$[0, .5]$ *by* $[0, 10]$

$[0, 10]$ *by* $[0, 20]$

Exercises 10.6, page 504

1. (a) Carrying capacity $= 1$, intrinsic rate $= 1$

(b)

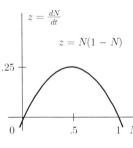

(c), (d)

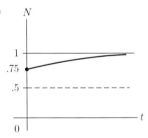

3. (a) Carrying capacity $= 100$, intrinsic rate $= 1$ **(b)**

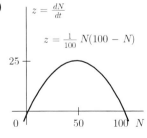

(c), (d)

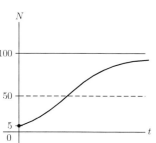

The graph is always concave down

5. $\dfrac{dN}{dt} = \dfrac{r}{1000} N(1000 - N),\ N(0) = 600;$

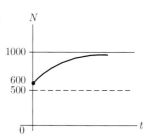

7. $y' = k(100 - y),\ k > 0$

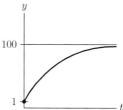

The reaction is proceeding fastest when $y = M/2$

9. $y' = ky(M - y),\ k > 0$

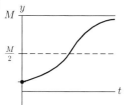

11. $y' = k(c - y),\ k > 0$

13. $y' = ky^2,\ k < 0$

15. $y' = k(E - y),\ k > 0$

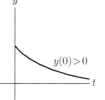

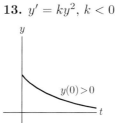

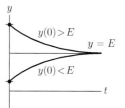

19. (a) $y' = .05y + 10{,}000,\ y(0) = 0$ **(b)** $y = 200{,}000(e^{.05t} - 1),\ \$56{,}805$ **21. (a)** $y' = .05 - .2y,$
$y(0) = 6.25$ **(b)** $y' = .13 - .2y,\ y(0) = 6.25$ **23.** $y' = -.14y$ **25.**

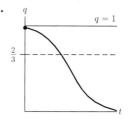

Exercises 10.7, page 510

1. 3   **3.** Increasing   **5.** $f(1) \approx -\dfrac{9}{4}$ **7.** $f(2) \approx \dfrac{27}{8}$ **9.** Euler's method yields

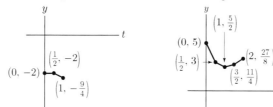

$f(1) \approx .37011;$ solution: $f(t) = \dfrac{1}{\frac{1}{2}t^2 + t + 1};\ f(1) = .4;$ error $= .02989$ **11. (a)** $y' = .1(1 - y),\ y(0) = 0$

(b) .271   **(c)** $y = 1 - e^{-.1t}, y(3) = 1 - e^{-.3} \approx .25918$ **(d)** error $\approx .01182$ **13. (a)** C

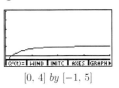

$[0, 4]$ by $[-1, 5]$

(b) A   **(c)** E   **(d)** B

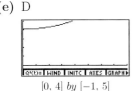
        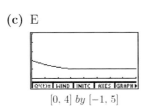
        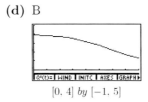

$[0, 4]$ by $[-1, 5]$ $[0, 4]$ by $[-1, 5]$ $[0, 4]$ by $[-1, 5]$

(e) D   **15.** $y_i = 1, .75, .6960, .7602, .9093, 1.1342, 1.4397, 1.8403, 2.3588; y = 1, .8324,$

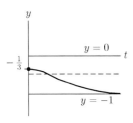

$[0, 4]$ by $[-1, 5]$

.7948, .8544, .9963, 1.2182, 1.5271, 1.9383, 2.4752, greatest difference $= .1163$

Chapter 10: Supplementary Exercises, page 512

1. $y = \sqrt[3]{3t^4 - 3t^3 + 6t + C}$ **3.** $y = Ate^{-3t}$ **5.** $y = \frac{3}{7}t + 3$ **7.** $y = \sqrt{4t^3 - t^2 + 49}$
9. $y(t) = \frac{1}{7}(t - 1)^5 + \frac{C}{(t-1)^2}$ **11.** $y = -1 - x + e^x$ **13.** Decreasing   **15.** y

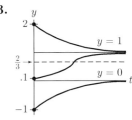

17.   **19.**   **21.**   **23.**

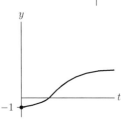

25. (a) $N' = .015N - 3000$ **(b)** There is a constant solution $N = 200,000$, but it is unstable. It is unlikely a city would have such a constant population. y **27.** 13.863 years   **29.** $f(t) = 2t, f(2) = 4$

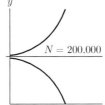

31.

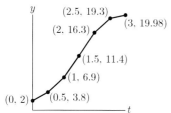

$(2.5, 19.3)$
$(3, 19.98)$
$(2, 16.3)$
$(1.5, 11.4)$
$(1, 6.9)$
$(0, 2)$ $(0.5, 3.8)$

CHAPTER 11

Exercises 11.1, page 520

1. $x - \frac{1}{6}x^3$ **3.** $5 + 10x + 10x^2 + \frac{20}{3}x^3$ **5.** $1 + 2x - 2x^2 + 4x^3$ **7.** $x + 3x^2 + \frac{9}{2}x^3$
9. $p_4(x) = 1 + x + \frac{1}{2}x^2 + \frac{1}{6}x^3 + \frac{1}{24}x^4$, $e^{.01} \approx p_4(.01) = 1.01005$
11.

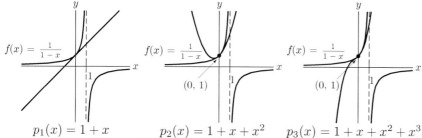

$f(x) = \frac{1}{1-x}$ $f(x) = \frac{1}{1-x}$ $f(x) = \frac{1}{1-x}$
$(0, 1)$ $(0, 1)$
$p_1(x) = 1 + x$ $p_2(x) = 1 + x + x^2$ $p_3(x) = 1 + x + x^2 + x^3$

13. $p_n(x) = 1 + x + \frac{1}{2}x^2 + \frac{1}{3!}x^3 + \cdots + \frac{1}{n!}x^n$ **15.** $p_2(x) = x^2$, area $\approx .0417$
17. $1 + (x - 4) + (x - 4)^2 + (x - 4)^3$ **19.** $p_3(x) = -1 + \frac{1}{2}(x - \pi)^2$, $p_4(x) = -1 + \frac{1}{2}(x - \pi)^2 - \frac{1}{24}(x - \pi)^4$
21. 3.04958   **23.** $p_1(x) = 19 + 33(x - 2)$, $p_2(x) = 19 + 33(x - 2) + 24(x - 2)^2$,
$p_3(x) = 19 + 33(x - 2) + 24(x - 2)^2 + 8(x - 2)^3$, $p_n(x) = 19 + 33(x - 2) + 24(x - 2)^2 + 8(x - 2)^3 + (x - 2)^4$, $n \geq 4$
25. $f''(0) = -5$, $f'''(0) = 7$ **27. (a)** 1   **(b)** $|R_3(.12)| \leq \frac{1}{4!}(.12)^4 = 8.64 \times 10^{-6}$

29. (a) $R_2(x) = \frac{f'''(c)}{3!}(x - 9)^3$, where c is between 9 and x **(b)** $f^{(3)}(c) = \frac{3}{8}c^{-5/2} \leq \frac{3}{8}9^{-5/2} = \frac{1}{648}$

(c) $|R_2(x)| \leq \frac{1}{648} \cdot \frac{1}{3!}(.3)^3 = \frac{1}{144} \times 10^{-3} < 7 \times 10^{-6}$
31. When $b = .55$ difference is approximately .11; when $b = -.68$ difference is approximately .087.

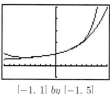

$[-1, 1]$ by $[-1, 5]$

33. When $b = 1.85$ difference is approximately .2552. When $x = 3$ difference is approximately 3.7105.

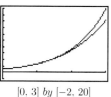

$[0, 3]$ by $[-2, 20]$

Exercises 11.2, page 527

1. Let $f(x) = x^2 - 5$, $x_0 = 2$; then $x_1 = 2.25$, $x_2 \approx 2.2361$, $x_3 \approx 2.23607$.   **3.** Let $f(x) = x^3 - 6$, $x_0 = 2$; then $x_1 \approx 1.8333$, $x_2 \approx 1.81726$, $x_3 \approx 1.81712$.   **5.** If $x_0 = 2$, then $x_3 \approx 2.79130$.   **7.** $x_3 \approx .63707$
9. $x_0 = -1$, $x_1 = -.8$, $x_2 \approx -.77143$, $x_3 \approx -.77092$

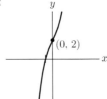

11. .703   **13.** 8.21% per month

15. 1% per month   **17.** $x_1 \approx 3.5$, $x_2 \approx 3.0$

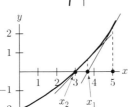

19. $-\frac{5}{4}$ **21.** $x_0 > 0$

23. x_1 will be the exact root.   **25.** $x_0 = 1$, $x_1 = -2$, $x_2 = 4$, $x_3 = -8$ **27.** 4; 31

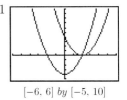

$[-6, 6]$ *by* $[-5, 10]$

29. (a) $\sqrt{2}$ (b) $-\sqrt{2}$ (c) 0

$[-2, 2]$ *by* $[-2, 2]$

Exercises 11.3, page 536

1. $\frac{6}{5}$ **3.** $\frac{9}{10}$ **5.** 3   **7.** $\frac{25}{124}$ **9.** $\frac{21}{10}$ **11.** Divergent $(r = -\frac{8}{5})$ **13.** 25   **15.** $\frac{3}{11}$ **17.** $\frac{2}{9}$ **19.** $\frac{4007}{999}$
21. $.99\overline{9} \ldots = (.9)\dfrac{1}{1 - .1} = \dfrac{9}{10} \cdot \dfrac{10}{9} = 1$ **23.** \$190 billion
25. (a) $100 + 100(1.01)^{-1} + 100(1.01)^{-2} + \cdots = \sum_{k=0}^{\infty} 100(1.01)^{-k}$ (b) \$10,100   **27.** \$1,655,629   **29.** 20
mg   **31.** 5 mg   **33.** (a) 2.5   (b) yes; 3   **35.** 6   **37.** $\frac{1}{24}$ **39.** $\frac{15}{8}$ **43.** 12   **45.** $\frac{1}{4} + \frac{1}{8} + \frac{1}{16} + \frac{1}{32} + \frac{1}{64}$; $\frac{1}{2}$

Exercises 11.4, page 542

1. Divergent   **3.** Convergent   **5.** Divergent   **7.** Convergent   **9.** Convergent   **11.** Convergent
13. Convergent   **15.** Divergent   **17.** $\sum_{k=0}^{\infty} \dfrac{3}{9 + k^2}$ **21.** Convergent   **23.** Convergent   **25.** Convergent
27. No   **29.**

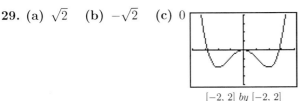

Exercises 11.5, page 549

1. $\dfrac{1}{3} - \dfrac{2}{9}x + \dfrac{2^2}{3^3}x^2 - \dfrac{2^3}{3^4}x^3 + \cdots$ **3.** $1 + \dfrac{1}{2}x - \dfrac{1}{2^2 \cdot 2!}x^2 + \dfrac{1 \cdot 3}{2^3 \cdot 3!}x^3 - \dfrac{1 \cdot 3 \cdot 5}{2^4 \cdot 4!}x^4 + \cdots$
5. $1 + 3x + 3^2x^2 + 3^3x^3 + \cdots$ **7.** $1 - x^2 + x^4 - x^6 + \cdots$ **9.** $1 - 2x + 3x^2 - 4x^3 + 5x^4 - \cdots$
11. $5 + \dfrac{5}{3}x + \dfrac{5}{3^2 \cdot 2!}x^2 + \dfrac{5}{3^3 \cdot 3!}x^3 + \cdots$ **13.** $x - \dfrac{1}{2!}x^2 + \dfrac{1}{3!}x^3 - \dfrac{1}{4!}x^4 + \cdots$ **15.** $x - \dfrac{1}{2}x^2 + \dfrac{1}{3}x^3 - \dfrac{1}{4}x^4 + \cdots$
17. $1 - \dfrac{3^2}{2!}x^2 + \dfrac{3^4}{4!}x^4 - \dfrac{3^6}{6!}x^6 + \cdots$ **19.** $3x - \dfrac{3^3}{3!}x^3 + \dfrac{3^5}{5!}x^5 - \cdots$ **21.** $x + x^3 + \dfrac{1}{2!}x^5 + \dfrac{1}{3!}x^7 + \cdots$

23. $1 + \frac{1}{2!}x^2 + \frac{1}{4!}x^4 + \frac{1}{6!}x^6 + \cdots$ **25.** $1 + \frac{1}{2}x + \frac{1 \cdot 3}{2 \cdot 4}x^2 + \frac{1 \cdot 3 \cdot 5}{2 \cdot 4 \cdot 6}x^3 + \cdots$

27. $x - \frac{1}{2 \cdot 3}x^3 + \frac{1 \cdot 3}{2 \cdot 4 \cdot 5}x^5 - \frac{1 \cdot 3 \cdot 5}{2 \cdot 4 \cdot 6 \cdot 7}x^7 + \cdots$ **31.** 48   **33.** 0

35. $\left[x - \frac{1}{3}x^3 + \frac{1}{5 \cdot 2!}x^5 - \frac{1}{7 \cdot 3!}x^7 + \cdots\right] + C$ **37.** $\left[x - \frac{1}{4}x^4 + \frac{1}{7}x^7 - \frac{1}{10}x^{10} + \cdots\right] + C$

39. $1 - \frac{1}{3} + \frac{1}{5 \cdot 2!} - \frac{1}{7 \cdot 3!} + \cdots$

Chapter 11: Supplementary Exercises, page 552

1. $x + \frac{3}{2}x^2$ **3.** $8 - 7x^2 + x^3$ **5.** $9 + 6(x - 3) + (x - 3)^2$ **7.** $p_2(t) = 2t^2; \frac{1}{12}$

9. (a) $3 + \frac{1}{6}(x - 9) - \frac{1}{216}(x - 9)^2$ **(b)** 2.949583   **(c)** 2.949576   **11.** 3.5619   **13.** $\frac{4}{7}$ **15.** $\frac{1}{7}$ **17.** 1

19. e^2 **21.** $\frac{9}{2}$ **23.** Convergent   **25.** Divergent   **27.** $p > 1$ **29.** $1 - x^3 + x^6 - x^9 + x^{12} - \cdots$

31. $1 + 6x + 27x^2 + 108x^3 + \cdots$ **33. (a)** $1 - \frac{2^2}{2!}x^2 + \frac{2^4}{4!}x^4 - \frac{2^6}{6!}x^6 + \cdots$ **(b)** $x^2 - \frac{2^3}{4!}x^4 + \frac{2^5}{6!}x^6 - \frac{2^7}{8!}x^8 + \cdots$

35. $1 + 2x + 2x^2 + 2x^3 + \cdots$ **37. (a)** x^2 **(b)** 0   **(c)** .3095   **39. (a)** $f'(x) = 2x + 4x^3 + 6x^5 + \cdots$

(b) $f'(x) = \dfrac{2x}{(1 - x^2)^2}$ **41.** \$566,666,667   **43.** \$120,066.66   **45.** \$3,285,603.18

CHAPTER 12

Exercises 12.1, page 561

1. $E(X) = \frac{4}{5}$, $\mathrm{Var}(X) = .16$, standard deviation $= .4$ **3. (a)** $\mathrm{Var}(X) = 1$ **(b)** $\mathrm{Var}(X) = 4$
(c) $\mathrm{Var}(X) = 16$ **5. (a)**

Accidents	0	1	2	3
Probability	.21	.5	.25	.04

(b) $E(X) \approx 1.12$ **(c)** Average of 1.12

accidents per week during the year   **7. (a)** 25%   **(b)** $100c^2\%$ **9.** $E(X) = \$90,000$. The grower should
spend the \$5000.

Exercises 12.2, page 569

7. $\frac{1}{4}$ **9.** $\frac{1}{15}$ **11.** 12   **13.** 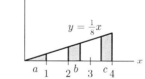   **15.** $\frac{1}{12}$ **17.** $\frac{1}{2}$ **19.** $\frac{3}{4}$ **21.** $f(x) = \frac{1}{4}(x - 1)^{-1/2}$

23. $f(x) = \frac{1}{5}x - \frac{2}{5}$ **25. (a)** $\frac{19}{63}$ **(b)** $f(x) = (x^3 - 1)/63$ **(c)** $\frac{19}{63}$ **31.** $2 - \sqrt{2} \approx .59$ **33.** 1.8   **35.** .6
37.   **(b)** $f(x) = 1 - x^{-4}$ **(c)** $\frac{15}{16}, \frac{1}{16}$

Exercises 12.3, page 574

1. $E(X) = 4$, $\mathrm{Var}(X) = 2$ **3.** $E(X) = 3$, $\mathrm{Var}(X) = \frac{4}{3}$ **5.** $E(X) = \frac{5}{6}$, $\mathrm{Var}(X) = \frac{5}{252}$ **7.** $E(X) = \frac{2}{5}$,
$\mathrm{Var}(X) = \frac{1}{25}$ **9. (a)** $F(x) = 10x^3 - 15x^4 + 6x^5$ **(b)** $\frac{53}{512}$ **(c)** $\frac{1}{2}$. On the average about half of the
newspaper's space is devoted to advertising.   **(d)** $\frac{1}{28}$ **11. (a)** 2. The average useful life of the component is
200 h.   **(b)** $\frac{1}{2}$ **13.** 8 min   **15. (a)** $F(x) = \frac{1}{6}x^2 - \frac{1}{54}x^3 - 1$ **(b)** $\frac{23}{27}$ **(c)** 412.5 worker-hours

(d) .5344   **17.** $E(X) = \frac{4}{3}$, $\mathrm{Var}(X) = \frac{2}{9}$ **19.** $3\sqrt{2}$ **21.** $\dfrac{3\sqrt{2}}{2}$ hundred hours   **23.** $\frac{5}{6}$ min

25. *Hint:* Compute $\displaystyle\int_A^B x f(x)\, dx$ using integration by parts.

Exercises 12.4, page 583

1. $E(X) = \frac{1}{3}$, $\mathrm{Var}(X) = \frac{1}{9}$ **3.** $E(X) = 5$, $\mathrm{Var}(X) = 25$ **5.** $e^{-1} - e^{-2}$ **7.** $1 - e^{-2/3}$ **9.** e^{-3}
11. $1 - e^{-2}$ **13. (a)** $e^{-1/3}$ **(b)** $r(t) = e^{-t/72}$ **15.** $\mu = 4$, $\sigma = 1$ **17.** $\mu = 0$, $\sigma = 3$ **23. (a)** .4032
(b) .4013   **(c)** .8351   **(d)** .9772   **25. (a)** 47.72%   **(b)** 47.72%   **27.** .1587   **29.** The Capital Beltway
31. 1.22%   **33.** *Hint:* First show that $\Pr(a \le X \le a + b) = e^{-ka}(1 - e^{-kb})$.   **35.** 62.15 weeks

Exercises 12.5, page 591

1. .0504, .0216, .0081   **3.** .4724, .3543, .1329, .0332, .0062, .0009, .0001

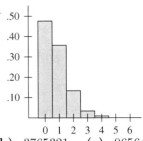

5. (a) .0000454   **(b)** .0027694   **(c)** .9972306   **7. (a)** .2231302   **(b)** .3765321   **(c)** .0656425
9. 22,105   **11.** .4, .24, .144, .0864, .05184, .031104

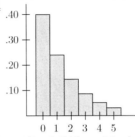

13. (a) $(\frac{3}{4})^n(\frac{1}{4})$ **(b)** .4219   **(c)** 3   **15.** $1 - p^n$ **17.** .04073   **19.** $\lambda = 2$ **23.** .74053326   **25. (a)** No
(b) .9979061

Chapter 12: Supplementary Exercises, page 593

1. (a) $\frac{1}{8}, \frac{19}{64}$ **(b)** $E(X) = \frac{3}{2}$, $\text{Var}(X) = \frac{3}{20}$ **3.** $f(x) = 1 - e^{A-x}$ **5.** $c_2 = \frac{1}{2}$, $c_4 = \frac{1}{4}$ **7. (a)** 5.01
(b) 100   **9. (a)** .96   **(b)** 1.8 thousand gallons   **(c)** $f(x) = 1 - x/2$, $0 \le x \le 2$ **11. (a)** $E(X) = 22.5$,
$\text{Var}(X) = 2.0833$ **(b)** 21.5   **13. (a)** $\frac{1}{300}$ **(b)** $\frac{3}{8}$ **(c)** \$17,222   **15.** $\dfrac{2}{\pi}$ **17.** \$54.88   **19.** $k \approx .35$
21. .4938   **23.** 69.15%   **25.** $a \approx .25$ **27. (b)** .6826
29. (a) $\Pr\left(-\dfrac{1}{k} \le X \le \dfrac{3}{k}\right) = \Pr\left(0 \le X \le \dfrac{3}{k}\right) \ge \dfrac{3}{4}$ **(b)** $1 - e^{-3} \approx .9502$ **31.** .1953668   **33.** 4   **35.** $\frac{2}{7}$

INDEX

Index of Applications